MW00582258

INAGUA

The Basilisk... A hope fulfilled in spreading sails and white hull

INAGUA

*Which is the name of a very lonely
and nearly forgotten island*

By

GILBERT C. KLINGEL

ILLUSTRATED FROM PHOTOGRAPHS
TAKEN BY THE AUTHOR

Dodd, Mead & Company, New York

ISBN 0-7414-5851-9

Printed in the United States of America

Published April 2010

INFINITY PUBLISHING
1094 New DeHaven Street, Suite 100
West Conshohocken, PA 19428-2713
Toll-free (877) BUY BOOK
Local Phone (610) 941-9999
Fax (610) 941-9959
Info@buybooksontheweb.com
www.buybooksontheweb.com

TO

EDMUND B. FLADUNG

BUT FOR WHOSE ENCOURAGEMENT
THE EVENTS DESCRIBED IN THIS
VOLUME MIGHT NEVER HAVE
HAPPENED

CONTENTS

PREFACE

INAGUA is a record of the highlights of two expeditions to that lonely and unfrequented island. In a sense, it is the story of an expedition that failed of its original purpose but which was compensated by certain unexpected and rather full experiences which otherwise would have been lost.

The technical accounts of these sojourns have been published in the *American Museum Novitiates* and in the bulletins of the Natural History Society of Maryland. In these pages instead have been transmitted some of the non-technical, and perhaps more human, sensations and happenings which have no place in a biological treatise.

Grateful acknowledgment is made to the Editors of the *Baltimore Sunday Sun* for permission to use portions of the chapters on "The Great Reef," "Creatures of the Night," and "Quest of the Firebirds" which had previously appeared in that publication. Also, a large portion of "The Edge of the Edge of the World" is here republished by the kindness of the Editor of *Natural History Magazine*.

INTRODUCTION

The author Gilbert Klingel spent most of his life on and around the Chesapeake Bay but in his early years he had a yearning to explore the West Indies. This book is the result of one of those Caribbean adventures.

In November of 1930 Klingel and his good friend W. Wallace Coleman, known in the book as Wally, set out on a scientific expedition in a sailing ship worthy of crossing the seven seas. Their chosen vessel was a replica of Captain Joshua Slocum's *Spray* in which Slocum was the first to sail single-handed around the world in the 1890's. They probably owe their lives to the sturdy construction of their 37 foot yawl for it proudly took them through the worst winter storm of 1930.

As they were leaving Norfolk, Virginia that November morning on their way out the Chesapeake Bay into the Atlantic Ocean, they could see the outlines of the large four-masted schooner Purnell T. White. Klingel writes in *Inagua* "She was a beautiful thing in the early light, sails all pink with the newly risen sun and white hull glinting against the green water. How could we know that in the short space of eight days this ship would be a sodden helpless wreck...Side by side we put to sea, the towering schooner and the tiny yawl. Our mast hardly reached her railing, or so it seemed, as she swept grandly past and headed for the capes and the rising sun. We watched her go with a feeling of friendly interest, for she was built by the same hand that with such care constructed our tiny ship."

Both vessels were to be caught in that terrible storm of 1930. Klingel reports that the waves were so high that at one point "...a wave broke over the top of the mast. *Forty-two feet five inches* our mast measured, and this breaking wave topped it by a yard." Coleman later noted in his journal: "You don't know what it is to be awed until you go to sea."

The book *Inagua* has been around for a long time. It was originally published in 1940 by Dodd, Mead and Company and was translated into several languages including German, Russian and Swedish. It also appeared under the title *The Ocean Island*. There have been several editions, a British edition in 1942, an American Museum of Natural History paperback edition (Doubleday Anchor Book 1961), and the most recent one in 1997 by Lyons and Burford.

In the forward to the 1961 edition Curator Charles M. Bogert wrote: "Biologists with literary talent are scarce. If naturalists with a flair for writing are difficult to find, however, journalists with the background and ability to portray life in terms acceptable to the biologist are downright rare. Gilbert Klingel proves to be one of these exceptional journalists."

When *Inagua* went out of print and out of stock it was still in demand, especially around the Chesapeake Bay where the author is widely known. This prompted me, the author's daughter, to publish a new edition with an introduction which would provide some insight about the man who wrote this unusual book. I also wanted to bring the book out of the past and into the present because recent events have generated renewed interest in Klingel's writings and accomplishments. This book will once again come alive and will now be available for future generations.

The cover design of this newest edition was done by graphic designer Stuart Coleman, the grandson of Wally Coleman who accompanied Gilbert Klingel on the expedition to the Bahamas. How this came about was quite extraordinary.

After their adventure on the island of Inagua the two explorers led different lives on opposite sides of the continent. Wally Coleman had moved from the East Coast to a distant part of Canada. Klingel had remained in Baltimore. The two friends are believed to have met only once in the 1950's when Klingel visited Wally at his home near Cleveland, Ohio. Although they may have kept in touch after that, their children had no knowledge of the whereabouts of their father's friend's families and were not even aware that there were any children. It wasn't until Wally's sons decided to find out what had become of their father's friend Gilbert that the children of the two explorers finally had the opportunity to meet in 2006.

Wally Coleman had returned to Baltimore after leaving Inagua in January of 1931. Later in 1931, he married and moved to Saskatoon, Saskatchewan, Canada, where he had accepted a position as the laboratory technician for a newly formed clinic. His interest in nature however continued as a photographer. Many of his photographs of birds in the wild were accepted for exhibition throughout Canada and in Europe. He continued his naturalist photography when he returned to the United States in 1948. He died in 1962 at age 55.

Thanks to the internet and the words "Grimstead,Va," "Mathews town" and "Gwynn's Island" that Wally had written in his autographed copy of *Inagua*, Wally's sons Walter (Walt) and Gilbert Wallace Randolph (Randy) were able to track me down and eventually come visit the boat yard where Klingel had worked and lived during his later years. They also had the opportunity to see the Gwynn's Island Museum where there is an exhibit about the life and work of their father's friend Gilbert. It was a wonderful rendezvous for all. Interesting to note here that Wally had named his eldest son Gilbert in honor of the friend he so admired.

How did the author of this book end up on Gwynn's Island in Virginia? That is another interesting story. Gwynn's Island is a small island located on the western shore of the Chesapeake Bay at the mouth of the Piankatank River and just south of the Rappahannock River. It has been connected to the mainland by a bridge since 1939. The island is part of Mathews County, Virginia.

Gilbert Klingel first came to Gwynn's Island as a boy in the days when steamers used to come down the Chesapeake Bay from Baltimore. It was most likely the steamer Piankatank which brought this young boy to Mathews County around the age of eight. He spent summers with his family at Hudgins House which is located just across the Narrows from Gwynn's Island. Here he learned to swim and sail and to appreciate the Chesapeake Bay. It was here also that his interest in marine biology was first awakened. His love for this area brought him back many years later to settle permanently.

In his hometown of Baltimore, at the age of ten Klingel was already a budding naturalist. He began by observing and photographing anything he could find in nature and because of this strong interest in natural sciences, he soon joined the Maryland Academy of Sciences. Wally Coleman also joined the Academy around this time (1919-1920) and within a few years had become a

Scientific Assistant in Entomology. While most boys of their age were out playing games, Gilbert and his close friend, Wally spent their free time studying plant and animal life along the shores of the Chesapeake Bay and its tributaries.

Dr. Edmund B. Fladung (known to his friends as "Doc" Fladung) to whom this book was dedicated was Klingel's mentor. It was Fladung who left the Academy and formed the Natural History Society of Maryland in 1929. Both Klingel and Coleman joined the organization and became curators as well as charter members. For several years Klingel served as vice president and curator of the Department of Marine Life.

A trip to the American Museum of Natural History in New York so impressed Klingel that he wanted to document more of the strange tropical creatures he saw on display. These were West Indian lizards, four and five feet in length, which were strongly reminiscent of a dinosaur. In the winter of 1928/29 he went to Haiti on a small tramp ship. He spent four months there studying the wildlife and took the first moving pictures ever made of rhinoceros iguana colonies. This study was published in the journal of the American Museum of Natural History in 1929.

Klingel soon wanted to return to the West Indies to search for new species. This time however he hoped to sail there in his own boat to be free to travel when and where he wished and to be more equipped for the journey. He decided to plan a scientific expedition for this purpose. He asked his boyhood friend Wally Coleman to join him in this adventure.

Under the auspices of the Natural History Society of Maryland and the American Museum of Natural History, a boat was soon built. It was outfitted as a research vessel. This replica of the *Spray* was completed at Conley's Shipyard in Oxford, Maryland in 1930 and was named the *Basilisk* after a Caribbean lizard that could run across the water.

Plans were made to sail from island to island in the West Indies to observe, collect, and gather information on rare species, especially lizards. The outcome of the voyage of the *Basilisk* is the focus of the first part of the book *Inagua*. Klingel returned to the island of Inagua with diving equipment for undersea work in 1938 to study reefs and marine life. These observations make up the second part of the book.

Gilbert Klingel was one of those people who despite great odds at times, and little funds to carry out projects, still managed through faith and quiet persistence to reach goals which otherwise would have seemed unattainable. Inspired to some extent by the under-sea adventures of Dr. William Beebe and his Bathysphere, Klingel, in co-operation with the Chesapeake Biological Laboratory of Solomon's Island, Maryland, set about to making his own new diving laboratory.

Using only make-shift equipment, such as a used boiler, garden hoses, and an automobile tire pump, he invented a steel diving cylinder in 1935 called the "Bentharium." With it, he made some of the first direct observations of the underwater life of the Chesapeake Bay. These studies, along with numerous field trips above and below the bay, eventually resulted in the publication in 1951 of Klingel's second and best known book, *The Bay*. It was this book that won for him the John Burroughs Medal in 1953 for excellence in nature writing.

This book soon caught the attention of the National Geographic Society and it requested his assistance in designing a new underwater diving device to photograph sea life under the Chesapeake Bay. Klingel's invention the "Aquascope" was built in 1952 and tested in the waters around Gwynn's Island in 1953.

The results of this research were published in the May 1955 issue of the National Geographic Magazine. The article was entitled "One Hundred Hours Beneath the Chesapeake." The amazing photos shown in the article were taken by National Geographic Photographer Willard R. Culver and were the first color photos taken under the Chesapeake Bay. The "Aquascope" is on display in the Calvert Marine Museum, Solomon's Island, Maryland.

Klingel's passion for marine studies led others to become marine biologists. Among them is Maryland author Dr. Kent Mountford, an environmental historian and estuarine ecologist, who contributes on a regular basis to the Chesapeake Bay newspaper the *Bay Journal*; and Mathews County resident Dr. Morgan Wells whose career in underwater research was inspired by Klingel's National Geographic article. Wells was former director of the NOAA Diving Program and was involved in habitat based and submersible research.

During the 1930's Gilbert had managed to make a living by writing for scientific journals, contributing articles to the Baltimore Sun papers, and by continuing research in the field of natural history and marine science. Research funds were soon depleted during the depression and Klingel eventually found himself jobless. He took a position with Armco Steel Corporation in Baltimore and soon specialized in metallurgy. He fell into this kind of work accidentally but it later served him well. He used this knowledge in building the "Aquascope" and later in constructing sailing craft out of steel.

Klingel's shipbuilding experience dates back to 1947 when he decided to build his own boat with a steel hull. Little did he know that this laid the foundation for his boatbuilding business. He built these steel boats on weekends at his home in Maryland until 1953 when he acquired the property on Gwynn's Island and began establishing his Gwynn's Island Boat Yard. He continued building boats part-time at that location until he retired from the steel company in 1963 and moved to the Island permanently. In all, he produced about 40 steel boats, ranging in size from 30 to 75 feet long. His third book *Boatbuilding with Steel* (1973), (1991) was the result of over thirty years experience pioneering the use of steel in yacht construction.

Though originally from Baltimore, Maryland, Gilbert Klingel chose to retire to Gwynn's Island, Virginia. This was the place he had visited as a boy. It was a place he never forgot and always wanted to come back to. It was here he returned for the National Geographic project and where during the last twenty-five years of his life he custom-built steel sailboats at his Gwynn's Island Boat Yard. He found a quiet life on Gwynn's Island and once said: "The prime rewards are in small things, like listening to seagulls in the morning, enjoying the sunshine and hearing the wind..."

Here too, I, his daughter, spent many wonderful childhood days around Gwynn's Island and have fond memories of watching my father working around the boat yard. In the early years, we would sleep on the boat anchored just off shore. During this time, he built the winch house, placed a railway, and began laying the bricks for the large steel beamed work shop. All this was done part-time over many weekends and holidays for he was still working full time in Baltimore during the week.

After constructing the boat yard, he built a small apartment on the second floor above the large work shop. How convenient it was for him to just descend to the ground floor on the elevator (which he had built himself) and go to work in the shop below. No commuting to work or traffic to deal with. From this apartment, one could see the sun rise in the east over Milford Haven and the sun set in the west on Hills Bay and the Piankatank River. After having lived in several different states and countries, I came to appreciate this place my father loved so much and also returned to settle permanently in the area.

Quite a few magazine and newspaper articles have been written about Gilbert Klingel over the years. The latest appeared in the August 2008 issue of Chesapeake Bay Magazine. It was written by science writer Lynn Teo Simarski and was entitled "The Man who Loved Gwynn's Island." Aubrey Bodine, the well-known Maryland photographer, came to Gwynn's Island in 1964 to photograph and document Klingel and his boat yard for a featured article in the October 11 Sunday Magazine of the Baltimore Sun.

The Gwynn's Island Boat Yard is still there but has changed hands and names over the years. The property became known as Pulley's Marine for some time. Pulley added a separate and smaller building for a boat shop and used the large building as a retail store for marine products. The upstairs area was used as office space and storage. After Pulley's Marine sold the property, it would have become a sailing school. When that didn't work out, it became privately owned.

As this book goes to print, the Mathews Maritime Foundation is leasing part of Klingel's old boat yard. The Foundation has a small museum in town, the Mathews Maritime Museum, but needed a waterfront location where donated boats could be cleaned up, repaired and sold. Boatbuilding projects will also take place here and the railway and dock will be put to use. This property will once again be a working waterfront continuing the tradition of boatbuilder Gilbert Klingel. If you ever come across the bridge to Gwynn's Island, you will soon see the sign *Mathews Maritime Foundation – Gwynn's Island Boat Shop* on the right not far after the Seabreeze Restaurant. A few more miles down the road is another interesting attraction, the Gwynn's Island Museum.

Klingel, a man of many talents, was a naturalist, explorer, award-winning author, inventor, metallurgist and boatbuilder. Of all these talents, however, he was first and foremost, a naturalist. His writings portray a love and understanding of all creatures, their cycles of birth, life, and death as well as their role in the ecological balance of nature. He knew that a breakdown of this balance would seriously endanger the environment of our earth. He was also ahead of his time in realizing the problems that development and population growth would have on the Chesapeake Bay.

Here was a man who enjoyed the simple life and the great outdoors. He was self-educated, an avid reader, and a naturalist who preferred to observe the natural environment first-hand. His keen sense of observation and detailed descriptions make his readers feel as if they are seeing and discovering things along with him for the first time.

There is another reason for issuing a new edition of *Inagua* at this time. My father had a great respect for the natural world and had a very effective way of describing it in his published books and articles. As our generation becomes more and more aware of the effect of climate change and the near and long term results of global warming, we need to increase our understanding of where our natural world is today and what has occurred since he sailed on the Basilisk in 1930.

A book like *Inagua* brings us back to a previous era when life was simpler and the natural world was more intact. It was a time before tourist boats descended on islands and a time before products from the outside world had changed the lives of native peoples. When Klingel came to Inagua the first time, aside from the one town on the island, Mathewtown, the island was not much different than it had been 400 years earlier when Columbus had first come to this area of the Bahamas. Klingel was able to see and describe for us an island in its natural state as it was in 1930-31 and this he did with great literary style. Rachel Carson once said that "Gilbert Klingel [has]...a rare ability to describe the life of a restricted area in terms that invest it not only with fascination but with rich meaning."

Klingel's experiences on Inagua ranged from elation at times to extreme disappointment. He mentions having the greatest feeling of despondency after Wally Coleman left the island. Wally had been on the island about a month and a half when he received word that it was necessary to return home to the States. He was able to catch one of the occasional steamers that stopped by the island.

Klingel's sense of despondency however did not last. "Inagua was too beautiful to be sad in and there was too much to do" he says in the book. Klingel was now alone in the little thatch hut by the sea with his only company being the big black and yellow spider who lived in the crack over the doorway. He would now continue the Robinson Crusoe lifestyle for several more months for he wanted to complete the research he set out to do.

The island of Inagua is roughly sixty by forty miles in length and breadth. Klingel writes: "Robinson Crusoe was happy in that he could survey his total kingdom from one hilltop. I was not so fortunate. Inagua stretches away...for fifty miles or more!...Without any of the side excursions which were necessary to accomplish my purpose the very minimum distance to be covered would be a hundred and fifty miles...all of it on foot, in a place where water was scarce..."

There were many surprises when landing on Inagua – both good and bad. The worst of these was that they had ended up on a coral reef and later were arrested for not asking permission to be shipwrecked on this island! A more pleasant and interesting surprise was that Klingel discovered while exploring the island that Captain Slocum had once stopped there and had left a photo of the Spray. Much more impressive than that however, was the discovery that Inagua had the largest flamingo colony of the Western Hemisphere.

Klingel writes in the chapter on The Great Reef: "There are two sights on this earth that are so unusual that they do not seem credible. One of these is the flamingos; the other the fantastic and exquisite world of the undersea barrier reef viewed from the point where the ocean bottom falls away into the great depths off the coast of Inagua. It is a strange paradox that the island of Inagua, which is so drab and forlorn in many respects, should harbor in its few square miles two of the earth's most magnificent spectacles." Klingel must have known there were some secrets to be found under the waters of Inagua for it was for this reason that the author returned alone several years later with diving equipment to study the reef and ocean marine life.

Excerpts from the *Inagua* book have been included in anthologies such as *The Book of Naturalists – An Anthology of the Best Natural History* edited by William Beebe, 1944. Here Klingel's chapter "In Defense of Octopuses" has been included. Beebe of course was a well-known naturalist, explorer, writer and another pioneer in undersea diving. It was Dr. Beebe who went to a depth of a half mile beneath the ocean's surface in his Bathysphere off the coast of Bermuda in 1934. Beebe said in his Anthology "If the volume *Inagua* is a result of natural science being merely a 'pastime and hobby,' I regret that the author has not devoted his life to the science of natural history." If it were not for the Great Depression, my father, Gilbert Klingel would most likely have gone on to be a full-time naturalist. Events beyond our control can certainly be life changing.

The final chapter of *Inagua* is included in *Green Treasury – A Journey through the World's Great Nature Writing,* selected and edited by Edwin Way Teale (naturalist-author), 1952. This chapter is the story of an undersea precipice and the life that dwelt along its edge. It is entitled "The Edge of the Edge of the World."

"Written with imaginativeness and beauty and rare perception, the experiences of Gilbert Klingel on the face of this odd little island...make one of the most extraordinary and delightful nature books that the publishers have ever encountered. Here, for sure, is a newcomer to the ranks of such popular naturalists as Thoreau, Hudson, and William Beebe." - Dodd Mead & Company.

Anyone who loves adventure and nature will truly enjoy reading this book *Inagua*.

Marcia Klingel Benouameur
Daughter of Gilbert Klingel
Mathews, Virginia
December 2009

INAGUA

INAGUA ISLAND

SCALE OF MILES

0   5   10

.... SEARCH FOR FLAMINGO COLONY
---·--- ROUTE FOLLOWED IN CIRCUIT OF ISLAND

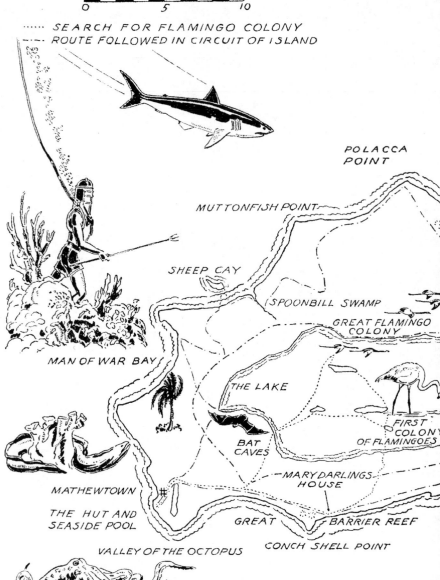

POLACCA POINT

MUTTONFISH POINT

SHEEP CAY

SPOONBILL SWAMP

GREAT FLAMINGO COLONY

MAN OF WAR BAY

THE LAKE

FIRST COLONY OF FLAMINGOES

BAT CAVES

MARY DARLINGS HOUSE

MATHEWTOWN

THE HUT AND SEASIDE POOL

GREAT

BARRIER REEF

CONCH SHELL POINT

VALLEY OF THE OCTOPUS

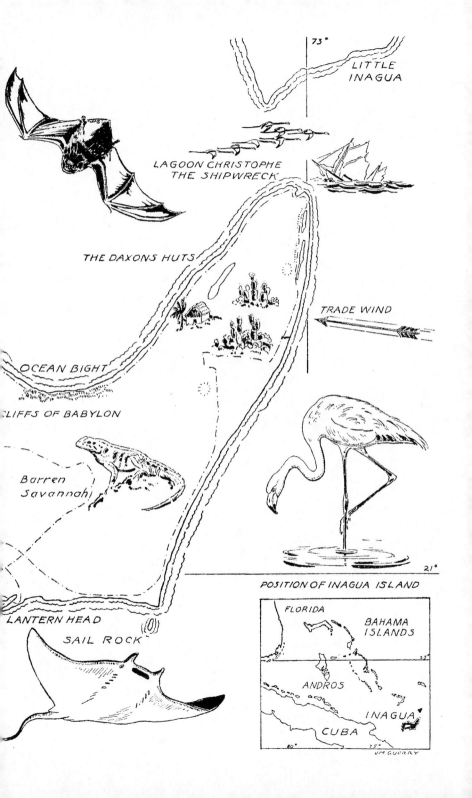

73°

LITTLE
INAGUA

LAGOON CHRISTOPHE
THE SHIPWRECK

THE DAXONS HUTS

TRADE WIND

OCEAN BIGHT

CLIFFS OF BABYLON

Barren
Savannah

21°

POSITION OF INAGUA ISLAND

LANTERN HEAD

SAIL ROCK

FLORIDA

BAHAMA
ISLANDS

ANDROS

INAGUA

CUBA

JM GUERRY

CHAPTER I

The Isles of the Indies

In the cold gray light of a mid-November evening our sailing ship lay becalmed. Evanescent wisps of fog swirled about her masts and melted softly into the blank grayness beyond. It was very quiet. Only the faint lap-lap of tiny waves at the waterline and the mournful cry of a gull, far distant and muffled by the mist, disturbed the silence. Close together on the slack sheet lines long rows of glistening moisture drops hung listlessly or dropped pattering on the sodden deck. I listened intently, straining my ears for the sound of ship's bells or fog horn, but heard nothing save a block at the masthead that was creaking a trifle. Once the distant gull broke the stillness again, but then even this plaintive sound ceased after a moment and was lost.

For five days we had been drifting like this, moving slowly through the empty fog, drifting from nothingness to nothingness, and on into the blank grayness again, sails barely filling or hanging limp for hours at a stretch. While I listened a faint breeze, smelling vaguely of salt marshes and decaying seaweed, stirred momently, straightened the drooping sheet lines, and then died as it was born. The spoked wheel rocked once, groaned as though inexpressibly weary, and then became immovable.

Disgusted, I knocked the ashes from my pipe, shook the water from my dripping oilskins and then opened the companionway slide. A breath of warm air came rushing out redolent of the good smell of cooking food and filled with the muffled anthem-like strains of Sibelius' majestic "Fin-

1

landia." Wally Coleman, my tall, blond, Nordic-looking first mate, chief cook and companion, gave me a cheery grin as I slid down the ladder and dropped sleepily on a bunk. With one hand he was balancing a frying pan filled with a mound of sizzling brown oysters over the galley stove and with the other preparing to lift the needle from the Sibelius record which was spinning on a small portable phonograph tightly bolted to a shelf near his bunk.

"No sign of wind yet?" he asked.

I shook my head and fell back on the blankets. I was a little worried. Hour after hour this fog had hung heavily about us, shrouding us in an unnatural gloom and retarding our progress. I was disturbed because I had the feeling that this prolonged quiet unbroken except for the intermittent blare of our fog horn was the prelude to something more violent. It was then past the middle of November and I knew that December was coming with December's gales and I was anxious to be clear of northern waters.

Through the portholes I could see that the light was waning and the gloom growing deeper. There was something intangible about this gloom, it had no depth or substance but possessed a certain indefinite quality that seemed unreal. This was the fifth night the daylight had vanished in shadowy emptiness.

Coleman lit an oil lantern set in brass gimbals and in its pleasant soft glow the feeling of depression vanished. Across a small table he shoved a steaming heap of oysters and potatoes, hot coffee and a prodigious pile of brown biscuits and yellow butter. We fell to with gusto, talking little, for the salt air had made us hungry. Then sated with good food we dropped back on our bunks to smoke and relax. But first I went on deck again, groped forward to the main stays where I found the riding light, lit it and placed it in its fastenings. The fog was so thick that its glow disappeared within eight feet. I then took a sounding and dropped the anchor for the night. From the depth of water I knew we were somewhere in the center of the Chesapeake Bay, but exactly where I was not certain.

Below decks again, I lit my pipe, drew on it for a few minutes and then let my eyes stray over the ship's cabin before me. It was a comfortable place. In it was contained everything that two men could possibly need for many months to come. It differed from the ordinary ship's cabin in that one entire side was taken up by a carefully constructed laboratory table of considerable length. About this table was grouped a considerable array of glittering chemical bottles of varied sizes and hues, and an odd assortment of instruments all tightly fastened with brackets to the wall so they would not shift with the motion of the ship. A binocular microscope shrouded in a watertight rubber case was bolted tightly to the table top and near it was a rack containing a half dozen hypodermic syringes ranging in size from a small 2 cc. glass syringe to a large affair of gleaming nickel with a capacity of nearly a pint. Likewise in a rack, was a case of dissecting instruments, clamps, hooks and chains, scalpels, needles and forceps. Below the scalpel rack was a dissecting board with drains leading to a shining monel metal sink divided in two portions. One division was free of all encumbrance but the other contained a complete set of developing and fixing racks with rinsing apparatus for photographic use. Adjacent to this was a compact printing machine, a timer and a number of holders for drying and processing film. Below the table a number of drawers held a considerable assemblage of materials, collecting nets, small dredges, cases of specimen bottles, unused film, guns and numerous other items. The remainder of the table area was taken up by shelves of reference works, mostly large volumes in dull gray or brown covers.

The science of navigation claimed the last five feet of the

table, that portion closest to the stern, as was evidenced by a set of charts securely clipped in position and by a chronometer which ticked steadily in a padded plush case. Next to the chronometer was another case containing a sextant and a set of night glasses.

Opposite the laboratory table and forward near the hold, partitioned off so the heat would not be oppressive, was the galley from which Coleman had conjured up the oysters, brown biscuits and coffee. Aft of this, one on each side of the ship, were our bunks tucked in roomy spaces beneath the deck beams. It was about these that we expressed our individualities, the only private space we had, for all beyond was common territory.

Coleman had a comfortable rack for pipes, easily reached by the turn of a hand. They were an amazing and considerable collection, for he was an inveterate smoker, and close by in a securely fastened humidor was a mound of yellow tobacco. Above his bunk and tightly screwed to the wall were three pictures—Franz Hals' "The Laughing Cavalier," a Japanese print showing a delicately limned egret poised daintily on one foot, and another more vigorous painting called "The Gulf Stream." This last, a work by Winslow Homer, showed a dismasted vessel, not much smaller than ours, rolling in an angry sea with a lone man reclining wearily on the deck, sullenly watching a great blue shark that was slowly circling the hull. Coleman had admired and purchased the picture long ago when we had first contemplated this voyage. For some reason it had struck his fancy and he had hung it in his room at home and then later on our ship as a taunt against the sea.

I liked the picture, too, but somehow the spirit in which it was hung stirred me to uneasiness. I felt that the sea should not be mocked with lightness, for I had seen it in anger too many

times, but Wally had laughed at my superstition and fastened
the frame in its place.

Both our bunks were surrounded with books wherever there
was space to place a rack to hold them. A glance at the volumes
showed a wide diversity of choice, a few volumes of poems,
a treatise or two on philosophy, a number of current novels,
a dozen or so biographies of ancient Romans, a pet subject of
mine, a few choice bits of literature and some others not so
studious. On Wally's side near the galley was a watertight rack
containing dozens of phonograph records, an assemblage pooled
from our separate collections, Wagner, Grieg, Puccini—and
Sibelius, whom Wally admired inordinately, and close by, the
phonograph which was again playing the majestic chords of
"Finlandia," for at least the eighth time since supper was put
on the table.

Here in the narrow confines of our ship's cabin were all the
necessities, both physical and mental, for an enjoyable existence
—dry bunks, a warm stove, tobacco, stores of food in the hold,
the choice of the world's most beautiful music imprisoned on
our records, good books—and an adventure looming ahead.

It was the laboratory table, however, that was the key to the
entire picture. Our ship, the cabin, all centered about its existence. It was the working heart of the ship, the reason for its
being and the entire excuse of the expedition.

All men have their dreams, their visions of affluence or even
affectation, their hopes of peace and security, of success and
ambition, some peculiar fantasy that each individual sets his
heart upon and pursues. These dreams are as varied as men
themselves and like the men that conjure them out of thin
emptiness or of need, they differ in intensity and substance.
Our entire cosmos is laid on the foundation stuff of men's
hopes and desires. So it was with our ship.

As far back as I could remember I had dreamed of owning a sailing ship, a sleek thing of tall masts, of taut gleaming canvas and smooth white hull. It is a dream common to many men. But as the years passed my hope grew in intensity and was fed by an increasing restlessness that is still with me and which I find difficult to explain, even to myself. Some dreams come of themselves, come unexpectedly and pass as quickly. Others and the more enduring ones grow slowly, gaining in stature with the years like children, spreading out, acquiring purpose and going on to realization. It was thus with this dream. From visions of mere adventure these fancies gave way to an object of serious intent. But there was first an interlude that shaped the ends of the dream so that it acquired dignity and became more fitting.

The interlude began in the strange little Republic of Haiti where I was engaged in biological research for the American Museum of Natural History. Prior to this time the pressure of financial and social obligations had forced me, like nearly everyone else, into business; and for a few years I was submerged in a welter of mercantile activity. My lifelong friend, Wally Coleman, with whom I had often discussed the ship of dreams and with whom I had planned long voyages, had drifted into medical work and it seemed that our much planned adventures would never mature. But then an opportunity came for a vacation in Haiti with the privilege of doing for the American Museum some research which had been my hobby for several years.

In Haiti I began to become keenly aware that I was leading a very pleasant life. As an amateur biologist I found ample excuse to indulge my hobby—to seek new places, new species, new habits of those species, and above all to have an opportunity to satisfy an inordinate curiosity about what lay in the next valley, over the curve of the mountain or beyond the turn of the coast. As the time to return home came close I became interested in a research problem that made it desirable to visit a number of the other West Indian Islands, particularly some of the small uninhabited and less frequented ones.

It was the spell of these islands, lying low under the horizon, that drove the dream into reality. Just beyond reach they lay, dozens of them strewn over the blue water from the reaches of the Bahamas to the deserty coasts of Yucatán. On many no student of natural science had stepped, or stepped only casually, lingering for a few hours at the most. It was my desire to remain at each until its faunal peculiarities were digested and understood. At that moment it seemed more important to seek these islands fully equipped to piece together the biological puzzle which interested me more intensely than anything else I could think of. Also, it was a splendid reason to justify the long latent dream. I knew from previous experience that native vessels were unseaworthy and uncomfortable, swarming with lice and sour with bilge. To work successfully one must be able to live in comfort, with a mind relaxed and at ease, to be free of insects and worrisome natives and also to have with one some of the more pleasant things, good clean food, stimulating books, music, when the monotony of the daily task was done. Why not give up business, seek the islands in one's own ship, in a vessel fitted expressly for the purpose?

Why not? Well, there was the matter of money. That puzzled me considerably. There was the matter of some eighteen hundred miles of open ocean between home and the islands of the Indies. There was the matter of storms and hurricanes, the mysteries of navigation to fathom and, above all, the problem of finding and outfitting a ship for the task.

So fired was I by the idea that I mailed a letter to my old friend Wally Coleman. Would he be willing to consider such a voyage? Impatiently I waited his reply. It came soon after.

"You bet," his letter said. "When do we start?" Hurriedly I wound up my Haitian vacation and returned to the United States.

Back in America the scheme did not seem so easy. Financing the project was the most difficult problem. For weeks and months we scrimped and saved, putting away a few dollars here, a few more there, until we thought we had enough. There were contacts to be made, arrangements with the museum to bring to completion, endless discussion about the scientific problems to be undertaken, how these problems had best be approached and correlated. There were nightly scannings of charts, mappings of itinerary, reminding us of the days long past when we had done the same thing in imagination.

Practical consideration of the problems involved, including those of finance, soon convinced us that ours was to be a small expedition. We could not afford a yacht nor could we pay a crew to man it. The needs of our research program demanded that we should be able to slip into little coves and harbors closed to ships of deep draught. It was essential in order to carry out this program that we utilize the smallest vessel compatible with the task in hand.

Such is the driving power of dreams that in due time we found ourselves with a snug little sailing ship, the backing of a great museum and an appalling sense of what we had started. But it was not as simple as that. A year and a half slipped by before we even found our ship. We did not just pick her up— our boat had to fill too many specifications. We needed a ship that would be seaworthy, staunch and sturdy. We had to have room in which to live and work in comfort; we had to be able to carry provisions and water for long periods so as to be independent regardless of location; we had to have a ship that could be sailed in any weather by one man, if necessary. Such a boat was not easy to find. We scouted all over our home waters, over the Chesapeake Bay. Nothing suited; all that we could find were too old, too narrow, too flimsy, too large or small—everything but what we wanted. Eventually, and unexpectedly, the search came to an end. In a small shipyard at Oxford, Maryland, in process of construction was exactly what we desired. Could we buy the vessel? We were told that we could not, for the owner also had his dreams, but that we could have one made like it. Within a month the contract was in the builder's hands.

We had chosen a famous model. In fact, we had chosen one of most famous boat models of all time. Our ship was to be an exact replica, except for the cabin and fittings, of the famous *Spray* of Captain Joshua Slocum who, it will be remembered, sailed the original around the world single-handed in the late 1890's. He set a precedent in maritime history and proved beyond all question that open ocean sailing in small boats was both practical and safe. All honor to him. As time proved, if we had searched the world over we could not have selected a better model.

But this was only the beginning. There followed long months of waiting—doubly weary for expeditionists anxious to be off—long hours of planning and planning again, outlining our scientific problems, working them out in the smallest detail. The success of any expedition, great or small, depends largely on the amount of beforehand planning—particularly so on an expedition as hazardous as this one. There would be days, weeks on end when we would be miles from the nearest settlements; there would be times of storm, times of calm, terrain of all sorts to work over and provide for; we had to be an entity within ourselves. Most important, we had to be able to care for our specimens and scientific materials when secured—all this in the limited space of a thirty-eight foot sailing ship.

There comes a time in the life of every individual, at least

every individual that deviates from the usual, when he pauses
in calm moment and considers what is before him. I think there
were times when both Coleman and I quaked in our shoes.
We were not so concerned about our bodily comforts—a lifetime of canoeing, tramping and camping had hardened us to
difficulties—but there was our responsibility to the museum
whose curator had placed sufficient faith in our idea to sponsor
the expedition. He was taking a chance, too, chancing expensive equipment, going to no end of trouble so that the expedition would be a success. We were anxious to prove that this
new departure in scientific expedition would be fruitful. It
was a radical departure from most sea-going expeditions,
nearly all of which had been undertaken in large schooners or
yachts, vessels with crews to man them and scientific staffs to
fulfill their special duties. But as these things were beyond the
reach of the average naturalist—most of them being poor people
at best—we were anxious to prove that two men in a small ship
could maintain themselves in the field for long periods, under
all sorts of conditions and return physically and mentally en-
riched by the experience and still produce work of value in
their special avenues of science. Could we? There were those
who thought we could not.

But a dream once started, like a snowball on a hill, grows
of its own momentum. In the rush of activity that followed we
forgot our doubts and tackled the task before us. There was
equipment to be stored, yet made ready for instant use. A year
and a half's supply of foodstuffs somehow disappeared by
magic—we shook our heads in doubt when two truckloads
arrived at the dock in Baltimore. Just how we were going
to stow two truckloads of food in a thirty-eight foot boat that
was half taken up by cabin and laboratory we did not know.
But we did it somehow, that and a lot more. And collecting
equipment, tins of preservative, nets, jars, specimen tags and all

those things peculiar to naturalists. Guns and cases of ammunition—seemingly enough to start a private revolution—typewriters, cameras and film in watertight cases, solution jars, and the thousand and one things incident to an expedition. All this and still more went into the bowels of our ship, disappeared into carefully constructed racks and lockers, so placed that all would be readily available.

Summer slipped into early fall, October into November, and the day of departure was at hand. Proudly we surveyed our vessel. We had spared no effort to make her seaworthy, spared nothing that she should be all the dream intended. Now the dream was reality, was a vision no longer, but a hope fulfilled in stout hull, stately masts and billowing canvas. We would not have exchanged places with the wealthiest banker in Wall Street.

There was no fanfare or blowing of trumpets when we left Baltimore, our port of registry. Our vessel, unheralded, unnoticed except for a few dock loiterers, slipped quietly out of her quay and headed downstream. Gently the bow turned outward, past the soil laden piers of Baltimore, past the great shipyards and the clouds of billowing smoke, and on into the open bay. Slowly the blurred outlines of the tall buildings melted into the haze, faded and passed from view. A quick breeze sprang out of the north, fanned out the spreading sails and pressed the hull far into the water. From down along the keel came the surge of moving liquid, an indefinable movement that pressed against the rudder face and transmitted itself into a keen vibration of the wheel. A sailing ship on the move! The white of sails and the islands of the Indies in the offing. What if the ship was only thirty-eight feet long?

Almost immediately after leaving the port of Baltimore, while still within sound of the bell buoys that clanged mournfully at the harbor entrance, the haze deepened, thickened and dropped lower and lower until the atmosphere was surcharged with clinging moisture. The breeze died and a fog settled that hid all signs of the shore. Hour after hour we lay motionless or crept slowly down the bay steering by compass alone. On all sides came the throaty whistles of invisible steamers feeling their way to port or the sound of their bells, strangely muffled, while they waited for the mist to lift.

Once a tall black gull-spattered buoy loomed out of the fog, towered high above the railing, and then passed on to vanish almost immediately. By its legend we reset our course and then drifted on again into space. Other than this in the whole five days we saw nothing but the still water at the rail and the encircling wall of swirling mist.

Down in the cabin we talked awhile, smoked our pipes to dead ashes, and then drifted off to sleep. Sometime after midnight I stirred in the blankets and awoke. Somehow I had sensed something wrong. Coleman was awake, too. We could hear the noise of waves slapping against the hull but they did not seem to have a proper sound. We went on deck in our pajamas. It was quite black, a darkness relieved only by the dull gleam of the riding light. The fog had lifted but it was so dark we could not see twenty feet away. We then noticed that although the fog was gone the stars were still blotted out. We moved up to the anchor chain, a new one untried. It hung straight down. We hauled on it. It came up—one foot, two, three—and then nothing. It had sheared off just under the waterline. We were adrift somewhere in the Chesapeake.

Then the storm came. It was preceded by a rush of cold air, a chilling breeze from out of the darkness that dropped again into a dead calm after a brief interval. When it ceased it began to rain and the drops sang on the water. Quickly we worked to get the ship under three reefs. We could not afford to be blown across the Chesapeake and on to a lee shore. That would mean the end of the expedition then and there. We had not quite finished our task when shrieking down from the northeast came the wind again, bitter cold, tearing across the waters, catching up the spray and pelting it against the house. There was a thundering of wet canvas, a crashing of blocks and the sing of air tearing through the taut rigging. Our vessel heeled to the blast, rolled far to one side and, like a startled thing, leaped into the darkness.

I caught one glimpse of Coleman in the gleam of the riding light—we had not yet had time to place the red and green running lanterns—a glimpse of a wet figure in soaked pajamas straining on the jib sheets. A second later darkness shut down on everything. Then pandemonium broke loose. The mizzen which we had not had a chance to reef had torn away, all except one corner. It was flapping like a great flag in the gale, flapping and thundering as only wet canvas can thunder in a storm. We thought the mast and entire stern rigging would go. Throwing the bow into the wind and heaving to as quickly as we could, we leaped for the stern. One corner of the sail caught Coleman a lashing blow on the shoulders and laid him flat on the slippery deck. He got up and tried again. It was like trying to fight a mad bull in the dark. The hard rope edging beat and smashed against our bodies, battered our arms and legs. We tried to get a line around the thrashing canvas, almost succeeded, only to lose it as an extra strong puff tore it away again. Once more I caught a glimpse of Coleman. His pajamas were gone, all except a portion of the trousers which were still hanging on. Water was streaming off his nude body and his hair hung limp and wet. It was bitter cold but we were perspiring profusely. Our fingers were becoming raw, beaten by the gaff which was still fast to the sail. Finally, by securing a line around a portion we managed to tame the thing little by little, a few inches at a time, until we had it firmly lashed in place. For a moment we rested, eased out the sheets—they were as taut as iron bars—and tacked into the storm. We were in a nasty position. A wind-swept shore behind us, we did not know how far, and a maze of shoals ahead. If we could only pick up a light. We beat on into the teeth of the gale for shelter. At last a light—Sharp's Island at the mouth of the Choptank River. We came about and drove for safety.

Minute by minute the storm increased in intensity until we were the center of a blinding screaming froth of water. If the Chesapeake Bay could act like this how would the mighty ocean behave? We voiced a hope that we would escape anything similar at sea and drove on in the darkness. We beat on and on, barely holding our own, until a faint glimmer crept through the clouds and showed the river mouth ahead. Vainly we tried to tack into it. Time and time again we were beaten back only to try once more. Noon came and passed and the storm grew in fervor. The hour arrived when we knew we had best give it up while there was still light to see.

We anchored that night only a few yards from shore in the lee of a small island some miles away. We hoped the spare anchor would hold. Three days we lay back of that island waiting for the storm to break, three days of anxiety, for we had much to do before setting out into the ocean.

If ever we should have doubted our ability to sail the isles of the Indies we should have doubted it then. But we didn't. The mere fact that we had weathered the gale—larger boats than ours were disabled in its path—gave us confidence.

This was only the first of a series of happenings. We had still half the length of the Chesapeake to go, a full hundred miles before we would be at the ocean's edge. We had yet to repaint our hull with copper at the shipyard in Oxford. It seemed that everything conspired against us. When we arrived at the shipyard the tide was out—driven out by the gale. It was the lowest in months and too low to approach the marine railway. While we were waiting for it to rise another gale screamed from out of the north, the northwest this time, and drove the tide still further. The new anchor and chain that we had ordered to replace the one lost was delayed, held up for no good reason at all. Early November passed into middle November, and still we were not ready.

But everything comes in time, and the day arrived when our vessel trim and newly painted slid off the railway into the calm waters of the Tred Avon River. We named her *Basilisk* after a Central American lizard that, similar to the water striders, has the power of walking on the water's surface. Like her famous progenitor the *Spray*, we hoped the *Basilisk* would make maritime history, a famous model put to a new use. That day our pride was unalloyed by any doubt. For the sun shone and all was life and activity. A gentle breeze caught our sails and carried us down the bay. We passed a fleet of milling oyster boats dredging on the bars and their crews waved greeting, for the news of the voyage had spread over the bay country. There seemed nothing to detain us then.

But there was. For that evening after the sun had set in a great gleam of yellow and red another dense fog had settled upon us and wrapped us up in its white mystery. Once again from all over the Chesapeake came the doleful clanging of ship's bells and the slow mournful whistles of the buoys. That day passed and the next and still the mist hung close, hiding all from sight and hushing even the sounds of the ducks that blundered away in the fog. On we pressed, stretching every inch of canvas for the breeze that scarcely moved. And we became depressed and blue at the never-ceasing delay.

Dark came, and light and darkness again, and still the fog remained. Once we passed a great ship, heard first her bell tolling in the gray, passed her and were swallowed in the murk.

A barred owl came from the land beyond and lit on our masthead and devoured a killdeer there. Otherwise nothing moved
except the translucent jellyfish that pulsed in the sea at the
waterline. If only the fog would lift—

When finally it raised, we beheld far ahead the gleam of the
great salt ocean and felt the roll of the long swells coming in
between the two capes with their twin lighthouses.

In Hampton, Virginia, at the ocean's edge, we received a
deluge of mail, letters and telegrams from men and boys anxious
to go along. Word of the voyage had reached the ears of the
press and while we were beating through the muck of a November fog the newspapers of the land had told the story. From
far and wide, from the little ports along the coast, from the
valleys and hills of the blue Appalachians, from the mid-west
prairies came letters, typewritten, scrawled, beautifully penned
some of them—all asking one thing. Can we go, they said? Can
we go? We will work for nothing if you will only let us go—
we will scrub decks, anything to go with you. Such is the spell
of the Indies, of white sails and trim hulls. Some of these letters were pathetic. The writers wished to go so badly. Henry
David Thoreau once wrote lines to the effect that most men
lead "lives of quiet desperation." Quiet rebellion against all the
established things, against the monotony of city life, of farm
life, against the drudgery of doing the same thing every day.
Wordsworth expressed it differently. "The world," he wrote,
"is too much with us; late and soon, getting and spending, we lay
waste our powers,—little we see in Nature that is ours, we have
given our hearts away—" And so the letters came—can we go?

Of course they couldn't. We would have needed a steamer
to have taken them, even a fraction of them. But we felt sorry
for those that wrote, they were so bound to their desks and
plows and occupations. It seems that the thick fingers of organized living press heavily on the souls of men, for they long to

be free, to move under the sky and over the sea if they have to scrub decks and work for nothing for the privilege.

Now that we were at the ocean's edge we were even more impatient to be gone. We realized that the longer we delayed the greater the possibility of running into evil weather. Consider again what we had started. We, two city-bred men, were about to sail into the open ocean in a thirty-eight foot boat. Before we could make a landfall we would have to cover a minimum of eighteen hundred miles of open sea. Not that it had not been done before. Old Captain Slocum had sailed the same model vessel around the world single-handed. But Captain Slocum was a seaman of many years' experience. We were two amateurs in every sense of the word. I had been to sea a number of times but never in the capacity of navigator. Coleman had never seen the ocean before. Furthermore, on our shoulders rested the responsibility of carrying out a scientific program of no small magnitude. It was more or less essential to this program that we cover a full itinerary of ten thousand miles, back and forth from island to island. Nor were these waters any too well charted or catalogued. Yet here was winter upon us before we had cleared our home shores. Already ice was forming on the decks in the morning, making them slippery as glass. Impatiently we watched the weather reports, hoping for clear skies and northwest winds. Finally the tidings came from the weather bureau—moderate winds and clear.

CHAPTER II

The Sea's Way

WE who live in the heart of great cities, who lead our entire
lives in deep straight canyons of brick and stone or on the
peaceful meadows of farms, forget in the security of our mode
of living that there is a sea, that only a short distance from our
Manhattan, Philadelphia or Boston lie miles upon miles of restless water, turbulent lonely reaches that stretch away to infinity and beyond. In our complacency we forget that the sea
is the greatest geographical feature of the earth and that it has
endured unchanged for long ages while continents rose and
fell, came into being and disappeared.

The sea is the last wild frontier. Yet here in constant change-
ful mood, nature reveals the entire scope of her emotions. No
sunlit meadow alight with flowers and with gauze-winged insects is more peaceful than a calm ocean, nor is there a land
scene more replete with life and vigor than a teeming seascape
in the trades where the white caps curling from the tops of the
waves hurtle forward and spend themselves in white froth
against the dark blue. Then there are the times when Nature,
brooding over her wastes, sends the clouds and the fog, deep-
ens the sea tones and spreads a mournful melancholy over the
depths. And yet again, the sea is a savage place, she sends the
gale screaming from the four corners of the world to remind
men that their proper habitat is the land. When this happens
the ocean becomes the most awesome spot on earth, a turmoil
of mountainous waves, of bubbly froth and swirling breakers.
Only those who have lived through a great storm at sea, who
have fought and battled with the ocean on its own terms, can

know what this means.

We forgot all this. A deep sense of awareness, once latent but brought to the surface by the leaving behind of land ways, filled our minds as we made ready to go. In the pale gray of early dawn we raised our sails and on the wings of a gentle land breeze slipped out of Hampton Roads. It was chill that morning and very quiet save for the soft hissing of the waves at the waterline. In the dim haze near Norfolk we could make out the stark outlines of a large four-master, the schooner *Purnell T. White*. As we watched, her sails rose, one after the other, stretched taut and filled as she came about.

She was a beautiful thing in the early light, sails all pink with the newly risen sun and white hull glinting against the green water. How could we know that in the short space of eight days this ship would be a sodden helpless wreck or that, three years later, refitted and repaired and once again in service, her captain and crew would all be dead men, lost off the Carolina Capes?

Side by side we put to sea, the towering schooner and the tiny yawl. Our mast hardly reached her railing, or so it seemed, as she swept grandly past and headed for the capes and the rising sun. We watched her go with a feeling of friendly interest, for she was built by the same hand that with such care constructed our tiny ship.

Fifteen miles ahead lay the capes, barely discernible in the haze, and beyond the open sea. Thimble Shoal passed astern and then Willoughby. Gently but swiftly, the promised northwest wind died and left us wallowing. The tide, now at full ebb, began to flow again, carrying us back whence we came. It seemed we were destined to remain permanently in the Chesapeake.

Just when we had reached the point of uttermost exasperation Providence, weary of playing a game of checkmate, re-

lented and sent aid in the form of a low-hulled Coast Guard
vessel. This Coast Guard ship had seen us slowly drifting on
the tide and in a spirit of comradeship had come near to in-
quire where we were going. We told some uniformed figures
on her deck that our landfall was to be San Salvador in the
Bahamas, whereupon we could hear the captain say something
that sounded like "Holy smokes," could hear the engines reversed, saw him direct a sailor to pass a line with instructions
to make it fast. Wondering, we did as directed, and a moment
later were pleased to find ourselves being whisked along at the
grand pace of eight knots straight for the open sea. Soon we
passed the tall black and white lighthouse at Cape Henry,
passed the land's edge and went into the blue. And I suppose
those jolly Coast Guardsmen would have towed us further had
not the line parted and cast us loose.

They came on board for a few minutes, examined our papers,
found them in good order and wished us pleasant voyage. As
they departed they gave us a salvo of whistle blasts and a chorus
of good-byes. Then, as if in answer to our prayers, a gentle
breeze came up and wafted us into the broad Atlantic.

Of what took place from the moment of leaving the Coast
Guardsmen until about three o'clock the following morning
I have little recollection. Much of the events of that afternoon
and evening is blotted from my mind and has been recon-
structed from Coleman's notes and from what he has told me.
It seems that after leaving the Coast Guardsmen we set a course
east south east into the open ocean so as to be well clear of the
land should the breeze change. We watched the shore slowly
fade and in time disappear altogether. And it seems the sun set
in a great lowering bank of clouds that hung in dark masses on
the horizon. But the northwest wind remained with us and we
thought nothing of it. Night came, and the stars that gleamed
with it, stars that gleamed with a brightness we had seldom

seen before. That is, all save the portion of the sky that was wrapped in gloom and from whence no light came except the faint loom of the lighthouse many miles away. We stood watch on and watch off, one man on deck while the other slept in the cabin below. The first watch came and passed and the second, and all this time the patch of gloom on the horizon spread, cutting off the stars one by one, blotting out the milky way, and drawing a dark cloak over the zenith. And by the time of the third watch the entire firmament was drowned in gloom and we moved only by the pale shine of the running lights and by the faint gleam of the binnacle. All beyond the decks was blackness, though a blackness that seemed alive if one could judge by the myriad water sounds that came from off the sea's surface.

A certain heaviness seemed to lie over the ocean that night, a heaviness that oppressed though it was cold on deck and the wind was sharp. And this feeling of heaviness increased when, toward the end of the third watch, the wind slackened and hauled to another quarter. Still we did not feel alarmed but continued on our way. Coleman was on deck and he had made the necessary wheel and sheet adjustments for the change of wind. It was then about two in the morning. At three o'clock he came down in the cabin and shook me.

"You had better come on deck," he said, "there is something brewing."

And there was. Even down in the cabin we could hear a new tenor in the sounds coming off the water, a certain restlessness that stirred above the wave whisperings.

We glanced at the barometer. It was extremely low. The lowest we had ever seen. Hurriedly we struggled into oilskins and jackets and ascended to the deck. From out of the sea were coming great smooth swells, much too large for the wind that was blowing. We knew what that meant.

For a moment I stood beside Coleman at the wheel.

"I think we had better take in some sail," I muttered, "while we can."

Hardly were the words out when the thing happened. A freak wave rushing from out of the darkness caught our stern, lifted it high out of the water and, catching the bow as it passed, swung our tiny ship to one side. And as the stern rose, the great spreading mainsail with its heavy boom swept to center and then jibed with a sickening crash. Hundreds of pounds of heavy canvas, iron and wood driven by a strong wind caught me a smashing blow full in the face and dropped me senseless to the railing.

How long I lay there I do not know. Coleman groped for my inert body in the darkness and hauled me to the wheel box where he sat with one leg entwined about my waist to prevent my slipping over the low railing. Then from out of the ocean came a low moaning sound that momentarily increased in volume, a swelling chorus of wind-lashed waves combining in a wild medley that knows no description. Only those who have heard it will understand. The thing we had most feared had come.

With a surge of cold air the storm broke. Our tiny vessel, still under full sail, heeled far to the blast, heeled until the lee ports were under water, until it seemed that we must turn over. And Coleman in all the welter of spray and churning water struggled in the dark to secure my body so he would be free to shorten sail; with one hand he spun the wheel to relieve the strain. Soon huge waves from out of the darkness were washing our craft from stem to stern. The wonder of it is that the sails were not blown away or torn to ribbons. But by some miracle they held. Before leaving our native Chesapeake Bay, the oystermen and yachtsmen had laughed at our heavy sails and rigging, were amused at the canvas they said was thick enough for a three-masted schooner. But this same stoutness saved us that night and in the days to come when without our forethought we would have been lost indeed.

A full half hour passed before I regained consciousness. At first I was only dimly aware of what was going on, but as surge after surge of cold water swept over me and dribbled into the scuppers I was brought into wakefulness. My head ached excruciatingly. And I was cold. Bitterly so—drenched with water and lashed by the icy wind. I can dimly recall Coleman's leg pressed into my side, could feel it strain and flex as he struggled with the wheel. I tried to remember what had happened but could not, nor can I to this day. On one knee I rose, fell again and then painfully and slowly struggled to a sitting position. My neck and shoulder muscles seemed almost torn from their fastenings. Ten more minutes passed before I was fully awake. Then, in spite of the pain and violent headache, I began to realize the gravity of the situation.

We must get those sails in.

As soon as Coleman saw that I was able to fend for myself he threw the ship into the wind so that we might reduce canvas. Then began one of the most grueling half hours we have ever spent. Reefing sails in normal weather is a simple enough job, consuming on a ship as small as ours only fifteen or twenty minutes. But in the midst of a storm, with the ship plunging and pitching, with waves sweeping the deck from one end to the other, it is a difficult task. As though this were not enough, every jolt of the boom and shake of the canvas sent shooting pains darting up and down my head. The greatest job was getting the mainsail down. This task took the combined effort of both of us and our utmost strength. The wind would catch the sail and with the force of a titan belly out the slack canvas, jamming the jaws against the mast. Only by catching it between squalls and exerting our united weights on the downhaul were we able to get it down and reefed.

We saved our sails. The immediate danger was over. We were so exhausted by our efforts we had to sit for a few moments on the deck to recover. Our hands and fingers were torn and burned by the whipping of rope. In all the melee the jib lazy-jacks had chafed through and were flying out from the masthead like pieces of string. Reefing a jib in a storm with the lazy-jacks gone is a nasty job. You must creep out along the footropes, feeling with your heels for the next strand, and hope that the oncoming waves do not wash you from the bowsprit to which you are holding with all your strength. As the surging water sweeps up and the bowsprit dips you are plunged over your head into icy water only to come up and be buffeted by the wild flapping of the sail. Lazy-jacks hold a sail in an even bundle, but with these gone the canvas becomes a battering ram that thrashes and thunders in the grip of the wind.

Even with the sails reefed we were not out of danger. We had to continue to beat off the coast, for the wind was coming out of the northeast and we were a bare forty miles from shore. Forty miles is not much in a screaming northeaster that in a few hours could pile one on the beach. Though we would have liked to have hove-to until morning we dared not, but beat on into the dark.

The hours of the first night passed and morning came, but the storm did not abate. Instead, it increased in intensity and low clouds scudded just above the water. By the light from the east we could see that the sea was no longer green but a deep indigo, a dull blue that showed in intricate openwork between the froth patches. We were in the Gulf Stream. And, in verification, a yellow, berry-floated strand of sargassum weed drifted by and disappeared in the wake. That was a comfort. We knew then that we could heave-to and get some rest. We sorely needed it. For we were wet and cold; our fingers were fast growing numb.

With the coming of full light, even though we thought the wind could not increase in volume, it redoubled its vigor. With a sudden blast it hurled out of the north and caught our little ship in its full grip. Coleman seized a lifeline and held on to keep from being swept overboard. The sudden surge momentarily flattened the water and whipped great blinding sheets of spray from the surface. Over went the hull until the deck was at such an angle that we could not stand, but slid on our knees. A convulsive shudder shook the boat from sprit to rudder and, with lee decks completely hidden, she leaped ahead.

But this was only the beginning. In a few minutes we could barely see the bow, so dense was the spray. The din was terrific. From out of the sea came a shrieking, sighing sound unlike anything we had ever heard before. It was the sound of wind-tortured water and the bass roar of huge breakers. Only those who sail the sea in small ships, who tread decks a foot or so above the surface, can hear this. It is a sound that hangs close to the sea's surface, an indescribable medley that those who travel on large steamers do not know. After the passing of ten years, when civilization and city living has dulled much of the details of the great storm, we can still hear those gale sounds, they are so indelibly impressed on our memories. Perhaps the most awesome moment is that in which one discerns vaguely through the driving mist the form of a great wave advancing before the wind. Then the wave thins at the top, curls, and in a ferocious roar sweeps all before it. It is a deep-throated sound, sullen and powerful. And the rigging sounds—low mournful whistles rising and falling in weird crescendos with the speed of the gale. Only the wind about the house eaves in a winter blizzard approaches it in tenor. Nor is this all, for there are the ship sounds, mighty creakings of wood, the groanings of mast and boom, the twanging of taut ropes and the noisome clatter from down below where loose objects are battering back and forth.

That blast nearly finished us. But like the stout vessel she was, the *Basilisk* bore under the strain and carried on. We were growing weak from exhaustion and cold. We could not stay on deck much longer, for the waves that were spilling aboard were tremendous and bid fair to sweep us into the sea. We had prepared for this emergency, however, and loosened the sea anchor from its lashings on the cabin top. Laboriously we made it fast to a heavy hawser and eased it over the bow. Swiftly the big canvas funnel filled out as the ship drifted back. In a moment the hawser was taut and the bow in the wind. We could now go below and let the storm blow itself out.

There was not much else to do. The wind was blowing so hard that we could no longer stand on deck. Swiftly we opened the companionway slide and slipped below, slamming it shut before another wave came aboard. Our comfortable cabin! It was a shambles. Much of the cargo that we had so carefully stowed and boxed had broken loose and was strewn about. Pots and pans, a barrel of potatoes, stove lids, notebooks, charts and tin cans littered the floor in little piles. And with each lurch these piles would slither from one end of the cabin to the other. For a moment they would remain quiescent, then with the tilt of the ship gather speed and bang into the distant bulkhead. Then back again with a crash, intermingled with the tinkling of glass and the duller sounds of metal. It was inconceivable the number of articles that had come loose. Items that we had nailed tightly in boxes and bins. How they ever got away was difficult to understand. But they did.

The coal stove in the galley was a mess. The iron doors were opening and banging with a clatter that sounded like the rush of a gang of riveters working overtime and anxious to go home. With every wave that swept the deck a gush of salt water came down the stove pipe and burst from between the grates in a miniature flood. That meant another trip to the deck with rope and canvas. We tried to salvage some of the material drifting about on the cabin floor. It was useless. As soon as one object was stowed another came loose. The flat stove lids replaced on the range jumped off again when the ship suddenly plunged to one side and then back with a severe jolt. This same jolt sent the pair of us spinning the length of the cabin to pile in a sodden heap at the far end. It was impossible to stand. Progress was feasible only by clinging tightly to fast objects and waiting for a lull. The best method was crawling. Even then the lurching and pitching would hurl us reeling into the far wall and back again. After a time we gave it up and let the jumble take care of itself.

Our bunks were made of canvas stretched between metal frames. On our knees and between slitherings we slacked the canvas until it formed a deep hollow; then we piled in. Only thus were we able to keep our positions. As it was, we had to maintain a constant grip on the sides to keep from being thrown out. We could not sleep. It was difficult even to doze. Hour passed hour in monotonous succession. Every now and then we could hear something give, vague splinterings and tearings that came to us through the howling of the wind. Time and time again great waves would smash aboard. We could see them coming through the ports. We thanked the gods that we had full steamer ports of three quarter inch glass instead of the flimsy things generally used on vessels as small as ours. We could see these huge waves mount up and up, could see the bow dip as if to plunge into the depths, could see the oncoming mountains suddenly rise and curl and then break in a dark blue welter of foam and solid water. When they hit it was as if we had run into a stone wall. How wood and iron could hold together under such hammerings was inconceivable. Suddenly the cabin would be darkened as the mass swept over the deck, burying it under several feet of indigo water. Then the ports would become luminous green holes in which danced hundreds of bubbles. Shuddering, the ship would lift, spilling the water off the decks in white froth.

At about two o'clock the sea anchor tore loose from the hawser with a dull snap. In a trice the bow swung around until we were broadside to the wind. Then, hurling out of the sea, came a tremendous wave that caught the cabin full amidships. I was suddenly lifted and thrown out of my bunk across the full width of the cabin on top of Coleman. On the return lurch we were both spilled on the floor. We struggled to our feet and as soon as the water had cleared, climbed on deck, slamming the companionway hatch hurriedly behind us.

The scene that greeted us was awesome. All that was left of the jib lazy-jacks were half a dozen short pieces of rope, fuzzy frayed things only one-tenth of their original length. The remainder had whipped away a little at a time. The bowsprit shrouds, steel cables, had torn loose on one side and the attached footropes hung in a jumble. Part of the solid oak railing was in splinters and an iron boom-rest had been yanked from its fastenings, carrying with it shredded pieces of wood and metal. Two water casks lashed to wooden supports were smashed and the anchor chain had been lifted out of its coil box and was hanging straight down in the depths. A full ton of it. Getting this last back on board nearly broke our backs. We had unshackled it from the anchor before leaving Hampton Roads so as to have a perfectly clear deck, and now we could not get it around to the winch to haul it in.

Hurriedly twirling the wheel we coaxed the ship around until we were flying under bare poles. But we were in an ugly position. Somewhere to the west and not too many miles away was Hatteras with its maze of shoals and streamers of thundering surf. There was no help for it but to beat into the storm again. Swinging about we got under four reefs and once again breasted the gale.

By this time it was getting dark. In all these hours we had eaten nothing, nor had we thought of food. Coleman crawled up into the hold and brought back a tin of canned beef which we devoured uncooked.

Captain Joshua Slocum, in telling of his voyage around the world in the original *Spray*, had claimed that for hundreds of miles his little ship had steered herself as accurately as if there had been a man at the wheel. Provided, of course, that the wind remained in the same quarter. The feat was accomplished by trimming and adjusting sail and rudder so that there was a perfect balance fore and aft. This claim has been disputed many times, but without foundation. We owe our lives to this one feature. For that evening, exhausted and weary, chilled to the marrow, unable to remain longer on deck, yet afraid to let the ship scud before the wind, we adjusted sail and rudder as Slocum had described. And in all that wild melee of storm the grand little ship plunged sturdily along, straight as an arrow, for the center of the ocean.

All through that night she sailed with not a soul on deck, tossed and beaten by the worst winter storm of 1929–30. Miles away the great schooner *Purnell T. White*, in whose company we had put to sea, was also fighting the gale and waging a losing battle. And far and wide, north and south of us that night on the broad Atlantic, sturdy steamers were sending out S.O.S. calls or limping into port with smashed houses and twisted decks. On and on we pressed, plunging through the waves, bobbing to the top and sliding down the valleys, proof that the old sea captain had not lied. A gallant little ship, the

Basilisk. There should be more like her.

The second day passed and the third, and when the fourth dawned in a gloom of gray we did not think we would live to see the evening. We were so exhausted by then that we could scarcely crawl from the deck to the cabin and up again. The exertion of adjusting sheets was so great that we would have to lie on the wet deck for fifteen or twenty minutes to recover. The wind was blowing as hard as ever and the waves were sickening to behold. Up, up they towered, great sweeping mountains that seemed to reach to the sky. If ever we felt small and unimportant, it was then.

Once a wave broke over the top of the mast. *Forty-two feet five inches* our mast measured, and this breaking wave topped it by a *yard*. Coleman was down below when it struck and I was crouched by the wheel box so that I would avoid the full force of the wind. Suddenly, and without warning, a great wall of water seemed to rise in front of the ship, rose with terrific speed, forced up by some tremendous pressure beneath, rose and towered above the mast. For a brief second I could see pale light shining through it, could see a yellow strand of sargassum weed high above my head. Then down it came with an ear-splitting crash. With stunning force it hit the deck, threw me against the aft railing and buried the ship under tons of water. It seemed that we would never come up. All I can remember is choking and fighting to get to my feet as the mass poured over the stern.

A minute later a dazed Coleman cautiously opened the companionway slide a few inches. He looked groggy and a great bruise showed on the side of his face. He had been clinging to his bunk trying to get a few moments' rest when suddenly the wave hit. In a brief second all light was blotted out and tons of falling liquid hit the deck. Water squirted in great streams through the seams in the hatch and companionway slide, dousing the cabin with water. For an awful minute all was dark and then with a sickening lurch he had been thrown out of his bunk. He came on deck fully expecting to find me washed away.

Three similar waves boarded us that night, straining the woodwork and opening many of the deck seams. Then it was that we saw the picture of the "Gulf Stream" run water. Gulf Stream water too, the sea's turn to laugh!

And though we did not think we would last through the night, we somehow plunged on, heading ever further into the ocean. In all these hours we had taken no sights, had no idea of our whereabouts other than by dead reckoning. We felt by this time, however, that we could afford to turn tail to the storm and run before it. As Coleman put it—"If we are going to hell, we might as well go flying." Running before the wind eased the strain somewhat, but was risky business. Added to the danger of jibing was the hazard of being pooped by a following wave. But by this time we did not particularly care. Anything seemed better than hammering into the gale,—hour after hour of terrific punishment and not getting anywhere was wearing on our nerves. Due south we headed the *Basilisk* and there began one of the most thrilling portions of the entire voyage.

With the speed of an express train we tore down the massive watery hillsides, tore on and into the south. Hour after hour the miles reeled behind us and were lost in the foam. While tearing thus before the wind we witnessed one of the most magnificent sights that the sea has to offer. We had just mounted the crest of an exceptionally large roller when from under our bows burst a great porpoise. Another came and another until the water fairly seethed with them. And at the same moment, from out of the ocean, from the depths that just before had been lifeless, from as far as we could see on the crest

of that gigantic wave, burst forth other porpoises leaping and
hurtling toward the ship. There must have been hundreds of
them. Sleek black things that surged and dived in effortless
gambol, all heading for our bows. There they collected in a
heavy muscled swarm, gloriously graceful, active and free.
Weary and tired as we were we could not help but feel a tingle
of pleasure at the sight. And as mysteriously as they came they
disappeared. All vanished as one, as if by given signal they
slipped into the depths at the same moment and were gone.
There was only the swirl of foam and bubbles where a minute
before was activity.

The porpoises made us feel better, helped to take away some
of the lonely feeling that had come over us in our exhaustion.
They were the first life that we had seen since leaving the
land. Later the same day two petrels swept by, little black
things hardly visible through the spray. We could hear them
calling, a plaintive whistle that somehow seemed to have a certain sad timbre. How could they live in that chaos of water
hundreds of miles from land,—how could they survive days
of gale with only the spray-swept water to rest upon? But they
do. Mother Carey's chickens! Brave little things, that fly on
sickle-shaped wings close to the water's surface, feeding on
floating tid-bits, stray things that the sea gives up, subsisting
on tiny crustaceans, larval fishes and pelagic eggs. Storm and
calm, hurricane and smooth sea, it is all the same to Mother
Carey's chickens. Their niche in the scheme of things is not
an easy one.

The gale lasted nearly a week and a half. Ten days of torture
and misery. There were hours on end when we thought that
every boarding wave would be the one to split us wide open
and send us to the bottom. We had taken in hundreds of gallons of water. The cabin floor boards had come up and were
sloshing about, mixed with a jumble of wreckage. We were

weary and tired, sick of the sea and the storm. We did not know where we were. There had been no sun to take sights from. The chronometer had stopped, beaten into somnolence by the terrific jolting. But it was becoming warmer. We no longer needed coats on deck. Long ago we had discarded every bit of useless apparel. In times of stress it is common custom to be rid of all superfluous appurtenances. We had thrown our shoes aside—could keep the deck better in bare feet. Our hands were a sorry sight. Calluses, open blisters, deep red seams, raw scale covered our fingers and palms. It seemed we had been to sea for an eternity. Ten days. In ten days we had got down to elementals. We were no longer concerned with a scientific program—we would worry with that later—if we survived.

But one morning the wind dropped, the sun burst from the clouds and nature once again smiled. Hungrily we drank in the warmth, basked in the golden light that streamed from the sky. We had almost forgotten there was a sun. It cheered us immeasurably. And though from out of the north the waves still came piling they did not break, but lifted us gently and passed on as if to say, "There you are, we wouldn't hurt you."

From out of the sea came flying fish, gliding creatures that skimmed from one wave crest to another. They cheered us too. It is good to see live things around even though they are no more than fishes. With hope renewed we set about straightening ship. It was a herculean task. As if half afraid the sea was playing us tricks, we carefully opened the hatch and bailed water. Gallons and gallons of it we dumped into the sea. Even when we had it all out, the cabin was still the dampest place imaginable, so much so that in the evening, rather than sleep below with all the wreckage to remind us of what we had been through, we lay on the deck beneath the stars.

We adjust ourselves quickly to new conditions. With life no longer a struggle for existence our thoughts once again

turned to the program before us. Where were we? We wished
to make the island of San Salvador where Columbus first made
landfall on that memorable morning in 1492. Here we were
to check on certain faunal conditions before proceeding to
other islands to continue our investigations. As nearly as we
could estimate from dead reckoning we were about eight hundred miles off the Florida Coast. With the chronometer stopped
we could not figure longitude. Latitude was an easier matter
though we had to break open the cabinet drawer to get out the
sextant, so swollen was the wood from the wetting it had received. Noon sights showed us to be in the latitude of Nassau.
We decided to continue south until we reached the parallel of
San Salvador and then make westing on the prevailing trade
winds.

On and on we sailed. At first we were almost afraid to shake
out full canvas, so fearful of the wind had the storm made us.
But the continued sunlight brightened our outlook and we
dipped gently on the wings of a mild breeze. A day passed and
another, and still no sight of land. Once in the early morning,
shortly after the sun had risen, a yellow-billed tropic bird had
come out of the west, circled in the blue and turned back again.
The following morning we saw a man-of-war bird and it, like
the tropic bird, circled and disappeared westward. Land was
somewhere over there. How far we did not know. The latitudes
of Eleuthra and Cat Island came and passed and still no land
showed up. We must be too far to the east. Noon sights gave
us the figures 24 degrees 3 minutes. San Salvador was due west.

As we swung the bow toward the afternoon sun the wind
shifted contrary to all rules of the trades and began blowing
briskly out of the west. Soon we were having hard going. Was
the sea never to be through playing with us? We held a consultation and decided to continue south again in the hope of

sighting Crooked or Mariguana Islands, or, failing these, the Caicos group. At any of these we could rest, clean ship and work back to San Salvador at leisure after once establishing our location. We must investigate these anyway and were bound to no order. On we went again. Ever southwards. Still no land. The wind continued beating out of the west cutting up a choppy, but not dangerous sea. Hour after hour we sailed, straining our eyes for a glimpse of green turf. There was nothing but rolling waves, yellow patches of sargassum weed and white caps. Several times Coleman climbed to the masthead. He could see nothing. Crooked and Mariguana were nowhere visible. Caicos then. Noon showed us to be exactly on the Caicos latitude. Water, everywhere water. We had never before realized that there was so much of it in the world.

Disgusted, we busied ourselves about the ship. At least we couldn't miss Hispaniola. We would sight it at sunrise. Coleman went below to tend to some duties and I became interested in the wheel ropes that had slackened badly and needed attention. Already the sun was setting, lowering in great banks of orange and red cloud. In a few moments it would be dark and I wanted to have the rudder in good shape. Busily I worked on, tightening the line and adjusting it about the drum. Casually I looked up.

There, strewn over the horizon, was land. Little mounds of it stretching in isolated lumps far in both directions.

"Land," I yelled down the companionway.

Coleman came bounding out and swarmed up the mast. It was land all right, good solid land silhouetted by the sinking sun. We had never thought that land could look so good. With big grins we shook hands in congratulation. Coleman went below again and returned a moment later with a pencil and a piece of soggy paper to make a sketch. He said it was such a pleasant

moment he wished to remember it. As for myself, I did nothing, just stood there and gazed. Now at last we could rest and
begin our work.

How little we knew!

CHAPTER III

Shipwreck

In the late afternoon of the following day we slowly climbed a low sandy bluff. At the top we paused a moment and then sank wearily to the ground. Before us the sand sloped away to a wide beach on which the shadows were lengthening rapidly. Even as we watched, little breakers slipped up the damp soil, hissed and sighed as they passed over the sand grains, and slid back again. As they slid they left on the beach myriad small objects—queer-shaped things that turned and rolled in the tide. Wreckage! Flotsam and jetsam that the sea had done with and was giving up to the land. Bits of spars, rope, sodden books, tin cans, instruments, bottles, boxes—and a picture of the Gulf Stream showing a man lying on the deck of a dismasted vessel, sullenly watching a shark that was circling by. The sea's turn to laugh. Journey's end.

Journey's end, indeed. Beyond the waves that sighed on the beach, beyond a lagoon of pale green water, glistened a line of seething white surf. A white frothy line that moved and pulsed, and emitted a constant throaty roar. The sound of breakers crashing on a coral reef. Squarely in the center of that seething line lay all that remained of a stout vessel. Each wave that rolled in lifted the hull a foot or so and with a resounding crash dropped it heavily into the spreading branches of coral. A sad ending for a stout vessel that had weathered a great winter storm and had gallantly carried its crew to safety when larger and better manned ships had gone to the bottom.

Journey's end and dream's end. There would be no sailing the isles of the Indies. It was a bitter dose. The irony of the

thing was that after going through so much, after living through
so much misery, so much cold and wetness, after all this, after
coming through a great winter storm we should meet disaster
on the very last stretch. And irony on top of irony; the wind
that was crashing the breakers on the reef was the usual trade
that we had expected to take us westward to San Salvador.
Too late now, too late to do us any good. The breeze that
should have carried us to safety was tearing our vessel apart
and spreading our gear on the bottom of the sea.

But worst of all was the stinging fact that we had met disaster
in a near calm. There was no excuse of storm or heavy wind
or great waves. The sea was like a millpond when Nemesis
boarded us. As flat and calm as a sea can be, save for a long
gentle swell from out of the east. Treacherous ocean! When
wind and wave had failed she had still one trick up her figura-
tive sleeve, a trick that we should have known about. The current—the smooth gliding current that, welling up from the
cool depths, glides its invisible intangible way to the surface.
The current had caught us unawares.

In the cool long hours before the coming of new day it had
caught us, had slowly, gently pulled us from our way, had
quietly without a sound dragged us to the waiting coral. Then
in a sudden last surge the swells had caught us and dashed us
onto the cruel coral. And the sea, in a last boisterous shout of
glee, had sent the wind, the trade wind to bring the matter to
conclusion. The sea had won.

After sighting land the evening before, reaction had set in
and we had fallen into a deep sleep. With the sinking of the
sun the wind had died, leaving us to wallow in a calming ocean.
For the first time since the ending of the storm we slept below.
utterly weary, confident that with hove-to sails we would wake
in the same spot in the morning. We would then approach the
land, establish our location and proceed to the nearest port.

All this while a strong current was carrying us northward where it swept around a point of land. But just before reaching this point it set directly into a maze of coral and reefs. On and on we drifted, nearer, ever nearer until the roar of the breakers must have reached the decks. But down below we slept on, exhausted by the days just past.

With a frightening crash we hit. Both Coleman and I were thrown to the floor. Dazed and sleepy, startled by the roar that came from outside, we rushed frenziedly for the deck. As we reached it another swell came from out of the ocean, lifted the ship and with a terrific lurch threw it on one side. Coleman grasped the railing and saved himself, but the lurch threw me spinning the entire length of the deck, through the jib sheets and over the bow into the foam. For a brief second I remember hurtling through the air, could dimly see the swirling surf beneath, and then plunged into the water. As I went down I was rolled over and over by the comber and into the arms of a great coral branch that held me in a strong painful grip. For another second I lay dazed. Off in the dark I could vaguely make out the mound of another roller, black against the stars. On and on it came, rose, curled and made ready to break. With a shout of alarm I quitted my painful bed of coral and dived headlong to one side. And as I dived the stricken ship rose on the tide and came down on the coral I had just left. Had I remained I would have been ground to a bloody pulp. The wave that so nearly finished me, rolled me a few feet further and then sucked me back to the bow. Hurriedly grasping the sprit chain I hauled myself inboard and onto the deck.

We made one last effort to save the ship. If we could only get one of our small boats overboard with an anchor and drop it behind the reef, we might still by quick action on the winch pull ourselves clear. With a knife that Coleman dashed into the cabin to secure we cut the lashings of the first boat and dropped it over the rail. Even as we did so another roller caught us amidships, lifted us slightly and brought us down on the skiff. It was mashed as flat as a flounder. The other boat fared a little better but was swamped a moment later.

It was no use. We were hard and fast. Every swell that came in carried us a foot or so further. A second later the rudder snapped off and was washed into the lagoon beyond the reef where it sank to the bottom. There was but one recourse—to save as much food and equipment as possible. A wind was coming up, the trade for which we had waited in vain. If we were to get anything ashore we must do it quickly. Food and water first. Particularly water. We knew that some of these islands were barren—dry waterless places where one could soon die of thirst. Quickly as we could on the careening deck we cut the lashings of the watercasks and with mighty heaves threw them into the surf. Disregarding everything else for the moment we jumped overboard, severely cutting ourselves on the jagged coral, and between crashing rollers edged the casks over the reef and into the calm waters of the lagoon. Satisfied that they would not float out to sea or be broken by surf we battled our way back to the ship again. Our feet and legs by now were bleeding freely from coral cuts and we were scratches and bruises from head to foot. Once again on the ship, we fought our way through the foam to the cabin. It was full of water. Somewhere underneath, the planking had torn loose and the bitter salt was surging in in a torrent.

The floor boards had come up and were rushing back and forth. They had the force of battering rams. The cabin was a fright. We leaped for our prize possessions. Frantically I clawed a cabinet apart to save my camera. It had accompanied me in all my jaunts in Haiti, in South America and at home. I would rather have lost a finger than that camera. Coleman dived for his microscope and other valuables. Holding them high above

our heads to spare them further wettings we made our way to
the deck. It was now careened at such an angle that we could
not walk on it. We slid into the water and struggled for the
lagoon.

Back again. This time for the sextant, motion picture camera,
ship papers, collecting equipment and choice books. Some we
got ashore, some we did not. It was a herculean task. The reef
was the worst of all, though swimming the eighth-mile lagoon
was not easy. By the third trip the hull had heeled so far over
that we could swim directly into the companionway. It was
heartbreaking. All our valuable instruments and materials were
being washed back and forth. Even as we tried to salvage them
great rollers would dash in the open companionway, snatch
them from our fingers and wash them out on the reef. The
white sand bottom for yards around was strewn with glittering tins, paper and brass. The cabin was a dangerous place.
Floating boards, boxes and weighty containers were being
hurled about with every entering wave. Every now and then
the ship would turn and roll on the opposite side. Then with a
mighty rush all these floating things would charge the length
of the cabin and slam into the farthest bulkhead.

Coleman had a narrow escape. He was in the cabin alone
trying to retrieve a valuable item that was packed low down
in one of the lockers. The missing object could not be found
and he had dropped on his knees holding his breath underwater
so that he could better feel with his hands. Without warning
the ship lurched far to one side, rushing all the water to his part
of the cabin, carrying with it loose boards and a floating bunk
mattress. One of these boards and the mattress wedged above
his body, pinning him tightly against the cabinet. He fought
like a madman to get free but could not budge the material.
Still fighting, he could feel the breath leave him in little bubbles,
could feel himself growing weaker and weaker, saw every-

thing turn black. And just when he was about to lapse into
unconsciousness a roller surged into the massed wreckage and
released him. He struggled to the companionway, crawled to
the deck and lay there panting and coughing water.

Morning came and passed and by late afternoon we were
still working. All this while the wind had grown stronger until
the hour arrived when we knew it was too dangerous to return
to the wreck. Wearily we swam ashore for the last time,
plodded through the soft beach sand, climbed the bluff back
of the beach and, there, exhausted, flung ourselves on the
ground.

The sea had won.

For a time we lay inert, too tired to move. The sun meanwhile dipped lower and lower, the shadows grew longer. Rous-
ing ourselves, we looked about for a sign of humans or human
habitation. There was none. Behind, the land sloped away to a
perfectly semicircular lagoon of emerald green water edged
by a pure white beach. Beyond that was the open sea again.
About five miles away could be seen the dim outlines of a small
island. To the south the land stretched away in low ridges and
shallow valleys. We were on the extreme tip of some large
island. A hundred yards further north our ship would have
cleared the reefs and been saved.

No use crying about it. The expedition was washed up—
literally. Through a tangled mass of thatch palm, round leaf
sea grape and cacti we made our way down the slope to the
lagoon. What a beautiful anchorage it would have made. Perhaps on the sand we would find some evidence of man. There
was. A jumble of cut sticks that had been severed from their
stalks months before, and some discarded conch shells that had
been broken open. Nothing more.

There was one thing more in store for us that evening. We
were to witness one of the most beautiful sights in nature, one

of the truly stirring spectacles that come the way of those who delight in color. We were treading our way back to the bluff overlooking the wreck, our eyes to the ground. The sun was setting, tinging everything with refulgent gold. From high above, from far up in the firmament came a faint crying—plaintive mournful notes like those the wild geese sing on the north wind. We looked up and froze in our tracks. From the interior of the island was coming a great flock of scarlet flamingo, wings ablaze in the setting sun. Like geese they were flying in V-shaped formation, guided by a leader. There must have been hundreds of them. As they moved, the scarlet of their wings flashed and flared, set in vivid contrast by the velvety black of their wing tips. Nearer and nearer they came, crying the while, reached the land's edge, circled and returned to the dark interior. And at the same moment the sun dipped beneath the horizon, taking the light away and plunging land and sea into darkness.

Under the glittering stars, with the song of the east wind in our ears as it rustled through the grasses and rolled the sand grains up and down the dunes, on the solid ground that smelt of dead and dying greenery, we slept the sleep of exhaustion. And though out on the coral that night the sea tore our vessel to pieces, growling through the teeth of the reef as it rended the timbers one from the other, we did not move.

Like Kim who lay on the ground and gathered new strength we rose the next morning, refreshed and with a brighter outlook. New days bring new problems, new tasks, new ideas. We were done with the sea, for the present at least—the land was our portion. What would we make of it?

The first thing that came to our minds was our whereabouts. Where were we? We knew only that we were on one of the Bahamas. But which one? We salvaged a chart from the rubbish on the beach and looked it over. Noon sights of the day

before had placed us in the latitude of the Caicos group. I was
of the opinion that we were on Grand Caicos on the eastern-
most fringe of the Bahamas. Coleman held out for Mariguana
on the basis that the sights were in error. But the low island five
miles to the north? Were we on Grand Caicos, the next island
should have lain northwest. On Mariguana no island should
have been visible, for the nearest group was the Plana Cays
which lay more west than north and were some twenty miles
distant. The only island that had another due north was Great
Inagua, the last and second largest island of the Bahama Archipelago. But this was impossible. To reach Inagua by sailing due
south we would have had to pass within a mile or so of either
Mariguana or Caicos. Certainly we would not have passed so
close to land without seeing it. We gave it up.

What to do? After a short consultation we decided that
Coleman was to remain with the wreck, salvaging what he
could, and that I would set out to find help if there was any
to be found. Half an hour later I shouldered a pack containing
some food, a canteen holding about two quarts of water and
a blanket. I was to follow the coast, wandering on until I had
located a settlement or, failing that, encircle the island.

First I went down to the beach and searched among the
wreckage for some clothes. Both Coleman and I were in rags.
Our trousers were torn and hanging in shreds and our shirts
were little better. We had seized the first things that came to
hand after getting our more valuable instruments ashore. We
particularly needed shoes, the tennis shoes that we had on were
nearly cut to pieces by the jagged coral. We located several
in the sand, washed them clean and put them on. They helped
to make us feel respectable though we were hardly objects for
a drawing-room.

Once again on top of the bluff, we bid each other good-bye
What direction to go? It did not make much difference, one

way seemed as good as another. Perhaps south would be best, particularly if we were on Grand Caicos as I thought, for several islands down the chain there was reputed to be a settlement. Possibly I could reach it by swimming the intervening channels. I trudged off on the crest of a sand ridge that paralleled the shore. Looking back I could see Coleman wading into the lagoon preparatory to swimming out to the reef. The last I saw of him he was bobbing about in the lee of the breakers, looking for an opening that he might reach the ship without being hammered against the coral.

Below the ridge on which I was walking stretched mile upon mile of gorgeous beach, pure white sand melting into a subtle green on the land's edge. Beyond the beach were the still waters of the lagoon, intense emerald and pale green where the bottom alternated from coral sand to growths of sea grass. On the outer edge of the emerald, as if to enclose it tightly, was the barrier reef, sweeping on and on in gentle undulations. On the reef the great sea swells broke in brilliant foam, intensified and brought into vivid contrast by the dark blue of the waters beyond. Further on, the bottom dipped down and down into the depths. Two thousand fathoms, the chart said, twelve thousand feet of dark blue water.

It was good to be on land again, even though the landing was not as we would have had it. From out of the island were coming deep pungent smells—the scent of myriad flowers, warm grass in the sun, of dried mud, and all those things that go to make up the earth-odor. It was good to feel the sand crunching under foot, good to have live things about, for even as I walked dozens of lizards dashed from their basking places and fled for shelter. One of these lizards excited me immensely. It was a new species, a type not yet described to science. I tried to capture it, missed, and ruefully watched it disappear into the scrub. Well, what difference did it make? I did not have

any formol to preserve it and we would probably be here for
a long time anyway. Plenty of time for that later.

But the lizard brought me a stirring idea. This island was our
portion. The sailing of the isles of the Indies was not to be. Our
scientific program was finished—before it had even started. Yet
here at our very feet was unexplored territory. On this island
should exist a complete cosmos of living things, an entity of
moving, crawling, creeping creatures, all living in the complex
ecological web of island life. We should learn everything that
was to be known about this island, this bit of water-enclosed
earth-matter. The mere fact that it was an island, that the
creatures and animals were imprisoned, held fast by the surrounding ocean, made the idea more intriguing. That is part
of the charm of islands, everything is so compact. Carried away
with the notion, I walked on. Great purple land crabs scuttled
from among the grasses and, like the lizards, dashed for shelter.
What was their niche in the scheme of island life? And those
snails hanging in clusters on the grass stems? What were they
doing and why were they on the grasses?

This was our portion, earth and sea and sky, the reef beyond
the land's edge, a world in itself, the pale green of the lagoons
—even as I looked a vaguely moving shadow showed the underwater trail of a giant sea turtle returning from an early morning egg-laying. And the beach itself, the pulsing, moving edge
of the sea, that belongs neither to the land nor to the sea, but
alternately to one and then the other. These were our portion,
these and the soil beyond.

Then, as if in gentle retribution for the egotism of thinking
that we should learn *everything,* a hummingbird swooped out
of a cluster of prickly-pear and hung before my face. Like an
angry bee it buzzed, humming and jerking its tail feathers. And
though the wings were an indelible blur, so swift was their
moving, every detail of the body feathering was visible. Swiftly

my memory raced down the list of hummingbirds, tried to correlate colors of gorget and ruff and nape with specie and genera. And I failed. I did not even know its name! With a great easy swoop the feathered mite swung to one side and quickly glided into the cacti as if to say, "So, you would know *everything?*"

Turning landward I examined the vegetation. It was tropical but not the exuberant, riotous vegetation of Haiti or Santo Domingo not too many miles away. Rather it was of a more subtle type, the type known as xerophytic, that tends to show its beauty in the sharpness of thorns, highly colored bark, spiny cacti and thick padded leaves. Thorns! They were the keynote of this island vegetation. Thorns, speaking mutely of a scanty existence, of the scorching of hot sun, of searing winds and dry soil. Desert vegetation. Half-consciously I felt my canteen to make sure it was full. A few thatch palms dotted some distant ridges and stood out starkly against the sky. There was a certain wild character about these plants, a certain impression that was at one and the same time forbidding and yet appealing. Perhaps this was due to their very sparseness, to their thorns, possibly to the open sand and rock that showed between the tree boles in little patches. Yet they were not devoid of flowers, for even on the cacti pads bloomed vivid scarlet and yellow blossoms. A subtly pleasing scene, tropical, yet not gaudy, the sort of thing that does not tire one too quickly.

There was one character that impressed. All the plants on the ridge and for some distance beyond leaned to the land. Theirs was an existence of sweeping wind, the interminable pressing of the trade winds that forced branch and leaf to their will. Day in and day out the breeze pressed its shoulders against their intricacies. And in defense these plants had turned their backs, had huddled close to the rocks. Here already was a chain of island life, interlocking links starting with the wind that had thrown up the sand dunes, that had borne the plants, that had provided the mineral nutrition for these plants, which in their turn were beaten flat again by the wind.

I trudged on. After a time the ridge dipped into lowland, dipped into a mangrove swamp. The swamp in its turn gave way to a long narrow lake that lay like a ribbon in the sun. Along the far edge were some of the flamingos we had seen the evening before. They were feeding, ambling along in crane-like strides, raising and dipping their reversed shovel bills as they walked. I edged closer, squeezing through the mangroves, but they took alarm and fled.

But I was wasting time. Or was I? Did it make any difference whether I found help today or tomorrow or the day after? But then I reflected that after all we must eat, and if I could quickly find help we might still salvage some of the tinned food from the debris that was lying on the bottom of the reef. After that we should see. It was not fair to Coleman to dally like this. On I pressed, mile succeeding mile as the hours passed. At noon I ate some of the food in my pack and sat down to rest on the crest of a sand dune. Then I thought I saw some figures way down the coast. Humans, two of them. Shouting, I darted down the sand, jumping over the grasses and waving my arms. To my astonishment the figures gave one look and dashed into the bushes.

CHAPTER IV

"Inagua Is a Queer Little Island"

I STOPPED in amazement staring at the spot where the figures had vanished, and then smiled. No wonder! I was a wild looking creature. My clothes were in tatters, torn by the coral from the day before; a battered old hat of disreputable felt lay draped over my head at a rakish angle and two weeks' growth of beard obscured my features. About my neck a dirty blue bandanna hung loosely; I had salvaged it from the sand to keep my neck from burning; and a shredded pair of gray ducks hung in ribbons about my knees. Until this moment I had not been conscious how I looked, so intent had we been on salvaging the necessities for our existence and in securing help in time to prevent our equipment from becoming a total loss. I must have looked like a renegade beachcomber. Ugly enough in any case to frighten timid natives. For several moments I remained where I was watching. There was no movement except the curve of the waves as they slid up on the beach in little streamers and the rippling of the beach grasses in the trade winds.

More sedately I continued. Soon I came up with the tracks, broad bare prints with splayed toes in the damp sand. The tracks led into a clump of mixed palmetto and mangrove. Hesitating for a moment I pondered. Idiotically, I wondered what was the correct procedure for approaching natives on an unknown island. Should I say, "Good morning, would you be so kind as to inform me what island I am on?" or would "Pardon me, but I am a shipwrecked mariner," sound better? Both sounded utterly silly but for the moment I could think of

49

nothing more appropriate. Feeling a little foolish I stepped up the beach and yelled "Hey!" at the green mangroves. No answer. Once again I called but received no response. "I say there, where are you?" I called again. For a moment nothing stirred and then with slow hesitating steps two small boys stepped from between some palmettos where they had been hiding.

I looked at them curiously. They were as inky black as it was possible for two human beings to be and they were nearly as ragged as I was. One youngster lacked pants but I soon discovered that he was carrying them tucked in a small grass basket slung to his back. The pair seemed quite frightened and appeared ready to bolt at the slightest move.

"I won't hurt you," I told them.

This seemed to reassure them a little, for the perplexed expressions on their faces slowly eased and they began to regard me with a little less fear. The boy minus the pants suddenly became conscious of his condition and hurriedly put on his trousers. I smiled at his embarrassment whereupon the pair broke out into broad grins.

"Could you tell me what island I am on?" I asked.

Instantly the grins vanished and the boys appeared ready to flee again. No doubt to them it was the most ridiculous question in the world. They looked at each other and then at me as if doubting my sanity.

"Don't run," I quickly told them. "You see, our boat was wrecked on the reef up yonder," and I indicated the direction from which I had come. "We were wrecked yesterday morning in the dark."

An expression of sorrow came over the two black faces and the larger boy broke out with, "Oh, suh, I berry berry sorry foh yo, suh, I feel berry hard foh yo."

Soon they became very voluble and told me that they had

been looking for turtle eggs when I had come upon them and that they lived on a "farm" some distance away. Here their parents and a considerable assortment of uncles and aunts dwelt in the summertime, but it was then winter and very cold (about eighty in the shade) and that they had only come to the farm to chase away the wild pigs that were rooting up the vegetables. The island, of course, was Inagua, everyone knew that.

So it was Inagua after all. That accounted for the small island directly north of the point of the shipwreck. How we ever slipped between Caicos and Mariguana on a due south course without sighting land I do not know to this day. The scene of our disaster was the northernmost point of the island and the lagoon where we had seen the flamingo was called Christophe. I asked the boys why it was named Christophe but they did not know. They said it had always been named Christophe. It occurred to me that possibly it was named after Henri Christophe, the Black Emperor of Haiti which was only eighty or ninety miles to the south. Later I found this to be the case, for a legend persisted that it was at this point that the builder of the famous Citadel near Cape Haitian was supposed to have constructed a summer palace. Here also in his last days before the coming of the revolution which caused him to end his life with a golden bullet, and which plunged Haiti into the dark period from which it is only now emerging, he was supposed to have cached a considerable sum of coin and bullion against a day of need. What truth there was in the legend I do not know, except that months later I discovered a number of cut stone blocks and a pile of debris half hidden by overgrowing palmetto and lignum vitae trees a short distance back of the lagoon.

I fished the chart out of my pack and looked it over. The map showed a very irregular island bearing the legend "flat and wooded." There was little else to set it apart from the

other islands of the Bahama Archipelago except its large size
and peculiar shape. On the opposite side of the island was a
settlement called Mathewtown. I asked the boys how distant
was the settlement. They replied that it was "far, far, far." The
repetition puzzled me somewhat but I found later that to repeat a word a number of times was a favorite Inaguan method
of emphasizing distance or quantity. The Lagoon Christophe
was only far, the farm far, far, and Mathewtown was far, far,
far.

I also discovered that there were some sailboats at the farm
and that the boys would be glad to lead me there. We headed
directly into the scrub, crossed a shallow lagoon and wound
into an almost invisible trail. It was a miserable thing at best,
beset with thorny cacti and was apparently used only by animals, for at shoulder height the branches locked together in
thorny embrace. This made it necessary to progress stoop-
shouldered, a most uncomfortable posture after a few minutes.

Occasionally the path dipped into muddy lowland or through
large patches of swamp mangrove. At times it vanished or became so vague as to be scarcely discernible. The noise of our
approach flushed large flocks of birds, hordes of tiny ground
doves that fluttered ahead for a few yards, settled and flushed
again. Wild pigeons burst away amid a sudden whirring of
whistling wings and once there was a great disturbance as a
hundred small parrots took wing at once screeching in anger.

Frequently we came upon small lakes or ponds with white
egrets and herons standing like figures from a Japanese print
along the borders. These were very tame and allowed us to
approach within a few feet before flapping away on gracefully
beating wings. The place was an ornithologist's paradise. Droves
of small sandpipers lined the edges of the ponds; myriads of
warblers slipped daintly among the branches, trilling and calling in the lighthearted way of warblers—among these I recog-

nized a Maryland Yellow-throat and was thrilled at the sight; and hummingbirds swooped dizzily between the thorn trees or hung motionless on vibrating wings as they watched our progress.

Presently the trail broke out on the beach again, the northern beach this time, and we continued to the west. The coast here was quite different from the lovely sand beach that marked the east coast. There was no fringing reef to break the force of the sea and the surf was piling in huge masses of foam and spray against a low bench of eroded gray stone. The bench was pitted and caverned out in great irregular holes and occasionally we passed places where we could hear the water roaring in the rock directly beneath our feet. In some spots the force of the incoming combers had broken away the roofs of the under-water caverns and great fountains of spray squirted up between the openings. Once a small geyser came up between my legs, wetting me thoroughly. The Inaguans shrieked with glee, thinking it a great joke.

A few miles further on the beach became exceedingly difficult to walk upon. Coral rock quickly erodes with the action of surf and spray and takes on the character and appearance of a magnified sponge, only a sponge of needle sharp stone. Great pits and holes, covered with a paper-thin layer of rock, await the unwary step that treads thereon. Unless one moves carefully the foot will slip into such a trap and slide down into a needle lined pocket that cuts the flesh to ribbons. Through the thin protection of my tennis shoes I could feel every irregularity. I wondered how the black boys could walk barefooted over such rock but when I examined the soles of their feet I understood. They were covered with a half inch layer of heavy callus almost of the consistency of horn. This horn extended some distance up the foot where it thinned at the instep. They were better protected against the rocks in bare feet than I was in tennis shoes.

In time we arrived at the "farm." We first saw a cluster of four houses nestling in the shade of some short cocoanut palms. At this point the rock bench had given place to a stretch of gleaming beach, and a circular coral reef provided a rough but reasonably secure anchorage. The houses were the usual thing for that portion of the world, little one room huts of white coral bearing brown roofs of palmetto thatching. They were exceedingly picturesque and melted intangibly into the landscape. Beyond I could make out a few more huts and then a long line of coast shimmering in the heat waves.

No one was about, but the boys said that we would find their parents back in the woods working the farm. Once again we plunged into the bushes. For some minutes we walked, pushing aside thorn branches, struggling with vines and threading between clusters of prickly pear.

"Where's the farm?" I asked.

The black boys looked at me with queer expressions and then with a sweep of their hands indicated the thorn scrub. "Heah, suh."

It was my turn to register amazement, for all I could see was a mass of tangled bushes and curling vines. But presently in all the melee of vegetation I began to discover an isolated corn stalk, a stand of two or three plants of some sort of grain, guinea-grain probably, and close to the ground some sweet potato vines. That was all. Good soil in the Bahamas is very scarce and on certain islands is only to be found in eroded pockets called "banana holes." Elsewhere the soil is only an inch or so deep, much too shallow for row farming. So the natives take advantage of every depression in which enough dirt has collected to grow their vegetables. Some of the individual corn stalks were fifty feet apart. A garden patch that in more prosperous parts of the world would cover fifty square feet must perforce in the Bahamas, or at least some of the Bahamas, be stretched out over a multitude of acres.

Suddenly, from the interior, came a great shouting and thrashing of branches and the sound of running feet. The noise increased continually, intermingled with a terrified squealing until out of the bushes there plunged a scrawny razorback hog holding a sweet potato in its mouth. The hog saw us, swerved careening in its flight and plunged at a tangent into the bushes. After him, carrying stones and clubs, raced two men and a woman who stopped when they saw us. The hog continued on and could be heard blundering away through the vegetation.

"Dom hogs," said the elder of the two men, "dey gobble eberyting on de place."

He came forward and extended his hand. The others came forward too and I shook hands in turn. Like the boys they were quite black, typically ragged, but seemed pleasant enough. They introduced themselves as Thomas and David Daxon and Ophelia. Ophelia was a long lanky woman clad in a dress that was vaguely Victorian and she had a bright blue bandanna wrapped around her head. Thomas was a small fellow with a goatee and a round cherubic face that beamed with typical negroid cheerfulness. The other, David Daxon, did not impress me so favorably. He was a great hulking brute with a crafty, almost porcine appearance.

I told them briefly of the wreck and of our situation. Thomas shook his head sadly. "Dat's a turrible ting for a mon to lose his boat," he said, "and in such a time as dis. I feel foh yo, suh, I feel berry berry hard foh yo, suh. But we help yo, suh, we salvage de wreckage, we salvage lots of boats, suh."

Somehow the remark that he had salvaged lots of boats did not strike me so favorably, perhaps some inflection or eagerness in tone, and in some way I must have shown it, for although I said nothing, he quickly added that he, Thomas, was a very respectable person, in fact he was a minister of the Gospel. I raised my eyes at this, for the Negro looked like anything but a minister of the Gospel. He was wearing a shirt of faded blue denim, an even more faded pair of pants with the seat and knees sewn with off-color patches, and he possessed a huge pair of bare horny scarred feet that appeared never to have had acquaintance with a pair of shoes. The hulking David was introduced as a deacon of the church. He looked the part even less than the smaller and more kindly appearing Thomas. However, I allowed the matter to pass without comment and made arrangements for their labor and the use of their boats which were drawn up on the beach near by.

While the Inaguans were getting their vessels ready I drew aside and sat down in the shade of a palm tree to rest and think. In the meantime a number of other Negroes had made their appearance and were helping with the launchings. I noticed that the big David had drawn a couple of these aside and was whispering to them. I did not like this air of secrecy and made a mental reservation to be on my guard. However, nothing further occurred to cause any suspicion and in the rush of getting the boats in the water I forgot the matter.

Nearly three hours later just as the sun was setting, tingeing the rock with orange and yellow, we sailed into the Lagoon Christophe. Two boatloads of us. Thomas and I in a small sloop with a ragged sail that threatened every moment to part from its boom, and David Daxon with some nephews and other relatives in a larger craft that had every appearance of disintegrating before our very eyes and plunging to the bottom. We hesitated near the sparkling reef outside the lagoon, sparred for an opening, and then with a rush slipped through a tiny coral-bordered channel. As we entered, two large greenback turtles swept out of the weed that lined the bottom, circled for a moment or two and then dashed with long curling sweeps of their flippers into the deeper water beyond the reef.

"Dey eat de grass," Thomas informed me, indicating the sea weed.

By this time Coleman had discovered us and came dashing down through the palmettos.

It was a jolly reunion. He had not expected to see me again for a number of days and had set about salvaging all he could. Time and time again, he had gone out to the wreck and fought his way inside to return with a load of tins and other materials. He looked tired and weary and I noticed that his fingers were wrinkled and drawn, like those of washerwomen, from being in the water all day. His face and neck were burned a fiery red from the glare and his shoulders sagged as he walked. But a considerable pile on the beach showed the results of his efforts. I introduced Thomas and David and then Ophelia who had walked up the beach preferring the needle sharp rocks to the boat which she said "made her stomach jumble."

By this time it was growing dark and Ophelia set about preparing a fire on a patch of sand between two thickets of mangroves. She asked if we cared to have her cook anything. We gave her some cans from the beach and some flour that was sealed in a watertight tank that we had had made for holding specimens. She wanted the flour for bread but we were wondering how she was going to make it with neither utensils nor oven. We then received our first lesson in island living.

She took a handkerchief full of the flour down to a flat rock on the very edge of the lagoon. There she dabbled sea water on it, kneading it the while until the dough was of the proper consistency. We watched, fascinated. The sea water gave the necessary salt, she said. I wondered how many isopods and copepods, with which the water's edge was teeming, were mixed with the dough, but said nothing. Satisfied that the mass was in proper shape, Ophelia returned to the fire, which by this time was a great heaping bed of coals. With a stick she dug a little trough in the center, lined it with hot sand and plopped the dough in the cavity. Hot sand was poured on top and red coals over the entirety. She then added more fuel to the fire and sat back on her haunches.

"Done soon," she said, and grinned.

The remainder of the meal was cooked in the tins that we supplied her. Somehow I was reminded of the philosopher and cynic Diogenes who lived in a tub and preached that owning property was vanity. It is related that the learned sage eliminated all his estate save the tub and one bowl which he used for drinking. One day he observed a boy drinking at a fountain with his hands. Ashamed, he returned "home" and cracked the utensil in two pieces.

In time Ophelia stirred herself and, with pardonable pride at our intense interest, raked away the coals and exposed a perfectly browned loaf. Coleman asked her how she knew it was finished and she replied that she "jedged the time, suh." Grinning from ear to ear, she handed it to us. Not a grain of sand adhered to the crust and only a faint powdering suggested the presence of ashes. We complimented her and she nearly rolled into the water with pleasure. We found it to be a little flat but a jar of jam that Coleman fished out of the sand along the beach made it very tasty indeed. The bread inside was as white and as pretty as that of a bakery loaf.

Further proof of the self sufficiency of these island folk was evidenced after supper when we hauled two folding cots which Coleman had salvaged from the wreckage down to the lagoon. On these we prepared our blankets and made ready for sleep. By the time we had them folded Ophelia and Thomas were snoring on the ground and the hulking David was keeping noisy accompaniment. Their only coverings were some thin rags which they wrapped, ostrich fashion, about their heads. The other Negroes disposed themselves likewise, sleeping like so many crocodiles on the bare sand.

For a time Coleman and I made a brave effort at slumber, for we both were near exhaustion. But the mosquitoes and sand flies would not have it. From out of the mangroves and from the ground beneath they came in swarming myriads to sing into our ears and burrow into our hides. We tried pulling the blankets over our heads like the Inaguans but it was too hot. We looked at the prostrate forms on the sand. The mosquitoes and sand flies might have been in Mars for all they cared. Finally we could stand it no longer.

"Let's get out of here," exclaimed Coleman and jumped to his feet.

In the dark we lugged our cots to the bluff overlooking the wreck. At last we had peace, for there the trade winds were blowing from off the ocean in a steady cool current driving the distracting hordes before them.

Early in the morning Ophelia came up the bluff to tell us that breakfast was ready. She appeared as fresh as a daisy. We asked her how she stood the mosquitoes.

She replied, "Oh, dem tings—dey don like black folk." And she grinned, "Dey's no skeeter now, wait till de rains come."

Some days later we had all our wreckage piled in one spot on the shore of the lagoon Christophe. It was a considerable jumble. A vast pile of tins glittering in the sunlight assured us of food for some time to come though we lost many in the heat of the sun which caused the cans to burst. At times the burstings sounded like miniature cannonades as can after can exploded, squirting jets of vegetable in the air. We remedied the situation by covering them with the leaves of palmetto. Our precious books, stained with water and gritty with sand, lay in piles where we had dropped them, and under spare canvas was the remainder of our instruments.

Off on the reef lay all that was left of the *Basilisk*. We had
stripped her of her canvas, of the running rigging and of
everything that would come loose. Meanwhile the surf had
ground a great hole in her side and she was badly splintered.
Most amazing was the distance which some of the wreckage
had floated. Bits of paper, splintered pieces of wood, tins of
one sort or another were strewn up and down the beach for
ten miles in either direction. We gathered in everything that
was worthwhile and piled it with the other material at the
Lagoon Christophe.

We then loaded the wreckage in the two ramshackle boats,
piling the tins in the bottom and the more fragile material on
top. The ship's papers and sextant I wrapped carefully in a
canvas and placed under a deck beam. When we were through,
the gunwales were only a few inches above water and we
began to doubt if we could progress as far as the houses without
swamping.

We set sail early the next morning shortly after the sun had
risen. I was sorry to leave the spot and with Coleman climbed
the bluff to take a last look at the wreck. For me it was an extremely bitter moment and I think Coleman felt likewise. In
the months that had passed we had become very attached to
our tiny ship. We had gone through the worst kind of misery
on her decks, we had spent sleepless sodden days in her cabin
but she was *our* ship and the parting came hard. Through the
dismal murk of a November fog she had carried us; through
the awful battering of a mid-winter storm she had fought with
us against the sea and we were loath to leave her lying broken
on the reef. But there was no way out of it and in the end we
quietly turned and made our way down to the lagoon. Even
the blacks felt our mood and made no remark as we climbed
into their boats.

On the wings of a billowing trade we swept out of the

lagoon and turned to the west. A mile or so away we could make out the white dress of Ophelia bobbing up and down as she scampered goat-like over the rocks. Although we had a strong wind behind us we were so heavily laden we did not catch up with her until we neared the huts. There we stopped for a few hours while everyone turned out for another spree of hog chasing. While the Negroes were in the bushes Coleman and I took the opportunity to examine the settlement. A total of six tiny dwellings nestled close together a few yards behind the beach. The hut walls were of broken coral rock plastered together with lime and neatly whitewashed with the same material. The lime, we learned, was extracted from the coral by burning. Four of the dwellings were thatched with palm leaves tied with a simple but ingenious fiber knot on a lattice frame; the other two were covered with grass and reeds. The doors and windows were constructed of planks that had drifted on the beach—on some we could still see the tell-tale mark of barnacles—and were hung with home-made, hand-carved wooden hinges. Total cost—nothing, except labor. None contained furniture other than a rickety table or two made from driftwood. The Inaguans, like most peasants in the out-islands, sleep on the floor on grass mats which they roll up and stow away in the morning. Here life was on its simplest terms.

In time the crew returned, satisfied that the wild hogs had the fear of man properly instilled in them. Once again we raised the ragged sails and turned down the coast. As I settled myself on the deck I could not help but marvel at the strange shaping of events that placed us in precisely the position that we had built the *Basilisk* to avoid. All our months of planning and planning again had availed us exactly nothing; we were again dependent on the natives and native boats. For a brief time we discussed the possibility of continuing our voyage in one of the native shells but when we saw that both ships had to pump water every twenty or thirty minutes to keep afloat we knew it was a hopeless situation. We were stuck on the island and there were no two ways about it. We began to examine the coast more carefully.

Mile upon mile it stretched away, a long low line of green that faded into infinity. Some distance in the interior a few low hills rose slightly and then sloped away again to the general level. Once in a great while we passed a series of palms shooting up from the shore like vegetable rockets frozen in mid-air. Back of these was an impenetrable jungle that lay somnolent in the sun. But it was a pleasing scene. Against the brown rock along the shore the incoming combers broke in great welters of foam, mounted high in the air and slid down again in pure white froth. We looked in vain for houses. David Daxon informed us that there were none between his "farm" and the "city." The "city" we deduced was Mathewtown.

At noon Daxon announced that he was going to roast some corn. From some debris on the deck he hauled out some sticks of wood and a box full of sand. In this he kindled a fire and shortly had such a hearty blaze going that it nearly drove us from the deck. Coughing and weeping from the smoke we watched him hold the corn in the fire until it was slightly charred. He then wolfed it down, smacking his lips in enjoyment. We tried some, but our palates, spoiled from years of civilized living, rebelled. It was about as dry and as tasteful as sawdust and about as easy to swallow. Coleman crawled down in the hold and fished up a tin from which the label had been washed but which proved to be Bartlett pears and more to our taste.

Daxon estimated that we would reach Mathewtown in about eight hours but at dusk all we could see was the long line of coast stretching away mile after mile. Just as the sun was setting a great bank of inky clouds began to form on the horizon, piling higher and higher, adding to their bulk, until in the gathering murk we could see the fitful brilliance of sheet lightning. I suggested to Daxon that we haul up on shore for the night lest we be caught in the gathering storm. He gravely indicated the barely visible line of barrier reef on which the surf crashed and thundered in measured cadence. In an unbroken line it extended to the west, curving and bending, but not showing a single opening. The nearest entrance he informed us was at Sheep Cay, three miles away. There if the tide was not too low we might find a safe anchorage.

Anxiously we watched the clouds, saw them gather in volume and spread over the horizon. Soon the sound of thunder came across the water, rolling and echoing, diminishing and breaking out again. Presently in the flare of sheet lightning we made out the low form of Sheep Cay, a small island lying close to the mainland. The barrier reef swept up to the edge of the cay, there terminated and continued on again on the far side. Try as we might we could not see any evidence of a channel. Daxon, however, seemed to know what he was doing and headed straight for the reef. For long moments we could see nothing, then in a glare of brilliance we could distinguish the long line of swells mounting up and up and then pouring over the coral in a halo of mist and spray.

"I hope this chap knows where he is going," whispered Coleman, "I've had enough coral for one week."

Closer and closer we drifted, dipping slightly on the swells, mounting to their crests and dipping on again. Rain began to patter with a singing sound as it hit the water and a chill breeze sprang and then died as quickly as it came. By the next flash we saw we were no more than fifty feet from the reef. Still we could see no channel but Daxon kept on straight for the beach. Once he swerved the tiller slightly and in the brief flash that followed I saw that he was lining up his bow with the edge of the island and a grove of palms on the shore.

On we drifted, ever so slowly then, for it was dead calm. The second flash showed us but three wave crests away from the coral, then two, and finally just when it seemed that we were about to crash a tiny opening appeared through which the foam rushed in broken torrent. To each side was a fearful welter and in the fitful light we could see the broad fans of coral protruding through the surf. We poised high in the air and then gently, accompanied by little windrows of froth, slipped into the lagoon and safety.

"Phew," sighed Coleman, as we slid weakly on the deck, "what a night!"

Momentarily, we expected the storm to break but seemingly disappointed at our escape, the clouds dispersed. Presently the moon shone through. But the evening's adventures were not yet over for just as we were congratulating ourselves on the way the weather turned out we ran hard on a sandbar and there stuck fast. We pushed and pulled, heaved and swore but that was all the good it did. Daxon sighed wearily, muttered something about waiting for the tide to rise and then sat down on the deck. He was soon asleep, his limp head rolling back and forth with the slight rocking of the boat. The relatives followed suit, slumping on the timbers, and a chorus of snores soon echoed across the rippling lagoon.

"I guess we might as well get some, too," I remarked to Coleman and slid down in the hold out of the reach of the wind.

The sound of voices and a trampling on the deck roused me from slumber. On the other side of the hatch I could hear Coleman twitching on the bed of canvas that he had made from the crumpled sails. I felt uncomfortably warm and perspiration oozed from every pore. It was pitch dark and from down along the bilge came the smell of long dead fish and foul water. I nudged Coleman, heard him grunt something about "Idiots that won't let people sleep," and then heard him crawl to the hatch. Together we pulled ourselves to the deck. It was still dark and a faint mist hung over the water hiding the shore from which we could faintly hear the surge of surf. Daxon was at the tiller again, but the relatives were still snoring in a tangled heap on the deck.

"Where are we?" I asked Daxon.

"Man-of-War Bay," he grunted. "We be Mathewtown by sunrise."

We looked bleary-eyed at the vague defines of the shore-line and once at the star-spangled profusion of the sky above. There was little else to be seen except the white outlines of the little breakers as they lisped along the rail. I lay down near the mast and Coleman slumped in a heap near the tiller. There we must have drowsed for when I again opened my eyes it was to see a faint glimmer of daylight in the east.

About a hundred yards inshore I could make out a high gray line of beetling cliff against which the surf rose and fell in lazy fashion as though tired from the night's calm. As I watched we gently turned a point of land and headed toward the south. "Mathewtown," Daxon grunted and nodded in the direction of the Southern Cross which was hanging lopsided on the horizon. At first we could see nothing. But then through the gray there began to loom the nearly intangible bulk of several buildings. Presently the light grew stronger and we could distinguish the scene more clearly. Near the beach rose a large square building with red shutters and back of that stood several other structures with tall flagpoles beside them looking like the masts of some gaunt ship that had been wrecked and lost its rigging. Dimly we could see some tall lanky trees that we recognized by their grotesque shape as cashurinas and clustered between them an assortment of other buildings grading in size down to little one room huts with thatched roofs.

Suddenly the morning quiet was broken by a frightful din. From the seemingly deserted streets came the crashing of metal, a tremendous blowing of horns and clanging of bells. Louder it grew in volume, appeared to be moving up one street and then another. Coleman and I sat bolt upright.

"Holy smoke!" exclaimed Coleman. "What's going on here?"

As he spoke the noise blared in sudden crescendo and burst from the street by the building with red shutters. Along with the noise there issued into view a motley group of people, a mixture of black and tan, a singing, cheering crowd that was waving flags, pounding on drums and kettles, rattling huge cowbells, strumming an assortment of stringed instruments and yelling its lungs out. The crowd turned into a street near the beach, marched for a block or two and turned inland.

"What is it," we asked Daxon, "a revolution?"

"No, suh," he grinned, "dey is serenading Christmas."

"Christmas!" gasped Coleman. "My gosh, I had forgotten all about it."

And I laughed to think of other Christmases; of long gray days in more northern lands, where the snow was drifted deep and where somber green pines stood dark against the white; or roaring fires and family gatherings. I thought of another Christmastide, several years past, when in a lonely little Haitian town a single white man and I had trudged miles up the mountainsides, past the area of royal palms and into the cool heights above that we might find a pine tree to decorate with finery for this man's children. I smiled again to think of how he had substituted painted gourds and alligator pears for Christmas balls and had cut tin foil from cigarette cartons for tinsel. And again, of the wonderment of these tropic-born children at this marvel of a tree brought from the heights three thousand feet above. From far and wide the Haitian peasantry had come to see this strange thing, this pine tree decorated with red and blue and golden spangles. Still another Christmas came to mind when I had deserted the family fireside, had loaded a canoe with tent and blanket and axe and had departed in the midst of a drifting snow storm in the heart of a great Eastern swamp. Though the wind blew in great gusts and the snow piled deep on the cat-tails and the leaves of the giant trees billowed to the ground in brown mounds, that was the most peaceful Christmas of all, for on the wings of the wind a certain contentment crept into my body, a satisfaction born of the beauty of wood and meadowland, of singing flakes and the rustling of long dead marsh grass. Once Christmas had come upon me far out to sea in a dirty, rolling fishing trawler, and that was a somber day when through all the hours we fought a gray cold sea and strove to haul nets and sort sodden, sharp-scaled fish.

But this was the strangest Christmas, this day when Coleman and I, perched on the deck of Daxon's boat, rode slowly into Mathewtown roads. Presently the noise of the serenaders faded into the back streets and then ceased as abruptly as it had begun. Daxon told us that it was the custom thus to usher in the Christmas season; every morning at sunrise and every evening at sunset the spirit of Christmas was serenaded for several weeks. What a strange habit, I thought, but then recollected that at that very moment, miles to the north, owners of department stores and haberdasheries were hiring professional choirs to sing carols on their door steps—mercenary hymns in the hope of attracting trade. They, too, were serenading Christmas, the music more sophisticated—but there came the gentle reminder that the makers of the frightful din ashore expected nothing more of the racket than the pleasure they had in making it.

My Christmas reveries were broken short by the swish of oars from a rowboat approaching from the beach. Sitting in the stern was a heavy jowled black man holding a furled umbrella across his knees.

Coleman, who is of a medical turn of mind, gave the Negro a quick look, then turned and whispered, "Three head tumors, confirmed alcoholic and bad kidneys—don't like him."

I nodded agreement although, not being medical, I had not noticed the presence of tumors or kidney symptoms.

"Who's this?" I asked Daxon who was sitting motionless by the anchor rope.

"Oh, suh, he berry important mon heah."

We turned again to look at this "berry important mon" and decided after a short scrutiny that we did not like him any better than before. In spite of the sun that was by then well above the horizon he was wearing a heavy coat and vest, raiment suitable for a northern winter, which was causing him to break out in a profuse perspiration. Pompousness oozed from his very being and was heightened by a thick linked gold watch chain of the vintage of 1890 which was draped ostentatiously across his chest.

"Wonder what this chap wants," Coleman whispered again, "or is he a sort of official greeter?"

The rowboat drew alongside and the man introduced himself as a Mr. Richardson. His business, he informed us, was that of handling ship salvage. It was the custom, he explained, for shipwrecked persons to turn over their affairs to duly appointed agents—of which he was the foremost—who handled all details of government tax, sale of wreckage and salvage fees. We, of course, would receive our portion—about eight per cent of the total value of the wrecked goods, or possibly a little less depending on the results of the auction sale which, as we no doubt knew, would be held over our property in the near future. When the island's commissioner permitted us to land we would find Mr. Richardson at home in the large white house near the government building where he would be very happy to discuss the matter further.

With this astounding information our newly formed acquaintance gave a wave of his hand and departed for the shore under the shade of the umbrella which he had raised against the sun. For a moment we were speechless, and then Coleman swore—vividly and luridly.

"How did that fellow know we were shipwrecked?"

"I'm sure I don't know," I assured him, "maybe this Daxon outfit got word to him—possibly we had better get ashore and find out what it is all about."

"What about going ashore," I called to Daxon.

"Yas, suh, Cap'n, jus' as soon as we gets permission from de Commissioner—he be down as soon as he eat breakfas'."

Eight o'clock came and passed, then nine. By nine-thirty the heat on deck was becoming unbearable. By ten both Coleman and I were thoroughly out of patience.

"If this chap doesn't come soon I'm going ashore anyway," Coleman grumbled. "What does he think we are going to do, steal his blasted island?"

He began to untie the painter of the small skiff which we were towing astern. His designs, however, were frustrated by the arrival of a small boat bearing two messages—one from Mr. Richardson requesting our attendance at dinner and the other from the Commissioner giving us permission to land. Attached to the Commissioner's message was a note asking our presence in the government building—the one with red shutters—to stand *trial* at one o'clock.

We looked at each other nonplussed.

"What do you make of that," I asked. "Did you murder somebody and not let me in on it? What are we supposed to go on trial for?"

"Search me," he replied, "I haven't done anything."

A few seconds later we slid up on the beach, jumped quickly

before the dash of the incoming combers and then with a pull
and a heave drew the small boat out of the way of the curling
surf. Above, the sand graded into a steep slope which we
mounted quickly and then strode into the first street of the
town.

The place was a ruin!

Vacant and broken windows stared at us from tumbled and
deserted houses. Roofs careened at crazy angles and through
great gaping holes in their surfaces we could see golden splashes
of sunlight that filtered into the darkened interiors. Flattened
fragments of long deserted garden walls lay in piles where they
had fallen, dislodged by the elements, and the flowers of these
gardens had long since run riot and were strewn in hopeless
profusion in a tangle of weeds and broad padded prickly pear.

The streets reeked with an air of desolation and economic
poverty, an atmosphere that was heightened by the fact that
the settlement must have, in a time long past, experienced a
wave of prosperity, a period of affluence. For the streets were
broad and well laid out, lined with gutters, and house succeeded house in trim design. But that was long ago, for the once
painted shutters hung crazily on rusted hinges, had disinte-
grated little by little or had dropped into the weeds by the wall
edges. Some of the houses lacked shutters altogether, so long
had these fallen or crumbled into dust. Through the gaping
windows we could see the remnants of smooth floors, barren
spaces drifted thick with leaves, broken debris and shingles
slipped from the roofs above. Here and there betwixt the
ruined buildings were houses still occupied but these, too, like
their ruined neighbors, transmitted a feeling of sadness. Only
the government building with its bright red shutters gave any
hint of prosperity or solidity.

Abashed and silent with the sheer poignancy of the ruined
village we failed to notice a barefooted mulatto who shuffled

up with a note reminding us that Mr. Richardson was waiting and that dinner was ready. Following the servant we entered a large house near the waterfront and ascended a flight of rickety stairs. We were ushered into a dim Victorian parlor from which we could look down on the beach and the blue water beyond. Here we waited for what seemed an interminable time before the curtains at the far end of the room parted and our host appeared.

He led us into another room and introduced us to his wife, a rather sweet-faced colored woman with graying hair who wore an expression of indefinable weariness almost in keeping with the feeling of sadness suggested by the desolate streets outside. Her expression was heightened by vivid contrast with the heavy features of Richardson. His lips were thick and pendulous and the flesh hung loosely about his jaws. Alcoholic dissipation showed plainly in deep rings under his eyes which were bloodshot and veined. He was not a pretty creature. But he seemed affable enough and motioned us to a table laden with dishes of green okra, peas and rice, and a meat which he told us was wild beef from the interior.

Dinner was not a success. Neither Coleman nor I were in any mood for conversation and with the passing moments we mistrusted our host more. It soon became evident that the invitation was not prompted by any spirit of friendliness but for the sole purpose of ascertaining our position and the value of our wreckage. The picture that Richardson unfolded was anything but encouraging. We were told of a long list of ships that had come to grief on the reefs of Inagua, of how only the year before a big fourmaster had piled up on the rocks beyond Man-of-War Bay and of how out of all the salvaged wreckage the captain was only able to realize a mere two hundred and fifty dollars, enough to secure his passage home. The crew were picked up and returned by passing steamers. He, Rich-

ardson, had handled the affair—we, no doubt, were familiar
with the details of the procedure. The government required
the sale of wrecked and salvaged goods, the proceeds being
divided between the wreckers, the agent and the government,
the remainder going to the original owners. The remainder,
we gathered, was very little. In fact, we deduced that if the
captain of a ship worth several hundred thousand dollars realized only two hundred and fifty out of his wreck our returns
would be so infinitesimal as to be visible only under a microscope.

It was really very unfortunate, but—we were informed with
a smile—there was really no use trying to circumvent the
matter, it was the custom and the law. And furthermore—here
Richardson settled in his chair and bit off the end of a huge
cigar—he, Richardson, owned most of the island, controlled its
affairs, the people did as he wished, all matters were referred to
him for decision. It was very unfortunate that we were shipwrecked but he would see that we were properly treated—

The man's condescending manner and arrogant speech were
becoming so irritating that we did not trust ourselves to speak.
But our silence did not faze the Inaguan a bit, for he swept
grandiosely on. He told us of how he started life with nothing
but his bare hands and a determination to get ahead, of how by
sheer cleverness he had overcome tremendous odds, and of
how little by little he had assumed control of the island's affairs,
until at the peak of his years he was master of it all.

It was a boastful, conceited story, baldfaced and presumptu-
ous in the details of how by one trick or another he had secured
property after property, all the island's wealth. I glanced out
the window and took in the sweep of deserted and decaying
houses and the thought crept into my mind that perhaps this
man's ambition was the cause of all this desolation.

On and on he continued until Coleman and I began to squirm

in our seats. The Negro seemed to sense our helplessness, for he grinned in evident enjoyment. Lolling back in his chair he bit off another piece of the big cigar and grinned again.

"You know," he said, and the grin twisted into an odd smile, "Inagua is a queer little island—in fact, you'll find it a damned queer little island."

CHAPTER V

An Island Existence

IN time we were to discover that Inagua was not only a "damned queer little island" but also one of those strange, exotic and truly fascinating spots where fact borders close to the marvelous. We were to find it a scene of almost unbelievable beauty where color and movement, the wealth of natural existence, was woven into a fretwork of intricate and absorbing pattern. Yet we were, withal, to know it as a place indefinably sad, a peculiar, pathetic, wistful place where human endeavor seemed to come to naught but emptiness and desolation. There are times when I think of it as a place of unsoftened newness, an island with the touch of the hard sea still upon it, raw, a geologic experiment thrust up from the ocean by the designing hand of nature. But paradoxically, and more often, I think of it as a place of intense quiet, even of contentment, a sea-born island of strange happenings where the beautiful, the mystifying and the purely spectacular change one with the other in kaleidoscopic variety.

But for the moment we knew none of these things and only thought of it in the light of Richardson's words. Inagua was a "damned queer little island." We felt there could be no doubt of it as we thankfully emerged from his doorway, happy to escape. It was good to be out in the open again and we wished that we were back at the Lagoon Christophe, that we had never come to this forsaken town. But there was no help for it so we stepped across the street to the red-shuttered government building. A small crowd of idlers lounging in the shade of some cashurinas stared as we approached; I was startled by the

74

inbreeding of races, the accidents of miscegenation, which were revealed by their features. Pale blue eyes peered out of faces that were unmistakably negroid, blonde hair with an irrepressible frizzy kink betrayed countenances that were English with thin English noses; British freckles fought for dominance with the pigment of old Africa; African lips hung thickly from light-hued Anglo-Saxon cheeks.

But it was not the racial mixture alone that caught the eye. There was no laughter in the faces, a certain light seemed to have gone out of them, some inner substance missing, leaving them lackluster and wan. There was even an air of sullenness, a sense of frustration expressed in the curve of eyes and the droop of mouths.

The idlers made way and we crossed the threshold of a long narrow room. At the far end was a small door through which gleamed the intense blue of the ocean beyond. Even as we looked a mound of surf curled up, broke, and slid on the beach in a layer of gleaming foam. We turned and glanced about. Beneath a British Colonial flag on a judicial bench sat a spotlessly attired colored man. His features were smooth, straight, a not unhandsome person. About his face hovered the trace of a half-amused, half-supercilious smile which, as the minutes passed, rarely changed. Next to him stood a middle-aged Negro resplendent in uniform of red and blue trimmed in gold braid. We were waved to a seat between several Inaguans.

"Are you ready, Captain?"

I replied that I was quite ready but would like to know with what we were charged.

We were informed that we had landed on British Colonial Territory without proper entry and that it was necessary to hold an inquest over the "tragedy of the shipwreck." I assured the Negro that the "tragedy of the shipwreck" was not of our choice and that we had not made improper entry into His

Majesty's dominions simply for the fun of it. The smile broadened perceptibly, then lapsed into its accustomed faintness.

Coleman was led from the room by the uniformed aide and the trial began. I took a solemn oath "to tell the truth, the whole truth and nothing but the truth, so help me," and sealed it by kissing a huge Bible which lay on the desk. On the Commissioner's request I told the entire story of the shipwreck starting from the day of departure, all of which was carefully inscribed in a book filled with flowing handwriting. I told of how we had put to sea, of our battle with the storm, and of how exhausted and weary, we had at last found journey's end on the reefs of the Lagoon Christophe. I told him the purposes of the voyage and how we had come on the deck of Daxon's boat to Mathewtown. But I might have been reciting "Mary had a little lamb" for all the effect it had on the ebony-faced Commissioner. The smile never wavered and the words went down in smooth sequence in the little volume.

When I was finished I was dismissed and waved to a seat again. Coleman was brought in. Once again we left the solid land, battled the hurricane and fought the wintry seas. One by one the words of the recitation entered the little book, near to overflowing with fine Spencerian script. At last we were through, over the reefs again, the voyage done. Coleman sat down beside me.

The Commissioner folded the little book, passed it to the uniformed Negro and sat thoughtfully for a minute, tapping the desk. From down on the beach through the open door we could hear the sigh of the surf, the sound of water sliding up on the sand and slithering back again. A full dozen times the swish and sigh of the breakers filled the room with their noise and subsided. At last came the decision.

"I suppose I can release you," said the Commissioner, "but I am afraid I will find it necessary to hold all your equipment pending the results of the auction sale which, as you probably have been told,"—the smile broadened again—"is customary with shipwrecked goods. The government retains one third of the proceeds, the salvoys an equal amount and the remainder is divided between the agent and yourselves. Possibly you will realize enough to secure passage home."

Filled with dismay at this turn of events I drew a sheaf of papers containing some correspondence relative to the expedition between the Colonial Secretary in Nassau and the Secretary of State in Washington.

"Here, do these alter the situation in any way?"

The Commissioner read them gravely and without a change of expression handed them back.

"I'm sorry, but until I communicate with the Government in Nassau, I will be forced to hold your materials. You are free to go now if you wish."

We strode to the door and out into the street.

"Well, what do we do now?" asked Coleman.

I replied that I did not have the faintest idea but thought that inasmuch as there was not much else in prospect we might as well find a place to camp. We had to sleep somewhere and until the Commissioner saw fit to release our equipment we had to make the best of a bad situation.

We turned up a long straight street bordered with ruined houses. The idlers dropped behind, that is, all except one who followed at a rapid pace. He called to us and we stopped and waited.

The man came closer, a sallow thin-faced fellow with bare scarred feet who introduced himself as D'arvril. He said he had something to show us, something very beautiful. Clutched in his hand was a tightly bound handkerchief. Carefully he unwrapped the cloth. Nestling in its folds was a tiny round object, an ovoid that shimmered with an iridescent gleam—a pink pearl.

It was about the size of a small pea. We could have it for $35.

Coleman laughed.

"Mister," he said, "that's a very pretty bauble, but if hamburgers were selling for a nickel a dozen I couldn't even pay for the steam to cook them."

D'arvril appeared mystified at the word "hamburgers"—and disappointedly wrapped up his pearl again. It was a pretty thing, all pink with the delicate conch hue and waves of scarlet light moved across its roundness. He explained that they came from the conch shells which were fished up beyond the reefs. But we were in no position to buy pearls. I had about twenty dollars in my pocket, Coleman had even less. All our traveler's checks had been ruined in the wreck and there was no place on Inagua to cash them even if they were available. We had no idea where supper was coming from, nor where we were going to sleep. So the Inagua pearl market went begging.

D'arvril, no longer interested, dropped behind and in a few minutes we were free of the houses. It was a very tiny town, a forlorn little place, sleeping out the hours in decaying somnolence, a desert island settlement that was rapidly returning to the soil from which it had sprung. We were glad to be clear of it and with quickened pace headed up the coast.

In a short time the beach gave way to a beetling wall of cliff, a frowning mound of brown coral against which the surf splintered and thundered in a thousand frothy fragments. With a rush and a roar the great mounds of indigo water came swelling in, rose mightily, mounted higher and higher and then with a crash poured over the rocks. Brilliant sunlight caught the tumbled water, vividly lighted it and dissolved again in liquid blue, a shimmering blueness that went down, down into the depths. It was so alive, so clean and free, in such contrast to the sadness and decay of the town that we caught our breaths and slid prone on the rocks just out of reach of the foam.

We rested silently, watching the seething water. It was the first time we had had in several weeks to be alone, to think a bit. Expedition gone, property tied up, money unavailable, greedy natives waiting to snatch our goods, we needed a few minutes to ourselves. The picture did not look too cheerful. What were the museum people going to think? What were we going to write them? How to explain the fiasco?

Coleman broke into the reverie.

"You know," he said, half thoughtfully, "this is a right pretty place, the way the surf slides up on those rocks, up there is a break in the cliff with a bit of sand beach, and there is a lot of cacti in back to give us privacy—why can't we locate here, possibly we could build ourselves one of those coral houses and save something out of this expedition after all? There is nothing for us down there in the town, and the inhabitants don't seem so cheerful. How about it?"

I glanced at the great mounds of swelling water, the brown coral rock, the sunlit beach, the green vegetation behind. It was a pretty spot. Why not? About us were tons of loose boulders and palmetto plants in abundance. There was plenty of material.

Why not? I jumped to my feet, hope swelling again. But then the thought came that we had no tools, not even an axe. Perhaps we could persuade the Commissioner to let us have a few necessities until he heard from Nassau. It was decided that I should return to the settlement and talk to the official while Coleman scouted around for a good location for camp.

The ebony-faced Commissioner, still faintly smiling, heard my request for a few necessities, hesitatingly agreed—he seemed not nearly so cold a fellow on second sight—gave the uniformed aide a key and told him to allow us to secure what we needed from our supplies which had been ferried from the boats to a stone shed. He turned to me then, explained that he was very sorry that he could not help me further, but that Richardson would probably make trouble if he turned our property over to us—apparently the letter from the Secretary of State and our other papers had made some impression—but that he would do his utmost until he heard from Nassau.

When I reached the cliff again, staggering under a load of canvas, rope and tin cans, Coleman was nowhere to be found. Dropping the load on the ground I wiped the sweat from my eyes and shouted. Soon he came plunging out of the bushes, face beaming. Beckoning for me to come, he turned and disappeared between a clump of bay lavender and some lignum vitae. I followed. He pointed ahead. Not fifty feet away, nestling between two massive cacti, was a dwelling, a tiny coral and thatch hut.

Somewhere from the list of books long since read and nearly forgotten a passage hurtled out of the dim recesses of memory and fixed itself at that moment on my mind. Homes, it said, were not made for man but for the spiders. Man only leases them for a while, builds them, fills their rooms with his voice, with his laughter, with his tears, quarrels and angers, uses them as a refuge against the elements, as a place to bear and rear his children, to sleep in and be comfortable in—only in the end to turn them over to their final inmates, the eight-legged spiders. It is the fate of all houses if they are not claimed first by fire, catastrophe or the destruction of war. Soon or late the gay voices are stilled, gone away or forever hushed. Children like birds leave the nest, old people die or go to greener fields, and the spiders move in quietly to spin their webs, to draw gossamer veils over the dust of things best forgotten.

The spiders had long since claimed this house.

A great yellow and black one slid silently to one side and vanished over the lintel as we pushed open the creaking door. Looking up I could see the faint iridescent gleam of its ocelli as it stared unblinking from the safety of a crevice. One of its webs brushed stickily against my cheek. I untangled it and it clung to my fingers. Drawing them aside the web fell away from the door jamb and exposed some dim pencil marks spread in half inch spans amid some scribbled dates. There were similar marks on the door jamb of my own home eighteen hundred miles to the north. These lines marked the tops of the heads of growing children as they sprouted year by year. The highest line was dated August 1914, the month of the year when the Great War began.

I pushed a shutter and it fell among the weeds with a crash. Sunlight streamed through the newly opened window revealing the dusty spaces of two diminutive rooms. This had been a very poor house, a roof and four walls, little more. But it did boast of a wooden floor that was still solid though it creaked mournfully in spots. The roof was almost all intact. A few palmetto leaves would make it tight. The walls were of coral, still faintly white with lime beneath the dust of a decade.

With a broom fashioned from a stick and a bunch of leaves tied with a vine we cleaned the place of webs and chased the spiders back beneath the rock walls from whence they had originally come. Only one was allowed to remain, the big black and yellow fellow over the lintel. We tried to coax it out but it only drew deeper into its crevice, glaring balefully at these trespassers on its rightful domain. Down to the sea we went with a square of canvas, dipped it in a surf-carved pool and returned staggering under a load of warm sea water. We splashed it mightily over the walls and along the floors until they ran with the flood. From one corner we kicked out the faded body of an orange and yellow land crab that had come there long ago to die. Its shell clattered across the floor and fell into a dozen pieces.

When we had it all clean, though still damp from the salt

water, we stepped back and admired our handiwork. We could not have asked for a nicer spot. The massed cacti in the rear broke the force of the trade winds sweeping in from the east, and our house so fitted into the landscape that a few yards away it was all but invisible. The weeds and prickly pear still hemmed it in and made walking in the yard difficult but an hour's work with the machete produced a very satisfactory clearing. When we had finished the sun was dropping close to the horizon sending long slanting shadows across the ground.

"Not bad," said Coleman. "If only we had something to eat."

"That's easy." I grinned and led him down to the beach where I had dropped the tins. We opened two with a machete, guessing at their contents, for neither had any labels—they had been washed off in the wreck—and found they contained salmon and Bartlett pears. It was an odd mixture but we wolfed them down hungrily and threw the empty cans into the sea.

"I feel better already," said Wally. "Let's go back to the settlement and see what's doing. It will soon be dark and we can move around without attracting much attention."

I agreed and we slipped between the cacti back of the hut.

Mathewtown in the dark was even more sad than in the full glare of daylight. Great splashes of moonlight filtered through the tumbled roofs and between the garden walls. Here and there a light gleamed from a crack in a window. The shutters were all boarded tight to keep out the night breeze—and not a soul moved in the streets. Like shadows we padded noiselessly by the buildings, paused a moment in front of Richardson's establishment and then filed into a back street. This, too, was deserted.

"Listen," said Wally.

I stopped and turned an ear to the breeze. Somewhere off in the maze of empty houses was a medley of voices, a singing and tramping of feet. But it seemed muffled and some distance away. We followed the sounds, listening intently. Presently the chanting became louder and then very plain. It appeared to issue from a wooden building near the back edge of town. We moved closer and slipped quietly to the walls. Light shone through a crack in the boards and we pressed our faces close.

Inside were David, Ophelia and Thomas of the Lagoon Christophe and a number of other Negroes. But they had undergone a transformation. No longer were they wearing the easy rags of a few days past. Mail order clothes adorned their bodies and patent leather shoes concealed their horny feet. But the greatest change was in their expressions.

The hulking David was pounding madly on a large drum and his eyes appeared about to burst from their sockets. Big veins stood out heavily on his forehead, sweat poured in streams down his neck. "Hallelujah!" he shouted and came down on the drums with a thunderous vibration. Ophelia was shaking with the ague and little bits of froth showed on her lips. Little Thomas was in nearly as bad a state and was shouting at the top of his lungs, "Hallelujah!" It was a good old-time southern Negro revival, garnished with a Bahaman flavor. I understood then what Thomas had meant when he said he was a minister of the Gospel. The other blacks were in like condition and they were clapping their hands and stomping their feet in time to the drum. The instrument increased in fervor and the entire congregation shook with the power of it. "Hallelujah!" they roared in one voice. "Hallelujah, praise de Lawd!" Ophelia rose unsteadily and began writhing with the ecstasy of the music. But soon her convolutions assumed the rhythm of the drum, beat and sway, beat and sway, and the tempo changed— slowly—then fast and sensuous. It was no longer religious revival but African Congo such as I had seen many times in near-by Haiti. The gentle and smiling Ophelia who had baked our bread in the sand at the Lagoon Christophe was a woman gone mad. She twisted and frothed and swayed with the vibrations. But suddenly Thomas raised his hand and with an abruptness that made us jump the chanting ceased. Ophelia looked startled, swayed uncertainly for a moment or two, and then still trembling and trance-eyed took her seat.

Thomas strode to a crude pulpit and began his sermon. I do not remember the words nor are they important but the theme of it was "Chillun, if yo don take de blessin yo gotta take de cussin." It was a powerful oration. He told of the children of Israel, of their trials and tribulations, of how the spirit—"de blessin" he called it—came upon them and guided them out of the wilderness. It was a marvelous story, an epic of struggle, of defeat and of victory. There were mighty wrestlings with "de debbil"; he related how the children of Israel fought valiantly and cast him out. The Negro poured his whole heart and soul into it. His voice shook with passion and he was an orator of no small ability. The listeners hung on every word, jumped when he crashed his fist. "De blessin is heah foh yo," he repeated again and again, "if yo don take de blessin yo gotta take de cussin."

We slipped away in the dark. Mounds of black masonry splashed with bluish moonlight stood somberly against the deep sky and high above the stars twinkled and glittered. Down the street we could hear the swish and sigh of surf, the sound of breakers gliding up the beach and falling back again. Once more the thought came that this island was our portion, earth and sea and sky, the deserted and decaying village, these people who shared the land with us. I thought of the braggart Richardson, the smiling suave Commissioner, the Negroes back in their primitive church—and of ourselves, islanders by accident. Sea-girdled people, all of us, enmeshed in a circling wall of foam and surf. And again, echoing down the empty street came the passionate voice of little black Thomas. "Chillun, de blessin is heah foh yo, if yo don take de blessin yo gotta take de cussin."

It was morning. Sunlight streamed through the open windows, crawled slowly across the floor, crept across our bodies and suffused the coral walls with a golden glow. Our figures, prone and sprawling, moved slightly, stretched, yawned and fell prone again. It was good to lie thus, soaking up the sunshine, drowsing away the morning hours. Reaction had set in. Tired from the sea, tired of worrying about museums and equipment, we were taking it easy. There was no hurry, for the moment at least, and we closed our eyes and drowsed. Beyond the tent, beyond a little slope of rock rose a faint murmuring—swish and sigh, swish and sigh again—the sound of a gentle, almost calm sea purring against the rocks. The trade wind had slackened and the breakers were hardly lifting—swish and sigh, they said, swish and sigh, like a faint watery metronome beating away the time. No hurry now, no hurry— A lizard crept by the open door, paused statuesquely a moment, and departed in quest of a bug. Birds began to call, vague whisperings of unseen wings, the gentle cooing of doves. From the soil beneath came clean, green smells, the odor of crushed leaves, blossoms, scent of prickly pear. It was an island morning —sea sounds, birds, peace and quiet, the glow of sunshine. We stirred again and opened our eyes.

Wally grinned, turned and yawned again.

"Damn it," he said, "I feel good." And he jumped to his feet, threw off his remaining clothes and raced down to the rocks. With a mighty shout he flung into the air and plunged into the depths. A tremendous splash rose skywards and he disappeared into the blue followed by a great streaming line of bubbles. I felt good, too, and for the first time in weeks felt relaxed. "De blessin" was already upon us.

After the swim we loafed on the rocks, soaking up the sunshine, watching the surf pile up on the coral and slide back again. A big four-masted schooner hovered far out to sea, com-

ing north out of the Windward Passage. She was heading back
to America, probably, loaded with logwood from Haiti. "We
might catch one of them," mused Wally, but I could see that
he was not serious. No, there was no use in going home. It was
cold back there, and the sun was not shining—not like this at
least—and there was no warm blue sea to swim in. True, we
did not know where the next meal was coming from, but for
the moment it did not matter—we felt good. Down on the
rocks, and above near the hut, swarmed myriads of slithering
crabs and dashing lizards; species new to us, many of them; and
birds, honey creepers, warblers and doves; and all the host of
sea creatures. We knew nothing about them, their ways, their
habits, their places in the scheme of things. Curiosity, if nothing else, would hold us fast.

But "de blessin" was not to come so easily, for we still had
to eat and all our equipment was in the hands of the negro
Commissioner. We walked down to the settlement again, hoping against hope that the government at Nassau would have
advised the Commissioner to release our materials. Mathewtown had one modern piece of equipment, a small radio station
maintained by the British Government. By this time some
word should have come. We thanked heaven for the miracle of
wireless for without it we would have been in a sorry plight
indeed.

Later in the day a message arrived and, as we expected,
the Colonial Government issued instructions to release all
our materials and to show us every courtesy. Still faintly
smiling, the Commissioner notified us of the decision and gave
us the key to the stone shed. Other than a very slight unbending
in his manner he never changed. He was the most rigid man
I ever met. Later I understood, for he had a problem on his
hands. As a Negro, with the destiny of the island in his keeping,
as the final court of appeal, as administrator of his tiny domain,

he had to steer a devious course between bitter jealousies, around the rancid hates of mulatto and black, and beneath the disdain of the whites and near whites. In self defense he had raised up a barrier, a frigid smile through which few could break. In a larger place this would not have been necessary but there are no jealousies more bitter nor ugly than those provoked by the frustrations of insularity. It would have been easy to have made fun of him, for he was so utterly precise in word and manner—too easy. It is simple to jest at scars when we have never felt a wound.

As soon as the news of the release reached the ears of Richardson, who proved to be but an empty braggart, he flew into a rage of disappointment and chagrin. In retaliation he sent us a huge bill for the dinner to which we had been invited. We refused to pay but when we saw that our refusal was going to result in a great deal of embarrassment for the Commissioner, we settled without further argument for the sake of peace though it took the remainder of our scanty cash. Richardson, it appeared, was the island's bad boy and was the source of trouble for everyone. Much to our relief and the general delight of most of the island's population he died suddenly some weeks after our arrival of acute alcoholism, heart disease and a series of complications too numerous to mention. We breathed easier after he was gone. The island seemed freer without him. But I suppose he had his excuse, he was a man with overweening ambition and no place to go with it. Inagua *was* a queer little island and it touched the lives of all who made it their home. Richardson it had affected adversely by bringing all his uglier characteristics to the fore. His overbearing attitude at the dinner had its inception in some injury, some cutting remark or disdainful attitude of a white man years before. Ever since that day he had been thirsting to return the insult, an eye for an eye, a tooth for a tooth. To make two white men feel uncomfortable and to cause them to squirm in their chairs was sweet revenge. That we were different white men was unimportant.

The Daxons were soon disposed of, though the elder David descended into one of the mightiest rages that I have ever seen possess a human being when he found that he was to be deprived of his share of the spoils. Under Richardson's prompting he had brought us a bill for seventy-five English pounds which we refused to pay. His face distorted into a savage leer, his eyes bulged and he worked himself into an insane frenzy. Throwing out a barrel chest he pounded, gorilla-like, on its immensity, bellowing curses at us. The island had touched him, too. Years of grubbing in its stony soil, with poverty always around the corner, had got the best of him and the hope of sudden riches in the form of easily acquired wreckage had upset his equilibrium. He was in debt to Richardson and his hope of canceling this debt had been dashed to the ground. We did not blame him, rather we felt sorry for him, and in the end he quieted down and was paid a fair amount for his services.

And thus it was that we became islanders, to dwell in a little coral and thatch hut by the sea. Over the door on a piece of soft driftwood which we picked up on the beach, we carved with our penknives the quaint and amusing motto—"If yo don take de blessin, yo gotta take de cussin." It became the essence of our island philosophy.

Although our house had but two rooms we managed quite nicely, for two rooms is about all the space anyone actually needs. We turned one room into sleeping quarters and the other into a laboratory. With two long boards that had drifted up on the beach a mile or so away we made a laboratory table. When we found the planks they were covered with barnacles and algae and housed a considerable collection of toredos and other marine organisms. But they were still solid, so we cleaned them and put them in place. For days thereafter our laboratory floor was littered with the bodies of tiny shrimp and copepods which had found shelter in the crevices of the boards and which as the wood dried crept from their hiding places to seek the cool water that had so mysteriously vanished. Most amazing was the length of time the scent of the sea remained. At night when I sat in the deck chair, which we had salvaged from the ship, and closed my eyes I could transport myself a thousand miles away by taking a deep breath of the aroma exuding from these water-logged boards. It was an odor that swept me back to the salt marshes and flats of the Chesapeake Bay, an indefinable aura of long-dead reeds, marsh mud and decaying fish.

There is something very basic and fundamental about the formation of a new home; some instinct within us that traces its genesis to a long forgotten century when a brutish two-legged creature crawled into a cave and barred its entrance with sticks against the elements. There comes first a sense of relief, an innate satisfaction in the knowledge that whatever comes, weariness, wetness, the bitter pinch of cold or scorch of sun, there is a haven in which to retire, in which to revive the sagging spirit, to contemplate and to prepare for the new day. It is in the very possession of a home—or a cave—that men are differentiated from the beasts. The first fire, kindled on the ledge of some Neanderthal cliff still casts its heat in the hearth-glow of a streamlined fireplace. The cave-dweller, tired from the hunt, who threw himself exhausted on an animal's skin on the floor of his troglodytic shelter is blood brother to the man who goes home to a bed. The quaint modern custom of elevation and the lapse of a thousand centuries is the only basic change.

I think I know something of the feelings of the cave man, or at least, I can claim closer kin because our house was so like his own. Except for the wooden floor ours was not unlike the barest cave, for only the thickness of coral walls and the thinness of thatch kept us away from nature itself. No draft nor winter's gale eddying about the mouth of a stone age refuge gave more the sense of nearness to the elements than the unceasing dirge of the trade winds that pressed at our shutters and whistled about the palmetto leaves on the roof. At night, particularly, these wind-sounds seemed to increase in tenor; the darkness seemed filled with a great unrelenting force that tore ever on into the west.

But primitive as it was it soon became home. From the vast accumulation of wreckage which we piled in a heap near the door we sorted out those things essential to our basic comforts: an oil lantern, two cots, blankets, the remaining books, our instruments, writing paper and tobacco. The rest we covered with a canvas to keep where it was. When, after a long day exploring the jungle, plodding the gleaming beaches or observing the movements of some animal that had claimed our attention, we saw in the last rays of the afternoon sun the diminutive white walls of our house it was always with a sigh of relief. Here at last was surcease from weary limbs, shade from the hot sun, food for empty stomachs and forgetful sleep. The primal man, on marking the dark hole that was his shelter, must have breathed an identical sigh.

As soon as we were established I sat down to one of the most difficult tasks I have ever undertaken. It was the unpleasant necessity of writing letters to all those who had placed faith in us explaining that we had failed. Day after day, on the excuse that there was no way of mailing a letter, I had put the task aside. But one clear morning a sail hove over the horizon to the north. It was the out-island schooner which called for a few hours once every fortnight and then left the island again to its solitude. This schooner, an infrequent call by a Dutch line of steamships, and an occasional cruising yacht were Inagua's only contacts with the outside world. With a sinking feeling I settled in a chair and began tapping the keys of our rusty typewriter.

It was difficult to admit failure, more difficult to acknowledge that there was little excuse for that failure. Only the excessive weariness from the great storm could explain our not posting a watch on deck while we lay becalmed off an unknown shore. What was there to say? As simply as possible I wrote what had happened and finished the letters a little lamely. That evening, when the schooner had gone, her sails melting into the purplish haze, a deep feeling of despondency settled over me, a depression that I could not shake. Even the sound of the surf echoing against the walls filled me with a vague dejection.

My courage reached its lowest ebb several weeks later when I saw the white clad form of Wally Coleman disappear on the deck of a steamer that touched at the settlement for a short while on its way north. Word had come making it imperative for him to return home. He had been a jolly companion and I was sorry to see him go. That night the little hut felt more empty than ever and the trade wind increased beyond its usual intensity, howling through the thatch and blowing out the lantern until I sheltered it behind some canvas close to the floor. Only on one other occasion, when I was seeking the nesting site of the flamingo, did the feeling of utter dejection so penetrate my being. For hours I lay awake tossing on my cot, listening to the dead leaves scurrying across the clearing and the hollow monotone of surging water.

This sense of despondency, however, could not last. Inagua was too beautiful to be sad in and there was too much to do. Life alone, though a trial at times, began to assume the proportions of an adventure. Even without stirring beyond sight of the clearing there was a host of things to claim my attention. Dozens of tiny Sphaerodactylus lizards, tiny brown creatures so small that they could curl comfortably within the space of my finger ring, made the hut walls their special domain. As their generic name implies they were equipped with almost microscopic five-toed feet, neatly furnished with cleverly formed adhesive pads that made it possible for them to cling upside down like flies to the smoothest ceilings. They were nocturnal, and in the dark of the evening it was a common sight to see their scampering forms darting all over the masonry. They were so tiny that I often mistook their shadowy scurryings for the movements of insects. These lizards were the subject of the first important discovery I made on Inagua, for when I examined their anatomy I found it differed from that of any Sphaerodactylus lizard yet described. They were a type new to science, and, as we proved, found nowhere else in the world except on this lonely island. I spent long hours watching their activities trying to glean something of their habits. I pulled the house eaves apart in an effort to discover where they hid when the brilliant sunlight sent them hurrying to cover. One little fellow, or rather lady, took up residence in the crevice of the laboratory table and there laid a single smooth, hard-shelled egg. Most amazing was the fact that this egg was as great in diameter as the lizard itself, a full quarter of an inch. How a lizard with a waist measurement of a quarter of an inch could lay an egg of equal dimension remained a mystery until I raised an entire family of them and attended the birth rites of several of the mothers. As obstetrician-in-chief to a jar full of lying-in-waiting lizards I made the interesting discovery that the eggs were quite soft when extruded, almost leathery in texture, and that after a quarter of an hour they assumed a smooth rounded shape and hardened to a beautiful, delicate, calcareous pink shell. I put these diminutive eggs in a safe spot and watched them each evening for two months before the first quivering baby cut itself a neat lid from the end of its prison, crawled out and went scampering forth to its fate fully equipped to meet the complex problems of adult lizard-hood. Consider what a marvelous provision this is. For these, the smallest reptiles in the world, there is no responsibility of parent to offspring, no weary hours of training and education. On the day of mating there is planted in the waiting ova all that is ever required for the baby Sphaerodactylus to know. It seems a divine attention is given to even the least of nature's children.

A family of scorpions lived in the interstices of the roof thatching and immediately under the ridge pole was the nest of a common house mouse. Like myself, it was an intruder, a foreigner, islander by adoption, having escaped probably by proxy of an ancestor several generations removed from the hold of some visiting schooner. I did not disturb it, nor did I make any further attempt to remove the black and yellow spider that was still occupying the crack over the lintel. I knew they were really harmless and I was well repaid for my forbearance by many hours of entertainment.

The most thrilling times of all were the evenings. Then the hermit crabs came out of their hiding places and began their nocturnal wanderings. Hermit crabs occur on Inagua literally in the hundreds of thousands, every hole and crevice shelters them, and night is their period of activity. These crabs are remarkable in that nature has taken away the hard chitinous covering on their tails, leaving these members soft, white and vulnerable. In order to protect these delicate appendages they thrust them in abandoned seashells which they carry wherever they go. The clattering and banging of these shells over the rocks made the night hideous. Every hermit crab thought its neighbor's shell was bigger and better than the one it carried and their midnight fights kept any but the sturdiest sleepers awake. Vague rustlings and creepings surrounded one everywhere; inside it sounded as though a vast army of prowlers were marching on the house.

But the greatest annoyance of the evenings was the herds of wild donkeys and cattle. During the day they disappeared into the bushes, into quiet retreats in the interior. But at night they came down to the water's edge and prowled about the beach. I did not mind them at first but finally they became so numerous I could not go out after dark without being charged by an angry cow. I determined to get rid of them once and for all. Among my equipment was a .410 gauge shotgun and a number of cartridges. I emptied a shell of its shot and replaced it with crystals of salt that I gathered from the rocks by the shore.

The next evening the cows were on hand as usual. Fully a dozen of them. They prowled about the yard, kicking over specimen cages and uprooting the piled tin cans. Quietly I opened a crack in the door and thrust out the muzzle. Not ten feet away was a big steer. I aimed for its rump. There was a frightful roar, a sudden blaze of powder, and a moment's silence followed by the most prolonged moo I have ever heard. The moo was followed by a whole series of snorts as the herd got into action. The yard became a melee of milling bawling forms. That is, all except one. The big steer had lit out at express train speed for the interior. With a mighty bellow it plunged through a wall of bristly cacti making a neat hole through a stone fence and over a wall six feet high, which it cleared by a foot. I had no idea a steer could jump so high. For almost fifteen minutes I could hear the animal tearing down trees and rooting up bushes in its path.

The next night, however, the cows were back as usual accompanied by a half dozen wild donkeys. This time I rigged up something different in the way of entertainment. From the wreckage I had salvaged a quarter ounce bottle of flash powder which I had brought for photographic use. A quarter ounce is a lot of flash powder, for it is a powerful explosive. I fitted it with an electric photo fuse and connected the fuse with a flash-light battery. I planted the powder in the ground in the middle of the clearing.

At eight o'clock, as usual, the yard was full of cattle. I touched the wires. There was a blinding flash of light followed by a thunderous boom and a hail of rocks and small boulders. A few came hurtling through the roof and bounced on the floor.

To have gone out in the yard in the next few seconds would have been suicide. Cows hurtled against cows and donkeys plunged over the lot. In a wild, screaming frantic horde they burst through a stone fence, knocking it asunder and went bounding into the bushes. After that evening I was never disturbed by another animal.

But the most amazing feature of my dwelling was the utter tameness of the birds. They came in the windows, perched on the table, hopped across the floor and bounced out again. The yard was the favorite resorting place of a half dozen ground doves not much bigger than good sized sparrows. These were so tame they allowed me to approach within a few inches. They belonged to a subspecies noteworthy for the paleness of its coloration and the excessive length of its scientific name which contained no less than twenty-nine letters. Oddly enough, the subspecies has been recorded from only two islands, Inagua and distant Mona which lies between Hispaniola and Porto Rico more than three hundred miles away. Yet on Mariguana only a short day's sail to the north is another variety of the same species. I captured one of these delicate brown doves and placed it in a cage. But it was so restless, flying against the bars, pacing ceaselessly up and down, never resting, ignoring the grain which I gave it, so obviously unhappy that I allowed it to escape.

Most fearless were the mockingbirds. These were much lighter in plumage than our northern mockingbirds and it was not at all uncommon to have them perch on the windowsills while I was busy working and sing out their hearts quite oblivious of my presence. There was one individual in particular that used the ridgepole for its nocturnal musings. In the quiet hours just before the coming of new day, when the trade winds had slackened almost to a calm, when all other sounds were hushed, this lone mockingbird would pour out its whole repertoire in the still air, note after note in liquid melody. It was the most entrancing hour of the island's day.

For sheer fascination and entertainment, however, none exceeded the hummingbirds. They were everywhere. Extremely tame, darting with lightning speed through the needle-lined passages of the prickly pear, feeding on the cactus blossoms, chirping in odd notes, hovering on invisible wings, they were irrepressible. The doors and windows were continually filled with their flashing forms and the rafters echoed with the buzz of their activity. In one corner of the yard near the stone wall was a remnant of what once had been a considerable bed of bitter aloe plants. When I first arrived these were in full bloom, tall composite blossoms of rich chrome yellow hung with long deep rows of tubular chalices. Their brilliant hue attracted the hummingbirds for acres around and I once counted as many as thirty hovering over the stalks at one time. They were completely without fear and permitted me to approach to within a few feet. Perfect confidence born of their marvelous powers of flight and years of living undisturbed by man made them indifferent to my presence. I have photographs in my collection showing them sound asleep on tiny twigs quite oblivious to my maneuverings with the camera. The supreme evidence of their assurance was shown one day when a hummer fluttered on vibrating wings no more than a foot from my nose, examined me carefully and then settled gently as a feather on the protruding lens of my graflex. I remained as still as possible and fully two minutes crept by before the tiny mite bestirred itself and then calmly, without paying me the slightest attention, opened its wings and melted into the green vegetation.

They were all of one type, a species found nowhere else in the world but on this one island. Their nearest generic relatives live today in the distant mountains of western Panama and in Costa Rica. How the Inaguan species arrived on the island is something of a mystery. One theory suggests that it is a remnant of a once abundant group distributed throughout the West Indies and which as the centuries slipped away became less and less numerous as its numbers were eliminated from island to island, gradually becoming extinct by accident, disease, capture by enemies, lack of food or whatever ill fate is peculiar to hummingbirds, leaving only the Inaguan species and one other type as testimony of their existence. The other theory, and the more dramatic one, is that the ancestors of the Inaguan hummingbirds were caught up in some great tropical storm of many centuries ago and flung the hundreds of miles across the seething waters of the Caribbean Sea to a safe haven on the level rocks of Inagua. The first theory is scientifically more plausible but I prefer to picture in my mind the scene that might have occurred if the second were correct.

There would have been a succession of calm, clear days, brilliant and clear in the tropical sunshine along the coast of Costa Rica, the usual prelude to hurricane weather. Undisturbed, the ancestors of my Inaguan species would have passed lightly from blossom to blossom as they had been accustomed to do from time immemorial. Doubtless not a breath of air was stirring to relieve the hot sun and in the unusual calm the hummers took to the higher branches of the trees to do their feeding. Then in the space of a few hours the clouds descended lower and lower until they scudded just above the tree tops. Still near to the ground there was no wind and the atmosphere was close and sweltering. But only for a short time. Roaring out of the expanses of the restless Caribbean came the hurricane, suddenly shrieking across the coast, snatching the leaves from the tree tops, breaking the branches and throwing the jungle giants to the ground in a gargantuan tangle of vines and twisted creepers. As the trees fell, the hummingbirds that took refuge in their branches were suddenly caught up by the great suction of the wind and in a few seconds tossed skywards toward the black racing clouds. Close together, a pair that had sought shelter on the same branch, were swirled heavenwards and, fighting valiantly with the gusts, sought futilely to reach the shelter of the forest. Their efforts were in vain. Their small bodies, weighing less than an ounce, were but chaff before the wind, they possessed neither the bulk nor the force to combat the howling gale. Then in rapid succession came great pelting sheets of rain, huge stinging drops that beat against their tiny bodies and soaked through their straining feathers. There was only one hope, to soar above the deluge. Side by side these hummingbirds permitted themselves to be swirled away on the updraft of the hurricane's funnel hundreds of feet above the ground. Then as quickly as it had come, the revolving, twisting demon shrieked away from the coast, leaving behind a scene of utter desolation. On and on into the limitless wastes of the blue ocean the monster howled, on past Cuba, on through the Windward Passage and out into the broad Atlantic. Probably hours passed and in all the roar of the hurricane two pairs of tiny wings beat at the swirling air; forty to fifty wing strokes to the second, tossed skywards one moment, down to the crests of the waves the next, on through the evening and into the horrible darkness of the night. But as the monster moved into the open ocean and on into oblivion, the hummingbirds were flung by sheer centrifugal force to the outer rim of the vortex. Weary, cold, hungry, the harassed pair saw the gray dawn come. Beneath was a seething expanse of angry ocean; huge waves, black from the great depths and white with foam, met the eye on all sides. No land anywhere. On and on the weary birds vibrated, scudding with the wind. All direction was lost; to keep aloft away from the waves was their only purpose. Somehow they were still together; only by sheer determination and the gift of marvelous powers of flight did they survive. The wind then died rapidly but the waves still mounted to the skies. Their wings moved slower, the grueling hours had taken their toll of reserve energy. Off in the distance they sighted a thin line of brown tinged with subtle green. An island! With a last burst of energy the hummingbirds moved straight as arrows to the land. It was low, flat, barely carpeted with vegetation, but land. Scarcely able to move, the mites sank exhausted on a plant. Their heads drooped, wings sagged loosely, they slept.

An hour or two passed. The regenerated birds moved again, chittering and calling to each other. After the hurricane all was quiet, the air so still, the roaring had ceased. A blossom nodded gaily on a slender fingered cactus plant, deep red with a yellow circle of stamens. One of the hummers settled on its lip and thrust its bill deep. It was joined by its companion. Tiny insects were snared on their wire-thin tongues. Another blossom provided sweet nectar and more insects, microscopic spiders and gnats. Presently the two slept again, side by side on a prickly pear spine. All through the night they rested, assimilating the energy of flower-haunting insects. Days passed and they hunted together, the dreary hours of the storm forgotten. Then came a day when, unlike all the others, the male felt bursting with energy; and as I have seen his grandsons do, it whirled round and round its placid, more neutral colored mate. At first she paid little attention but as his attentions increased, she could not disregard their manifestations. He began swinging back and forth on invisible wings, twisting, turning, going into a frenzy of activity; he moved as though suspended by an invisible pendulum, more and more swiftly; the dead leaves underfoot rustled with the blast of air from his wings; they emitted an angry buzzing as he reached the climax of his love dance. She could not ignore him any longer and they drifted away through the cacti to culminate their courtship on the bristly spines of a cactus pad. In a tiny cup of soft fibers from the silk-cotton tree decorated with gay lichens and minute fragments of dead plants the female laid the fertilized eggs of this first island mating. It was thus, I like to think, that the race of Inaguan hummingbirds was begun.

One breezy afternoon I was seated in the hut banging away at my typewriter when an angry humming at the door attracted my attention. One of the descendants, a thousand generations removed, of the first Inaguan hummingbird had entered the open door and was vainly trying to penetrate the transparent screening of mosquito netting that I had tacked across the windows. I picked it off the mesh, placed it in a near-by lizard cage and continued writing. It was a male. I had hardly started when another began buzzing at the screen. I captured it too. For a few moments I admired the gorgeous pair preening their ruffled feathers in the cage. Although I had handled them as gently as possible my clumsy fingers had pushed their plumage all out of arrangement. This did not seem to disturb them, however, and they went about their feather cleaning quite methodically, chirping the while in thin trilling notes, and paying me not the slightest bit of attention. Even when I picked them up again they did not struggle but lay quietly in my hand. This sort of behavior was a new experience in my ornithology; never before had I seen wild creatures so confident of good will. After a bit I opened the cage door and permitted them to escape. They flew up in the rafters and began darting back and forth. As I settled in my chair they seemed to have forgotten my presence. I lay back and watched.

One was perched on a rafter, readjusting a microscopic feather, when the other backed the entire length of the hut and rushed headlong at the sitting bird. The impact knocked it off its perch but it recovered before it had fallen far and retaliated with a rush. They seemed ablaze with hatred, the hut walls hummed with the sound of their fury. Back and forth they swept, wings ablur, squeaking and calling in trilling crescendos. Then to my utter amazement they suddenly declared a truce and sat side by side on a convenient rafter and began carefully preening their plumage. The open door and I were ignored. The battle, if battle it was, started again. The impacts of their meetings were terrific; they drove headlong at each other from opposite sides of the building meeting in a swirl of feathers and beating wings. Again the birds rested.

Half an hour they were still at it, bristling with energy. My neck was tired from staring up at them; a task called me outside. Carefully, I propped the door open so they could escape. On my return I looked in vain among the rafters for the birds. They were not there. My glance fell on the cot. In the center was a tiny fluff of bedraggled feathers. It was one of the hummers. The creature was still alive but very weak. Its feet twitched convulsively, its tongue hung drooping from the end of its long bill. I could find no blood and I pulled out its wings to see if they were broken; they seemed undamaged and I folded them closed again. Presently it drew in its tongue and began sending up series after series of faint discordant squeaks.

No sound that I have ever heard, except possibly the voices of tiny meadow mice, was exactly like it. I stroked the bird for a moment then took it out in the sunlight to a large prickly pear plant. Turning the little thing right side up I placed its feet on the edge of a big yellow blossom and steadied it. It teetered drunkenly and then began to acquire its equilibrium. Plunging its bill to the base of the blossom the bird drank once, twice, rested, drank again and then very weakly spread its wings and flew between two cacti and out of sight.

CHAPTER VI

Dwellers of the Surf

THERE was one thing on Inagua that was inescapable. When all other memories of the island will have faded, merging indistinctly with a horde of other recollections, and when the shape of all the birds, animals and people with whom I had contact will have become but hazy shadows and dim evanescent figures, I shall need only to close my eyes in a quiet place to bring it all back once more. Then rushing through the darkness will come a sound, a roaring sighing sound, low, sibilant, or at times throaty and powerful, increasing and falling in tone, on and on in endless reiteration. It is the sound of the surf as I heard it day after day against the rocks near my dwelling, swirling, surging, boiling, boisterous, angry, or gentle and murmuring, week after week, hour after hour until its cadences were etched in indelible gravings on the cells of my brain. Day and night it set the tempo and the mood of the island; calm and soothing when the wind was low; deep and fretful when the trades grew angry and topped the waters with white caps.

The surf was the tone background of island existence. The mere sound of breaking waves is all that is necessary to bring back to memory the long succession of tropical days steeped in dazzling sunlight, the recollections of the hot still bush and the shimmering, dancing heat waves, of bending palms leaning seaward over pure white beaches, of curving sand dunes, barren and white in the glare, of stark fingers of cacti, mounds of prickly pear and gaunt thorn trees, the pale ghostly hue of sedge and sea grape, the darker verdure of lignum vitae and bay lavender. It was the theme music to the velvety atmosphere

103

of the warm dark nights, to the steely blue shine of moonlight
glowing on ruined walls splashed with leaf patterns, leaves
themselves fretted black against the stars, dark sweeping clouds,
the glittering zenith spangled with a billion flashing lights. Inescapable. The sound of the sea was always present, growling
against the reefs, swishing over the sand grains and slipping
back again.

The longer I dwelt on Inagua the more certain it became
that the day's activities would terminate within sound or reach
of the surf. When the inner jungle became too hot to be toler-
ated and seemed devoid of any life; when the interior plains
and the ponds of bitter salt sweltered barren and motionless
under the heat of the midday sun; when the white sand dunes
were silent except for the rustle of the wind-blown grains; and
when the lizards had crept out of sight in their burrows and the
birds had gone to other places, seemingly vanished, it was in
sheer relief that I turned to the edge of the sea. Here always
was life and movement, cool air and activity. Magnetism, or
perhaps the same instinct that draws a convict to his bars, im-
pelled me to gravitate at one hour or another to the island's
borders. My feet, sore and burning from the hot sand of the
interior, automatically led first to home to dispose of the day's
notes and specimens, then to the sea for a swim and an hour of
contemplation on the warm rocks. Surf loitering, first casual,
became frequent, then habit.

This habit partly began because of the scarcity of drinking
water which made washing in the surf a necessity. Inagua is
a vast flat island of barren rock, dry loose sand and salty mud.
There are no springs or streams, the only source of fresh water
is the infrequent rainfalls. Even rainwater becomes salty after
it has lain on the ground for a few hours. There are a few wells
in the settlement but these produce a brackish liquid that is
quite unpalatable. Most of the Inaguans depend on rainwater

which they collect in stone basins and wooden casks. I had one keg of good clean, northern spring water which had been saved from the ship, which I propped up outside the house and used as sparingly as possible. Until it rained again I knew it would be a considerable task to replace it.

To save water I washed everything in the surf. Soap would not lather in salt water but by pounding and diligent scrubbing I kept things reasonably clean. Pots and pans were most difficult but were not as bad as they might have been, for I had no grease. The Daxons had made away with the lot of it. Coleman had personally lugged ashore from the wreck three cases of tinned shortening but they had mysteriously disappeared somewhere between the Lagoon Christophe and Mathewtown.

Fortunately the vast pile of tin cans under the canvas in the yard made the use of water for cooking largely unnecessary though eating out of tin cans which had no identification made meals always a matter of surprise. The labels had all been washed off in the wreck and though I tried segregating the containers by shape and size I never quite succeeded in telling them apart. The most dismal meal was served late one afternoon when after returning ravenously hungry from an all day trip in the field, I opened four cans in a row and found they contained no less than four varieties of lima beans. It was the third consecutive day that I had inadvertently opened lima beans but I knew I could not waste food so I resignedly gulped them down. I had some very weird combinations. Opened cans soon spoiled in the tropical heat and I had to eat whatever came to light. Salmon, siruped cherries and canned pumpkin were perhaps the worst.

For my personal use I had the privilege of a magnificent bathtub. This was no modern one with gleaming metal and delicate porcelain but was a pool hollowed out of the rocks by the action of the surf. It was about four feet deep and was

----

kept continually filled with fresh water by the spray which
dashed over the rocks. The sun, beaming on it all day, kept it
heated to a perfect temperature, neither too hot nor too cold,
exactly at blood heat or slightly cooler. It was such a pleasure
to use this natural pool that I found all sorts of excuses to swim
in its crystal depths. I seldom used soap in it, however, because
it seemed to irritate the hundreds of small fish which made it
their home. These fish were all the colors of the rainbow, blues
and golds, gleaming silver, reds and purples, and there were
even a number of little fellows with vivid black and yellow
stripes. These last were very friendly and nibbled at my bare
back and toes. In this activity they were joined by a host of
pale brown fish the exact color of the rocks. Like ghosts they
slithered along close to the bottom, squirming beneath the
shadows of my legs, tickling with their fins.

When I first found the pool it contained four beautiful sea
anemones which looked for all the world like big pink carna-
tions. I pried them from their resting places and placed them all
together in one corner where they seemed to thrive quite contentedly, a living bouquet. There was one resident, however,
that I had to dispose of, a big black velvety sea urchin with
needle-sharp spines six inches long. I pried it loose, too, and
moved it to another pool where it seemed to do very nicely.
Perhaps the most marvelous thing about this seaside bathtub
was the constant change of inhabitants. With every high tide
fish came and went, though how they got in and out was something of a mystery, for only the thinnest sheets of spray lapped
over the rock edges. Along with the fish there were always
appearing and disappearing an incredible assortment of invertebrates, ghostly shrimp and prawn with sides so transparent and
clear that one could see their anatomies working and what they
had for lunch; hermit crabs carrying sea shells festooned with
moss and algae, a few bristly worms that lurked in the crevices

and even at times a half dozen or so thimble jellies, pinkish lavender wraiths that floated with no visible movement other than a slight pulsation of their umbrellas.

When I tired of the still waters of the tub I could change its comforts for the more invigorating waters of the ocean simply by walking ten feet and plunging in. From the edge of my bath the coral rock sloped gently down to a vivid yellow moss-covered shelf overhanging twenty feet of the bluest water in the world. The surf crashed on this ledge and then poured back again exposing the under surface of a fantastically adorned submarine cliff. I had to be careful, however, in coming to shore again, for the waves hit with stunning force. The trick was to catch the exact moment, to slide in on the tip of the advancing comber, then land feet first on the moss-protected shelf and quickly grasp the rock to keep from being swept out again. It was glorious fun but I gave it up for a time when a monstrous green moray measuring six feet or more swam leisurely under my thrashing toes when I passed too close to its hole in the cliff. The beast gave me one of the nastiest scares I have ever had. I did not suspect its presence until I saw its long sinuous green form with a row of stiletto-like teeth out of the corner of my eye as I was coming in to a landing on the shelf. I descended with a thump, quickly grasped the rock and scrambled up to safety. Morays are among the most savage fish that dwell in the sea and it is their custom to lie hidden in shadowy crevices and holes waiting for some luckless fish to pass. They belong to the family of eels and although apparently sluggish they can move with amazing rapidity. That this one did not take a piece out of my anatomy can only be attributed to the fact that it probably was not particularly interested; my white body only excited its curiosity. But the adventure shook me somewhat and several weeks went by before I got up nerve enough to go swimming off the rocks again.

By lying on the very edge of a boulder close to the water and catching glimpses between swells when the water smoothed out, I could make out its den about twelve feet down. During the middle of the day the creature was generally out of sight but as the afternoon wore on it usually came to the opening and protruded it head. I determined to capture it if possible and rid the neighborhood of its presence. From the pile under the canvas I extracted a length of quarter inch line of Manila originally intended for jib lazyjacks. For a hook I bent a steel rod that was used as a small spreader on the ship and filed one end to a point. There was no way of making a barb but I felt that if I could keep a taut line I could prevent the moray from slipping off.

Late the same afternoon when the tide had dropped I clambered out to the farthest boulder overlooking its den, captured one of the fish frequenting the pool, and thrust the hook through its back. With a penknife I slit the sides to make them bleed freely and then dropped it over. The moray was not in sight but I thought perhaps it might be a foot or two back in its crevice. The bait swirled back and forth but by a little juggling I managed to hold it exactly over the opening. A number of small fish came darting close, swimming excitedly about the morsel. Because of the motion of the surf it was difficult to see but in about ten minutes the ugly green head slowly began to project. Never have I witnessed more cautious action. A bare fraction of an inch at a time my intended victim slid forward, creeping sinuously between the algae. The smaller fish hung at a respectful distance, interested but not daring to approach. Deliberately the mouth opened, exposing a row of straight ivory teeth. The head slid forward again; anxiously I moved the bait closer until it was almost touching the moray's snout. The inner lining of the exposed throat was clean and white. The jaws closed carefully over the dead fish, exasperatingly slow.

The beast gulped and then glided backward. With all my strength I pulled on the line. There was a sudden swirl of blue water and the cord whipped out through my fingers, burning them as it passed. Quickly I caught a turn on a knob of rock and hung on. The line was as rigid as a bar of iron. Down it went and curved back under the cliff. Catching a hitch on the rock I seized the taut portion and heaved with all the weight of my 190 pounds. The line did not budge. I tried again but the big eel had backed into its den and had wedged itself tightly in place.

For ten minutes I heaved and pulled, then sat down on a rock exhausted. The line had not come forward an inch; the moray could not retreat. We were checkmated. Rushing back to the house I grasped a small block and tackle left from the rigging and dashed down to the surf again. The line was still rigidly taut. As rapidly as possible I made a seizing about the portion closest to the water. The other end of the tackle was fastened to the knob that held the line. Once again I heaved but without result. The tackle gave me the strength of several men but I could not move the moray out of its hole. What prevented its throat from being torn away I do not know. Stretching the tackle tight again I made the loose end fast to a point of coral and then threw my weight against it. It seemed to budge a little. Once again I tried. Dashing up to the house I retrieved another short piece of rope and made it fast to the piece I was pushing, catching the loose end around another corner so as to retain whatever advantage I won. Inch by inch I dragged the moray out of its crevice. It fought stubbornly, twisting its body violently, gained a little and then suddenly gave way. In a frenzy of hate and pain it flung itself into the surf and attacked the line. With a rush I pulled it up on the moss-covered shelf and then turned to free the tackle so that I could drag it out of reach of the water.

But I did not reckon with the blind hatred of the gasping eel.

In a series of flapping dashes it threw itself across the algae, striving to reach me. I scrambled out of the way, dropping the line and bounding toward the upper rocks. Its teeth snapped savagely, making a noise like castanets; its mouth was dripping with blood. I knew that one bite of its teeth might result in a festering wound that would take months to heal; I also knew that the blood pouring from the mangled throat mixed with an open cut might very likely prove dangerous, for the blood of most eels is highly poisonous, so much so that a few cubic centimeters would be enough to cause an agonizing death similar to that produced by a rattlesnake wound. Vividly I remembered a laboratory experiment I had once seen when a rabbit was injected with the substance derived from the blood of the common eel, ichthyotoxin it is called; the poor bunny died in convulsions. Also, I have seen the hands of fishermen swollen and infected from cutting eels for crab bait when the substance had seeped into open splits on their fingers.

The beast slid into the water again and strove to get away. This time I grasped the line well out of its range and dragged it high out of the reach of the surf where it lay gasping and thrashing. It took quite some time to die; almost four hours passed before I ventured to examine it closely. Several times when I had thought it dead and prodded it with a stick, it suddenly turned and snapped at the wood. One piece, nearly an inch in thickness, was ground into slivers. The hook was well down into its stomach and had to be extracted with a knife. The skin of the creature was thick and leathery with no visible scales and was covered with a heavy layer of slime. This mucus had been scraped away where the skin had dragged over the rocks and showed a bright blue integument beneath. The slime itself was brilliant and translucent; the combination of blue skin and yellow mucus made the animal appear green. Altogether it was a very unsavory looking beast. Its eyes were small and evil;

ferocity was etched in every line of its narrow ugly head. When it was dead I cut it in two pieces and threw them into the sea. Its stomach contained the remains of several squirrel-fish and the ground up fragments of a crab.

The moray, however, was only an incident although a memorable one. The real marvel of the surf and the cliff by the sea did not become apparent at once or in one evening. Like some of the more intricate passages of Wagner or Beethoven, it had to be assimilated little by little, becoming more under-standable, more wonderful with repetition. At first glance the cliff seemed a lifeless place except for the magnificent action afforded by the sweeping roll of the surf, but I soon came to know the twenty feet from the top of the rocks to the level of the sea as one of the most complex organizations of animal life in existence.

My seaside bathtub served a dual purpose. It not only pro-vided a place to swim and relax; it also enabled me to sink gently out of sight and observe, without being observed, the host of animals that made the surf their dwelling place. Few of the birds and beasts that came to the cliff seemed to associate my bobbing head with the anatomy of a human being; hence I was not an object of suspicion. Also my submersion made it possible to look at existence from a snail's-eye view for the edge of the pool was exactly on a line with the uppermost swirl of the advancing combers. By sinking up to my eyes and re-clining sideways, like some ill-proportioned manatee, I could place myself on an equal plane with the mussels and anemones, slightly above that of the fish and just below the stratum oc-cupied by the dashing Grapsus crabs. Poised midway between land and sea I commanded a view of both, belonging to neither; by merely shifting my eyes, I could look straight down to the shadowy depths or up at the racing clouds.

Discovery is largely a matter of point of view. I have often walked down a street without being aware of its existence. The same avenue from a thirty-story window or from the sanctuary of a manhole between the car tracks belongs to two different worlds; people assume the proportions of scurrying ants or conversely loom skyward like Brobdingnagian monsters. From a thirty-story window a man appears but a mote in a horde of swirling insects, from a manhole he dwarfs the street in which he walks. My submerged position in the pool placed me in the manhole category and put a new value on everything I saw. Only when I have begged, borrowed or stolen an airplane and gazed at the Inaguan surf from the height of a thousand feet will I feel that I have begun to exhaust its potentialities.

I do not know if snails and other gastropods are conscious of color; certainly my assumption of a snail's viewpoint placed me in a world in which pure brilliancy of hue was the dominating factor. I was surrounded by a weird cosmos of yellow in which great scarlet carpets spread crazily between corridors of mauve and lavender. Emerald green towers, splotched with iridescent pink, stood out boldly against lacy draperies of orange and warm Van Dyke brown. Behind all this was a vast heaving horizon of deep indigo, an azure space that oddly was never quiet but advanced and rose to the clear blue sky, where it rapidly altered to pale green and then sheer molten gold, which in its turn changed to dazzling white, pure and glittering, edged with shimmering halos of rainbows. Then the horizon receded and the world was tinged with yellow again amid great floods of cerulean blue and glitterings of royal purple; there were protruding spaces of leaf green, islands of dark saffron and deep shadows of russet.

It was a world studded with volcanoes, perfect symmetrical cones like that of Fujiyama, each with a crater at the top, only unlike Fujiyama, these volcanoes were of pale green daubed with large splotches of rose pink. On all sides and alternately smothered by rivulets of bubbly water, were a number of huge pincushions with barbarous needles, grotesque affairs of the most intense purple, almost black, but which showed thousands of tiny facets of scarlet and lavender iridescence. The needles themselves were graven with delicately etched lines like the blades of old Damascus steel; the tips were fretted with cruel hooks. Beside these were a number of armor plated tanks with the armor set in parallel rows overlapping to give utmost protection. These rows were banded with a flexible rim that extended to the ground and which was studded with closely set jewels, emeralds and sapphires, a sprinkling of garnets and amethysts, crystals of beryl and zircon. These were set in combinations, emeralds and garnets in wavy bands so as to give an impression of studied but unsuccessful camouflage.

Nothing was in proper proportion. The volcanoes were dwarfed by the gigantic pincushion, the armored tank was nearly as large as the emerald towers and the scarlet carpets stretched away for acres and acres. Only by raising my head and adjusting the focus of my eyes did creation come back to normal. Then the yellow world resolved itself to a slope of leathery algae, the carpets of scarlet became encrusting sponges, the volcanoes assumed the dimensions of limpets; the jeweled tank turned into the back of a chiton; the monstrous pincushion, the prickly body of a purple sea urchin; the heaving horizon, but the summit of an advancing wave.

The armored tank, however, gave the clue to the entire scene. This was a world of warfare, a place of continual strife where only those creatures equipped with heavy armor plating, cases of rigid shell, steel sharp spikes or other armament were able to survive. Nowhere in all the realm of nature is there a more bitter struggle for existence than that which takes place by the edge of the sea. The region bounded by high and low water is an area of instability, of alternate dry and wet, a place

of cold and intense heat, of smashing waves and thunderous
boiling surf. Only the most hardy can persist. Yet in the area
between tide lines have occurred some of the most profound
events in the history of our globe. In comparison the doings
of the Caesars, the Alexanders, the Napoleons, pale into in-
significance. The measurable results of the victories of the great
generals extend at most over a few centuries, then fade into the
background of things past and over with. This cannot be said
to be true of tide lines, for here there developed a vast array of
creatures which because of their success in this maelstrom
between tide lines were able to conquer new worlds on
land.

There is a law of nature, somewhat disputed in its exact details, but generally agreed upon by scientists, which states that
those creatures subjected to constantly changing conditions and
environments are more prone to physical change or adaptation
than those organisms which live a sheltered existence. Crinoids,
for example, ancient marine forms which dwell in the still quiet
depths of the sea where each decade is like the one that went
before, exist today nearly as they did millions of years ago
because the conditions under which they live are precisely
what they were in that remote age when they reached their opti-
mum. For them there was no need for alteration. On the other
hand our own distant relatives the ancient Amphibia evolved
from giant fresh water fish caught in drying Devonian swamps.
Nowhere more than in the area swept by the rise and fall of
the tide do more varied, difficult or changing conditions exist.
Hence it is not surprising that various dwellers of the sea in
crossing this barrier have become changed to land creatures.

I had only to drop again in the warm waters of my pool to
understand what a tumultuous life these surf creatures must
lead and to marvel at the wonderful variety of methods which
they used to combat their first strongest enemy, the surf itself.

Day in and day out great walls of surging water flung themselves at the cliffs, dashed high in the air and fell back again, roaring. The tumult never ceased, the air echoed to its thunder; high on the tops of the cliff great blocks of coral and sandstone weighing many tons were piled in a long rampart where they had been deposited by the ocean during storms. Some of these blocks were more than a foot thick and several yards in circumference. Yet they had been tossed more than thirty feet as though they had been but cordwood. But just before my eyes was a cluster of delicate hydroids, flower-like animals with tentacles so diaphanous and translucent as to be illusory. Near by hung long tendrils of filmy algae, looking like the finest Castilian lace, tiny interwoven threads that parted at the touch. How could they survive the tons of surf that poured on them every few seconds? Simply by giving way before it, by swaying in the direction of the water, a passive resistance created eons before Mahatma Gandhi was ever thought of. The water can secure no hold on them.

People can be divided into castes or groups, convenient classifications by which we describe their modes of existence. We are liberals or conservatives, fundamentalists or free thinkers, independents or stand-patters. Even yes-men have their place and survive in a world of rugged individualists. This is true no less of the denizens of the surf. The anemones and lacy algaes belong to the yes-men society; they persisted because they eternally agreed with the superior force confronting them. To resist or argue was unthinkable. The chitons, limpets and gastropods were the fundamentalists and stand-patters; the world changed and roared by them; they moved not a single inch; clad in impenetrable armor, imprisoned behind walls of ivory or unyielding calcium, they sat immobile; neither force of wave, heat of sun or attack of enemy caused them to change their mode of living one iota. Nor did this simile seem so unreasonable when one day I made an extensive collection of a species of limpet from an area both above and below the line of the surf and found that those individuals which lived at the places of the most violent action had the thickest shells. How like the fundamentalists were these mollusks; the more variable the world, the more case hardened they become.

The mussels, those purple-black bivalves that grow together in thickly crowded clumps, used a system of resistance unlike any other creatures of the surf. By some marvelous chemistry they derived a substance from the sea water which they spun in long silken ropes which they cast out in all directions, like the warp lines of a schooner, anchoring them firmly to the rocks. The number of lines which they put out seemed to be in inverse ratio to the safety of their position. These anchor lines are known as byssus, and it was from their substance that the tough but silky garments known as tarentum were manufactured which graced the bodies of the lords and ladies of medieval Europe. Because the mussels were so unusual I was hard put to think of what human category they might be linked with; then it occurred to me that they were not unlike those sedentary people who go in for life insurance policies and annuities, who buy gilt-edged securities and low interest bonds; forever throwing out lines to windward against the vicissitudes of life. And like these people, when the surf overcame them they always went down in masses, the entangled strands of byssus giving way all at once, precipitating them into the depths to be gobbled up by hungry fish.

Exactly opposite to these were the Grapsus crabs. They lived about the pool in the dozens; their sizes varied from little fellows a half inch in width to massive individuals measuring eight inches from claw to claw. They wore brown suits of wavy strips and mottled checks exactly the hue of the rocks.

They reminded me of the racetrack touts who also wore checkered raiment and who, like these surf crabs, subsisted by grabbing things on the run. Theirs was a life of dash and abandon, a series of intermittent scuttlings between the breakings of the waves. These crabs were the most nervous creatures I have ever seen. Only by lying utterly motionless could I induce them to approach me at all. Then they would creep close, eyeing me narrowly with glistening eyes mounted on a pair of stalks, watching timidly for the slightest movement, sidling forward cautiously, dashing back a few feet and then inching forward again, ever on the alert. Once I allowed a full dozen to collect about the borders of the pool where they began feeding on microscopic tid-bits which they lifted daintily to their mouths, which, by the way, worked sideways instead of up and down. Suddenly I raised my head. Instantly the rocks became alive with racing streaking forms. They moved so fast that their legs were barely visible and some of those near the top of the cliff threw themselves heedlessly into the open air and into the roaring surface of an incoming comber. There was no thought or consideration of what lay beneath, their only reaction was to be away.

For a long twenty minutes the rocks were empty of life, then from between the crevices they cautiously began to emerge once more. Those that had flung themselves into the foam came sidling out of the surf, dripping and unharmed by the experience. They resisted the deluge by grasping the seamed rocks tightly in their sharp claws and dropping close to the boulders so the water could not get underneath them and tear them away. Their stalked eyes made it possible for them to see in an arc of almost 360 degrees; the waves never caught them napping. At the precise moment when the water struck they flattened out until it was passed, then raised again and moved forward until another wave came in. Their zone of existence was bounded by the cliff tops on one side and by the roaring surf on the other. They were found nowhere else on the island; here they mated and deposited their eggs, found their food, kept an eternal watch for their enemies, lived and died. The very spirit of the surf itself, their lives were a vivid illustration of how the dry barren land came first to be peopled with crawling animals. Where the limpets, anemones and sea urchins were still completely bound to the ocean, perishing miserably of heat and dryness when it left them for long, the Grapsoid crabs were able to forsake it for hours at a time. Strictly speaking they were still creatures of the sea, but they were also land animals in process of transition. While still restricted to the twenty feet bordering the area of the water's edge, they had advanced further toward a life on dry land than had any of their companions. Only an incomplete anatomical transformation from gill to air-breathing lung requiring frequent wettings in the salt ocean held them in place. Laboratory experiments have shown that they can survive with gills completely dissected out in dry air for several hours, an operation that would kill any normal sea-dwelling crab.

Centipedes are noted for the amazing number of their feet. But they are amateurs in the art of pedal dexterity compared with the sea urchins. Sea urchins are the porcupines of marine life; only a person with cast iron fingers would dare pick one up, for every inch of their bodies is protected with long pointed spines which are mounted in cleverly designed ball and socket joints. They lived by the pool and along the cliff in great scattered masses, giving the rocks the appearance of being festooned with giant cockleburs. To fall on one would be a painful and dangerous experience, for their spines are frequently very poisonous, being covered with germ-filled mucus that produces festering wounds difficult to sterilize. Often the spines are barbed and very brittle, breaking off where they enter the flesh. One such injury in the fleshy part of my leg gave me no end of trouble until I dissected it out with a scalpel; even then it required more than a week to heal. The under sides of their barbed and pointed bodies are literally a mass of feet, strange sucker-like affairs arranged in symmetrical rows radiating from the round centrally located mouth. By means of these they progress slowly from place to place, advancing by a series of wavy rhythms. These tube-feet are capable of considerable contraction and expansion and no matter how uneven the surface on which they rest, they have a firm grip on the ground at every point. Thus they are able to cope with the surf, staying firmly in place while the water bubbles and roars over them. Sea urchins are considered to be but stupid automatons, headless creatures without a thought or flicker of intelligence. This is literally true, for they are the original scatterbrains. The only nervous system they enjoy is distributed in a series of ganglia in a circle about their spherical bodies. Thus the sea urchin functions because its ganglia are stimulated by its moving parts. One moving part generates activity in its neighbor; the animal is managed by its own activity. It might be said that the essential difference between an animal with a brain and one without, as for example, a dog and a sea urchin, lies in the fact that a dog moves the legs, in a sea urchin the legs move the animal. But be this as it may I could not help admiring the manner in which these living cockleburs had carved a niche for themselves in the face of terrific odds. Any animal that can survive in a world of crashing surf while managing several hundred separate feet at once, brainless or not, is a creature of no small attainments. Most of us have trouble enough at times managing two.

How very wonderful these sea urchins were I did not know

until I had watched them for a long time from the sanctuary of my bath. One of the things that always astonished me was the immaculate appearance of their bodies. Although the surf at times piled loose carpets of torn seaweed over the boulders and cast up gritty piles of loose gravel and coarse sand, and although all the other animals, the snails, mussels and chitons, had a rubbed worn look, or were covered with parasitic barnacles, the sea urchins were always spotless; no grains of sand, strands of algae or blotches of parasites marred their jet black coats. This was particularly remarkable when one considered that their spines should have been catch-alls for all manner of debris. They had a very clever system of keeping themselves clean. When a fragment of sand or dirt fell between the needles, it was grasped by a tiny clamp or pincers equipped with a triple set of jaws, like those of certain types of dredges; these were mounted on a flexible shaft of muscle and skin which transported the debris to the next claw which carried it to another, or to one of the tube feet which were also scattered over portions of the creature's upper surface, and so on until the offending fragment was dropped into the water. Small parasites that slipped between the barrier of spines were not treated so gently. The moment they touched the urchin's side the claws began snapping, opening and shutting until they seized on some portion of the animal's anatomy. Once a pincers secured a grip it held on tenaciously and then if a struggle ensued, other claws came to its rescue until the captive was held rigid by myriads of tiny clamps. Only death of the parasite caused the grip to be relaxed; the corpse was then passed from claw to claw, foot to foot until it reached the urchin's mouth and was devoured.

The hundreds of tube feet were not the only method these animal cacti utilized in retaining their position in life. Great numbers of them lived in cavities in the rocks; their bodies were larger than the entrances to their caves. These cave-dwelling individuals were about as safe as it is possible to be, for they were guarded by their spines and could not be approached from any direction except directly in front. They paid a penalty, however, for their security for they were hopeless prisoners. Early in life when they had stationed themselves at some favorable spot they secreted a powerful corrosive which crumbled the soft coral rock beneath them. Soon they were well out of the way of the driving water, safe in their holes. But then as they grew it became necessary to expand their quarters; the acid and the surf etched away the walls until they fitted comfortably but the openings remained comparatively small. They reminded me of those human beings who spend a lifetime carving niches for themselves only to find that in the end they are completely enmeshed by the fruits and habits of their ambitions. All about the pool were dozens of these imprisoned urchins. They seemed as healthy and as fully formed as their freer relatives. The free individuals, however, probably found food more abundant, for they lived on seaweed and algae which they ground up in their peculiar five-sided jaws; the prisoners had to be content with whatever the passing waters brought them—the inner surfaces of their dens were eaten quite clean and barren.

The sea urchins were not the only surf inhabitants who relied on their ability to bore into the rock to protect themselves from the shock of thundering waves. By lowering myself slightly over the edge of the pool and into the aura of mist that hung just above the tops of the bubbles I could see that the coral at this point was pitted with numberless small holes. Similar holes also were to be found in the shells of many of the gastropods that dwelt in the area. At first scrutiny, there seemed to be no life in the cavities but with a dissecting needle it was possible to tease out small pieces of brown matter which proved on more thorough examination to be the life substance of sponges. Like the urchins, these sponges drilled into the rock with acid. Some of the holes were as neatly formed as if shaped with an auger bit.

The last word in hole drilling, though, came to light when I took a piece of rock containing a number of these cave-dwelling sponges up to the house and examined their structure under the microscope. Inside the sponge, which itself was not more than a quarter of an inch in total diameter, was the fairy-like form of the young of some indeterminate crustacean. The early stages of so many of the crustaceans are so totally unlike the adults that I found it impossible to discover its identity; its structure was long and angular, and apparently it spent its earlier stages ensconced in the interstices of the sponge, gathering substance and strength before venturing out into the violent and dangerous world of the surf. I would have given much to have been able to visualize its life history, to have seen the hour when it burst from its egg case, to have known how it swam its way into its darksome abode in the entrails of a boring sponge.

Where certain of the surf-residents survived by making sticking plasters of themselves like the chitons, holding so tightly to the rock that they could be moved only with a heavy screwdriver, and where others hid in holes or crevices like the boring sponges, or dashed rapidly about like the Grapsus crabs, or like the snails and gastropods crouched in thick houses of shell, the anemones resisted the elements by virtue of their sheer versatility. There were several species scattered over the rocks; the most numerous were the large pink variety similar to the ones which I found in the pool, and which I moved to one side to prevent their being crushed, and a delicate brown species which lived in swarms about the edges. These last were so utterly beautiful, so translucent and frail in their structure as to be almost unbelievable. From the tips of their tentacles to the base of their cylindrical bodies they were soft mouse color, a neutral tone that derived its beauty from the shine of golden sunlight through clear tissue. The larger pink anemones were somewhat garish in their aspect, but these smaller ones were loveliness in monotone. They belonged to the peculiar group that believed in passive resistance, and with every motion of the water their long filamentous tentacles swayed back and forth, quivering and swirling. Although they were completely resilient, so perfectly designed was their anatomy that never at any moment did they assume an awkward position; complete gracefulness was their most conspicuous characteristic.

When I first became interested in them the tide was high and their bodies were being constantly bathed in the uppermost ripples of the breakers; when I again looked for them the water had dropped several feet, leaving them dry and helpless. Their forms were nowhere to be found but in their places were a number of disks of dark fleshy matter hardly one-fifth the bulk of the original animals. When I ran my finger over them, they felt thick and rubbery. It seemed impossible that these shapeless masses could be the beautiful creations of several hours past. I prodded one with a knife and it split open and oozed a mass of turgid liquid. Later when I again examined them they had shrunk still further. The hot sun beamed down and all life appeared to have gone out of them.

Yet when the tide came in again at four in the afternoon they were all out in flower again, as delicate and wraith-like as ever. This was a very wonderful thing; for nearly six hours these ocean-born creatures had been subjected to the dry air and blistering heat, conditions for which they had never been designed. It seemed they must be devoid of all sensitivity to endure such extremes and to prove it I reached out and gently touched one. Instantly it snapped shut, the graceful tentacles contracted and disappeared, the anemone once more became a shapeless blob of dark flesh. Interested, I let it alone and settled in the water to watch. For a long time it did not stir, but, then when my patience was about exhausted, it began to pulsate and quiver. The top unfolded slowly revealing a radially symmetrical surface, the color lightened perceptibly, light began to penetrate the loosening tissue, the tentacles emerged, reminding one of the slow motion pictures of the opening of a blossom, the flesh became translucent and filmy. Relaxed, the animal once again swirled and flowed with the current.

At that moment my attention was attracted by the frantic rowing of a small crustacean which was darting across the pool apparently trying to reach some haven of safety before one of the gaudy fishes became aware of its efforts and gobbled it up. I turned to inspect it and my shadow cut across its path causing it to turn violently to one side. This action was its undoing, for it blundered squarely into the expanded tentacles of a neighbor of the anemone I had just been watching. Then, in a small sort of way, I saw a very horrible thing happen. The creature ceased its motion as if it had been hit by a miniature bolt of lightning, as indeed it was, for the tentacles at the moment of contact shot hundreds of poisoned nematocysts into its flesh. The paralysis that seized it was complete. Other than a spasmodic jerk or two it did not so much as quiver; the creature never knew what happened. The long sinuous tentacles folded Medusa-like about its helpless body, then slowly curled inwards toward the mouth at the center of the anemone. Through the transparent flesh I could see the crumpled corpse of the victim as it began to dissolve under the strong digestive juices that poured on to it from all sides.

The anemones are most wonderful in the delightful versatility of their modes of reproduction. They can quite casually split themselves in two, either crossways or vertically, and become in a short time a pair of identical twins; or perhaps not desiring to lead a dual existence they can assume the characteristics of the flowers which they so much resemble and sprout buds on their stems. Unlike flowers, however, these buds are not allowed to come to fruition but are pinched off by a constriction near the base and are dropped near by on the rocks. Righting themselves these buds grasp the boulders and begin their individual lives by expanding their newly formed tentacles for whatever fate or the currents may bring them. If neither of these methods will suffice the anemones have still another system; the eggs may be cast forth to be fertilized at the will of the water or they may be retained in the cavity of the body until they become full-sized embryos. This versatility is their insurance that the race of anemones will never die.

I thought I had exhausted the potentialities of these organisms when I picked a boulder out of the bottom of the pool and cast it over the edge. It slipped from my hand and as it fell it rolled heavily through a cluster that was growing like a small suburb near a larger city of anemones. The suburb was all but wiped out. Many were terribly crushed and mangled, tentacles were torn off and split, several individuals were cut in two. Certainly, I thought, this would be the end of the little colony. But it was not. In a few days the missing tentacles were regenerated; the split individuals became two animals instead of one, each half burgeoning out fully formed and complete; the mangled sections were all healed and repaired. This was their ace in the hole. When every other method of resistance to their stormy environment failed them and when the force of the waves tore them to shreds or they were ground against wave-cast boulders, even when their tentacular arms with which they secured their food were destroyed, they were still not without hope. By some remarkable magic hidden deep within the complex workings of their body cells, they were able to re-create the damaged tissues and continue life as before.

A long line of green–with here and there a line of palms
shooting upwards like vegetable rockets frozen in mid-air

In the center of the seething line lay all that remained of the stout vessel.

Shipwreck camp. Beyond the land sloped away to a semicircular lagoon of emerald green water.

Cacti–speaking mutely of a scanty existance,
of scorching sun and parched soil

Nesophlox lyrura, the Inaguan hummingbird, is found nowhere else in the world. A female.

The blossoms provide sweet nectar and microscopic insects, a male *Nesophlox* hummingbird.

Every hermit crab thinks its neighbor's shell is bigger and better than the one it carries. Their midnight fights keep all but the sturdiest awake

A lizard paused statuesquely in front of the door
and then disappeared in search of a bug.

The surf–an area of bitter struggle

Sea urchins–the original
scatterbrains

The *Anolis* lizards–delicately colored creatures of gray
tinged with pale violet, soft yellow or warm brown.

Sphaerodactylus–the
smallest lizards in the
world. Their scur-
ryings in the dark
remind one of the
movements of insects.

An *Artibeus* bat–the most gargoylish, demoniacal yet humanlike face. None of the frowning stone figures on the high parapets of Notre Dame are more weird.

On the very edge of the sea the nighthawk deposited its single egg. During the day it drowsed and went forth in the evening to feed–with the bats and the owls.

An *Ameiva maynardii*–a lizard of the lee, a vivid reptile of jet black, bright yellow stripes and a stomach of ultramarine.

In the interior the crabs had piled up white mounds of loose sand and retired to their burrows to escape the heat of the tropical sun

For they have become laden with eggs–in a purple black mass they hang beneath thier aprons, glued together in viscid mass.

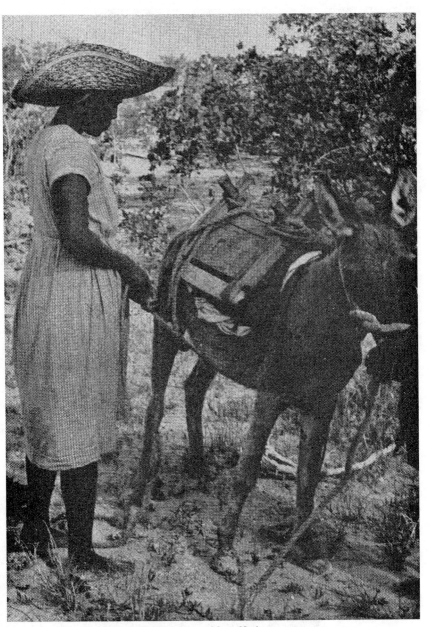

Mary Darling–a self-sufficient woman.

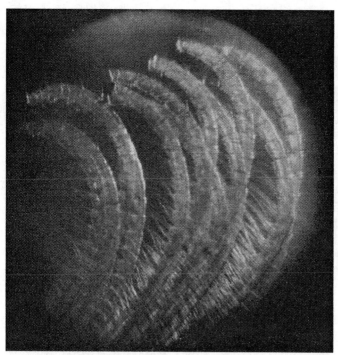

A barnacle's legs–transformed by the mechanics of need into living seines

On the slopes of the underwater hillside grew great clusters of feathery mosses, brilliant red sponges and purple sea fans. There was not a sound, although only twenty feet above the air was filled with the sullen roar of the surf.

The half-beaks–silvery creatures of the dark

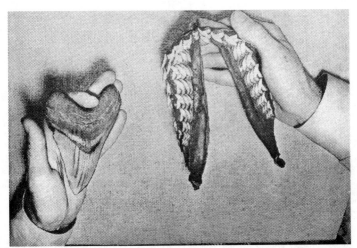

The modern and the ancient. A jaw full of modern shark teeth compared with a tooth of a monster of the Miocene.

Only a few flamingos remained. These moved disconsolately about the shallows.

A pair of newly constructed nests containing two chalky white eggs. The first flamingo colony.

CHAPTER VII

The Making of an Island

I⊤ is almost an accepted routine for shipwrecked sailors on tropical islands to make a circuit of their respective domains, if for no other reason than to satisfy themselves of what they already know or suspect—that they are on an island. This custom was originated by no less a person than that doughty and personable character Robinson Crusoe himself. As a full-fledged castaway I felt bound to follow the established tradition although I had as an excuse the more logical purpose of determining the essential topographical and ecological characteristics of Inagua in order to proceed intelligently with a study of the island's inhabitants. The brief glimpse of the wild bush as Coleman and I saw it from the deck of Daxon's boat was enough to convince me of a considerable diversity of environment and the coast was sufficiently beautiful and intriguing to provide the additional incentive of pure curiosity which, after all, is the driving force behind most scientific endeavor.

There was, also, another and more personal reason for the trip. Word had reached me through the medium of a small sailing boat that touched at Mathewtown that the hulk of the *Basilisk* had been lifted out of its grave and cast over the reef by the strong gale that came up the evening after Coleman had departed. The surf had thrown it high and dry on the beach. I also heard that the Daxons and other natives were cutting the remaining timbers apart to secure the bronze and galvanized fastenings. These tidings disturbed me considerably. There was no earthly reason, perhaps, why the Inaguans should not be free to despoil the wreck, but the sentiment which I attached

to my ship made the fact irritating. That the sea should tear
the vessel apart was reasonable and acceptable, that the Daxons
should hack at her with axes was a form of sacrilege.

Robinson Crusoe was happy in that he could survey his total
kingdom from one hilltop. I was not so fortunate. Inagua
stretches away, headland succeeding headland, for fifty miles
or more! Except for the few acres surrounding the settlement
it is as wild and desolate as on that memorable day in mid-
October over four centuries ago when Columbus first sighted
the Bahamas. It is a strange piece of irony that the islands which
were the first land trod by Europeans in the new world should
remain to the very last the most forsaken. Without any of the
side excursions which were necessary to accomplish my purpose the very minimum distance to be covered would be a
hundred and fifty miles. I knew that this was going to be a
tough trip, all of it on foot, in a place where water was scarce
or only to be found in far distant waterholes. No rain had fallen
since the light shower the evening we ran aground off Sheep
Cay, nearly two months before.

At most, with the other equipment which I must take to care
for my specimens, all the water I could comfortably carry
would be about three or four quarts. Even this would be an
intolerable load. I eliminated every possible bit of luggage.
There was no need to take a tent, rain was very unlikely, day
after day the hot sun glared in a clear blue sky unmarred except
for a few racing clouds; the tropical heat made blankets unnecessary; the air grew cool at night but by making some sort
of crude shelter from the wind I knew I could sleep undisturbed. In a light but cleverly woven native grass bag with a
shoulder thong I thrust a vial of formaldehyde and a small
hypodermic syringe with a roll of gauze for wrapping and
preserving specimens. I decided to restrict my collecting to the
lizards and other reptiles, as the biological problem with which

we were originally concerned dealt with these creatures. Along with this equipment I placed a wide-mouthed jar for keeping specimens once they were secured. A box of matches, a knife and a small bar of soap completed the pack. In the other grass bag I placed as many tins of corned beef as it would hold. I selected this meat as it seemed about as light and as nutritious as anything I had at hand; for other nourishment I had to depend on the .22/410 gauge game-getter which I demounted from its stock and slung at my side as a large sort of pistol. The .22 shells which were loaded with dust shot would serve for my specimens, the .410's would do for doves and sandpipers and other small game. A single shirt, a clean pair of strong white ducks, socks and a new pair of canvas shoes were all the clothing I needed.

When I closed the doors of my dwelling before dawn the next morning, sending my friend, the spider, scurrying back into his crack in the lintel, the air was light and cool. The trade wind had slackened and was whispering faintly through the grasses; in the east the sun had not yet risen, pale shafts of gray light were just stealing above the horizon; a pair of tiny fly-catchers was bubbling prettily somewhere off in the dark; the stars were still glittering in the heavens although they had paled slightly; the surf purred listlessly on the rocks below. A sense of expectancy permeated the air; it was that magic moment which exists briefly before the creatures of the day have begun their activity and when the dwellers of the night have departed for their hiding places, leaving the world momentarily hushed and still. Caught with the elation of the hour, fresh from a good night's sleep, I lifted the grass baskets, adjusted them on my shoulders and stepped lightly into the path which I had worn through the cacti down to the village.

It was quite deserted. My footsteps echoed emptily between the ruined houses, only the muffled sound of snoring coming from between a few black doorways gave any hint of habitation. The same deep sense of poignancy that overwhelmed me when I first stepped ashore in the town swept over me again. In the gray light Mathewtown appeared more desolate than ever. There seemed little hope that it could survive more than a few years. The island's one industry, the harvesting of sea salt from a saltpond in back of the town, had ceased to exist, the laboriously built pans were becoming filled with silt and mud, the crude wooden windmills that sluiced the sea water into the drying basins were falling to pieces, their timbers decaying from dry rot and neglect. Near the waterfront a huge pile of grayish salt lay waiting for the steamer that would never call. Unless the "salt," as the Inaguans termed the industry, returned the town was finished.

I followed the road to the saltpond and reached it just as the sun came above the horizon. The pond was about two miles long and the shores were piled three or four feet deep with a thick layer of white foam which the wind had whipped off the water during the night. The bubbles held their form tenaciously, layer piling on layer until it seemed as though some playful giant had used the lake as a washbasin and daubed the edges with prodigious quantities of shaving cream. I waded through some of this bubbly froth and it clung to my clothing where it dried in little crystals. Wiping some off with my finger I tasted it. It was saturated with salt.

Turning away from the lake I found a worn path leading to the north toward Man-of-War Bay. This bay cuts a deep groove in the coast before it swings to the east. A magnificent coral reef protects it from the sweep of the rollers and this barrier was the scene of the first event in the history of the island of which there is any accurate record. The chronicle is dated in the year 1800 and is from the report of an English naval officer. It contains only three short paragraphs which state simply in terse official style that "the British Man-of-War, *Lowenstoffe*, and eight Jamaica ships, her convoy, were unfortunately cast away on the reefs and destroyed. . . . The crews perished in attempting to land . . . and were swallowed in the breakers." As an added footnote is the cheerful information that even if the survivors had succeeded in reaching shore they could have expected "but little hospitality as the island was inhabited by one man—a fugitive outlaw accused of evil and wanton murder." Thus, in tragedy and death did the written history of Inagua begin.

The trail was ill-defined and wound between thick clumps of tangled thorn trees and stunted bushes. In a few seconds after leaving the saltpond the soil underfoot changed from shifting sand to a hard floor of smooth gray rock. Scattered helter-skelter over its surface were dozens of slabs of loose flat stone. These varied in thickness and in size from small dinner plates to irregular sheets seven or eight feet in circumference. The rock floor seemed hollow and boomed cavernously even under the soft tread of my canvas shoes. Whenever I stepped on one of the loose slabs it rang with the resonance of a bell, the tone varying through several octaves depending on the width and thickness of the plates. The sound was clear and metallic; the effect was startling. For a half mile around my presence could be detected by the clang of rock on rock. I felt as though I were walking on the keys of some gigantic piano or harpsichord, strangely off tune and prolonged as though an invisible player had his foot on the sustaining pedal. Once, far off in the distance a wild medley of discords came jangling through the thorn bush. The sounds came nearer, increasing in volume, until a small herd of wild donkeys burst through a glade in front of me and went clattering away again. The noise of their going sounded like a carnival of mad bell players. Some of the plates had a light tinkling sound, others

gave off a deep ecclesiastical tone somewhat like the resonance of an organ in the shadowy lofts of a cathedral. By way
of experimentation I tried ranging a series in a row to see if I
could play a tune. With a big stick and by dint of much dashing to and fro, for some of the pieces were too large to haul
conveniently, I managed to bang out the first five notes of
"My Country 'Tis of Thee" but I got stuck on the "sweet land
of liberty" part and could go no further. The slabs needed
tuning badly and the music sounded horribly flat, but it had
possibilities.

The land beneath the surface must be honey-combed with
holes and caverns, for this hollow sound is common to many
parts of the island. Inagua, like many of the Bahamas, can be
compared to a gigantic stone sponge. In places the sea pene-
trates far underground. Ocean holes, clear blue ponds of salt
sea water which rise and fall with the tide, frequently occur
a dozen miles from the coast. They are quite different from
the shallow lakes of dull green or pinkish water which abound
everywhere. I found one of these holes several days later about
four miles from the beach on the north side of the island. It
was roughly sixty feet in diameter and was filled with the same
liquid blue water that washes the reefs. The sides were crusted
with red sponges and deep down below the surface I could
discern a few anemones and the white marks of barnacles. There
was no bottom. Although the water was so clear that the walls
were visible for a hundred feet the hole disappeared into infinity. Somewhere down in the dark a tunnel pierced its way
out to the ocean. I would have given much to have been able
to explore its fastnesses. Did it emerge beyond the reefs along
the edge of some towering submarine cliff or did it lead for
thousands of feet down into the black depths of the ocean?
What fantastic creatures lived in its dark passages; ghostly
white anemones, possibly, forever shut off from the light of

day, giant morays similar to the one that frequented the hole
near my bathing pool. Such a trip would require a brave heart,
and diving equipment of a type as yet undeveloped. It would
be a weird dangerous excursion down into the wet bowels of
an island; a jaunt that might lead anywhere. The age of exploration is by no means completed.

The sun was now high and the trade wind had resumed its
daily vigor. But down in the glades between the trees, the air
was still; the temperature climbed steadily. Presently I was
bathed in perspiration, my shirt hung clammily to my skin.
Soon the heat was unbearable. Even the lizards, which normally
basked in the sun in the more open places, lay prone under the
slabs of stone waiting patiently for whirling insects to come
within convenient reach. The bare rocks were hot to the touch,
so much so that to sit on them was uncomfortable. The heat
began to assume the proportions of a blast furnace. I was beginning to get thirsty. Stopping at a small pool in a hollow of
a rock I tasted it. Like the foam from the lake it was steeped
in sodium chloride. A mile further on I tried another; it was
like the first. I wet my mouth with the canteen, sparingly; there
was a long way to go. Everywhere the ground was saturated
with salt. Even the roots of the trees growing in the hollows
of the rocks were encrusted with the crystals. How they survived was a puzzle. At home a sure method of destroying a
plant and ruining the ground for a long time was to pour salt
around the roots. Yet these trees thrived in it. By way of experiment I broke a thick padded leaf and chewed it. The tissue
was full of moisture, unpleasant to the taste, but the moisture
was not salty. In some way the vegetables of this saline land
filtered out the chemical before it entered their tissues. Even
the earth itself was impregnated although some of the deeper
holes filled with a reddish brown earth derived from the decay
of drifted and dead leaves were quite fresh. In compensation,

the trees which grew in these holes were a shade greener than
their brothers. But even these were dull and ghostly in hue.
For a tropical land Inagua is remarkably drab. In Haiti and
Cuba, but a day's sail away, the vegetation is lush and brilliant;
on Inagua grays, silvery whites and pale greens predominate.
Only the flowers are vivid.

With a sigh of relief, I saw that the trees were commencing
to thin, permitting the wind to steal through. The breeze cooled
my hot body and allayed the feeling of fatigue that was starting to steal over me. The musical rocks became scarce, the
ground began to be covered with a thin layer of light silt
which was slippery and wet. Obviously the soil was only a
fraction of an inch or so above sea level; there was no place
for the water to drain. The crystals of salt became more common; the trees were smaller and more stunted; only one species
resembling the quivering aspens of northern countries still
grew to any height, about twenty feet. Even these were sparse
and straggly. The leaves of these trees were pure silver, touched
only lightly with a suggestion of chlorophyll; they had a burnished look which caused them to glint metallically as they
danced in the wind.

A burst of air hit me in the face as I rounded the last cop-
pet of trees; the landscape had suddenly become empty. As
far as I could see there was not a sign of life nor any evidence
of vegetation other than a sparse layer of yellow grass growing
between puddles of stagnant water. Near the fringe of trees
from which I had just emerged a half dozen tall thatch palms
were making a brave stand against the elements; beyond these
was utter desolation. Mile upon mile a level plain stretched
away into the heat waves. Far in the distance the glint of sun
on a large body of water loomed in a bronze flare above the
horizon. This would be the great inland lake which the natives
had told me covered the entire central portion of the island.

The wind whistled across this plain with a violence that was amazing after the quiet of the hot forest. But it was cool. Bending against its pressure I followed the trail which wound sinuously toward the northeast. At noon I found myself well out in the middle, and seeking a dry spot I sat down to rest and eat a little lunch. The corned beef did not help my thirst so I washed it down with another swig from the canteen. While I rested I examined the soil. It was derived almost entirely from living matter; there was no sand mixed in it. Only an inch or two beneath the surface was a layer of solid rock; thousands upon thousands of fragments of tiny ceritheum shells made up its substance, diminutive spiral mollusks hardly more than a quarter inch in length. This soil had its origin largely in the decayed material of these animals, and in the accumulated residue of millions of their droppings which were derived from countless billions of feedings upon equally diminutive algaes. How many hundreds of years and trillions of lives had been necessary to produce this skim of earth I could not guess. Some of the skim had been lost, no doubt, whirled into the sky as dust on the wings of the trades. Equal amounts had probably been dissolved by the rains to drain back into the sea again. A few other creatures had added their quota to the sum total of this inch of earth, but not many; a few stray feathers and the crushed carapaces of land crabs were the only other evidences except the sparse straws of the struggling grass. The grasses appeared to be newcomers, for they were not numerous and were scattered in distant clumps. Around the grass clumps were some mounds of whitened sand brought up from crevasses in the base rock by great yellow land crabs with unbelievably monstrous claws. But these crabs were hidden in their holes; their existence was only indicated by a number of the shells of their dead bodies scattered over the plain where they were bleaching in the sun.

After an hour or two in the open savannah I was as happy to leave it as I was to find it. The wind allowed no peace and the plain was so utterly desolate as to be depressing. The place gave the same feeling as I imagined one would have if suddenly transported back to the early morning of the fifth day of creation. The earth and firmament were there and the grasses of the third and fourth days were waving in the wind, but in the early hours only the crabs and mollusks had been devised. The remainder of creative existence was yet to come.

The trail turned sharply toward the coast again and as I entered the outposts of vegetation, life began to be apparent once more. A black crowned night heron rose from an amber pool where it had been standing pensively thinking of the minnows it had for supper the night before or of whatever it is herons dream about; the liquid trilling of the little flycatchers rose from between the thorn trees—it was the same sound I had heard at dawn. These flycatchers, called Tom-fools by the natives, are exceedingly curious. Their lives are a continuous burst of song; happiness is their specialty. From branch to branch they followed as I moved along.

Before long I heard a familiar sound through the trees. It was the surf again. The rocky soil disappeared and was replaced by white shifting sand. Defiling from the trees I emerged on the beach. It was Man-of-War Bay where the British squadron was destroyed and where so many men gave up their lives. But there was no hint of violence then; instead the sea was calm and blue; a short distance from shore a sextette of pelicans was gliding and flapping above a school of fish; even the reefs were barely visible. The Bay was gorgeous. For several miles a long row of tall cocoanut palms overhung the beach; it was much more colorful than any portion of the island I had yet seen. Beneath the palms were a long row of white houses. These, like the dwellings in Mathewtown, were in ruins. A few still possessed roofs but the majority had long since crumbled into dust. I passed one after the other. They were of coral, simple creations like my own house. Fully a half thousand people must have dwelt along the shores of the bay. There was even a church; it, also, was vacant though some of the pews and a portion of the pulpit were still in place. It seemed that all man's endeavors on Inagua were foredoomed to failure.

A slight spiral of smoke from between a row of palms attracted my attention. I strode down the beach toward the point where it was curling between the palms, topped the ridge back of the beach and found two diminutive houses still in good state of repair. Beside one of them was an old man. He turned slowly as I approached, then bade me welcome. His hair was white and a long beard fell down on his chest. Pale blue eyes looked at me from between wrinkled brows; I guessed his age at between seventy-five and eighty; although he was bent with the years, he was not feeble. A battered old straw hat covered a matting of thick white hair; ragged shirt and trousers hung loosely on his frame; his feet were bare and thickly calloused.

I spent the afternoon and evening with the old fellow. Over a supper of fish, dried corn and conch meat he told me his story. As a very young man he had come from one of the more northern islands and settled on Inagua. His ancestors were English and they had come to the Bahamas shortly before he was born. With some other venturesome souls he had established himself at Man-of-War Bay and had lived there ever since. He had a number of children but they had left home and had either departed from the island or were living in Mathewtown. From his description I recalled a daughter I had seen about the settlement. She had married a man of mixed blood. Years later I saw her daughter married to a coal black Negro; there was not much choice in Mathewtown. One by one the families about Man-of-War Bay had moved away until only the old man remained. There were only a few years left; he could see no reason to follow. The sea and the forest behind provided all the necessities of life, thatch for the roof, fish and conchs to eat, the clearing grew a little grain, enough for his few needs.

In my turn I explained how I came to Inagua, how our ship was wrecked and why I was heading out into the bush. When I described the *Basilisk* to him he became quite interested. Moving over to an old cupboard he extracted from some papers a faded and creased photograph. I turned it over and looked at the picture on its face. It was a photo of the *Spray!* Captain Slocum had stopped at Inagua on one of his famous voyages and had given a lecture at the tumbled down church. As a memento of his visit he had left this photograph of his ship.

In the morning I refilled the canteen from the rain barrel beneath the eaves, ate a few pieces of conch meat and once again went into the bush. Until I reached the houses near the Lagoon Christophe there would be no more water unless I could find the waterholes which the old man described to me. This was unlikely since he had not visited them for over twenty years.

By evening I had walked about twenty miles zigzagging back and forth between the coast and the barren plains near the inland lake. As I went I shot a series of the lizards and injected them with the syringe and formol, packing them in the jar with little strips of paper beneath their gauze wrapping describing the localities where they were captured. When I reached the beach again late in the afternoon as the shadows were lengthening, I was very weary; my shirt and ducks were smeared with dirt, and I was sticky with perspiration. Thorns had scratched and torn at my arms and legs. I had tried to be as sparing of water as possible but the canteen was half empty. Another day like this and it would be gone. The heat had been intolerable. I sat down on the sand and opened a tin of beef.

It disappeared rapidly and I was hungry enough to devour another but refrained as there were not too many left. In a day or two they, too, would be gone and I would have to depend on the gun. After a short rest I stripped and swam for a few minutes in the surf, then came to shore and donned my clothes again. By this time the sun had set and the moon was coming up.

I slept on the bare ground that night and dreamed that a vast army of crabs was coming out of the sea to surround me. In my slumber I could hear their armored bodies clicking over the rocks, their large yellow claws were raised menacingly and they crept closer and closer. Soon I could see the facets of their eyes raised grotesquely on bulbous stalks. Their bodies were yellow in color and they waded in deep furrows of sea shells, long spiral turrets shaped like those of ceritheums. They were ceritheums, and strangely they began to multiply, piling deeply, hundreds, thousands of them, appearing out of nowhere. Even the crabs had trouble combating them but they pushed them aside with their yellow claws and steadily moved closer. Suddenly the great pile of ceritheums vanished, dissolving liquidly into a brown slime. The slime ran between the legs of the crabs and then solidified into a crust exactly an inch thick. Then just as the crabs were about to reach me the ground became warm and the air thick and heavy.

I awoke, damp with perspiration. My head was buried in the crotch of my arm and a pile of loose sand had worked under my shirt. The moon was out, nearly full, and in its blue glare I could see the shapes of a dozen hermit crabs crawling through the grasses. It was their clacking that I heard in my sleep. For the rest of the night I slept fitfully, alternately dozing and then waking. The sun beaming in my face aroused me in the morning. I felt stiff and dirty and went down to the surf again to wash. The cool clean water made me feel better and I shouldered the grass baskets and set out once more up the coast.

About noon I reached the lagoon opposite Sheep Cay. The cay lay about one half mile from shore and was separated by a channel of shallow water about the color of emeralds. In the hope that the islet might contain some types of lizards unlike those on the mainland I decided to try and reach it by swimming the portion that I could not wade. Most of the way the water appeared to reach about to my armpits, the portion over my head was not more than an eighth of a mile wide. The tide was low; in about an hour the channel would be impassable. Quickly I stripped and deposited my shirt and ducks on the rocks to air and sun. I then loaded the chamber of the gun with dust shot and with the thong of the grass basket tied it to my hat to keep it out of the water. In the band I placed some extra shot.

The first quarter mile was easy; the bottom was composed of fine hard sand and the water was so clear as to make it easily visible. As I came closer I could see a long row of cocoanut palms along one shore of the cay, the central portion appeared to be covered with a large clump of vegetation covering a low hill. The channel was wider than I expected. I eased into it, striving with my toes to touch bottom. It was too deep. A strong current was sweeping through, bearing to the west and toward the coral reef on the outer edge of the cay. Holding my head high I breast-stroked toward the palms. In the center of the channel the bottom shoaled again and by stretching my toes I could just keep my head out of the water.

This gave me a chance to rest and like a submerged toe-dancer I edged forward, fighting against the current to prevent being swept toward the reef. I had just reached the outer rim of the shoal and was preparing to swim again when a sudden commotion to the left attracted my attention. There was a loud splash and a large black tail fin rose above the water and came down with a smack. The spray flew skywards and a moment later a dark dorsal fin cut the water. It was a large shark. A cold wave of apprehension swept over me. The beast apparently had not yet seen me and was playing in the shallows where it possibly was feeding on small fish or mollusks. Quickly I looked about and gauged my distances. The cay was closest, the channel terminated about fifty yards beyond the bar on which I was standing, from its edge the water shoaled within a few yards to about a foot in depth. If I could make this I would be safe.

As quietly as possible I slipped into the channel again and shoved hard for the shallows. I did not dare use the crawl for fear the noise would attract the creature's attention. Out of one eye I watched the fin rising and disappearing above the ripples. Then my blood ran cold; it turned and came straight for me. The hair at the base of my scalp began to creep, and for a moment I almost gave way to panic. About fifty feet away it veered again, swept back of me around the shoal in the center of the channel. Then it began to approach from the right. I trod water waiting for the attack. But it did not come. Instead the shark began circling, slowly and leisurely, describing a circle about thirty feet in diameter. Once it swept toward me and I tore the gun from my hat and thrust it under the water in its path. I knew it would be of no use but I thought the explosion might scare the fish away. As nearly as I could estimate, the shark was about nine feet long. When the beast circled back of me I turned to keep it in view. Fortunately it stayed near the surface and I could make out its every movement. The current was momentarily becoming stronger and the edge of the channel was slowly slipping backwards as I was swept toward the reef. In another two hundred yards the shallows would be out of reach. Throwing caution to the winds, but still not daring to make too much of a commotion lest the beast think I was frightened, I slipped into a side stroke and strove hard. The circle grew narrower; soon I could see flashes of a white belly as the shark turned and rolled. I was thoroughly frightened and I was growing a little tired. The twenty-mile hike of the day before was beginning to tell on me. The beast stopped and idled. Thinking it was going to make an attack, I grasped the gun from my teeth where I had been holding it and sank beneath the surface. The salt water stung my eyes but I could see clearly. Only ten or fifteen feet away the shark was gliding again through the water, circling. Then it turned sharply and slid by to my left and disappeared behind my back. With a sudden surge I lunged to the surface and frenziedly swam with every bit of remaining strength to the edge of the channel. As soon as I hit the sand I struggled up the slope and dashed for the shore, tripping several times amid great fountains of spray. When I reached the beach I dropped panting on the sand, shaking in every muscle. It was one of the most terrifying experiences I have ever had.

Until that time I had had no personal experiences with sharks. Later, in the light of calm reflection and with the accumulated knowledge of several years of working with diving equipment, I am convinced that my fright was somewhat unreasonable. In fact, from recollections of the anatomical features of the individual that swam around me that day at Sheep Cay, I am now certain that it was one of the nurse sharks, a perfectly harmless group that assails nothing more vigorous than the mollusks and crustaceans on which its members feed. The attentions of this particular one were probably due to plain inquisitiveness. Certainly if it had desired to attack me it would have done so for I was completely at its mercy.

As might be expected, the lizards of Sheep Cay did not differ sufficiently to cause them to be classified apart from those on the mainland. There was only one type, a member of the genus Anolis, beautifully tinted reptiles varying in hue from pale gray suffused with a suggestion of lavender to a rich chocolate brown. These were capable of rapid color change and within a few minutes could assume a complete alteration of tone, blushing yellow, pinkish or green-gray as their mood dictated. I collected quite a series, shooting them with the dust shot after shaking the water out of the gun and laying it in the sun to dry. By some strange accident my hat remained with me and provided me with sufficient shells. But I was hardly an example of what the well-dressed herpetologist should wear roaming about the island stark naked except for a wet hat which flopped loosely about my ears.

Sheep Cay was truly a remarkable place. It was occupied by two species of trees, a few small bushes, three genera of crabs, a large variety of mollusks, one kind of lizard and one mammal—myself. This was the island's total population with the exception of a little green heron which screeched in alarm and fled when I arrived and a host of stinging mosquitoes and sand fleas. The trees were the most obvious living organisms, thirteen in all. Twelve of the thirteen were cocoanut palms and they were distributed along the shores of a little cove which penetrated the island near the middle. The other tree spread over all the remainder of Sheep Cay and was the most magnificent individual of its species I have ever seen. There is a possibility that it was composed originally of more than one plant but these had so coalesced as to be indistinguishable. This tree possessed no less than several hundred separate yet united trunks and perhaps three or four thousand upraised roots which supported these trunks on a raised platform well above the level of the salt water. The roots were intermingled and entwined in an indescribable maze; the branches twisted and wove their way upwards, fusing in countless places, locking arms, bracing one joint against another, until an impenetrable fretwork of timber supported a canopy of dark green leaves.

Only the strongest light rays filtered through this screen; the upper reaches of this gigantic vegtable mesh-work gave the appearance of a great gloomy cavern. The green cavern was filled with a low humming as of the whirring of countless insects; as indeed I discovered it was when a horde of mosquitoes settled on my bare flesh and busily sank their probes. Scrambling outside I brushed off the pests and walked around this monstrous tree. It covered at least half an acre. In Kingston, Jamaica, there is a renowned banyan tree that is large enough to fill a small plaza; this great mangrove, for such it was, would have swallowed the banyan and left room for another.

This tree was the center and the axis of existence for all the creatures of the islet. The Anolis lizards, being arboreal, were restricted to its branches; the barrier of leaves protected them from the sweeping force of the trade winds and provided the quiet atmosphere essential for the maintenance of the mosquitoes and other small insects on which they stuffed themselves until their bellies were distended like small balloons. Even the crabs, a land species of yellow and purple, depended on the mud and debris about the bases of the roots to furnish them with the microscopic bits which they gleaned between the dead leaves; outside in the hot sun these crabs were not to be found. Life on the island existed because of the tree; or more exactly the tree was the foundation of the island itself. But for this arboreal giant Sheep Cay would be nothing more than a bar of white gleaming sand, forever shifting, drifting at the mercy of the wind and currents. Only under the branches was there any hint of solidity: here the calcareous sand, held tightly by the binding roots, had settled and metamorphosed into gray carbonate of lime.

Sheep Cay had, no doubt, first appeared above the rushing surf when a portion of the fringing reef became too interlaced to permit the free passage of water and had bogged down with sand. As time progressed this sand had crept upwards, filling up the coral branches until it reached the surface. At the surface the waves and currents tore at the shifting grains, tossing them about, piling them up and tearing them apart, forming and re-forming the bar with every change of tide. I walked up to the outer edge of the cay and found just this sort of action going on. The magnificent curve of foaming coral reef swept up to the extreme tip of the island where it terminated in a great pile of white sand. The rollers coming in from the sea swirled over this area, churning it into a milky silt which surged back and forth with each ebb and flow of the waves.

Returning to the little cove and dropping on the sand preparatory to getting ready for the swim back to the mainland again I saw the second phase in the drama of the building of an island enacted before my eyes. The tide had reached its lowest ebb and was beginning to flow again. Inch by inch the water crept up the slope of the sand, sending tiny ripples lapping gently on the beach. Rolling in these ripples was a long spear-like shaft of reddish wood about a foot in length. The lower end of it was shaped like a javelin, tapering to a smooth point; the upper was peculiarly sheathed with a circle of shriveled and torn fibers. The javelin was the radicel of a mangrove seedling, and it had drifted from somewhere on the mainland.

Mangrove trees live in an area of ever-changing surface, marshes of soft mud, in the treacherous space of the tide lines washed by strong currents and still stronger waves. Their seeds if distributed like those of other trees would soon be washed away, drowned by salt water or smothered in piled up silt. To compensate for this insecurity nature has provided a method of propagation ensuring a firm anchorage in whatever shifting element the tree is to grow. Instead of casting the mature seed to fall and be washed away or buried, the mother tree retains the product of its blossoms until it has produced a long stiff radicel or spear-like root which hangs downwards from the branch. This is held intact until one of two events occurs. Either the spear will reach the ground and attach itself by rootlets and begin its growth as a separate tree, breaking loose from the parent; or it will suddenly part its top fibers and plunge straight downwards like a javelin and bury itself in the soft ground. By its own weight it fixes itself upright until the roots can take hold and consolidate their position.

Something had gone awry with this seed-root. It had fallen on its side, deflected by a branch and floated away on the receding tide; or it had struck some hard object beneath the mud, a shell or buried log, and failed to secure a purchase. The tide and the trade wind had brought it to Sheep Cay. Whether it would survive after having arrived was a moot question. But not twenty feet away was another radicel half buried in the sand. From the top of this was emerging a pair of green tissues, dark and lanceolate, the first leaves. Beneath the soil long fibrous roots had anchored themselves firmly entwining the wreck of a long buried conch.

In just such a way did the great tree in the center of the island secure a hold. Its early existence must have been a terrific struggle, a battle with salt spray, sticky foam, with the shifting of sand grains and the swirling waves. But it had triumphed. The first rootlet had become two, then four, then sixteen, a hundred and a hundred thousand. The newly sprouted leaves drank in the brilliant sunlight and by the magic of their green chlorophyll transmuted its energy to tissue of trunk, and tendril and blossom. Branches dropped additional rootlets, these pierced the sand and raised new shoots, from these came other branches, other leaves, more blossoms, seeds and the pointed fingers of seed radicles. These in their turn had dropped off and sprouted, fusing with the parent, until for yards around the shifting sand bar had become stabilized and assumed the status of a permanent island.

The cocoanut palms had arrived the same way, drifting on the beach as ripe and fertilized nuts. They had come long after the mangrove and by some trick of the beach had lined themselves in a straight row just out of reach of the tide. In the debris and jetsam of the tide lines were the decayed shells of a number of other cocoanuts which just drifted in; these nuts could not have belonged to the trees already on the island, for the bar had enlarged since the trees had reached maturity and the first comers were a number of yards inland.

The cocoanut shells gave an indication of how the lizards came to Sheep Cay. They could not have arrived on a mangrove radicel; they would have been quickly chilled and drowned. On a cocoanut shell, however, a lizard would have had an excellent chance of survival; the casings are buoyant and ride high out of the water. If the weather were calm and the tides set right an agile lizard or even two would have had no difficulty in navigating the half mile from the mainland. There is even another possibility. An entire bush may have been torn from its fastenings and been blown out to sea by a storm with a whole family of arboreal Anolis ensconced in its branches. This seemed more logical as none of the ground-living species which abounded on the mainland had as yet made their appearance on Sheep Cay.

So far, the flying insects, the Anolis lizards, the few bushes and the two species of trees were the only dry-land organisms which had survived. The crabs and mollusks could hardly be included, for although they were terrestrial in their habits they were, strictly speaking, marine, being forced to return to the ocean sooner or later to breed or wet their gills. How many years had been needed to reach this stage of population I could not guess. Sheep Cay, very likely, was not more than a century or two old. The oldest map which I can find is dated 1860 and shows the island as an unnamed point. Presuming that it is a hundred years old this would give a rough average of approximately only one new permanent resident each quarter of a century. This is probably a very high figure, yet, on this basis each millennium would see only forty additions divided equally between the animals and plants.

Therefore, I felt exceedingly fortunate in being present at the introduction of two new inhabitants, one of which was animal, the other vegetable, a full half-century's quota! As a matter of fact I was directly responsible, for when I reached in my water-soaked hatband for another dust shot with which to secure a supplement to my series of Anolis I was surprised to see emerge from the wet cloth the gaudy body of a spider. It was a very small spider and it appeared to be damp and be-draggled though it moved quickly on its eight legs. Attached to its body was a spherical sac which contained several dozens of diminutive eggs. Carefully I carried the mite up to the shelter of a fallen palm leaf and deposited it on the dried fibers. It sat quiescent for a few seconds and then retired into a crevice lugging the sac with it. There I am confident a new race of spiders was begun.

The sixth resident I was not so sure about. Neither was I certain of its identity. In the hope of finding another spider as mate for the first I turned the hatband inside out and examined it carefully. There were no more arthropods but nestled in a fold of the felt was a very small peculiarly shaped seed. It was formed somewhat like the head of a lance except that the butt end was twisted and curved in the fashion of a lyre. Microscopic engravings were etched over its surface and it was cleft lengthwise with a deep fissure. Several weeks later I ran a net through a number of the grasses thinking I might find a duplicate but nothing I secured even remotely resembled it. Possibly the seed had fallen into my hatband while I slept;

again it might have come all the way from North America, for the hat was an old one. In the shelter of one of the palms I scraped together a little soil, planted the seed and ringed it about with a circle of conchs to mark the spot. It was a bare hope, for even if it sprouted, unless the plant were one of those remarkable creations which fertilized itself or reproduced freely, it was foredoomed to failure. Nearly ten years later when I returned to Sheep Cay for another purpose I remembered and looked for it in vain. The circle of conchs had vanished and even the cocoanut had died and fallen to the ground where it was rapidly becoming a portion of the beach.

While I was musing over the plant I thought the island was to add still another resident to its tiny quota, for the flickering yellow body of a Catopsila butterfly floated by on the wings of the wind. But the insect made no attempt to reach the cay and drifted over the foam of the reef and was blown further out to sea. It reminded me of the mystery of a late September afternoon in 1927 when I saw a great horde of Tieris butterflies, tiny creatures with wings of yellow and orange edged with black, gather together on the hot sands of the beach midway between Lewes and Rehobeth in Delaware and then suddenly rise on a gentle west wind and drift out in a great streaming ragged line into the darkening wastes of the Atlantic Ocean. They went to a certain death. One by one their fragile bodies fell to the waters to flap dismally for a few moments, to float quietly on the waves for a while and then, waterlogged, to slip down into the cold green depths. Thousands of them. A few have been known to reach Bermuda where they have been reported on rare occasions only to disappear as mysteriously as they came. The Catopsila butterflies, which belong to the same great family, have been seen doing the same thing along the coasts of northern South America, setting out in great swarms into the Caribbean from which there is no re-

turn. It is the same form of madness which at times mysteriously seizes the migrating lemmings of Norway and causes
them to plunge in hordes over the fjord walls into the sea where
they drown in the hundreds, an insanity which seems to be
due to an epidemic disease resulting from overcrowding. Perhaps the same urge which causes the land-living butterflies to
gather suddenly and permit themselves to be swirled to a death
on the ocean and which causes the lemmings to depart on their
seemingly hopeless migrations has the same biological root as
the unexplainable urge or "will-to-follow" which afflicts as
a kind of disease normally peaceful and sedentary humans,
catches up their emotions and coalesces them into war-mad
nations intent on self destruction. The sudden burst of energy
that centered about the person of Genghis Khan and swept
like a whirlwind over the steppes of Asia, and the similar
unaccountable flare of power which hurled the force of the
Crusades out of a Medieval Europe on an unsuspecting Jeru-
salem, the great swirl of human emotion which brought down
on Rome the restless hordes of barbarians from northern Europe, or the more modern will-to-power of a Führer-following
Germany have a deeper significance than the leadership of one
man, or group of men, however magnetic they may be. The
leader is but the spark that sets the energy in motion. Men or
mice or butterflies are all subject to their madnesses; these differ
only in effect and potentialities.

The making of an island is a long and tedious process. I can
plow up my back yard, turn under all vegetation, burn off the
residue, plow it again until the soil is seemingly barren of all
life, a patch of yellow brown dirt. Unless I persist, however,
this patch in the short space of two or three weeks will become
a carpet of green weeds, plantains, daisies, morning-glories, Jim-
son weed, phlox, violets, grass, moss, curling vines, small sap-
lings, stems of blackberry and bramble. The small six acres of

my Maryland farm, woodland and cleared space, dry soil and wet, probably contains more different species of animals and plants than all of Inagua Island, though, of course, not the numbers of each. An oceanic island achieves its fauna and flora by long methods of trial and error; a dozen creatures arriving by wind or wave or on the bodies of animals or birds perish to every one that survives. A single storm on an islet as small as Sheep Cay can destroy in one night the accumulated contributions of a hundred years of favorable circumstance.

I patted the soil about the newly planted seed, adjusted the conchs once more, gathered up the gun and my limp hat, and then with my heart thumping with apprehension waded out to the edge of the shoals and slipped quietly into the water.

CHAPTER VIII

The Wind

IT was well that I did not tarry much longer, for the current was swinging through the channel at a quickened pace and was pouring swiftly toward the open reef. Only by swimming with my utmost strength did I succeed in reaching the last bar a few feet from the place where it terminated. Beyond this bar the lagoon opened up into a wide expanse of water where it deepened considerably; if I had not made this point as soon as I did I would have had a long struggle before reaching shore again. As it was I arrived nearly exhausted. Constantly glancing over my shoulder I kept a watch for the shark but the beast did not put in an appearance. I was much relieved when I waded wearily ashore and slumped on the sand near my clothes to rest.

While I relaxed I got out the vial of formol and the syringe and injected the group of Anolis and placed their corpses in the jar for safe keeping. I was thus engaged when a series of strange croaking calls attracted my attention. Looking up I saw a long wedge-shaped formation of roseate spoonbills flying between the mainland and the cay. Like geese they were in military formation, each bird flapping a little to one side and close behind the individual preceding so as to take advantage of the aerial waves pushed aside by the advancing flock. Their wing beats were slow and graceful and occasionally the leader set his wings and glided, each spoonbill in succession doing likewise in perfectly timed sequence until the entire flock skimmed motionless just above the water's surface. Then the birds would resume their flappings, starting at the front end and taking up the motion one after the other for the length of the line. The precision of this movement reminded me of the evolutions of chorus girls.

No chorus girls, however, were ever arrayed like these spoonbills. With the possible exception of the flamingo I have never beheld a more gorgeous sight. Spoonbills are dressed in a plumage of lovely pink, of a hue that is quite unnameable. To say simply that they are pink is like stating that the sky is blue. Spoonbill pink is a color that contains something of the iridescence of pearls, a little of the crimson of the sunset, the brilliance of flame and much that is completely evanescent. This pink is a living tone which flares and dims with the light, becomes in turn delicate and pale, or dark and carmine. A twist of wing, flash of sunlight, shade of cloud and the dress of spoonbills reflect vivid scarlet, old rose, deep salmon or the color of Mediterranean coral. Contrast this raiment against a seascape of deep indigo, the lucid green of a coral lagoon, the heavy olive of mangrove trees, a sky of cerulean blue and the golden yellow of a sun-drenched tropical beach and you have a faint approximation of spoonbills in their natural haunts.

The hour is rapidly approaching, unless something is done for their protection, when the last roseate spoonbill in this quarter of the globe will build its last nest and lay the last spoonbill egg. Great flocks of these birds once occurred in the southern regions of Florida, along the Gulf of Mexico and in the West Indies. The Florida colonies are all but decimated, and in the West Indies the only remaining breeding flocks are those in Cuba and Hispaniola where they are on the verge of extinction, and on Great Inagua Island. When these are gone there will have perished forever one of the loveliest and most peculiar of our native birds.

A spoonbill appears to be a cross between a stork and a duck. Actually it is neither of these but is most closely related to the

ibises with which some students of ornithology consider it to
be classed although at present it stands aloof in a family all its
own. Its unusual bill sets it apart from all other birds and gives
it a truly amazing appearance. This organ is not pink like the
remainder of the animal but is dull greenish-blue, shading to
gray at the base. The lower end is flat and spoon-shaped and
looks like the business end of a spatula. The creature's head
and nose are bare and the effect when seen head on is that of
a bald-headed Cyrano de Bergerac with a monstrous nose.

Hastily gathering my pack and donning my clothes I hurried up the coast after the flock. The flying wedge followed
the shoreline for a half mile and then turned inland between
some large clusters of mangroves. When I reached the spot
the birds had disappeared and I saw that they had entered the
mouth of a large creek which penetrated the country for some
distance. The waterway was lined with hundreds of mangroves
which crowded together in an impenetrable barrier, denying
access to the shore. Somewhere in this mangrove swamp there
should be a nesting colony of spoonbills. It was then the fif-
teenth of February and from what I remembered about their
breeding dates the season was about due.

To go chasing spoonbills was not an altogether reasonable
thing. There was still more than three quarters of the island to
circuit, my water was half used up and in a few days I would
have to start living off the country. While spoonbills were an
interesting feature of the landscape, they were nevertheless a
definite digression from the problem at hand. But the possibility of seeing these rare and rapidly vanishing birds on their
breeding grounds was too good an opportunity to miss.

The waters of the creek appeared to be shallow, not much
over knee depth, and I estimated that I could follow its course
back into the interior, gaining solid ground beyond the mangroves and then cutting diagonally back to the coast again. On

the way I could collect a series of lizards and examine the topography. By this casuistry I salved my conscience although I knew that I could accomplish that result in one quarter the time by crossing the creek at its mouth and passing the barrier of mangroves. But then the spoonbills would have been lost to me.

In a small boat the exploration of this lonely creek would have been but a matter of a few hours, nor would there have been any difficulty if there had been a shore to walk along. Instead the tangled roots of the mangroves thrust out everywhere, forcing me to keep well out in the center. At first the bottom was smooth white sand, hard and firm under foot; presently this became soft and fine, oozy and then mucky. I should have turned back then, and would have done so, giving up the quest as hopeless, but just as I was about to retrace my steps I caught sight of the spoonbills again. They were wading in the shallows, feeding with queer graceful lateral motions of their bills. These were thrust into the water and passed rapidly back and forth as the birds scooped up the small shells, tiny minnows and small fry on which they feed. Leisurely they took to the wing again and flew up the river.

Late afternoon found me well up into the labyrinths of the swamp. Seven or eight times I had been on the point of turning back but always the hope of finding the nests urged me on. The spoonbills kept tantalizingly out of reach. The mangroves were literally alive with waterbirds. Great droves of migrant plover and sandpipers trooped in regiments about the mud flats. Several flocks of pelicans alternately glided and flapped above the green water or dived with great splashes after fish. Little green herons were legion; they swarmed everywhere, under the mangroves, between the shallows; the air was filled with their guttural clacking; dozens burst into the air with frightened squawks, flying a few yards and then settling again to flush once more. The great lank forms of Louisiana and great Blue Herons were poised motionless on single legs waiting for luckless minnows to pass, then rose and flapped heavily away, looking like ancient pterodactyls against the sky; several pairs of Black-necked Stilts raised a terrific hubbub when I startled them away from their feeding grounds; their notes reminded me of the yapping of ill-tempered dogs. There were dozens of herons' nests, all deserted, and in the shallows in carefully hidden places, the half floating platforms of the Dominican Grebes. These too were empty and were in the process of decay though their owners were swimming and diving all over the creek. These grebes are the smallest of their race, resembling small ducks except that their bills are compressed vertically, and their legs are placed so far back that they can progress on the ground only at a slow drunken shuffle. They seldom fly, but in the water are marvels of seaworthiness; as submarines they reach their peak of efficiency, underwater they can swim for long distances, forcing themselves rapidly along with the broad lobes of their aquatic feet. The life of a Dominican Grebe is spent wholly in the water, either above or below it.

I was a long way from the coast when the last rays of the sun caught up with me. The spoonbills had disappeared, losing themselves in the tangled growth of the mangroves. The white, chalky mud was exceedingly thick, it clung to my canvas shoes and my trousers and dragged at my feet. Suddenly I began to realize how tired I was. The two grass bags felt as though they were loaded with granite, the thongs cut my shoulders, the sun had burned my neck and face until they smarted at the touch, my eyes were heavy from the glare of the sun, the salt water had cracked the skin of my legs and wrinkled the flesh. I looked for a place to sit down. There was none. The mangroves hedged in any solid ground. Even the mud bars offered no resting place.

To break through the trees was impossible, their tangled roots formed an impassable barrier through which only the slim bodies of herons and sandpipers could have slipped. The sun dipped lower and lower, dropped behind the somber trees, tinting the clouds with pink and crimson. The gloom deepened; a star appeared, glinting palely at first; the sky altered swiftly from blue to blue gray, then became dark. A low singing sound came to my ears, the hum of mosquitoes. In vast multitudes they poured out of the shadowy mangroves and settled on my face and arms. Frantically I tried to brush them off. Dozens were crushed; my arms became smeared with broken wings and blood—my own blood extracted by the mosquitoes. The crushed insects were immediately replaced with newcomers; they flew into my eyes; my ears were full of their beating wings; my lips, already sore from the sun, swelled to negroid proportions; even my nostrils became clogged with mosquito bodies. I could feel the flesh of my exposed forehead become turgid with bumps; I tore out a handkerchief and draped it below my eyes, bandit fashion, but the pests flew up underneath and were worse than before. My shirt was no protection, the mosquitoes pierced the thin cloth as though it did not exist. In desperation I tried wetting it, thinking this might discourage the insects, but it made no difference, the fabric only clung stickily. I even tried caking my face and neck with mud but the slime would not cling; it ran down my shirt and across my body in little rivulets. I cursed the spoonbills, cursed my own stupidity, cursed the predicament in which I found myself.

In a sense I was not altogether to blame, even though I had gone into the swamp against my better judgment, for since the evening when Ophelia had baked our bread in the sand at the Lagoon Christophe there had not been a sign of a mosquito. Somehow in spite of the salt water, the mangrove swamp

provided breeding places for them and after dark they came
to life in the countless thousands. I have spent evenings in the
Jersey swamps and in the cypress marshes of southern Georgia
where the numbers of these insects have produced a sound like
that of a dozen droning airplanes, but never had I encountered
anything like the myriads that came upon me that night in the
spoonbill swamp.

I had to do something and do it quickly. The pain of the
accumulated bites was beginning to drive me frantic; the humming was worse; my ear drums vibrated noisily to the high-
pitched din. There is no sound more nerve-destroying than the
hum of mosquitoes. I came nearer to panic than I have ever in
all my life. Only by grim determination did I fail to give way
to temptation and throw away the heavy pack and run as fast
as my legs could carry me to the coast. There was nothing to
do but retrace my steps and do it carefully lest in the dark I
take a wrong passage and walk up a blind waterway. Doggedly
I plunged through the mud, trying not to slap the mosquitoes.
Fighting them only served to set them buzzing more wildly
than ever and excited my already overwrought nerves. Minute
after minute I slugged through the tepid water, falling into
holes and tripping on buried sticks, rising and falling again and
again. By concentration I tried to obliviate the sensation of pain
and soreness that was stealing through every fiber. Vaguely I
recalled reading of the Hindu ascetics who rendered themselves insensible to suffering by focusing their attention on
beautiful thoughts or abstruse philosophical themes. Resolutely
I set my mind on a familiar poem, repeating it aloud as I struggled through the dark. It was the strangely mournful and stately
"Thanatopsis."

*To him who in the love of Nature hold communion with her
visible forms,* my voice echoed wearily through the mangrove
trees, *she speaks a various language; for his gayer hours she has a*

voice of gladness—how utterly silly the usually beautiful words sounded then, Bryant could have known nothing of mosquitoes —*and a smile and eloquence of beauty*—cursed spoonbills, I thought,—*and she glides into his darker musings with a mild and healing sympathy that steals away their sharpness ere he is aware.* I fell into the water with a loud splash. Rising again, and brushing the mosquitoes from my eyes, I continued, *When thoughts of the last bitter hour came like a blight over thy spirit, and sad images of the stern agony, and shroud, and pall,* —my eyes were beginning to swell shut—*and, and—breathless darkness—make thee to shudder, and grow sick at heart,*—what a poem to have picked—*Go forth, under the open sky, and list to Nature's teachings, while from all around—Earth and her waters, and the depths of air—comes a still voice.* The word trailed off in a whisper, for a dozen mosquitoes had settled on my lips and were probing all at once.

Yet in a few days and thee—and thee—the all beholding sun shall see no more in all his course; nor yet in the cold ground, —I was not cold but hot; perspiration ran out of every pore— *cold ground, where thy pale form was laid, with many tears, nor in the embrace of ocean, shall exist thy image—*

A soft light stealing across the water distracted me momentarily; it was the moon creeping blood red above the trees; through the stinging hordes before my swelled eyes I could just see the coppery hue lighting the edges of the leaves. Grimly I began again. *Earth that nourished thee shall claim thy growth, to be resolved to earth again, and, lost each human trace,*— No one would ever find me if I became lost and collapsed in the swamp.—*Surrendering up thine individual being, shalt thou go to mix,*—the wild clatter of a heron echoed across the water— *forever with the elements, to be a brother to the insensible rock and to the sluggish clod*— The words slipped from my mind and for a few moments I gave way to a frantic clawing at the halo of mosquitoes about my hair. My face seemed puffed to twice its normal size, the skin of my lips was stretched and hard, the poison of hundreds of bites was seeping into the tissues of my arms, making them stiff—once more I gained control and began repeating the words again,—*the sluggish clod which the rude swain turns with his share and treads upon. The oak shall send his roots abroad and pierce thy mould. Yet not to thine eternal resting place*—I would have given anything for a place to sleep—*shalt thou retire alone, nor couldst thou wish couch more magnificent.*

I was only deceiving myself, the pain and annoyance was maddening; "Thanatopsis" helped only for brief seconds at a time. I was finding difficulty in remembering the words although I knew the poem by heart. Blindly I sloshed on, trying to repeat the familiar cadences. *The gay will laugh when thou art gone, the solemn brood of care plod on, and each one as before will chase—will chase his favorite—favorite phantom; yet all these shall leave their mirth—and——and—their employ-ments——and shall come, and make their bed——with thee.* Numbly I resisted crying out at the mosquitoes.

The events of the remainder of that evening stay with me as a miserable dream. Utterly weary, too tired to go much further, half frantic with insect bites, I eventually emerged about two in the morning and limped down to the beach. Here the trade winds brought relief and drove away the swarming myriads. I dimly remember slumping down on the sand in the shelter of a mound of rock and slipping off into unconsciousness. I may have been still muttering the lines of "Thanatopsis"; I do not recall.

In the morning I roused myself sufficiently to strip and wash in the surf, laying my muddy clothes in the sun to dry. My face was still badly swollen and puffed and big lumps stood out all over my body. I was burning up with fever; I thought it was malaria but it was only the resistance heat of millions of corpuscles combating the acids of the mosquitoes' bites. Extreme lethargy pervaded my being and for hours I lay still and drowsed, stirring only to put on my dry clothes again and to eat a tin of corned beef. The fever made me consume large quantities of water; by late afternoon there was less than a pint. Before the sun set I gathered up my two bags and walked a short distance up the coast to a place where a bench of solid rock came down to the water's edge and where I was sure there would be no mosquitoes if the wind failed.

I slept most of the night on the hard rock and wakened several hours before dawn to find that I no longer burned within and that the swelling had all but disappeared. I also felt refreshed and physically able once more; my muscles were a little sore from the unaccustomed rock but with action this stiffness would pass. Best of all I felt more mentally alert than at any time since the wreck; the slim diet of the past several days and the distress of the night in the swamp together with the utter weariness of two long days' marches in the heat had apparently induced a compensating sharpness of nerve reaction. I am firmly convinced from this experience and from two somewhat similar episodes that the ancient religious customs of fasting and self-induced privation have a sound physical basis for their origin. The brain, normally moving in a smooth course, becomes stultified and requires a deeply disconcerting physical hardship to burgeon it into full activity. Many of the truly brilliant decisions of the old prophets came after periods of physical discomfort and days of fasting; lest we consider this gross medieval fantasy it should be remembered that even a certain man of Nazareth subscribed to this theory and spent forty mysterious days in the wilderness.

No brilliant decisions, of course, came my way as I lay that early morning under the stars but I did find myself more than usually sensitive to and keenly aware of the forces encompassing me on all sides. The moon was still high in the heavens and was flooding the world with cold blue light. The Pleiades flared in a scattered mass low on the horizon; the planet Jupiter stared unwinkingly out of the dark background of infinite space; in the north the pole star glittered faintly, half hidden in the sea haze; around it revolved the tremendous galaxy of a million solar systems. The great somber ocean stretched darkly away into the night, suggested rather than revealed by the soft loom of the moonlight on its surface; it gave the sensation of a great sleeping monster whose rhythmic breathing was audible as low deep thunder. The waves rumbling against the island's barrier were not visible but they filled the air with guttural sobbing, a subdued moaning that began heavily and then faded into an audible sigh. The earth seemed divided between two great and tremendous powers, one which was firm and stable, the other surging and fluid. Swelling behind these forces was the sound of another, and seemingly all-pervading, energy.

This third force seemed to come out of the emptiness of outer space; the wail of its pressure dominated the whole of existence. It did not rise and fall in rhythmical sequence like the surf but maintained a constant tenor, a deep organ-like lamentation that swept on and on in constant reiteration, never ceasing. The sound was the howl of the trade winds as they poured over the earth in a continuous stream. I had never noticed it quite like that before. The entire firmament seemed alive and on the move; the slight pocket of still air behind the mound of boulders where I lay accentuated, by contrast, the sense of power flowing by on all sides. The earth was being washed by a vast river of rushing gas—intangible, invisible but nonetheless potent.

By listening intently I could separate the hundred components that combined to make up the majestic sound. There were weird soft whistles, countless hundreds of them, so low as to be barely audible, ranging in scale as the pressure fluctuated slightly, the rending of air as it was torn in fragments over needle-sharp spires of hard stone, over the sponge-like encrustations of weather-decayed coral; close upon these low flute notes was a faint pattering that at first was indefinable. It was composed of billions of mote-proportioned explosions, Lilliputian particles of sound that broke in swelling crescendos of rhythm through the medley of other tones. I lay listening a long time before I was able to place them; then suddenly recollection came to me; I heard this once before in a golden wheat field just before the August harvest; the sound was the tapping of millions of grass plants in the wind, the tiny clatter of blade against blade, of stem against stem, bending and straightening, nodding one blade to another. Turning I verified it immediately. In the moonlight were the shadowy patches of beach grass, swirling, alternately lightening and darkening as they were pressed close to the earth and released again.

From higher in the air came a sweet tuneful whispering, that before this night I had associated with only one scene. By half closing my eyes I found myself transported thousands of miles away; the tropical vegetation melted away and I was lying in a forest of great green pines, the whisperings were the breeze sounds filtering between the needles, the sighing that with increase of wind becomes great roaring moans and then subsides again to gentle singings. It was the voice of evergreens talking one to the other, confiding secrets of the good rich earth, of the dry carpets of smooth brown needles, of sky-topping clouds and of warm rain. Then presently, and at first all but unnoticeable, came another rustling, impinging slowly on the ear, becoming perceptible only after it made itself known. Even more vividly than the pine-whispering, this new sound brought memories of the north country flooding back to mind. It was a murmur akin to the swishing of old silk and taffeta, and, briefly, I thought of Victorian ladies clad in multi-hued petti-coats moving in old-fashioned parlors. But this memory van-ished swiftly and once again the green pines dominated the scene. Except this time the air was not warm but was frosty and cold. Down through the interstices of the somber needles were drifting swirling clouds of tiny white motes, the falling of new snow. The gyrating horde of six-shaped crystals danced across the clearings and fell on the carpet of dead leaves. Their falling and bumping against the dried vegetation combined in a mysterious murmuring that ran up and down between the aisles of the trees.

I opened my eyes once more. The same trade wind that was bringing the rollers in was drifting the beach sand, rolling the countless grains up and down the beach, tumbling them into one another, piling them into drifts and sweeping them on again. The sound was not snow but the movement of tropical beach sand that was causing this whispering, billions of infinitesimal sounds accumulating one upon the other, the noise of grain against grain, of lime rasping against lime. The wind was blow-ing the sand, tearing the island apart, building it up, scouring the slopes of the dunes, etching graven lines in the soft rock.

Gaunt and stark in the moonlight the ghostly silhouettes of a thousand thorn trees crouched blackly against the luminous sky. From these came the tones that I had mistaken for the whisperings of the pines. These trees had all grown to an equal height, stretching supplicating fingers to the heavens and then like old men had all become bowed—curtsying evenly in one direction—pointing to the west. They seemed to suggest that in that direction moved the stream of life. Vainly their branches had sought to resist the current, growing in normal tree fashion until the uppermost twigs emerged from the still zone close to the earth and felt for the first time the ceaseless pressure of the moving river. Then slowly they had turned, bent by a force greater than themselves, turned and followed the lines of least resistance. Life flowed all in one direction. A series of whisperings higher in tone than those given off by the trees near by called my attention to a whitened corpse of a nearly dead lignum vitae. Through the years its gnarled trunk had resisted the surge of air, but age and unrelenting struggle had got the best of it. One by one the leaves had curled into brown crisps and fallen off, the bark had whitened, even the iron hard wood had become etched and graven, glistening palely in the moonlight. The foliage had slipped from limb after limb, leaving them bare and lifeless until only a small cluster of green remained on the very last and most western twig. Life had literally flowed from this plant, was pushed by the force of the wind from fiber after fiber and from twig to twig.

I rose from my shelter and stepped out into the stream. Its force was surprising. While I had slept the trades had increased in intensity until they were blowing half a gale; the loose fabric of my shirt and trousers fluttered in the breeze; the temperature was slightly cool and I shivered. Striding down to the water I stopped at the edge and listened. Here, too, the air was alive with sound, with the liquid splash of wave on wave, the sing of salt spray. But these sounds were mostly further out, and I remembered that I was still in the lee and that the full power of the wind would not become apparent until I passed a headland called Pollacca Point a few miles up the coast. Returning to the shelter I gathered together the contents of my two bags, ate another tin of beef, and set out again determined to cover a few miles before the heat of day.

From that hour early in the morning the wind became a personal enemy, a hostile and relentless antagonist which gave no peace, chilling my body when I slept at night huddled behind a rock, catching up the shimmering heat waves during the day, blasting them against my face and forehead, singing, howling, whistling. I could escape the sun by hiding beneath the trees or crawling in the shade of boulders; the wind granted no amnesty. Eddying, swirling, it worried me endlessly; drifting sand covered my bags when I set them down, the tiny grains filtered into my food, making it gritty; my clothes flapped ceaselessly, breaking my rest, irritating me during the day. Not for an hour, not for so much as a minute, did it slacken. In my hut back in Mathewtown I had been conscious of the trades in a vague sort of way: they whistled through the palmettos, and rustled the grasses in the clearing, but behind the snug walls of my home the wind did not exist; I could sleep, eat and live unmolested. The clearing was in a semi-vacuum, its position in the lee of the island sheltered it from all but the most violent gusts. The trades roared overhead and then passed on out to sea again.

Inagua lies squarely in the path of the trades. These winds at times blow incessantly for weeks, at others fall to near calm or gentle zephyrs, more often they are vigorous and galelike. Usually they increase and decrease in intensity, slowly building up velocity over several days, holding it for long or short periods and then gradually waning again. My exploration of the island was in a period of increasing intensity.

About dawn I passed the last of the lee. From Polacca Point the coast swings southwards in a long sweeping bay known as the Bight of Ocean. Somewhere in the center of this was a fabulous place known as Babylon which I had been told I could not pass. I was curious to see it. Polacca Point was visible long before I reached it by the curtain of white spray surging up from the windward side. There was no sheltering reef to guard the coast from the onslaughts of the huge swells that were running; the bottom dropped straight down for fifty or sixty feet; the water hit the blank wall with nothing to slow its impact; white sheets of dazzling foam shot skywards and were whipped into long streamers by the wind. The roar could be heard for miles.

The spray drenched my clothing when I passed. Even though I crawled far back into the tangled vegetation, the wind carried the moisture yards inland. The land here was very low to the water's surface, seven or eight feet at most. The waves appeared ready to overflow at any moment. In some time long past this very thing had happened when a hurricane had burst on this section of coast, for although time had smoothed out the evidences of violence, the fury of the long distant storm was still visible everywhere. Back of the level bench of gray stone which fronted the beach was piled a huge rampart of monstrous boulders which had been wrenched from the sea's edge. Mixed with these were huge masses of brain coral and yard-thick branching trunks of madrepores which could have come only from the bottom of the sea. Some of these lay half buried a hundred yards from the breakers; a hundred feet down were the living counterparts of the dead masses on dry land. It did not seem within the bounds of possibility that any wave could have accomplished this feat. The wind on that terrible day must have screamed at a hundred and fifty miles an hour. For miles around the land must have been awash; the waves that came pounding in must have hit the cliff at the island's edge with the roar of a dozen cannon, must have spouted a hundred feet into the air, to be caught and flung by the shrieking wind in a tearing, blinding deluge of hundreds of tons of water. In this maelstrom the surge of the moving mountains must have swept down to the ocean bottom, scouring the sea floor and tearing loose the living coral. These had been flung high above the rampart and then rolled by the wash into the drowned valley behind.

The rampart provided some little shelter from the wind. A short distance down the coast the tangled vegetation melted away and there opened up a long narrow valley which ran parallel to the beach. This valley was filled with a deep desposit of loose white sand. The sand was pitted with hundreds of long depressions, oval hollows of almost equal length. Thousands of tracks crisscrossed back and forth between these and the wall of vegetation on the far side of the valley. Their identity eluded me for a long time; the sand was too loose to make clear impressions, but the mystery was solved when I rounded a clump of bushes and came upon a nest full of baby pigs. I almost stepped upon them and they dashed madly about squealing with fright, bumping into one another. Dropping the pack I ran after them in circles thinking I might secure one for supper but they were too quick for me. Stopping, I loaded the .410 and prepared to shoot but the mother hog came running up and they dashed to her for safety. She looked mean and angry and advanced with her head lowered menacingly. The .410 would hardly have stopped her if she had charged and I decided that there was no sense in having an angry sow on my hands, so I edged cautiously away, leaving her with her brood. They turned and trotted away into the bushes.

For the next mile or two I moved quietly, hoping to find some more young pork and was so intent on watching the ground that I failed to notice until I came close the towering hull of a great schooner piled high upon the rampart. It was the four-master that Richardson had told us about during the dismal dinner on our first day in Mathewtown. She had been a magnificent vessel. Two of her masts were still standing and the remnants of her rigging were strewn in long piles along her decks and over the sides. She had hit the rampart head on and the impact had lifted her nose high out of the water until the great bowsprit rose heavenward in a tangled mass of foot-ropes and cordage. The hull was stove in in a dozen places and the water rushed in and out in foaming torrents. I tried to climb up to her decks but her sides were too steep and the few lines that were draped over the rail parted with rot and decay when I pulled on them. Great beams and planks were strewn for yards around and her woodwork was bleaching to a silvery white from the sun and salt spray. There is something infinitely sad about the wreckage of a beautiful ship.

The ruins of the schooner reminded me of my own errand. It also called to mind the distance I had yet to go. The sun was growing hot again and the wind was gushing down the sand valley with the intensity of a volcano. The water bottle was practically empty and the mysterious land of Babylon had yet to be crossed. There was nothing even faintly resembling a waterhole. Beyond the valley the interminable limestone stretched away into the center of the island. Somewhere in the interior there must be water; the pigs had to drink. The idea of utilizing a sow's drinking cup was not enchanting but the water could be boiled. Caching the pack in an interstice of the rampart I headed inland, taking only the canteen, the gun and some dust shot in the event I saw some interesting lizards.

The wall of vegetation proved to be well-nigh impenetrable. There were few lizards, fewer birds, great mazes of green tree cactus, acres and acres of gray limestone, more musical rocks and billions of needle-sharp thorns. Little else. Low pig trails ran everywhere. I crept along several of the more used ones, hoping they might take me to water. They led nowhere. The vegetation sprang out of crevices and holes in the rocks. I dug the dirt out of a number but the soil was dry down to the ends. No rain had fallen for several months. I did find one small hole with a few drops in the bottom but it was too narrow to admit my hand and there was no way of withdrawing the liquid. It was probably salt anyway.

After an hour I gave up the search and returned to the cache in the rampart. I could do without water for a while, at least until I reached the huts near the lagoon. In the meantime the country might change character. This did not seem likely but there was always the possibility.

Instead the thorn scrub became more wild than ever. A maze of tough prickly branches denied entry in a solid front all along the edge of the valley. Gradually the inner wall became steeper and eventually developed into a concave recessed cliff that stretched out mile after mile in the heat waves. There was a peculiar character to this wall that excited my curiosity. In some manner it had a vaguely familiar look, some idiosyncrasy of construction that set it apart from all other rock ledges that I had seen. I searched my memory for a long time before a recollection flashed into mind. This wall was exactly like the cliff wall which towered over my bathing pool at Mathewtown. The odd construction was caused by the scooping action of surf; the signs were unmistakable. It was as hard as flint.

The wall itself offered further proof. Half cemented to its base and frozen by the chemical action of decaying lime were the remnants of dozens of varieties of sea creatures; the shells of ancient whelks, faded to chalk white; crushed and broken conchs; pieces of old coral, bleached by the sun and half melted by the elements; the curved pieces of the armor plates of chitons; broken fragments of mussels, piled deep; the calcareous remains of echinoderms and the worn spirals of a dozen varieties of gastropods. This was an old sea cliff where the surf once thundered and foamed. I looked out to the present sea front. It was about fourteen feet lower down and nearly four hundred feet distant. At no very remote period, geologically speaking, Inagua had been a dozen feet lower down in the sea. Much of what is now dry land must have been shallow lagoon and rolling water. The Bahamas are considered to be in a period of geological submergence, they are slowly slipping into the ocean from which they came; there is much evidence, however, of local uplift; mother earth breathes deeply at times; a mile down in the depths the sand-heaped granite platform on which Inagua rests must have pulsed upwards, suddenly thrusting the old beach out of reach of the ocean and forming a new one out of what had been a submarine cliff.

The geological history of the Bahama Islands is very complex. For countless centuries they have been isolated by great deeps from all other land; they have fallen and risen rhythmically into the depths; whole islands and archipelagos have emerged and disappeared, have been connected and disconnected; the waves have built them up and torn them apart again, scattering their sands over the floor of the blue ocean. They have always been islands of the sea. Never at any period of their history, even during the glacial era when the level of the waters dropped three or four hundred feet, sucked up by evaporation and deposited as ice at the Poles, did they join or connect with any continental mass. Much of the evidence of this struggle between the sea and the land is obscured, drifted away on the wind and tides or lost forever in the abyss of the ocean. Yet in this valley wall in one breathless sweep was the last page of the story. Inagua was a relatively new island; the sparse soil of the great inland plain, covered only with the thin skim of decayed ceritheum shells and with the grasses,—the figure of speech linking these grasses to the third day of creation was nearer the truth than I imagined—gave added credence to the evidence of the wall.

The wall terminated abruptly in the first outlying crags of the place called Babylon. I reached these crags just before sunset. A more forbidding vista would be difficult to imagine. Were it not for the fact that I knew that the Bahamas are entirely sedimentary in their structure, I would have believed that this was the brim of an active volcano which had just finished erupting, belching out great masses of lava and scoria. The crimson rays of the setting sun cast a flame-colored hue over a maelstrom of violently tumbled rocks, slag-like ridges of razor-edge cinder and cavernous pits of deep maroon. In the half-light it appeared weird, unworldly, almost Martian. Babylon is a magnified sponge acres in extent, a sponge which has for its tissues the needle-edge spires of flinty stone. It is a gigantic fiber of pitted and decayed lime, sharpened by the elements into sword-thin blades of carved and jagged mineral.

Babylon was the end of travel for the day and I withdrew to the shelter of the concave cliff where I lit a fire of driftwood. Immediately beyond the aura of light cast by the flames, the ancient sea cliff plunged directly into a wall of sheer stone that formed an angular shelter from the wind. This was mysterious in itself. The valley and the cliff ended too abruptly and gave the feeling that under the vast pile of eroded limestone that was called Babylon they continued on and on, smothered under an eighty foot thick blanket of rock.

The wind that night howled louder than I had yet heard it. The fire flickered and flared and weird shadows slid across the ledges. Deep organ-like notes came out of the darkness, different from the low whistlings and whisperings of the night before; the rushing air pouring through the million holes and crevices of the spongy rock assumed an ecclesiastical tone, a low harmonious medley common to the vaulted naves of great cathedrals. The sound disturbed me deeply; it was so utterly mournful, penetrating; not to listen was difficult, there was little else to do except tend to the fire.

I roused myself before dawn, devoured another tin of beef—this food was beginning to get monotonous—and in the light of the waning moon climbed out of the valley floor. In the moonlight the world was more strange than ever; pale blue light edged the jagged rocks; the shadows appeared as empty black holes that seemed to pierce the center of the earth. The valley glistened as a long narrow ribbon between the dark rocks on shore and the old sea wall. Eighty feet below a seething line of pale blue marked the waves breaking against the blank cliff.

Once years before in the dazzling white glass-sand quarries of the Ordovician in West Virginia I climbed two hundred feet from the bottom over sheets of loose shale and fragile sandstone to reach an almost perfect fossil of a crinoid which I had seen through my field glasses and, having secured it, hung helpless for several hours, too frightened by the treacherous character of the rocks to descend, expecting at any moment to be precipitated to the quarry floor; and, once I spent a miserable half hour clambering over steep projections on a narrow ledge high above the Susquehanna River in upper Pennsylvania where I had gone seeking the nest of a Duck Hawk, cautiously hoisting myself from stone to stone, scraping the flesh from my knees and fingers as I hugged the cliff wall, and lowering myself between sharp crevasses. On the latter occasion a portion of the ledge had crumbled behind me, shutting off all means of retreat and forcing me to drop from ledge to ledge, some of which were hardly more than eight or nine inches wide, until I reached the valley floor a hundred and fifty feet below. These experiences led me to believe that I had some knowledge of the technique of climbing over rock. I had not then seen the crags of Babylon.

There was no danger of falling any great distance but a drop of a few inches in this amazing place would have meant frightfully lacerated limbs and mangled flesh. Hundreds of thousands of stone needles and curved knife blades of razor-edge limestone thrust up everywhere. Every crevice and hole was lined with them; deep fissures were barbed with recurved hooks; there was scarcely a spot level enough or large enough to place a foot. Thin sheets of sharp stone covered deep spiked pits and crumbled at the weight of a body. The thin soles of my tennis shoes afforded no protection. Frequently I had to stop and rest my feet. Sitting was a problem, solved only by perching on top of the grass bags.

Daylight revealed a strange and wild vista. Curving along the sweep of the Bight of Ocean was a great line of magnificent stone cliffs rising and falling into the distance. Against these the brilliant blue of the ocean beat in a frothy white line, throwing spray high into the air, pulsing and roaring. The water was unbelievably clear and the bottom was easily visible a hundred feet down. It was strewn with gigantic boulders and crags apparently crumbled from the cliff walls. Between these were moving a number of dark shadowy forms, the bodies of large sharks and slow lumbering groupers. In one spot a group of immense blue parrotfish hovered about an algae-covered boulder, revealed by flashes of deep indigo as they twisted to munch the filmy covering. About a mile away a bright scar showed where a small landslide had slipped from the cliff and tumbled into the sea. On the land side the jagged rocks swept away in a series of rolling hills toward the interior where they were covered with an impenetrable scrub.

The sun was well above the horizon when I reached the new gash on the upper rim of the cliff's face. Cautiously I edged my way down until I was on a level with the center. A great chunk had fallen away, undercut by the waves. The stone underneath was white and filled with sand, slightly soft but firm, and resistant to the fingers. A small object imbedded in the rock attracted my attention. With a penknife I extracted it carefully and rolled it between my fingers, crushing off the loose grains. It was the shell of a land snail, a long curved spiral of delicate form, exactly like those which covered the grasses of the valley and which occurred elsewhere on the island, clinging to vegetation in great multitudes. The place where I found the fossil was at least thirty feet from the crest of the cliff.

These snails are not creatures of the sea; their entire lives are spent on dry land far from the sound of salt water. This shell could only have dropped centuries ago from the frond of some plant, a blade of grass or leaf of some sea grape; immediately after drifting sand must have covered it over, protecting it against the elements. Drifting sand! This was the answer to the mystery of the disappearance of the ancient sea wall into the heavy blanket of solid rock. Drifting sand—once more I bent close and examined the new exposure. Not far below the matrix impression of the snail I found a long brown streak unlike any other discoloration in the cliff. Excitedly I dug it to its source—the crushed and stained mold of the base of a frond of palmetto palm. There was no tissue remaining but there was enough impression to identify it beyond all doubt.

Drifting sand—this was truly the land of the wind. Centuries before on this spot a great series of dazzling white sand dunes had been rolled up from the ocean, grain after grain sweeping with the wind, piling in long rows, making ripple marks, long curving lines like those in the sea when the tide is out. On and on, higher and higher the wind carried the fleeting sand, burying the ancient sea wall, marching inland, sloping and gradual on the windward face, steep and abrupt in the lee. Dune grasses sprang up momentarily, bore families of snails; these lived their lives and died, dropping in dozens to the shifting floor; the wind sprang up again covering these shells and obscuring the grasses beneath tons of tiny particles. Palmettos grew and were buried in their turn. Month in and month out the wind never ceased; night and day, the dunes shifted and re-formed. In a continuous stream the particles came billowing out of the ocean, tossed up by the crashing waves. Ground up fragments of sea creatures, the drifting dust of pulverized shells, the delicate houses of microscopic foraminifera, the silica spicules of sponges, the broken and powdery carapaces of giant crayfish, the wave-rolled residue of coral, all went drifting away on the gales. In great mounds a hundred feet high this vast pile of the wrecks of a hundred million living creatures lay in large yellow hills. I crumbled some of the buried particles between my fingers and looked at them closely. They were all formed of the corpses of once living matter. These hills were hills of death.

Truly the land of the wind; the record was there to see, preserved by remarkable chance. The dunes had formed, grown to full dimension—and then frozen. Literally frozen; not by chill of temperature, nor snow, nor blanket of ice but congealed by the slow corrosive chemistry of grain against grain, of lime against lime. The fresh seeping water of downpouring rain had melted the sand, fused it together in one hard flinty mass. One sees this story repeated everywhere in the Bahama Islands. The blue ocean casts up its tons of dead sea creatures and the winds and the rains solidify the dunes into enduring stone before they have marched far. There are places where series after series of frozen hills line up opposite windy shores like regiments of marching soldiers; the outermost still soft and yielding, fresh with the marks of the sea; the innermost hard and flinty, pitted and scored with the scars of slow dissolution. Even hills have their youth and old age; their flexible years and their set and hardened decline. To be born; to grow and reach maturity; to exist awhile and then crumble to dust again is the fate of all substance; mineral and animal, the animate and inanimate, all must pass this cycle.

This is a universal picture.

CHAPTER IX

The Web of Island Life

EVERY event in nature has its inception in the alteration of substance or change of action that preceded it. Spring is born of autumn; today's roses are nourished by the fragments of last year's leaves; the liquid burble of a wren outside your door is only the energy of yesterday's insects whose crushed and digested bodies are transmuted into song and joy, into flight and avian activity. Living comes of dying; a fallen tree is home for myriads of boring beetles which would never have existed but for the toppling of the trunk; the comforting chirp of crickets, the haunting calls of whip-poor-wills, the mellow droning of bees hurrying from flower to flower, flowers themselves, are only possible because last night, or last week or last year something passed its time of usefulness and fell to earth, or was devoured, or was dissolved into the elements from which it came. Every flash of bright color from fur, scale, or feather, the graceful movements of living things, the vibrant darting of hummingbirds, the impelling sweep of migration, the slow majestic soaring of an eagle or albatross, the thud of pounding hoofs, the curve of rippling fins, all these are made possible by the perishing of some creature or plant, or because of the modification of some mineral or action of the elements.

Living might be considered a chain, or, better yet, a mesh of chain links, like the chain mail of the knights of long ago. Only the simile is not quite complete for the mesh of the knights was composed of a single metal, of bronze or silver or gold, according to the station of the wearer. The chain mesh of organic existence instead is of variegated mesh; a tangled web in which one strand is brightly illumined with the glow of day, in contrast to and unlike its neighbor which is dark with the shadows of night. It is an enjoined tissue in which one coil is life and the next is death; and, there is a great intermingling of patterns, as of design shuttling between one portion of the mesh and another.

All individual creation has its beginning and its ending. Stars wing their way into existence in a burst of flame and then die as cold, blackened spheroids; birds begin as eggs and complete their course as smudges of brown earth or heaps of bedraggled feathers; the winged seeds that drift over the spring meadows become in the fall clumps of charred and frayed tissue; continents rise and disappear as geologic time overwhelms them; even epochs start with hope and promise; the new year pushes out the old and in its turn makes room for another.

On Inagua nearly the whole of existence began and ended with the wind. To be able to compute with exactness the potency of the wind in the lives of the creatures of the island would require the services of a super-statistician and the combined efforts of a complete university of technicians, miles of graphs and years of patient research. Even then the picture would be clouded with uncertainties. Yet the factor of the wind is everywhere present and everywhere obvious. Even the most undiscerning soon discover that the birds pay allegiance to its force when they sleep at night; their bodies are all oriented to the east, facing the breeze. Herons, flamingos, sandpipers, doves, warblers, hawks, perching in branches or crouching on the ground, singly or in flocks of hundreds, all turn and face the direction of the sunrise. I adopted this habit myself, except when in the shelter of a boulder, snuggling low to avoid the current. Even the lizards which burrowed underground delayed the hour of their morning appearances when the wind was strong. I kept a careful record of the times of their emergence and of the velocity of the wind and found as much variation as two hours between slack days and times of semi-gale. The humans, too, were affected by the wind. When the saltponds near the settlement were reopened ten years later I recall the exasperation of the operators when the wind went unaccountably slack for an unusual period; with no wind there was no evaporation of brine, hence no salt, reduced earnings and no work for the laborers, unrest and discontent. The scorching sun was not enough to evaporate the sea water; without the wind the entire economy of the island was disrupted.

These were the more obvious evidences; Inagua itself was wind-created, born like the dunes out of the sea. It would not be altogether an untruth, nor an overstatement, to say that hummingbirds exist on Inagua because over the American mainland, in Central America, in Colombia and in Venezuela great columns of hot air are arising, creating a vast semi-vacuum as they mount skywards which the trades rush in to fill; nor to declare that the cactus blooms from which these hummingbirds glean their meals of nectar and insects have their being because a thousand or a hundred thousand years ago the wind picked up newly dried fragments of surf-ground dead sea creatures and whirled them into the air to place them within reach of the fresh warm rain. Sea and clouds, wind and hot sun, the bodies of tiny foraminifera, living coralines, drifted barren sand dunes, a tinge of green vegetation, flower blooms, blossom-dwelling insects, insect-feeding hummingbirds; these are a chain of events, a mesh of existence, a transportation of inanimate and animate, a death for a life, a fiber of existence beginning with the wind.

The cycle of birth and death was nearly complete at Babylon. Life had come and gone. Snails and palms and hummingbirds, grasses and seeds had their brief hour and had been cast aside by the breeze to be buried and dissolved. The same wind that brought the dunes into existence was etching away the solid rock, stealing it a particle at a time, hollowing away the weak spots, boring holes, leaving sharp ridges and spines. The sea, too, had advanced and was gnawing steadily at the cliff face, breaking up the boulders and crushing them into sand again; into whitened grains to be drifted once more. The task was half done, the hills were carved neatly in twain. In a few years, or a few centuries, Babylon would be returned to the Mother Ocean which gave it birth.

The trip over the cliffs occupied the better portion of a day and cut the bottoms of my inexpensive sneakers off my feet. The bladed stone swiftly sliced the crepe rubber to ribbons, tore out the crinkled latex bit by bit, stripping the soles and heels away. In linear distance the ancient dunes did not extend more than six or seven miles; but for every foot of forward progress I climbed or descended two or three; each inch had to be negotiated carefully, painstakingly. These shoes had been adequate for the yielding sand of the beaches and for the flat rock of the interior but three hours on the razor rocks of Babylon ruined them forever.

Modern living has unfitted us; we are too dependent on the habiliments of civilization. Without shoes I was as helpless as a day-old rabbit. We take our foot coverings for granted, giving them scant attention except to polish them daily; to groan temporarily, perhaps, when they are new and stiff; or, perhaps, to make certain we are clad in the most proper and latest styles. Like handkerchiefs, or knives, or forks, or napkins, we become acutely aware of their existence only when they are absent. Within the short space of three hours my thoughts altered from the problems of Aeolian geology and the ecological relationships of lizards to shoes; the lack of shoes changed me instantly from a student of natural science to a limping automaton intent only on the problems of feet. The sudden demand for footgear dominated my universe, canceled all other considerations. Even the dryness of a growing thirst and the threat of an empty water bottle failed to penetrate the shell of my shoe-consciousness.

Never again shall I laugh at the Haitian peasants who, once having attained the social and financial status of shoe-proprietorship, carry these precious belongings perched precariously on their heads to the edge of town where they don them before entering. Their shoes are too valuable to waste on dusty country roads; the possession of footgear is their badge of dignity. Only the very poor and the primitive have the misfortune—or the good sense—to do without them.

I sat down in the midst of the wilderness of Babylon and pondered. What to do? I tried swathing my feet in lizard wrappings, donning the canvas uppers to retain the gauze, but the soft cotton quickly shredded to ragged lint. By walking bow-legged on the edges of my soles where the rubber had not worn through I managed to creep down to the water's edge near a low spot in the cliffs. There I found a fragment of a water-soaked plank and with my penknife whittled out two inner-soles and forced them into the wrecks of my sneakers. These made flexion impossible and forced me to walk flatfooted like a duck.

However, as though in compensation for the soreness of my feet, the cliffs ended as abruptly as they began in a smooth stretch of level sand that curved northward as far as the eye could see. The ancient sea wall did not reappear and presumably vanished beneath the sea or terminated under the blanket of rock. Instead a stately row of cocoanut palms lined the shore for miles. These all leaned gracefully seaward and were laden with nuts. Gratefully I twisted off several and sliced the tops. The liquid was sweet and cool, and so intense was my thirst I drank the contents of three in quick succession. Their juice was the first liquid in over twenty-four hours. To make certain I would not be dry again I drained several into the canteen although I suspected that the milk would quickly go rancid in the hot sun.

The glades back of the palms swarmed with lizards. Instantly I forgot my feet; these lizards were of a new type. I shot several and examined them carefully. They obviously belonged to the genus *Ameiva*, a group characterized by exceeding nervousness and by the rapidity with which its members are able to run. When alarmed, these lizards fling themselves across the ground with an abandon that has to be seen to be believed; their legs move so quickly as to become invisible blurs; occasionally they stop and dash suddenly off in a new direction, vanishing from sight because the eye, unable to adjust itself so quickly, follows their original course and loses them in so doing.

I was greatly interested in this genus because I once spent several months working out the life history of a related Haitian species, *Ameiva chrysolema*, and had discovered that the females of this lizard congregated when pregnant and deposited their eggs in a communal burrow; each clutch in a separate compartment; a type of reptilian maternity ward, as it were; a most unorthodox proceeding, for most lizards deposit their eggs singly and apart from one another. The new *Ameiva* in my hand was colored unlike any other that I had ever seen. On the far side of Babylon another species, *Ameiva maynardii*, was common wherever there were sandglades as far as the settlement. But this new lizard was totally unlike *maynardii* in that it was uniformly colored a soft olive tan which faded into a light blue on the creature's stomach and undersides. *Maynardii*, in contrast, is an intensely vivid lizard of jet black marked with two brilliant yellow stripes traversing the length of its body. Its undersides are ultramarine; an altogether gorgeous creature. As nearly as I could discern the anatomy of the two lizards was identical, scale for scale, plate for plate. This later proved to be the case when a large series were compared in the laboratory; for this reason the new lizard did not merit the status of a new species but was relegated to the position of subspecies.

The classification of the new lizard did not interest me so much as the fact that the rocks of Babylon were the dividing line of the spheres of influence of the two types, so alike in everything except color. They were obviously derived from the same parent stock; and, although in the weeks that followed I traversed every inch of the island, their ranges did not overlap except in the last few miles of the circuit before reaching Mathewtown. At the points of overlap I collected a number of intergrading forms, specimens that were half *maynardii* and half *maynardii uniformis*, as the new subspecies came to be called. A line drawn from the rocks of Babylon to the last occurrence of the new lizard would divide Inagua exactly in half at *right angles to the wind! Maynardii* was a lizard of the lee, *uniformis* a denizen of the windward side of the island. The same line also divided Inagua in relation to its vegetation. The lee vegetation was thick and tangled, at places completely impenetrable; the plants on the opposite half crouched low to the rocks, were sparse and in places missing altogether. This is a curious circumstance. It is, also, a yawning trap for a scientific misstatement.

Henry David Thoreau once declared that a trout in the milk was circumstantial evidence. On the basis of circumstantial evidence it is easy to jump to the conclusion that this new lizard was a direct result of its windy environment. Because the vegetation was stunted and because the scouring wind had blasted life out of all but the most hardy, it would seem reasonable to assume that these lizards had appropriated their drab color because of some relationship to the wind, because perhaps their food was different from that of their neighbors, or because they had suited their hue to a condition with which their relatives in the lee did not have to contend.

Such a conclusion would be reasonable except for the fact that new species or subspecies do not happen that way, except possibly under very rare circumstances. Animals fit themselves marvelously to all sorts of environments, adapting themselves in a thousand ways to meet the incidents of life; but as recent research has shown, they become new types because of some mutation, some peculiar alteration of energy deep within their egg cells that sends individuals off in new directions. Animals become new species or types because they cannot help themselves; the change is beyond their control. If the alteration does not combat the environment they live and flourish; if not, they struggle as best they may or eventually perish.

Somewhere in the island's past, if the evidence of modern research is correct, a family of dull brown *Ameiva* suddenly made its appearance, either all at once or over a number of generations, and bred true. The wind had nothing to do with the mutation except that it altered the topography of the newly risen island so as to separate permanently the two forms, permitting them to breed unmolested. The sand hills of Babylon suddenly sweeping out of the sea may have been the original separation, or Inagua may have been two or more islands which later connected. The possibilities are legion.

The finding of the new lizard put a new spring into my hobbling gait and I decided to press on. Naturalists are queer people; it takes surprisingly little to please them. The Lagoon Christophe was at least fifteen miles away but so elated was I that I determined to sleep that night by the wreck.

By sunset I passed a cluster of coral and thatch huts where I replenished my water supply from a barrel set beneath the eaves to catch the rain. The water was dark brown, almost coffee color from the thatch drippings and from the soot which had accumulated during the years. Mosquito larvae swarmed in the liquid and it had a bad taste. But it was better than nothing so I filled the canteen to the top. There were about thirty houses in all, most of them little more than rude shelters from the wind, all with dirt floors and all deserted. They were arranged near the beach in clusters, the group belonging to the Daxons farthest up the coast. When I passed these I was limping badly though I had long since taken out the board inner soles and substituted palm fiber which was more flexible but which chafed miserably. How I was going to navigate the remainder of the island without shoes I could not guess.

I stopped for an hour to eat a tin of corned beef and to bathe my feet in a tidepool. By this time I was feeling considerably tired and somewhat dejected. The elation of finding a new lizard had worn off and the exertion of crossing the rocks of Babylon and the miles of soft sand had wearied my muscles. Once again, as in the spoonbill swamp, I marveled at the predicament in which I found myself, and wondered what was so important about the distribution of the Lacertilia that I should subject myself to mosquito bites, hot sun, dirty water and a few ounces of corned beef daily for food. I recalled lecturing before a class of college students and glibly stating that no well-planned expedition was subject to adventures. Yet there I was half a hundred miles from base with no shoes, no food and a quart of chocolate colored water. I grinned a little ruefully.

The moon had been up scarcely an hour when I limped onto the curved beach of the Lagoon Christophe and climbed the bluff back of the wreck. High out of the reach of the waves the hull of my once beautiful ship lay on her side in the sand. The moonglow lighted her timbers softly and for a brief moment she looked almost undamaged. A lump came in my throat and I slid down the steep bank bringing a pile of loose sand with me. Then I saw what had happened. Great gashes had been sheared out of her sides, the decking was stove in and masses of splinters

hung everywhere. The mast was broken off just above the deck
and the bowsprit hung loosely at a peculiar angle. On one side
a great hole had been ground through the massive oak and a
large piece of branching coral was tightly wedged in this space.
I crawled through the open deck and found the interior a mass
of tangled timber and loose boards. There was nothing left of
the table, of our book racks or the bunks. Dimly in the half
light I could see the marks of axes around the bronze fittings of
the ports and elsewhere wherever there was any visible metal.

Crawling out again I retrieved my bags and returned with
a box of matches. I piled a mass of small strips and splinters
at one end of the ruined cabin and another in the hold. Waiting
until the flames caught I moved forward in the flickering light
and set fire to the second heap. The heat soon drove me out
and I stood on the beach and watched the flames mount skywards. The sun-dried wood caught quickly and turned the interior into a brilliant mass of light. The beach was crimson for
yards around; in the glare the squat bodies of the ghost crabs,
surprised in their nocturnal wanderings, cast long flickering
shadows as they retreated or dived in their holes.

On top of the bluff I solemnly watched my ship go up in
flames. The plankings burst one by one as the spikes charred
loose, casting showers of sparks, and fell smoking on the sand.
The deck boards caught all at once and crumbled together,
leaving only the stark outlines of the ribs and beams. The tough
oak burned fiercely, crackling and exploding; the stout stem
and samson post were wrapped in sheets of flame, the massive
stern roared with the pressure of the wind and with the heat;
presently it collapsed and fell on the beach. The floor pieces
melted soon afterwards, dropping the ribs to the ground where
they lay in curved arcs of flame in a bed of glowing coals.
Gradually they dissolved into the general mass; the glare subsided, grew faint; became dull cherry red and then a dim scat-

tering of glowing sparks.

Snuggled behind the rise of a small dune I dropped off to sleep with a feeling of intense satisfaction. My ship was beyond the reach of despoilers. To have her go up in flames was a more fitting end than to lie splintered and crushed on the desolate beach to dissolve slowly of dry rot and decay. The act removed the last regret I might have had; from that evening the affair of the wreck became a past event.

I awakened in the morning feeling better than I had all week; my appetite was enormous and I looked about for something to eat. There was no more corned beef and, although there was nothing else in sight, I was glad of it. Strangely, too, the feeling of loneliness which had begun to creep over me was pushed into the background of my consciousness; the dejection of the night before was all gone. In several ways the burning of the *Basilisk* marked a turn of events. Most important, the evening's happenings were the climax of physical discomfort occasioned by the misery of the spoonbill swamp and the unaccustomed hardness of a bed on solid ground with no protection from wind and sand, from the glare of sun and the monotony of a slim diet. The days just past served as a conditioning rendered unpleasant by fresh comparison with the comforts and protections of my coral and thatch home.

The inference of the events leading up to the attainment of the goal of the wreck and the long miles to the Lagoon Christophe is that I would stagger half starved and thirsty, crippled and with swollen feet back to the settlement. Nothing would be further from the truth. Too many volumes are written picturing the islands of the West Indies as savage jungles out of which the explorer staggers half mad. There are few actual jungles anywhere on these islands and there is no excuse for anyone's becoming involved in a near fatal episode. Inagua is by far the wildest island of the entire series and the most desolate. The only very serious problem is that of water. Food is abundant provided one is willing to cast aside prejudices and go on a diet of wild ducks, doves and conch meat and is willing to eat these unseasoned and cooked over a fire of brush. There are even a number of herbs which produce excellent tea, some of these are very sweet and refreshing.

The shoe problem was my first concern and I solved it by throwing away the useless uppers which were chafing my feet and by making a set of moccasins from a scrap of canvas which I found buried in the sand near the pile of ashes. This canvas I recognized as a portion of our hatch cover; it was heavy, well waterproofed, and yet was soft and yielding to the flesh. With a little experimentation I cut a shape that folded satisfactorily and tied it with a strip peeled from a green thatch palm. When the moccasins were finished I was quite proud of them; they were very comfortable and gave the pleasant feeling of walking barefooted. At the same time I cut an extra pair and stuffed them into the grass bag along with the preserved lizards.

For breakfast I shot six tobacco doves and two sandpipers. The doves proved to be sweet but slightly tough. The first mouthfuls were dreadfully flat but a few crumbs of sea salt gathered from a tidepool supplied the necessary condiment. They were infinitely better than corned beef but when skinned and cleaned were hardly larger than sparrows. The sandpipers, however, were a disappointment, for they tasted fishy and were as unyielding as seasoned leather.

The breakfast of fresh meat served to ease my mind about the food problem; I felt I could proceed, checking the terrain carefully without danger of going hungry. After eating I walked down to the beach, washed my greasy hands and took a swim in the lagoon. The sun and wind soon dried me and I put on my soiled shirt and ragged ducks. I was amazed how refreshed I felt after the dejection of the evening before; the miles ahead did not seem so appalling.

Only the wind remained to tantalize. While I was cooking the doves it swirled the smoke into my face, scattered the ashes and ruffled my hair. The tatters of my shirt vibrated noisily; my trousers flapped and clung about my ankles. I plodded down the beach in the same direction I had taken the day we were wrecked. Fortunately there had not been much wind then, for had it approached the intensity of this latter date we would have been lucky to escape with our lives. The surf on the outlying reefs was tremendous; the wind had free sweep all the way from Portugal over two thousand miles away.

Soon I reached the lake where I had seen the flamingos. Curious, I eased down the rampart dune and through the bordering mangroves. The lake was quite deserted except for a few gallinules which disappeared between the roots. Behind the far shore was a low matting of vegetation, grass and thatch palms which covered a low hill and which continued into the valley beyond. These palms were very small, not over four feet in height. In other portions of the island the same species reached twenty or more feet; here the rush of air had stunted their growth. All the other plants were in proportion; sea grape, usually head high, scarcely reached the knees. The effect was startling. I felt as though I were gazing at a tall mountain side instead of a sand dune not more than thirty feet high.

While crossing the lake to examine these dunes I made a momentous discovery. The smooth silt underfoot suddenly became hard and jagged; irregularly so. Reaching down I prodded with my fingers in the chalky mud. I came up with a piece of coral in my hand. It was reef coral, the uppermost branches of staghorn. Digging deeply I shoved aside the clinging muck; as far as I could go were other branches, still in perfect condition. This was the line of the old reef! By walking down the center of the lake and criss-crossing I verified my fact. The site of this shallow pond was once the outermost sea barrier, and at no greatly distant period the surf crashed and thundered over its intricacies.

Walking back again to the nearly barren rampart dune I surveyed the scene. Mile upon mile the existing reef curved away into the distance. Behind this was a shallow lagoon, then the rampart dunes, the parallel lake and a series of low hills rolling into the interior, becoming more covered with vegetation and obscure. Inagua was growing into the wind. The reef was most luxuriant where the surf was the most violent; ever outward the tentacled polyps were reaching, seeking the swirling water with its billions of micro-organisms, striving to escape the bogging sand of the lagoon behind. There were even a few spots where at low tide one could almost walk dry shod to the very edge of the reef. The story of the buried reef in the pond would soon be repeated; before long a new reef would be formed further out, growing up from the clean water and burying the reef behind. Then the wind would take up its task and drift the sands into another rampart, possibly forming another shallow pond and covering up the existing lake in turn.

The present pond was filled with diminutive shells of ceritheum, those tiny mollusks on which the flamingos depend for their sustenance. Flamingos and ceritheums are synonymous; without ceritheums flamingos would probably cease to exist, their anatomy is specialized for the sifting of these shells from the silt of the lake bottoms. The occurrence of ceritheums in this newly formed lake was interesting. How did they get there? Certainly not overland, the nearest pond was several miles away. Not by the ocean, for these particular snails do not thrive under marine conditions. There was only one answer. By air; these mollusks probably arrived on the feet or bills of birds from other ponds.

This was interesting speculation. How many other organisms

had arrived on Inagua in similar manner? After I returned from the trip around the island I spent several days shooting any birds I saw in prolonged and direct flight and examined their bills, feet and stomachs for organisms. From the feet and legs of sixteen spotted sandpipers which arrived from the direction of Mariguana I rinsed and scrubbed into a dish of sterile water enough mud to cover an area the size of my little fingernail; from this earth I separated exactly eleven seeds visible to the naked eye; two species of beautifully geometric desmids, microscopic green algaes which probably had come from a pond much fresher in content than the bitter saline lakes of Inagua, since most of these were so laden with chemical as to inhibit the growth of these primitive plants; and a number of amoeba-like organisms which my limited protozoology prevented me from identifying. I tried to sprout the eleven seeds but they all failed to grow except one which perished in birth, so to speak, for as soon as it gave signs of life it gave up the ghost and died. The amoeba, however, did very well in an infusion and the desmids flourished in a glass of water from the contents of my diminishing barrel. When one considers the vast number of sandpipers and other birds which each year sweep down through the Bahamas on the winter migration from North America, and considers the tremendous number of seeds, spores, microscopic algaes and one-celled animals that must be carried on their feet, tucked in crevices between their claws, under scales or clinging to their bills, the wonder is not that there are so many animals and plants on Inagua but that there are so few.

I do not believe the average of eleven seeds, two algaes and one amoeba per sixteen birds across the water is exceptionally high, for from the corpse of one little green heron whose legs were caked with mud I took 78 separate seeds provided with downy strands of whitish silk similar to the fluff of the cat-tails.

This heron had walked through them with its sticky feet and collected them as it brushed against the pod.

The web of island life had been spun a little way. Also, like the nets of certain spiders, some of it had been retracted. A death for a life; the corals and anemones had to live and breed and grow that there should follow ceritheums and flamingos; whole hosts of fishes and crustaceans had disappeared with the corals; gallinules and clapper rails splashed and waded where the surf had thundered; mangroves and beach grass existed because gorgonians and sea fans had perished; the wind was the binding thread, the warp and woof of island existence. Dependence upon dependence, a thread on a thread; coral polyps fed upon microscopic sea-animals which were brought by the wind; these polyps manufactured forests of rigid stone, immovable calcium trees which strangely bore no leaves and which, even more amazingly, reached their barren branches towards the wind which, paradoxically, did not exist for them. This has the sound of an old fashioned riddle but is nothing more than the plain statement of truth; the trees of coral thrust their fingers towards the direction of greatest current, towards the path of the incoming waves, which is the direction of the rushing trades. Here the polyps find the most abundant food; anchored to their stony homes they cannot pursue their prey; it must be brought to them; that is why coral reefs are always most abundant and spectacular on the windward side of an island. The stone trees in their turn shelter the lagoons; the lagoons capture the drifting sand; the sand provides footing for beach grass; these plants supply shelter and sustenance for insects; birds feed upon these; except for my breakfast of doves I would have gone hungry and would not have been sufficiently interested to note these happenings; the editor and the proofreader would not have been bothered and this chapter of this volume would not have been written.

The relationship between coralines and flamingos is not as fantastic as it might seem. Darwin long ago proved the connection between cats and clover. Field mice destroy the combs and nests of humble bees, the red clover depends upon humble bees for its fertilization. Over two thirds of the humble bees in England are destroyed yearly by these mice; near towns and villages the nests of humble bees are more common than elsewhere, a fact that must be attributed to the number of cats that destroy the mice. No cats, lots of mice, fewer humble bees, less clover seeds. Therefore clover depends upon cats; or to carry the illustration further it is the old maids of England who keep the clover going; for without old maids there would be a dearth of cats.

The concept of life as an intricate web puts a new aspect on our biological approach. There is no such thing as isolation; nature is a vast system of interlinking and ramifying co-ordinations. If one thread is pulled a hundred are shaken or loosened; the vibration is transmitted to the whole. There are webs which are concerned only with the maintenance of life, with the provision of sustenance in which the capture of one creature provides food for another, and which on its demise provides a similar bounty. Other webs are concerned with the functions of creation. Any person who is father to children is a link in a chain which has been forging since the beginning of time. The Chinese long ago grasped this idea and have made it an integral part of their philosophy; the grandfather and grandson are separate and successive molecules in a stream of life. Evolution, too, is only a woven fabric of complex pattern in which the design is controlled by time. Even emotions foster a chain of events; even after the lapse of two millenniums, the kindly hand of Jesus of Nazareth is visible in the halls and corridors of dozens of orphanages and hospitals; conversely the sequence of hatreds which had their genesis in the sorry turmoil of 1914 are indirectly slaying thousands of men on the battlefields of Europe though a quarter of a century has passed.

In a great city, or on a continent, the separate threads of life are not readily discernible. They are submerged in a tangled mass of fabrics superimposed one upon the other with connections so intricate that they are difficult to separate and follow. This is one of the joys of a tropical oceanic island. Life is tightly enclosed in a wall of surf, the strands begin and end within narrow borders. Because of this they may readily be traced to their conclusions or their general patterns are discernible.

An island might be compared to a prison. It is a prison without bars or cells, the only walls are the lines of gleaming surf, molten and shining as silver; the warden is circumstance. To be born on an island is to be a prisoner, few escape. The very fact of insularity sets the creatures of an island apart. The lizards that frequented the clearing of my hut often dashed down to the parapet of rocks overlooking the sea and there stopped as though they sensed that this was the edge of their world. They never ventured beyond this prescribed limit. Even the hummingbirds, which should have been free, terminated their whirling flights at the borders of the vegetation. There was nothing to hold them back; yet I never saw one venture beyond. That their close family relatives, the Ruby Throats of North America, would unhesitatingly fling their diminutive bodies across the whole five hundred miles of the turbulent width of the Gulf of Mexico is one of the wonders of the world; the Inaguan species never went beyond the surf. The impelling tide of migration passes them by; the whole sphere of their existence is bound, delimited by a wall of water.

How very wonderful and intricate this web of island life could be I had yet to learn. But the thought persisted. In the evening when I had camped in the shelter of a sand dune and devoured my scanty meal of doves and one wild duck shot during the day and roasted over a fire of driftwood, I pondered the idea and resolved to experiment by seizing on the first tangible event and following it through to its conclusion.

The event arrived sooner than I surmised and, as might be expected, arrived on the wings of the wind. Somewhere, out of the maze of low vegetation came a strong pungent odor. It was a sweet heavy smell, reminiscent of the fragrance of locust blossoms, or even of the cloying scent of sweet peas or lily of the valley. I knew it could be none of these and my curiosity was aroused. Here was an aural beginning for an adventure that might lead anywhere. The moon had risen and the soft sand was suffused with a delicate blue light that cast deep purplish shadows. Standing up I sniffed expectantly. The odor was gone, swept away on the gale. The only means of tracing it to its source was to creep close to the ground, trailing it in the manner of a hound following a rabbit.

For a few moments I was tempted to give it up, for to go crawling over the ground in the moonlight seemed sheer idiocy. So I laughed a little at my fancy, hesitated, and then decided to persist. The trail led down the slope of the dune and into a sandy valley. The scent was hard to trace, for it was shielded and disguised by a horde of other odors, by the rich hay smell of beach grass, the dry parched aroma of sun-caked earth, the musty reek of dead leaves and rotten wood. There were hundreds of similar fragrances, strange perfumes that I did not know existed until I concentrated on them. This was adventure in a new world.

The sense of smell is a neglected faculty. We may admire our friends' possessions, touch them, feel them and exclaim at their beauty or oddness, yet we dare not smell them. Only posies and perfumes are exempt; and even perfumes are to be sensed rather than remarked. This is a mistaken custom. Few sensations, for example, are more delectable than the clean smell of well-tanned leather, or the pleasant aroma of an old library. Yet to sniff a book frankly is unthinkable.

No sense is so apt to arouse memories as that of smell. The odor of tar, no matter where encountered, places me instantly in the center of a shipyard amid the busy tapping of adzes and the sonorous whine of band saws; the peculiar pungency of iodoform brings back the anxious evening in the hospital where my wife lay ill, and a vista of a long hall down which white clad interns and nurses scurried on seemingly interminable errands. The fragrance of maple immediately conjures up visions of crisp brown waffles and cups of steaming tea; asafoetida and an old-fashioned drug store which I used to visit are inseparable. The smell of new-mown hay is more potent than the sight of it; and there is no more stimulating experience then the released fragrances of damp earth after a summer thunder shower.

The odors that came pouring out of the thornbush were strongly reminiscent. A leaf that I crushed gave forth the spiciness of sassafras and I unconsciously fingered it to see if it was, though I knew that the nearest sassafras bush was nearly a thousand miles away! A beetle blundered into my face and I slapped it, crushing it between my fingers. Immediately they reeked of musk, a vile, unpleasant stench. Although I rubbed my fingers in the sand I could not get rid of it; it almost nauseated me. The musk attracted other beetles of the same species; they whirred and zoomed about my head; seemingly the purpose of the scent was for attraction.

The beetle smell nearly drowned the odor I was pursuing; only by diligent effort was I able to trace it to its source, a stunted tree from which hung thousands of tiny blossoms. These gleamed faintly white and when I shook the branches a cloud of filmy pollen went drifting off in the moonlight. The wind again; this plant depended on the currents of air for its propagation. What a squandering of pollen cells there must be!

Literally millions of powder-fine sperm-molecules went to waste that a few would chance on a receptive flower and complete their function. I struck a match and examined a blossom. It was very small and its stigmas were much enlarged and branched, almost plume-like, a thoughtful provision providing greater sticking surface for the drifting grains.

I settled back in the sand at the base of the bush. Seemingly I had reached the end of the trail. I had followed the strand of the web and it had led me nowhere. Instead I was faced with a mystery. Why, if this plant depended on the wind for its fertilization, did it exhale such a strong perfume? Certainly not to attract insects. Unlike the flowers of the prickly pear and the cactus it had no use for insects. Why then? I had to confess I did not know, and seeing nothing further I turned and started back to camp.

I had not taken three steps before a voice at my elbow said very softly—WHY? And I jumped and turned in the direction of the sound, and again it said—WHY?—or maybe it was just OH!—and then again and very softly—OH!

Perched on the ground beneath the bush I had just left was a small dark shadow. It was bobbing up and down rapidly as though immensely excited, and in a second began chattering in a low voice. Once again I struck a match, shielded it until it caught, and reached the flame out at arm's length. It flickered faintly and then revealed the rounded form of a small Speotyto burrowing owl. Just beneath its body was the dark shadow of its underground home carved out of the soft soil beneath the roots of the tree. I caught a brief glimpse of a pair of gleaming eyes staring fixedly at me before the match spluttered out. Dropping to the ground and crawling closer I lit another. The owl backed up a foot or so but did not flee. It was quite the smallest owl I had ever seen and in the yellow light it was mottled and barred with a pale earthy brown fading to cream and pale umber. Its plumage was smooth and rounded, and it was devoid of ear tufts or other appendages, which gave it the appearance of a soft sleek ball.

Its antics were ludicrous. It cooed and jabbered to itself, uttering chorus after chorus of droll notes, at times plaintive, then vociferous, or soft and pleading. Its tameness was amazing. Even when I stretched out my hand it did not fly but merely bobbed faster and shuffled to one side. When I reached my fingers towards its hole it went into a perfect frenzy of motion.

A sudden blast of air coming over the top of the ridge blew out the second match and left me in darkness. By the time I had adjusted my vision the owl was gone and even though I reached my arm full length into its burrow I could not grasp it, presuming it had disappeared there.

Returning to camp I dug a hole in the sand for my hips, curled into a knot, and drifted off into a deep slumber. Before dawn I awoke, chilled from the cool morning air; off in the dark the owl was calling again; the notes were more placid then, the low cadences flooded the dunes with their complaining. As soon as there was light enough to see I rose and walked over to the burrow. The owl was perched on the exact spot where I had seen it the night before. When it saw me it stopped chattering and sat motionless. With a feeling of regret I raised the .410 and fired. The poor creature dropped in its tracks, quivered once or twice, and was still.

With a knife I slit its abdomen, extracted the stomach and laid it on a palmetto leaf. It was full and I squeezed its contents on the green tissue. The stomach contained the partly digested remains of a small anolis lizard, the disjointed segments of a scorpion, and most amazing, the nearly complete, if crushed, carapace of a *Panopeus* crab. *Panopeus* are tiny crustaceans, scarcely more than an inch in width, and they are clad in drab mud-colored hues. The lizard and the scorpion were not surprising, for these are normal articles of burrowing owl diet; the occurrence of the crab shell was beyond all expectation. My single strand had now become three; two threads led landward, the third towards the sea. Discarding the lizard and the scorpion, I cleaned off the remains of the crab, tucked it in a vial, and shouldered the bag.

Sometime during the night the burrowing owl had ventured somewhere along the coast and snatched the body of the crab in passing. Just where was a puzzle. I searched along the beach closely. There were no mud crabs in evidence. Still more puzzling was the fact that mud crabs seldom if ever venture in open air; their bodies are not equipped for prolonged exposure. The chain of events had led me from the *why* of the perfumed bush to the *how* of the owl, two queries that confront the naturalist constantly. How and why; the how is sometimes answerable; the why almost never.

I did not solve the question of *how* until a day later when I swam across the beautiful green channel of Lantern Head more than thirty miles from the place where I had seen the owl. In the meantime the strand of the scorpion forced itself on my attention. I was busy stripping the bark from some fallen palm trunks looking for lizard eggs and for new lizards when I carelessly thrust my fingers into a crevice. Several unseen scorpions occupied the crack and resented my interference. One antagonistic individual nabbed me in the end of my index finger with its tail and then scampered away to the shelter of some undisturbed bark. With an exclamation of pain I hung on to the injured member and gritted my teeth. The finger throbbed violently and stung virulently. Momentarily I expected to see my hand swell as the poison took effect. My first thought was to get back to the settlement as quickly as possible, but then I reflected that a much more sane course would be to take things easy. Still gritting my teeth I sat down on the sand and tried to relax for a few moments. In ten minutes the finger had not shown signs of swelling and the pain had subsided slightly. In twenty minutes it stung no worse than if a bee had pierced it; ten minutes later the pain was completely gone, the only evidence of the injury being a tiny red dot where the barb had entered. Like nearly everyone not fully acquainted with scorpions, I had believed scorpion sting a serious poison. Since then I have been bitten several times and the result has always been the same, a painful half hour with no further infection.

Lantern Head is a deep indentation in the Inaguan coast, a landlocked shallow natural harbor with a peculiar rock formation at its mouth from which it derives its name. In places the shore is lined with mangroves; clinging to the roots of these was a thick culture of small oysters and mussels, many of which were raised well out of water when the tide was low. The oysters were a welcome addition to my diet of doves which was beginning to pall. I pulled several bunches off the outermost arched roots and found a half dozen *Panopeus* crabs stowed in the crevices. These scampered away and sought new shelters. No doubt my burrowing owl had lit somewhere on a mangrove root and spied the moving form of a mud crab and devoured it on the spot.

The third link of this zoological chain was forged quickly. One of the *Panopeus* crabs fell on the smooth mud beneath the mangrove roots and was immediately seized by a larger mangrove crab, a brilliantly colored crustacean with scarlet claws and legs which rushed up and down with a quick motion and tore out the *Panopeus'* pincers, rendering it helpless. The mangrove crab then did a brutally cruel and savage thing. Holding the helpless mud crab in its claws it deliberately pulled off its victim's legs a joint at a time and let the fragments fall on the silt where they lay with tiny bits of shredded muscle quivering at the ends. The bestial action was heightened by the sardonic, never-changing face of the crab with its bulbous stalked eyes which appeared to regard the proceeding with diabolical calm. The seemingly quiet world of the mangrove roots was a place of deceit; life there was merciless; to relax for a moment was to court sudden and painful death. Everywhere existence was the same: the animals of the pool near my hut spent their lives pitting their talents and forces against the elements and against a horde of hungry carnivores; the owl lived because a lizard and a scorpion relaxed once too often and too well.

Struggle, bitter, unrelenting, never-ceasing strife is the portion of all earth's creatures. Conflict is as much a part of heritage as is form and instinct. Those creatures that do not go forward fall back; the weak are eliminated, only the strong survive; the defenseless must develop swiftness, the slow acquire armor, spines like the sea urchins or other means of resistance. There is no mercy for the swift that do not run, nor for the slow that do not use their protection—nor for men that do not cultivate their brains, the only weapon nature has given them. Crabs or lizards, men or nations are all actuated by the same basic principles: the *Panopeus* was dismembered because it failed to watch; likewise the civilization of Ancient Rome crumbled for much the same reason, the three hundred year peace that followed the Augustan Age brought with it security and ease—and carelessness and disintegration. The cruelty of crab to crab and man to man can probably be matched incident for incident. I have a very vivid recollection of a day in the small town of Samana in the Dominican Republic when on the orders of a high official a prisoner was forced by the police to lay his hands on the stump of a tree, and bayonets were driven through them and twisted in order to secure information in regard to a thievery. I also recall the finding of a man's mutilated body on a small island in the harbor of the same town literally hacked to pieces by machete blows—because the man belonged to the wrong political party. The Samanas of the world can be counted in the hundreds, they are the mangrove swamps of human existence.

The trail from perfume to bestiality was only a matter of three links, so it was not surprising that the fourth should carry me back to beauty again. Life is like that—a cosmos of contrasts. Unpleasantness and kindness exist side by side; loves and dislikes sometimes abound in the same household; the well-fed and the hungry live within a few blocks; donkey carts creak along the same roads that bear streamlined automobiles; jazz and symphonies are produced from identical instruments.

To my surprise, the mangrove crab did not eat the dismembered carcass of its smaller relative, so it was, at least, saved from the stigma of cannibalism. Instead it dropped the crushed body on the sand and stepped daintily away, no longer interested. This action, which was wholly unexpected, rendered the proceeding utterly futile. Why did the mangrove crab fail to make use of the food it had earned? What strange dictate of instinct urged it to commit wanton brutal murder? Did it derive joy in the sheer pleasure of killing? The eternal why again; there must be a reason—or need there? So many events in nature seem beyond explanation, completely wasteful and directionless. The spectacle of migrating robins perishing miserably in blizzards into which they prematurely blunder is a common example. Is the force which drives them out of the warm southland directionless or purposely extravagant? Here natural history approaches the realm of metaphysics.

The fourth link arrived in the body of an American egret, readily identified by its vivid yellow bill and black legs and feet. It did not see me, for after the incident of the *Panopeus*

I retired to a small bluff overlooking the waterway and sank out of sight on the sand to rest between two ghostly green sea-lavender bushes. The egret was sheer beauty. Dressed in plumage of spotless white, the bird gracefully floated down to landing on the edge of the water and poised expectantly, then slowly and elegantly stalked along the edge of the mangroves. Egrets are among the most artistic of living birds; they suggest purity and chasteness, both in hue and line; their lives are a succession of beautiful poses.

The egret earned a brief place in the chain of existence I was pursuing when with a lightning jab of its beak it impaled a mangrove crab, either the one that barbarously tore the *Panopeus* to pieces or one of its cousins several times removed, and devoured it. The bird was as merciless as the crab had been but its hunger was understandable; it did not indulge in any unnecessary tortures. And, having satisfied its appetite, it passed from the sphere of my observation by springing lightly into the air and flapping away on snowy pinions.

The departure of the egret put an end for the moment to my little game of what-comes-next. It also set the stage for the interweaving of the next strand. Because, but for the going of the bird, I would not have become acquainted with the blenny, nor would the great philosophical principle which the blenny illustrated have entered the course of the web which was being woven thread by thread. Thinking that the flight ended the search I walked over to the point where the egret had last stood and looked at its broad triangular tracks threading along the edge of the roots. They were evenly spaced until they reached the point where the mangrove crab had met its Nemesis. Here they left the silty mud and continued into a shallow pool of water between a clump of mangroves where they terminated abruptly under water at the place where the egret had taken its exit. Near the last print was a claw of the devoured crab which had become detached and fallen in the water.

The claw was the excited center of attention of a host of tiny fishlets which were crowding around the manna which had literally dropped from heaven. Here at one swoop were a hundred divisions to the main thread; strands that went off at a tangent. The fishes were accidental beneficiaries from the hunger of a creature which to them was purely nebulous, except possibly for the sight of a thin leg or long black claws reaching from the bottom of their world to its very top. An egret to a fish is a pair of feet and a vague shadow. Occasionally it is the shadow of death, when a long bill lashes out and with a slight splash snatches a minnow to the world of upper air from which it never returns.

The wave of excitement of the small fishes spread out in a widening circle as the innermost scrambled to the feast. Some came streaking hurriedly, thrusting aside smaller minnows and in their turn being thrust aside by still larger ones. The claw rocked and swirled at the pushing and shoving; once it started off on a straight line as a larger fish seized hold, but it was torn away again and mobbed by a fresh horde of hungry creatures.

Then I saw a very interesting thing. On the very edge of the melee of food-crazed animals was the algae-covered remains of a long dead razor-clam. Once this mollusk had stood upright in the sand but then it lay on its side in the water with the valves half open. Peering out of this shell was the head of a dark brown fish with a face so old and gnome-like as to have belonged to a book of fairy tales. Strange little tufts of fringed tissue took the place of hair and the eyes were soft and golden. There was almost an expression of amazed good humor, a look half of surprise and half of doltishness; yet an appearance of stolidity. It was a hairy blenny, a fish that was common in shallow places all around the island.

The blenny stared fixedly in its comical way at the surging minnows and did not move so much as a muscle. Even when the struggling multitude swept over my bare toes and within a few inches of its door it did not stir except to open and shut its mouth rhythmically as though it were chewing a wad of gum. When the crab claw was disposed of and the schools of feasting fishes had gone I stooped and very gently thrust my fingers toward the shell. The blenny stood its ground and it was not until I actually touched its body that it consented to retire into its den. Softly closing the valves I lifted the clam out of water and withdrew to the beach.

The bivalve contained a mass of fifty or more eggs all glued tightly together on the bottom half of the shell. Closely curled about these was the blenny. When I tried to pick it up it wriggled loose and once again curled about the spawn. I even held the opened shell in the water but the blenny would not leave; the eggs were its charge and it was guarding them to the last.

My experimental chain had reached the final link, for I returned the blenny and its eggs to the water to whatever fate the mangrove lagoon might have for them. The blossoms and their mysterious perfume, symbolizing the beginning of life, had started me on a trail in which death and beauty and primitive savagery were separate stations; the blenny and its eggs pointed out a truth that I had very nearly missed. Nature is cruel; she is wasteful; but she is also provident and kind and prodigal. Like the blennies which guard their eggs when they most need guarding, the young of the earth are protected in their hours of need, or are provided with a sum of guiding instinct, like those of the Sphaerodactylus lizards of my hut which went their way fully equipped to meet the ways of lizard life. Similarly, we are born with a mother's protecting arms

ready to receive us. Strife and brutalities and lost causes hem
us about and edge us in on all sides; but in compensation, the
force of love or of creation, if only evidenced in the blind
maternal instinct of blennies, which functions without reason,
is as potent as the powers of destruction. This is an old idea
which even the non-scientific ancients recognized, and forms
the basis of much of religion.

The evil and the good, the bountiful and the scarce, the hard
and the easy, struggle and peace, ugliness and beauty are only
successive links in the chain of life. Success for one is failure
for another, the price of living is dying; every action is transmitted equally and exactly, though perhaps in altered form, to
its next component. Between these extremes is beauty, sweet
perfumes and impelling experience. Had it been possible to
follow the chain of circumstance which began with the perfume and ended with the blenny to its ultimate and nethermost
ramification, there would have been evolved the entire scheme
of island life. The completed fabric would contain all there is
of living, the sum total of experience, of philosophy and of
science.

An island imposes restrictions on its inhabitants, places on
them limits which they cannot overbound; yet existence on an
island is not greatly different from that elsewhere. It is only
more visible and tangible. There is beginning and ending, frustration and compensation, ebb and flow; the essential diver-
gences are only those of quantity; the quality is the same.

CHAPTER X

The Creatures of Darkness

ONCE, I remember seeing in an art gallery a masterful painting depicting the death of the philosopher and poet, Goethe. The dying man was portrayed lying on a massive bed in a somber room with paneled walls. Through the closely drawn shades a fine pencil of golden sunlight was streaming, catching up the dust beams, and focusing on the invalid's lined face. One hand was outstretched, as if in supplication; the features wore an agonized expression and the lips were half opened, as though a word had just escaped.

Tacked on the frame was a tiny gold plaque, such as is universal in art galleries, giving the name of the artist, a few pertinent facts about the work and in larger letters the title. This was the expression—"Light, more light!" believed to be Goethe's last words, a cry interpreted to signify the yearning of a great mind, slipping helplessly into oblivion, for greater knowledge, larger understanding, for intellectual brightness in the darkness of his time.

It is a pretty story, and one that is worthy of the death of a man such as Goethe, but it is more probable that the cry for "Light, more light!" was really the agonized complaint of a very human person whose optic nerves, paralyzed by the approaching hand of death, no longer functioned and who was being enveloped in an increasing world of darkness.

A man is a creature of day and sunlight; in the dark, unless, like the blind, he has developed special senses, he is helpless and confused. The time of his activity is during the bright hours; without candles, electric bulbs or the benefit of the moon, his evenings are curtailed and rendered useless.

Nature has divided the animals of the earth into two spheres, the hordes of the day and the equal swarms of the evening. Large multitudes of creatures prefer the evening hours, some because of the protection it gives them from their enemies, some because their food is about at this time, and some because of the restful quality of velvety darkness. Yet most of these see well as is testified by the high development of their optic systems. Thousands of species of moths feed upon nocturnal flowers, many of which are beautifully colored; and these same moths hide in the shadow of leaves and under pieces of bark at the approach of the glaring, too obvious daylight.

Consider, for example, the owls. In the dead of night when human eyes are ineffectual, they go hunting. Flying low over the meadows they seek tiny prey, mere meadow mice, brown shadows in a black world—and find them. Compared to the perceptions of an owl our own vision is a dull thing, susceptible only to the most blatant colors. To an owl the shadows of a deep woods or the starlight over a marsh must be as daylight is to us. Can we say with any degree of certainty that an owl does not find the night-light as full of tone as we find the sunshine? And, may it not be a more restful coloring? Temperate climate people who live long in the tropics soon tire of the gaudy colors of that region and yearn for the softer, more pastel greens and browns of northern zones.

Shortly after my return from the trip around the island, which was completed two days after the passing of Lantern Head, I had an interesting experience. I arrived home hungry, inexpressibly tired, and unbelievably ragged. As soon as I had taken care of my specimens and had jotted down the observations I did not want to forget, I cast thoughts of work aside and spent the next few days relaxing, catching up on lost sleep, and indulging in the luxury of doing nothing. I loafed in the pool by the cliff and spent long hours on the beach watching the surf and the pelicans fishing near the reef.

One day I strayed further than usual up the coast to a point where the stone cliffs disappeared and were replaced by a long ribbon of gleaming white sand that stretched endlessly away as far as Lantern Head. Back of the beach were a number of old cocoanut palms, some of which had fallen and were decaying on the ground. Among these I found some fragments of lizard eggs of a type I had not seen before. Becoming engrossed in locating other clutches or perhaps the lizard that laid them I stayed quite late. Then, when I caught a fleeting glimpse of a sleek brown body that scrambled away under the bark leaving a wriggling tail in my hand as proof of its existence, I became very much interested and finally succeeded in capturing the owner, a dark brown, soft looking lizard with great liquid eyes which had golden yellow vertical pupils. It had no eyelids and the eyes moved under a crystal-clear cap somewhat like the crystal of a watch. Its skin was coated with tiny granular scales which gave it the appearance of fine velvet. Under each of its toes was a broad adhesive pad which enabled it to climb vertical tree trunks and even run rapidly upside down under branches. It was a gecko, and as subsequent examination proved, a new genus and a new species.

Although I had been over the same area many times I had failed to discover it before although the palms swarmed with *Anolis* and *Sphaerodactylus,* and the ground with *Ameiva* and *Leiocephalus* lizards. The vertical, cat-like pupils showed me the reason. This lizard, like the tiny insect *Sphaerodactylus* which was much more common, was nocturnal; its round of movement began when I, and all the other creatures of the day, had gone to sleep.

The next half hour's search failed to locate any more specimens and I decided to give it up and return another day with more equipment. Winding down to the beach again I sat down on the sand to watch the setting of the sun. The trade winds had slackened and a great mound of clouds were piled high in the direction of Cuba. They were rain cumulus and I hoped they would spread, because it had not rained for many weeks and my water supply was getting low. Presently the light began to turn yellow, then orange and a deep hush settled over the world. The pelicans stopped their fishing, the wind fell almost to a calm, the grasshoppers ceased their chirping, only the lapping of the waves broke the quiet.

The tide had fallen and near the top of the beach lay a long pile of seaweed that had been washed ashore and was strewn in narrow arcs as far as the eye could see. The sun turned cherry red, then became elliptical, and in an angry blaze settled behind the clouds, sending a momentary flash of green light before it disappeared. This green luminescence was almost a nightly occurrence and lasted for fifty or sixty seconds at the exact moment of the sun's sinking. Shortly after the sky became gray and then purplish.

Then in the darkness, from the piles of seaweed at my side came a faint rustling, like the swishing of fine silk. As I listened the sound became stronger, reached its maximum and continued steadily. I lit a match and looked downwards. There on the beach were hundreds upon hundreds of beach hoppers, little translucent crustaceans a half inch or so in length. They were hopping and jumping over the sand in a frenzy. It was the combined scrapings and bumpings of millions of these creatures that blended to make the rustling. Where were they a bare fifteen minutes ago? What brought these myriads of crustaceans climbing upwards through the damp clinging sand at the exact moment of nightfall? What invisible crustacean time signal told them their hour of activity was at hand down in the wet and the dark? Yet there they were, swarming where all day had been only blank sand and swirling water. Then, even as I watched, a number, disapproving of my presence, dug themselves in again, sinking smoothly and evenly as though let down by an invisible elevator.

The coming of nightfall was the signal for the coming of other nocturnal animals. The bushes and grasses began rustling with the movements of the hermit crabs; whirring moths swept past my ear and went on into the dark; beetles droned across the glades and blundered into my hair; a few mosquitoes sang busily, taking the places of the flies that had buzzed all day and were then asleep on the under surfaces of leaves. Back in the interior the low notes of a pair of night herons echoed across the surface of the saltpond and faintly I could hear them splashing in the shallows. High in the zenith the faint geese-like notes of a flock of flamingos came filtering down; every evening after dusk they circled the beach and then settled on the far side of the lake back of the settlement. Here they spent the night gabbling to each other; their tones were reminiscent of the chatter of old ladies at a sewing circle.

There were, however, few of the cheerful night noises of home. Inagua has no frogs. There are no shrillings and liquid callings of these joyous beings. There are no crickets, and no hearths for them to sing upon. There is none of the vast chorus of stridulating katydids such as fills any northern woods in mid-summer. The Inagua night sounds are all mournful and sad; or weird and plaintive. In some portions of the island, in the barren savannahs and in some of the dried salinas, there is only utter silence, unbroken except by the howl of the wind. The great interior lake was an exception; there the air was filled with a vast roar of screams and calls, with wails and complaints; the tone of sadness was still present but it was fortissimo.

Later in the evening, after I had deposited my newly found lizard in a safe cage, I went down to the rocks and sat for a while, listening to the noises and trying to identify them. Presently, out of the darkness came a sound that could only be described as *wop*. The *wop* was followed by a whistling sound and a long silence, then *wop* again. Straining my eyes I tried to see some form of movement; then, against the stars was the shape of a rapidly moving body which plummeted to earth. Sliding back to the house I seized a flashlight and went in the direction of the noise. The rays of the flash lighted the eroded coral, throwing the worn spires into gaunt fantastic shapes; on the very edge of the cliff was a pair of gleaming yellow eyes. The eyes did not move. Walking quietly in my tennis shoes, I crept nearer.

Suddenly the orbs disappeared and I caught a brief glimpse of a flash of brown feather and the curve of a long sickle-shaped wing. I thought the creature had gone but a sudden *wop* as it hit the ground directly in front of me announced its return. The brown feathers resolved into a long sleek body surmounted with a round head with a tiny bill. It was a nighthawk. Instead of flying away it shuffled across the rocks and then very deliberately sat down near a pile of seaweed. I walked over and crouched beside it. Accustomed as I was to the tameness of the birds of this lonely island, this did not seem reasonable. I thrust the flash in its face. It closed its eyes as if intensely annoyed, as no doubt it was, and remained in place.

The nighthawk was a perfect example of a nocturnal creature. The eyes were large and sensitive and their brilliant gleam was direct evidence of night living habits. Its plumage was drab and well camouflaged; among the open glades and gravel beds where it rested during the daylight hours it was all but invisible. The seemingly tiny mouth was deceptive; I knew that it was capable of tremendous extension, and acted as a highly effective net or scoop. The strong recurved wings gave it the darting flight with which it captures the insects on which it lives. These are snared in flight in a series of swift aerial evolutions.

With my hand I very gently shoved the nighthawk to one side, and as I suspected, disclosed an egg which was laid on the barren rock without benefit of padding or nest. At the touch of my fingers the bird flew into the air but was back again in a second and again shuffled over the precious shell. In the morning I returned and took a series of pictures with an ordinary folding kodak, and so willing to pose was this amiable creature that I was able to shove the camera in its face and even turn it slightly around so the light would strike it more favorably. In all my years of nature photography I have never had a more agreeable subject.

Soon the wind began to pick up again and I returned to the cliff near the hut where there was more shelter. The bare stone was still warm from the heat of the day and I spread out to rest and listen. The warmth crept into my body and before I knew what was happening I was asleep. For nearly an hour I dozed and when I awoke I became conscious of some vague sounds that I had not heard before. There were queer squeakings and clickings, the fluttering of wings and the rustle of branches. I rolled over and listened. The noises were very distinct. They seemed to come from the shadowy outlines of a tamarind tree just back of the beach. I moved up to the dark branches. There was a rush of wings, a sudden crescendo of shrill squeakings and a horde of bats swept from the tree. I could feel the air from their wings as they fluttered by my head. For a time they whirled in the sky, silhouetted by the stars, and then one by one disappeared into the blackness.

In the morning I went again to the tamarind tree. It was in full fruit. Light brown seed pods looking like fat, shortened lima beans hung on the branches in profusion. I plucked one and tasted it. It was mildly sweet, partly gummy in texture and contained two round seeds about the size of cherry pits. Numbers of the fruit had been chewed, and on some was the imprint of tiny sharp teeth. The bats had been feeding on the tamarind.

It was not this fact that intrigued me, for I knew that many tropical bats fed upon fruit, but the size of the creatures. In the starlight they seemed huge; besides I knew they might be a new species, or at least a form peculiar to the island. Inquiry among the Inaguans brought the information that back in the interior were a number of caves where the bats went in the daytime between their nocturnal excursions for insects and tamarinds. Here they were supposed to hang from the walls in the countless thousands. Knowing the native tendency for exaggeration I discounted the tales by about fifty per cent but thought the place would be worth exploring.

In order that I might reach the caves in some degree of comfort I traded a few odd articles of ship salvage for a donkey to carry my water and food, which is to say I traded my good possessions for one of the most cantankerous, puzzling, obstinate bull-headed beasts in all creation. I should have known better, for I saw the smirk in the eyes of the Inaguan who traded with me, and I should have seen the leer in the eye of the donkey. But I did not. In fact so elated was I at my acquisition that I felt almost like Shylock for driving a hard bargain, and when the animal patiently trotted after me up to the hut and permitted itself to be loaded with a vast bag of tinned meats and water I was certain I had a jewel. Even the faint brown stripe that reached from shoulder to belly escaped my attention and, in my ignorance, I did not realize that this was the mark of a wild ass only recently tamed from the interior.

The Inaguan who was the animal's owner neglected to tell the creature's name, so I christened it Griselda, the patient one. Patient indeed was this donkey. I finished the pack, strapped it tight, made sure I had a jar of formol to preserve any unusual specimens that came my way, and set out once more to explore. I was feeling very good that morning and for the first time in months found myself singing. It was "de blessin" again. The tangy smell of highly fragrant leaves filled the morning air; the trade whispered softly in the tree tops; its cool pressure fanned against my chest. A sense of well-being permeated my body. It was good to be alone with the sun and wind for company. The song finished, I began to whistle. *Tales from the Vienna Woods, Humoresque,* snatches from *Peer Gynt,* the *Meditation* from *Thaïs* went echoing down the glades. *Amaryllis,* minor notes from Puccini's *Butterfly, Old Man River, Orpheus,* the *Fledermaus;* I had no idea my repertoire was so varied. I was whirling to a climax on the dulcet notes of Debussy's *Afternoon of a Faun,* intent on the proper scaling of the music, when suddenly I was yanked unceremoniously from my feet and flung lengthwise on the ground. Dazedly, I looked up. Griselda was heading full tilt for the thorn jungle. She reached the edge of the bushes, turned, brayed demoniacally and then disappeared between the trees. I jumped to my feet and ran after her. She was nowhere in sight; food, water, everything had vanished. In the distance I could hear her clattering between the cacti.

Fully half an hour elapsed before I caught up with her. She was wound up in a lignum tree, snared hopelessly with the lead rope. Both her heels let fly as I approached, my camera and equipment were strewn all over the ground. Angry at being so rudely snatched out of the blandishments of Debussy and sore from the thump on the ground, I retaliated with a stout club. For a moment we had it hot and heavy, then Griselda quieted down and I reloaded her pack. I started out with the lead line; abruptly reached the end of the tether and came to a sudden halt. Griselda refused to budge. I beat her, I pushed, I yanked. She was adamant. In the depths of despair I even built a fire under her. She only moved a few feet to one side and stood still again.

I had about given up hope when for no good reason Griselda trotted ahead as quietly as a lamb. She was to have her fun in another way. Each large tree that was passed was used to dislodge the pack and crush its contents. Then she would turn her head and grin—I could almost swear it. Eventually I shoved her ahead until we emerged into a semi-open plain where there were no large trees. Here, I thought, I would have no trouble. But Griselda slowed down to a queer waltzing gait, almost a snail's pace. She would go no faster, certainly no slower. For the remainder of the day she acted miserably. When evening came we had progressed only ten miles—a very poor day's travel.

In a vile humor I unloaded the pack, tethered the donkey to a bush and spread a blanket. I felt hot, dirty and out of sorts. From the heights of elation I was plunged into the depths of dejection. Instead of Griselda I renamed her Timonias, after Timon of Athens, the famed Greek misanthrope who passed his days cursing all mankind.

That night will long be remembered as one of the most weird I have ever spent. I had hardly settled in my blankets when a horrible scream burst through the air. It was followed by another and still another. I sat bolt upright, seized a small pistol, and sprang to my feet. It was pitch dark and all around I could hear the scratching sounds of myriad crabs crawling over the rocks. Once more the high-pitched scream pierced the gloom. It was answered by another some distance away. Close by, Timonias was thrashing at her tether. I walked over and was met by a flail of thudding hoofs. They missed me by inches. She came at me with bare teeth; only the tether kept her back.

The loud ringing of hoofs on the bare rock soon told me the cause of her actions. She had caught the smell of her wild brethren and was anxious to join their company. In the dark I felt around for a club. There was none available. I had no idea what was the proper thing to do, my experience with donkeys was limited.

Through the dark I could hear the hoofs pattering as the herd circled the camp. The night became hideous with the sound of their braying. No African veldt with lions, baboons and hyenas resounded more violently to the howls of wild animals than the Inaguan bush did that night. I sat down, sweat pouring from my back. There was nothing I could do. Between the intervals of howling, giant land crabs with yellow claws crept all about, keeping me alert with their clatter. The din died down about an hour before dawn and I dozed into a fitful slumber.

When I awoke the sun was high above the horizon and the heat waves were dancing, making wavy images. My eyes were heavy from lack of sleep. Even Timonias drooped wearily. I cursed the day I acquired her. In a brackish pool, brown with the steeping of tamarind roots, I washed my face and doused my hair. It refreshed me considerably but dried with a sticky feeling. Sleepily I reloaded the pack, and turned again toward the center of the island.

Everywhere the ground was covered with tracks, long sinuous trails with double lines that marked the trails of the yellow crabs, scores of prints of little round hoofs and the cleft ones of wild cattle. There must have been hundreds prowling about, their imprints were everywhere. Once a splendid horse burst from a glade, snorted and plunged away again. The interior of Inagua must contain several thousand of these wild animals.

I found one of the caves later in the day. Its entrance was obscured by vines and was partly obstructed by rocks. After tying Timonias to a tree, I unloaded the flashlight and camera and stepped inside. The sudden change from glaring daylight

----

to darkness blinded me and some time passed before I could
see. Presently in the light of the flash I could discern a low
winding tunnel that vanished in the distance.

Moving forward, I found the ceiling becoming lower and
lower until I had to drop on my knees and crawl. The floor
was covered with a brownish, half-moist loam which smelled
like ammonia. It was guano, the decomposed droppings of
thousands of bats accumulated through the centuries. The loam
was several feet thick. The fumes were stifling and the air
seemed dank and heavy. There was a sudden clatter at my side
and I swung the flash in time to see an orange colored land
crab scuttle into a hole in the rocks. Presently the walls began
to widen again and I emerged into a big dark open space. The
floor at my feet dropped away for six or seven feet, and in the
dim light I could see a large pool of black water. The pool was
bitter salt. Everything on this island was steeped in salt, even
the caves. The reflections of the flash cast eerie lights over the
stained walls. Fifteen or twenty feet above my head the ceiling
soared away into the distance, supported by tall limestone pil-
lars covered with green mineral. Ghostly stalactites hung from
the roof and great shadowy holes went off in all directions.

I turned the flash into one of these recesses. Far up near the
top hung a living portiere of bats. They stirred restlessly, opened
their wings and shut them again with a noise that sounded like
the swishing of cloth. The air became suddenly filled with a
chorus of high-pitched voices, shrill falsetto squeakings and
rustlings. These echoed back and forth under the vaulted arches,
rising and falling in waves of sound that diminished eerily in
the distance. Feeling around the floor I picked up a stone and
flung it against the walls. It clattered back and forth, echoing
hollowly, and fell with a loud splash into the water. Instantly
the cave became alive. With a thunderous throbbing a thousand
wings beat the air at once as the bats poured out of their hiding

places. In great bunches they swept the length of the cavern; the vibrations of their wings pulsed through the arched ceilings. They milled about the flashlight by the dozens. The glare seemed to confuse them for they swooped close to my body. I could feel the cool gusts of air created by their fluttering wings and several times the leathery tissues brushed against my face and arms.

I hurled another stone. This threw the creatures into a panic and they rushed madly from one end of the cavern to another. Giving them time to subside, I unloaded the camera and flash gun. Propping the camera on a little ledge, I focused it on a hole full of bats. I then filled the flash gun and stepped around a corner of the cave, first opening the shutter. I pressed the trigger. There was a blinding flash of light, a thunderous boom and choking smoke. Coughing, I went back and closed the camera shutter. Then I noticed that not a bat was flying, though a number were twitching restlessly, no doubt disturbed by the smoke. I turned on the light again. The bats were all hanging in their holes where they had gone when they first quieted down. The flash powder had made a report like a cannon but not a bat stirred. I picked up another stone and tossed it against the walls. Instantly the cave was alive with fluttering forms. Another discharge of the flash powder produced the same re-sult. They did not seem to hear the artillery-like report of the ignited chemical; it was too heavy a sound for their finely adjusted ears. Their hearing was attuned to faint scratchings, the sing of insect wings, the rustle of leaves. For them the thunder of the flash powder did not exist.

With a net I scooped a half dozen from a recess in the roof and placed them in a bag. They made a terrific racket, fighting and squealing, struggling to get free. Laying the flashlight against a stone I pulled one out, carefully avoiding the needle-like teeth. It stretched and pulled, shrilling in high notes, angrily striving to bite my fingers. The great tissue wings wrapped about my hands, clawed to get free. I held the creature close to the light. It had the most gargoylish, yet human looking, face I have ever seen. None of the frowning stone figures on the high parapets of Notre Dame in Paris are more weird. And it had a most peculiar nose. A leathery tissue resembling a fleur-de-lis stood up stiffly on the end of it. The tissue must have been highly sensitive, for when I touched it the bat went into a perfect frenzy of squeaking. Its rage went beyond the bounds of mere anger; it vibrated from the end of its ludicrous nose to the tips of its recurved toes; its face twisted into unbelievable contortions; the teeth chattered like castanets. The eyes were malevolent, with an evil glint that belied their true character. For these bats—and most bats—are really harmless creatures, mammals which ask no more than to be let alone.

From its peculiar nose I identified it as a leaf-nosed bat belonging to the genus *Artibeus*—one of a tropical family related to the blood-sucking vampires. It is by means of their strangely convoluted noses and their ears, which are equipped with long delicate lobes and tissues, that the bats are able to find their way about in the dark. The wing tissues are also extremely sensitive. These are richly supplied with blood vessels and nerve endings; a bat may be said to be alive to its finger tips. I was reminded of the now classic experiment of that indefatigable Eighteenth Century naturalist, Lazaro Spallanzani. This incurably curious person filled a dark room with an intricate maze of threads and wires extending in all directions, and so arranged them that there was just enough space for a bat to pass between the obstructions. He then operated on a number of bats so they could not see or smell. Although the creatures flew back and forth for several hours in the room, at no time did they so much as touch a wire. The wing tissues and the nose and ear appendages are attuned to minute vibrations too fine for human perception. Thus a bat is able to capture insects in mid-air or find its way on a dark night through a forest of entwining twigs.

A bat is the very essence of nocturnalism. It is also one of the most remarkable animals in existence. The western world regards the bat as sinister, fit company for witches, a denizen of graveyards, companion of ghouls. The Chinese have the good sense—and the felicitation—to judge the creature in its proper light; to them it is a symbol of happiness, and is so pictured on their exquisite silks and embroideries. The fact that these people have recognized the animal's good qualities is an indication of their fine sensitivity and powers of observation. When nature produced the bat she succeeded in creating a very finely tuned mechanism, and accorded it a place which no other animal of creation can fill as well.

Bats have the distinction of being the only mammals which are endowed with true powers of flight. All the others which make pretense at the art are but clumsy performers, novices on a road which the bats traveled centuries ago. Flying squirrels, phalangers and similar mammals are but parachutists; they can glide or plane; only the bats can truly fly. Few of the birds can approach them in aerial dexterity; hummingbirds, swifts and petrels are, perhaps, their closest rivals; even these must acknowledge inferiority in control. A bat is capable of reversing its direction in its own length or of turning a complete right angle within a few inches while in full speed, feats attained by it alone.

Also, the bat is the only animal in the world which flies with its fingers, although a few hundred million years ago the reptiles went it one better when they produced the Pterodactyls which flew with the little finger alone! Some of these Pterodactyls attained a wing spread of twenty-five feet; the bats reached a maximum of five—but are still in existence while the reptilian digiti-aeroplanists have been out of circulation for an eon or two.

The bat uses all its fingers except the thumb, which is free and which functions as a grasping claw; the third, fourth and fifth digits are longer than the remainder of the arm. If an average man's fingers were produced in proportion they would reach from his shoulders to the ground and would be about the thickness of a lead pencil tapering to the thickness of a knitting needle at the ends. These finger bones are unbelievably elastic and may be bent almost double before they break. Yet they are so perfectly designed that they support the wing tissues rigidly while in flight.

The marvelous wing membrane, which is a very fine flexible tissue, is kept well lubricated with a special grease which occurs in the region of the nose and eyes. The care which is given to the wings is as great as the attention the birds give to their feathers; and a bat's wing is capable of a great many more uses than the pinions of a bird. Its actual lifting surface in proportion to bulk is much greater and is extended over a greater area. Even the space between the hind legs is utilized and most bats are equipped with peculiar spurs which are attached to the heels to help support this inter-femoral membrane, as it is termed.

This membrane, stretching from leg to leg, and further supported in some species by a flexible tail, serves a dual purpose. It is, first of all, used as a baby-basket, for the newly born young have been observed resting in its curved surface as in a pouch until the parent is able to transfer them to a more permanent place near her breasts. The membrane is also used by certain species as a retainer for food while devouring an extra large insect, such as a beetle. This in itself proves what wonderful aerialists bats are, for the action of eating the beetle is performed in full flight high in the evening sky. The difficulty lies in crunching the insect without losing the grip of the jaws or wasting precious fragments. The bat solves this problem by suddenly lowering its head to its skin basket where it chews its prey without danger of losing it. While this action is progressing the animal tumbles wildly in the air, plummeting downwards, but it is so perfectly adjusted to such acrobatics that it recovers in an instant and continues its flight.

Searching about on the floor of the cave beneath the holes where they slept, I found great piles of tamarind seeds. Apparently these *Artibeus* bats carried the fruits to the caves and chewed them at leisure or swallowed them whole at the tree. With a net I filled the bag to overflowing—a quarreling, squeaking mass of fur and leathery wings—and crawled outside into the sunlight. One by one I examined the creatures and permitted them to escape. Of the fifty-three that I captured only four were females. All the remainder were full-grown males. Lady *Artibeus* must be at a premium; the competition between males must be keen.

One of the females was carrying a baby, a queer little mite with a face that looked at least eighty years old. It was clinging tightly to her breasts, snuggled close into her fur. The mother tried to protect it and folded one of her wings over its body. I let her go and she soared into the sunlight. Between wing strokes I could see the huddled form of the infant hanging upside down clutching its mother. Until they are able to fly these baby bats must ride along with the parent as she wings her way in search of insects or tamarinds. They do not know how to fly at birth but must undergo a slow period of maturation. Unlike birds, baby bats have no nests in which to rest, and as the mother spends all her hours either flying or hanging from a cave wall suspended upside down by her feet, the babies must grasp from the day they are born.

It is a strange and paradoxical thing that the closest relatives of the bats are the insectivorous shrews and the moles. The shrews are almost all nocturnal, the moles irrevocably so. It seems a far cry from a mole burrowing in its damp tunnel of earth, down among the beetle grubs and the garden worms, to a bat with its tissue wings high among the stars. Yet in their general anatomy and particularly in their dentition there is a very marked affinity. Somewhere along the long road of evolution, marked with the milestones of failure and success, with the coming and going of a hundred species and genera, is a forked trail, one side leading into the airy spaces of the sky, the other into the depths of the clinging soil. The bats took one path, the moles the other.

Few accomplishments are attained without sacrifice; the bats have paid their penalty to nature. For the privilege of flight under the glowing lights of the evening sky and for the advantage of being able to pursue their insect prey or seek the fruit they subsist upon instead of crawling through the mud and leaves like their relatives, they have relinquished the ability to walk. A bat on the ground is a caricature of the creature that dodges among the clouds. In order to perfect the mechanism of flight they have been forced to reverse the position of their knees which are turned outwards and backwards like our elbows. Hence the best most bats can do is an awkward shuffle, although a few such as the Vampire still retain a mouse-like quality. They have also paid another penalty, for the reversal of the knees has made it impracticable for them to stand upright. From birth to death they must hang head downwards, forever suspended between heaven and earth.

Once I kept a number of little brown bats in a cage through a northern winter. From the first cold days of November to the warmth of early April they hung immobile, head downwards. At times their huddled bodies were covered with a coating of hoarfrost until they looked like rows of suspended snowballs. To the touch they were as cold as marble and as stiff as though *rigor mortis* had set in. There were times when I was certain they were dead; but deep inside their bodies, that wonderful gift called life still persisted, and in the spring on the first warm day they relaxed and began squirming and chattering. The total number of days they had hung suspended was one hundred and twenty-seven; in all those hours the feet never relaxed, nor did they change their position. That is a long time to hang in one place. An equivalent action would be for a man to pass the winter asleep on his feet, though, no doubt, many business men would be willing to swear they have witnessed a comparable display among their employees. How very tenacious this suspension is, however, I did not realize until I found the second cave.

This cave turned out to be a magnificent place of dome-like arches and fretted ceiling. In places the roof had fallen in, leaving jagged holes through which the sunlight streamed in long fingers. The light gave the cave a soft unearthly glow which faded in the distance to utter blackness. I had difficulty finding the cave and only vague direction to guide me. If it had not been for the bats I probably would not have found it at all. With Timonias tied safely to a tree, I was making camp, chopping some wood for a fire and preparing a scanty supper. The sun had gone down and the sky was becoming tinged with deep purple. To my surprise I saw what I thought was smoke issuing from a distant hillside. I knew there was no one within miles and the geology of Inagua was not volcanic. The wisplike smoke grew thicker and I dropped what I was doing and dashed over. When I came closer I saw it was not smoke but a horde of bats coming out of one of the holes in the roof. The twilight had deceived me. Hundreds were pouring out of the cavern; in a steady stream they rose out of the ground and disappeared in the velvety dusk.

Early the next morning before the sun had risen I found the entrance of the cave with a flashlight and went inside. I wanted to see what happened when the bats returned. The cave was very dark and mysterious, a feeling helped, no doubt, by the fact that I was alone. Only a few bats were visible. Why these had not gone out with the others I could not guess. In one place there were three hanging close together. I reached out and touched one. It was dead. Only its skin held it together, for inside it was dry and powdery. My fingers dislodged the mummy and it went fluttering to the floor. The others had died similarly. Old age, disease, or whatever causes the demise of bats had come upon them in their slumber. But although their flesh and tissue had become dried and mummified, though the life had gone out of them, their tiny claws still held them in place just as they do when they are in dreams. Even death could not relax their hold upon the rocks.

I made myself comfortable in one corner of the cavern and waited. Presently I dozed, for when I wakened a faint radiance was streaming through the opening in the roof. The bats were returning. Vaguely against the sky I could see their forms fluttering above the hole and could hear the vibrations of their wings as they entered. More and more came to the hole and fluttered into the cavern. Soon the place was filled with their chirping and mice-like squeaking. They must have brought back some tamarinds with them because I could hear them munching the fruit and dropping the seeds on the floor. I sat very quietly so as not to disturb them. Some even hung themselves near my head. I could feel the air pulse as they swept by, and could hear the soft thuds as they swooped upwards and caught the rocks. Presently the gray began to turn pink. A great mass of them was pouring in the hole then and the vibrations of their wings filled the air. At times the sky was completely darkened as they swept across the opening.

They were fleeing from the light. Into the darkest portions of the cave they went, far into the shadowy corners. Little by little the chirpings and the squeaking ceased, the flutterings and the shufflings became still. One by one the bats suspended themselves in the crevices—living portieres of brown fur and wrinkled wing, row upon row, tier upon tier—and went to sleep. The pink glow around the hole turned red and very gently a ray of sunlight stole into the cavern. The day had come, with its activity for half of nature, and its complete stillness for the bats.

CHAPTER XI

The Mysterious Migration

Because of a wedding party in which I had neither part nor interest, I happened to see a very wonderful thing. Like so many tropical weddings, these nuptials began some months too late and ended quite a few hours too early. They celebrated the climax of a romance, somewhat gone stale, between a mulatto girl whose name I cannot remember and a black boy called George. The fact that the bride was about to be delivered of a child, and was already the mother of several children by virtue of previous adventures, did not dampen the ardor of the wedding guests, but served to increase their joy, helped, no doubt, by copious quantities of rum purchased from a tiny liquor shop in the settlement. The noise of the celebration, augmented by a pair of monstrous drums and several guitars, by some queer trick of acoustics carried across the glades and flooded my clearing with clashing sound until the small hours of the morning. Finally I could stand the din no longer and, weary from hours of tossing to and fro listening to the hundredth repetition of a chorus which stated over and over again that the singers wanted "no peas no rice nor cocoanut oil," I dragged irritably out of bed, donned shoes and shorts and went out into the moonlight.

For a time I wandered aimlessly about and then turned into a donkey trail that wound down to the seashore. Presently I emerged from a great bed of cactus and prickly pear near a huge mound of rocks on the very edge of the beach. Here the surf was sliding up very gently, slithering in long creeping fingers between the rocks, etched in vivid highlight by the gleam of the moon. Far away the pulsations and shouts from the belated wedding still throbbed in the night air but these sounds were no longer of any importance. Instead the roar and sigh of the gently rising surf occupied my half-conscious hearing. The air was warm and heavy with perfume; the trade winds had slackened to an unusual calm. For the first time that evening I felt soothed and dropped on the smooth sand where I drifted into a heavy sleep.

On and on I dozed and did not stir for nearly an hour. But then into my half conscious senses there crept a multitude of little sounds that I had not heard before—faint scratchings and clatterings, queer little noises barely audible above the surf. Once a mockingbird in the bay lavender back of the beach broke into liquid melody, trilled half-heartedly, and then lapsed into silence. But the scratchings continued.

Presently they became more frequent, more pronounced. I raised my head. Up on the white beach, gleaming silver in the moonlight, were moving small shadowy forms. In long windrows they were gliding out of the dark bushes and creeping down to the surf. Faintly I could see the glisten of the salt water as it reached their bodies and drenched them with its coolness. For a second their forms showed half smothered in foam and then they disappeared. It was their clattering over the seashells that had awakened me.

Some moments passed before I realized the full significance of what I was watching. The shadowy forms were crabs—not the checkered *Grapsus* crabs of the surf nor the crustaceans of the dark blue water, nor yet the ghost crabs that flitted like shadows along the sand just back of the beach, but land crabs— queer round-bodied creatures that lived in holes far back in the interior. They did not belong on the seashore, but had their being in those dry portions of the island where big cacti reared their heads above the soil. There were two kinds of land crabs on Inagua, in addition to the ubiquitous hermit crabs—small purple crustaceans about as big in body as a clenched fist and big yellow fellows with tremendous saffron claws. I had seen them miles from the seashore, as far back as the borders of the great central lake where they rambled about the tangled thorn glades and the barren savannahs seeking the twigs and bits of green vegetation on which they feed. But they had not been visible for a long time—ever since the period of high wind when I burned the wreck of the *Basilisk*. No rain had fallen for weeks in succession and the crabs were keeping close to their holes, sleeping away the hours in drowsy somnolence. Back in the interior it had become very dry and the mud had split in jagged cracks and the dust rose as one walked.

Strange that they should be there on the beach. I looked again. In a continual stream they were pouring out of the bushes and sliding down to the sea. There must have been hundreds of them; and there was an air about them of something very important; something that would not be brooked. Even when I jumped to my feet and strode up the sand they did not pause but merely scrambled to one side and continued down to the surf.

Then I remembered.

Far back in the hinterland of the island, miles away, it had rained that day, a downpouring drenching tropical rain that filled the dry salinas to overflowing and flooded the hollows. The rain had lasted for several hours and had turned the feathery dust into slimy slippery mud. The drops had not ceased until just before sunset and the slanting rays of the sinking sun had flared into the sky, making a long arched rainbow which stood out vividly against the dark mass of clouds behind. This rain then was what the crabs had been waiting for, hidden deep in the cavities of their holes. And when the precious water came down, wetting their bodies and turning the land into a miniature sea, these crabs knew in some unexplainable way that their hour had come. In the countless thousands they deserted their underground houses and ventured forth into the open air. A sudden urge had taken hold of them, all at once, an urge that with magnetic power turned them all in one direction.

The time had come to return to the sea.

Many hours had passed, a full year had gone since they left their mother ocean and it was time to return. But not as they came. The beaches and bush trails had swarmed with them that day a year gone, so thick that one could scarcely walk without crushing their bodies. They were very tiny then, barely an inch in length, and the larger birds had held joyous revel and had stuffed themselves with young crabs until they could hardly fly. They had seemingly come out of nowhere; for a few days they had swarmed and then little by little they disappeared into the jungle, into their lonely retreats in the interior. Creeping over boulders and stones, threading between the lignum vitae, struggling under the tangled masses of the prickly pear, they had made their way, meeting death and disaster in a thousand forms, growing the while—some of them— until the inland country had swallowed them up.

In the moonlight I cornered one of the advancing crabs, a purple one with yellow spots, and picked it up. Beneath its body was a great purplish mass tucked under the shelter of the apron. The crab was female and the purple mass was her eggs. She struggled to get free, bit at me with her claws. I dropped her to the sand and tried to make her go back into the bushes. But an instinct stronger than fear possessed her that night. Stepping daintily sidewise, moving each of her legs in consecutive precision, she menaced me with her claws and ran to pass between my feet. I let her go and she dashed the remaining distance to the surf and was swallowed in the bubbles.

There, I knew, though I could not see it, for this is the way of these crabs, a wonderful thing would happen. In the cool depths, in the shelter of some dark crevice safe from hungry fishes the weary mother would shake off her burden of purple eggs. Just below the area of the surf where the bubbles churned the water into silvery spray the eggs would hatch, casting forth their spawn. And the female, exhausted by her long journey, by the vicissitudes of her life on dry land, would try to struggle back to the interior again. Some succeed to live a short while before they leave their whitened bodies in the rocks to bleach in the sun; others fall easy prey to ravenous carnivores, perishing before they are out of the surf; but it does not matter, for their hour of labor is finished, their destiny fulfilled. And I also knew that if the life history follows the pattern of most other crabs in a few hours or days the sea near shore would be afloat with vast swarms of micro-creatures, the spawn from the purple-colored eggs—queer, gargoylish, outlandish looking spawn that in no way could be conceived to be crabs.

Scientists call these spawn zoea, which is a word meaning life. Smaller than the head of the smallest pin these transparent apparitions float through the water, looking like Martian mosquitoes, unbelievable creatures invisible save under a strong lens. For days their function would be little more than to drift, kicking vigorously with feather-like legs, peering into the water with big black eyes, seeking the light, and devouring everything that came within reach. Hundreds would disappear down the craws of other creatures, larger than themselves and equally voracious. Some would perish in the folds of the stinging tentacles of the coral polyps; other hundreds would be cast ashore to desiccate miserably on the dry sand; still others would be carried out to sea and would be lost. But in the end there would still remain many thousands to moult their skins and change to a new form.

In the new form, retaining none of their original characteristics, they would be known as megalops, which is to say, they would still be outlandish looking creatures. But in this new shape they would bear some faint resemblance to a crab, although a horrible misshapen sort of crab with a wriggly tail and a pair of claws in proportion to nothing except its appetite. In this megalops stage the crab-to-be turns cannibal and greedily devours its younger brothers and sisters which, not so fortunate as itself, have not yet attained full megalops-hood. Nor does it satisfy itself with young zoea, but munches its grotesque way through life devouring everything in sight, shedding its skin, and growing the while until it moults for the last time and emerges, wet and ever so tiny, on the beach as a perfect crab.

But not yet is this midget a land crab, for that is a matter of training. Its ancestors, back in the remote centuries, took a few hundreds of thousands of years to accomplish the transition from sea to land, at first clambering on the rocks of some ancient sea, poking their heads into the air and then dashing back again. So this baby crab recapitulates the history of its ancient relatives. In the dark of the evening, for it becomes nocturnal and no longer seeks the light, it creeps up on the pure sand of the beach. But not very far. The sea is still its mother and like a chick with a hen it dashes back to her for protection. And it needs protection, for death stalks the beach in a thousand forms.

The greatest danger is that of drying up. Tucked away under its eighth-inch body is a set of diminutive gills, tiny little fringed tissues hidden ingeniously away where the gritty sand may not reach and injure them. In the deeps of the water these gills had served it well, gathering the oxygen from the brine, distributing it through the tissues, and in all its babyhood these gills had been comfortably wet. But when the epic moment arrived when the baby crab, drawn by some unaccountable instinct, struggled its way through the last inch of foam and stood wet and dripping in the open air, it must have felt a surge of well being. The gills, which before had laboriously separated the water-clinging oxygen, must have drunk in the free air, soaking it up in quantities.

It is a cosmic thing to step suddenly from one world into another. However, it is probable that the baby crab did not think it cosmic at all, for baby crabs function chiefly by blind instinct. Instinct coupled with activity caused the crablet to struggle further up on dry land, fully six inches out of the surf. It must have been a terrific struggle, for, remember, the infant is probably an eighth of an inch in length. Tiny sand grains must have been as great as boulders; a half-buried sea shell a veritable mountain.

Presently, back in what serves the creature for a mind, comes a feeling that all is not well. There is a tight feeling around the gills, a dry, uncomfortable, oppressive sensation. Panic-stricken it dashes back to the sea. But only for a time. Soon there is a desire for the air again, for the warm wind that glides over the beach, rustling the leaves back of the sand.

And so for a period, the tiny creature repeats the story of its ancestry, the stepping on dry land and the returning to Mother Sea again. Little by little, the dry land gains ascendancy of the instincts of the tiny mite; only it is not so tiny now, for it has moulted a number of times, casting aside its shell and increasing in stature. The gills have become accustomed to the air, though they must still be kept moist. To aid them the body has become equipped with an air chamber which takes over the duties of breathing, relieving the tender gills.

In time there comes a day when in a vast horde the swarming beach crabs desert the shore and step back into the dark mystery of the island. It is the crossing of their Rubicon. For a full year they will not see the ocean again, and when they return their life's purpose will have been accomplished. Many will never see it again. But dauntless they move ahead. Go inland, their instinct says, go inland to the very center of the island.

Hundreds fall by the way. Some are killed by birds, some perish by accident, falling into deep holes from which there is no escape. The latter die of starvation and thirst, for the islands are places of little water. Only by nibbling on little twigs and on green vegetation can they secure the water they need so badly. The gills still must be kept moist. Should they dry, even slightly, death will quickly follow.

Above all they avoid the sun. Ten minutes' full exposure in the sun means certain disaster. Crabs have no sweat glands to keep them cool and, when the tropical rays beat down on their purplish backs, their shells become so hot they can scarcely be touched. But the crabs do not live that long. With the first sudden rise in temperature they become drowsy, their legs fold wearily under them, and they fall to the ground. Once fallen they never rise again.

I discovered this quite by accident one day when I cornered a crab in an open glade. Frantically it tried to reach the shade. It even lost all fear of me and tried to scramble between my legs. But I did not know the reason for its panic and kept it in the open. Hardly three minutes had passed before its claws fell weakly to the ground and it toppled on its face. A moment later it was dead.

Out of the thousands that die by the way a certain number reach the appointed place and distribute themselves over the land. In the shade of the bushes and around the roots of the trees they excavate deep holes, long curving cavities in the soil.

With their claws they dig out the loam, roll it into little balls, and carry them, one at a time, to their doorways. In the warm tropic nights they go forth to feed, clipping the succulent jungle twigs and carrying them back to their dens.

In the months that follow they grow, casting aside their shells, becoming more and more amazing in appearance. By November they are fully adult--purplish creatures with grotesque gnome-like faces. And to make them even more weird their eyes are set on stalks and their mouths open not up and down but sideways.

The rainy season passes and afterwards the sun shines with tropical fierceness. The ground dries out to powdery softness and great cakes of hard mud take the place of lakes and ponds. The vegetation withers, loses its succulent greenness, and becomes dry and dull. And these are the gray days for the land crabs, for they dare not venture forth to feed. Only in the cool of their holes is there moisture enough to keep them alive. February glides into March and March into April. The sun becomes more intense and only the cacti appear to remain green and fresh.

Particularly do the females need the dampness, for they have become laden with eggs. In great purple masses they hang beneath their aprons. There are hundreds of these eggs, each about the size of a pin head, all glued together in a viscid mass. It is time to go--if only the rains would come.

A female stirs in her burrow. There is a feeling in the air. Off in the distance somber gray clouds are forming, gathering in sullen masses. Thunder rolls fitfully and dies away. The trade wind is gone and the air is still--very quiet and heavy. It is terribly hot. Across the dry salinas the heat waves are dancing, making queer images. The clouds pile up, higher and higher, jet black in the middle. Thunder rolls again. The sun drops towards the horizon, tinging the world with refulgent gold. From the direction of the clouds a new odor drifts across the jungle. It smells fresh and green and cool. Suddenly from the gathering darkness there comes a rush of cold rain and in a pouring, drowning deluge the water beats into the soil.

Down in their burrows the crabs are frantically removing the walls of their dens. Hastily they roll aside the little pellets of brown soil and carry them away. Through the newly formed openings the water seeps in in an ever growing stream. It soaks into the soil, turning the round pellets into oozy mud. The time has come at last.

In vast hordes, from far and near, the crabs break out of their dens and creep through the rain-soaked vegetation. Their shells glisten with the moisture and the lightning throws their bodies into high relief. It is the hour for which they have been waiting, day after day, week after week. Nothing turns them aside. Over rocks and vegetation, through slimy mud and tangled vines they come. In some unaccountable manner each purplish body has become polarized towards the ocean. Fresh water does not deceive them, nor the brackish pools left by the rain. It is sea water they want, the bitter salt ocean and the crashing surf. Possibly they recall in some unknown way the scenes of their grotesque babyhood, when as zoea and mega-lops they had their being in the blue ocean. Hour after hour they move onwards without stopping to feed. The eggs must be spawned before the ground dries up again, the eggs that carry the whole hope of the race.

I stirred on the rocks and looked up again. Far in the east was a faint glimmer of gray and I noticed that the moon was very low. For nearly four hours I had sat watching the crabs pouring out of the interior. Wave after wave had marched out of the bushes and had flung itself joyously into the foam. In a few days a new horde of crabs would be born to go through the same cycle again. What strange power did the

ocean hold over these errant children of hers that she should
call them forth that they might give life again? And by what
means did she guide them the weary miles out of the interior?
Was it the roar of the surf, the swish and sigh of the breakers
that beckoned them on, or some vibration too fine for human
ears?

I listened intently, straining for some hint. Even as I heark-
ened, the east began to turn pink. For the first time I became
aware that the drums from the wedding party had ceased.

CHAPTER XII

The Quest of the Firebirds

AFTER the migration of the land crabs a change seemed to come over the round of life on the island. The continual howl of the trade wind slackened; frequent gusts of pattering rain fell, dried in a few hours and fell again. There was not enough moisture to fill the salinas but enough each day to make the air heavy and humid. Mosquitoes began to make their appearance in the evenings, breeding in holes in the rocks where a little water had collected. It was no longer pleasant to go prowling at night in the moonlight or to sit on the rocks by the sea. The great saltpond back of the settlement, which every day had been filled with companies of flamingos and sandpipers, became a great empty space glittering in the glare of the sun. The heat increased and the glare on the white salt was almost intolerable. The sandpipers had gone north on their long migration, disappearing during the night; the flamingos had filtered away in twos and threes, heading in small groups for the very center of the island.

It was then the first of May. A deadly spirit of monotony seemed to pervade the atmosphere. This was particularly noticeable in the settlement. There the only relief was the nightly religious orgies of the Daxons; the pulsations of their drums throbbed endlessly through the saddened streets. Before and after these celebrations a few gangs of blacks and mulattoes hung in groups on the deserted corners. There was little gaiety. The groups hushed when I approached, then resumed talking in low tones when I had faded out of sight in the dark. They did not laugh and joke, or play pranks as a

similar gathering would have done in Haiti. The general air
of hopelessness and shiftlessness was apparent everywhere.
The world of these surf-encircled people was crumbling to
pieces around them; instead of bending their energies to re-
creating it they were allowing themselves to be swept along
with the tide of easy dissolution. Even doorsteps which could
have been repaired in ten minutes with a few strips of wood
or fragments of stone were permitted to fall of dry rot; it
was simpler to do without them than to rebuild.

There was no leadership on the island. The one family of
mulattoes which might have, by force of example or unselfish-
ness, contributed to the welfare of the settlement was passing
the days in careless somnolence, or exploiting the little remaining resources of the island for its individual benefit. The black
commissioner was helpless. He was doing his level best, but
like the others he was enmeshed in a web of circumstance.

Monotony and frustration were written on every face, in
the very deportment of the inhabitants. I cannot be sure I
blame them too much. For all my interest in natural phenomena
and my fresh background of the outer world I was beginning
to slow down. The heat had something to do with it, the complete sense of isolation fostered the condition; lack of outside
stimulation, of literature and music, gay companionship, caused
a slackening of activity. Birds and beasts, as wonderful as they
are, pall at times. I began finding excuses to sit and loaf. Yet
I had been on the island scarcely half a year; these people had
been born here, had been faced with insularity from the moment of their genesis. Even this, in many cases, was not under
very happy circumstances. Illegitimacy was common, blacks
bred with mulattoes, mulattoes with whites—as white as these
were—and these with the blacks again. The moral code was
low, a status to be expected in a colony that for long years had
fostered slavery and had promoted promiscuous breeding to

increase the working stock.

So, I was not altogether unhappy when I received a letter from the Museum requesting me to go to Santo Domingo and collect a series of *Hemidactylus* lizards for experimental purposes. Several weeks later I gathered together all my materials and engaged passage on one of the rare passing steamers for Port au Prince, Haiti. I closed the door of my little hut, saw my friend the spider emerge after I was out of its short sight and begin to weave its web across the lintel. I wondered if I would ever see the hut where I had spent so many quiet hours again. And, as the lumbering old Dutch freighter passed the rocks of my cliff I caught a brief glimpse of its brown roof nestling between the leaves. It seemed very tiny across the expanse of blue water.

I asked the captain if I might climb the mast for a last look at the island. From the height of the crow's nest I could see the full extent of the saltpond a mile inland glittering in the sunlight. A bright pink mass in one corner showed the position of the last remaining group of flamingos still in the lake. All the others which for weeks had stalked in its shallows had gone inland. Even as I looked the pink mass began to pulse, then broke into a scattering of scarlet motes. The flock climbed high in the sky, turned toward the beach, circled above the hut, and then with a faint crying noise, scarcely audible above the swish of the water, turned inland. In a few minutes they were gone and as the distance increased the island became a long thin line of green that faded into the haze and disappeared from the face of the earth.

Of what befell me on the Island of Hispaniola, of how I languished in a Dominican jail because a stupid official could not read my permit to carry a collecting revolver, and of how I quite inadvertently started a small inquisition, and in turn had the revenge of seeing half a town incarcerated in the same hoosegow, and of how I collected the necessary *Hemidactylus* is a long story and one that has no place in this volume. It is sufficient to relate that I returned home in time to witness the collapse of the era of inflation and the beginning of the American depression. The island of Inagua was frequently on my mind; but as a year slipped into two, two into four, and four into eight, I saw no possibility of returning to complete the tasks I had begun. The sight of the flock of flamingos leaving the coast for the interior particularly haunted me, and I resolved to return some day and make a series of photographs of these magnificent birds on their nesting grounds. I also intended to take a diving suit with me to continue my explorations where I had left off on the edge of the cliff by the sea.

The years of the depression were not altogether unfruitful ones. In co-operation with the Chesapeake Biological Laboratory at Solomons, Maryland, I engaged in some research problems dealing with the Chesapeake Bay and in order to further this program invented a steel diving cylinder in which, with my colleagues, I was able to spend long hours beneath the surface making observations of the sea life that came to our big plate glass window. The sights that we saw in the Chesapeake began an interest in the world of undersea that has never been satiated, and the possibility of exploring the reefs of Inagua loomed ever larger in my mind.

Desired accomplishments, however, frequently require a spark to cause them to crystallize into reality. The spark that returned me to Inagua was quite accidental. I had been to a musical show with some friends, and after the performance, stopped in a restaurant for late sandwiches and coffee. A newspaper lay crumpled on a chair and, the conversation lagging, I idly reached over and picked it up. The paper contained the usual round of daily happenings and I was about to lay it down again when a small headline caught my eye. Instantly I was all attention.

REVOLUTION ON TROPICAL ISLAND

Eight Americans and Twenty Employees Flee Uprising on Island of Inagua—Settlement in Flames

There was a brief and uninformative report of a riot and a battle between two factions. Little more. The article had apparently been inserted to fill space and the editor had clipped the story to its barest essentials. What Americans? What had happened to Inagua? The editor's office could give me little additional information. Unsatisfied, I was left to wonder.

After that I was unable to get the island out of my thoughts. I remembered the air of sullenness and despair, the whispering groups that loitered on the darkened corners. But more strongly I remembered the scattering flamingos that swept into the sky the evening I left. If I could get to the island in four weeks I would arrive on the exact date I departed. I could continue where I left off.

The first time I landed on Inagua I came like Neptune, striding out of the sea dripping with seaweed and with salt foam running between my fingers. The second, I arrived in the manner of Icarus, also of mythology, who for a time soared dizzily through space only to be hurtled to earth again. Only, unlike Icarus, I did not land with a bump but so gently that the impact scarcely disturbed the precarious balance of the baggage clutched between my legs. It was such an unorthodox way to land on a tropical island and was so startling that it was some seconds before I could recover sufficient composure to thank the almost naked but bronze and smiling gentlemen responsible for my temporary flight to heaven.

Actually I was delighted at what had happened. Not every-one has the good fortune to land on a tropical island in the mode of two Greek deities. It had all been very surprising. My steamer, a small freight and passenger vessel, filled to over-flowing with vacationing shopkeepers and vacuous tourists off on a West Indies cruise, dropped her anchor off the island a little after midnight. There was no moon, nor could I see the shore, but out of the east came the familiar nostalgic smell of jasmine and lavender that is so characteristic of the island. And with it came the roar of the breakers pulsing over the rocks, bringing a flood of memories.

I was glad to be back and impatiently waiting for a boat to take me ashore. After a half hour, in which the captain cursed and swore in voluble Dutch at the delay, for the only excuse for stopping at Inagua was my getting off, a motor boat came bouncing out of the dark bearing a stern-faced white man and a younger chap who spoke with an unmistak-able Georgia accent. They disappeared into the captain's cabin, performed mysterious rites over the ship's papers and then took me, after a brief inquiry as to my designs on the island, down to the launch. I was reminded of the trial when I first landed on Inagua. We had scarcely reached its deck when the steamer, tourists and all, signaled full speed ahead, scarcely waiting to pull up the anchor, and surged off leaving us in a world of darkness.

We rolled in close to shore and backwatered near the break-ers. Suddenly to my amazement there was a fierce blaze of electric lights and a whirr of machinery as a wooden platform hung on rope slings plummeted out of the sky and slowed to a halt beside the boat. Above my head towered an immense steel crane which supported the sling. Hurriedly we clambered aboard and clung to the ropes.

The platform swooped skywards, reached a zenith, swayed dizzily over the surf and then rocketed to earth on the top of the stone cliff. Somewhat flabbergasted, I stepped off and stared about. Six nearly naked young men, clad only in tennis shoes and shorts, stood draped in various queer attitudes about some boxes of machinery, while another crouched over a whining puffing winch. Above, a whole cluster of electric bulbs brilliantly lighted the scene. There had been no electric lights eight years before, no crane to hoist one, Icarus-like, out of the reach of the surf—nor were these nearly nude young men native islanders.

One even addressed me in a Harvard accent—and I realized what had happened. The "salt"—the island's one hope—had returned.

A tall slim chap—he with the Harvard accent—grinned welcome. He was coated, as were all the others, with a gorgeous coat of sunburn, a deep reddish brown almost of copper hue. Dabs of grease streaked his legs and arms and when I shook hands I felt a palm that was worn and callused. Obviously, this was not a man afraid to dirty his fingers. Somehow it was startling to hear this Harvard accent coming from a man who looked the color of an Indian.

Remarkable changes had taken place. Beyond the glare of the lights I could see some new buildings, all aglitter with steel and aluminum paint. The old ruins with gaping windows and holes in the roof were still there—looking like ghosts, as indeed they were—but the settlement carried a new air. A desert island was waking from a long sleep. In a moment I sensed that in the hands of these keen-faced, bronzed, athletic figures rested the fate and future of an island.

The story of these men and their industry is a dramatic and creditable one. They are the brothers Erickson, a trio of New Englanders, and their enterprise is a chemical business having

the harvesting of sea salt as its basis. Inagua was chosen because
of its highly saline sea water and because of the brilliant year-
round sunlight and sweeping trade winds which are necessary
for the evaporation of the brine. From the very beginning
they were faced with tremendous obstacles. The old salt beds
had to be completely reconditioned, ruined houses had to be
repaired and made livable, a machine shop had to be installed
—one of their expensive loading trucks fell into the sea while
being transported from ship to shore and had to be salvaged
from the depths—laborers had to be trained and educated to
the new scheme of things, and a power station created out of
thin air—a considerable task for seven pairs of hands even as
hardworking as those of the Ericksons and their colleagues.
The mechanical difficulties were conquered step by step but
the Ericksons reckoned without one condition—the accumulated poisons of years of monotonous insularity.

The Inaguans, some of them, had slipped too far down the
scale of decay and degeneration. In spite of the revivifying
and clean energy of the Ericksons, the smouldering tide of discontent and frustrations swelled into dangerous proportions
and burst into flame, first against the island's newly appointed
commissioner who was wounded with a shotgun and then
against the Ericksons who came to his rescue. They were be-
sieged in their home and their new machine shop and several
other buildings were burned. One employee was killed and
Jim Erickson was shot. They made a break for the boats to
stop a passing ship and drifted all the way to Cuba when their
engine broke down. In one brief hour all their efforts went
up in smoke.

Undaunted they began all over again and a new order has
come to Inagua. The old resentments are fairly well burned
out and a new cheerfulness is beginning to make itself apparent. If the Ericksons are given half a chance Mathewtown

will be transformed over the course of years from a place of creeping desolation to a pleasant peaceful tropical village. For these brothers are putting something more than mere hours of labor into their industry and their island; they are installing a sense of pride and, I believe, a portion of affection into their speck of sea-girdled earth. I should like to write more about the events leading to the uprising and the causes in back of it, for they are an intricate and absorbing story, but Jim Erickson has asked me not to. He says there is no sense in reviving old hurts or recalling events that had best be forgotten. I respect his wishes and admire his forbearance.

There was one disappointment. My old hut had completely crumbled to pieces and could no longer be used. Instead I took up residence on the outer edge of the settlement where I acquired a two-room house in fair state of repair for the magnificent sum of $3.00 a month. For an additional $3.00 I acquired the services of Celestina, a middle-aged black woman who did my wash and prepared my meals but whose most interesting accomplishment was singing "La Cucaracha," a result of several amazing years in Mexico. She did this with such great spirit and inflection of tone that I would have willingly have retained her for the sake of hearing her sing.

Although she did her best in the culinary arts, her meals were distinctly Inaguan and, as such, highly indigestible. Fortunately I received a reprieve now and then from her kindly attentions by dinner invitations from the Ericksons and a number from the commissioner. The Erickson dinners were always a riot of fun and the evenings spent with the commissioner in the tiny residency will long remain with me as among the most pleasant I can remember. Over our cups of English tea we swapped yarns and compared notes late into the night while outside in the dark the land crabs clattered and banged over the residency yard. England produces, in certain of her colonials, a very high type and Mr. J. V. Malone, appointed administrator of Inagua after the uprising, was typical of the men that make England's far-flung empire possible. Like the Ericksons he placed a considerable amount of affection into the affairs of his island.

There was another surprise. My old acquaintances the Daxons had prospered. Religion had become good business. I met them both the morning after my arrival. Thomas was arrayed in a magnificent yellow suit with half-inch stripes running the length of it and a white "lion hunter's hat." David looked equally sublime in a race-track check of mail order origin purchased via the out-island schooner. Thomas had reached the imposing position of "Bishop of Haiti" and, as he gravely assured me, no longer had to work. Late one evening I strolled down to their church building and listened outside, hoping to hear another sermon about "de blessin" but was disappointed, for the service was ingeniously devised to make the collection as convenient and as pleasant as possible. This was achieved by permitting the congregation to dance and clap around the pews in company to the boom of drums and the rattle of gourds. Everyone was having a grand time and the file was arranged to pass the collection box each time around. An occasional rattle of coppers denoted the success of the scheme. The old sincerity of the Daxons seemed lacking. There was no question, however, of the whole-hearted and evident enjoyment of the congregation. They appeared to fully appreciate the privilege of dancing in church.

Once beyond the settlement and the tiny sphere of influence of the energetic Ericksons, the island remained as it had been since Columbus found the New World. Steeped in brilliant sunshine, blasted by the wind, it appeared exactly as I had left it. When I contemplated the hunt for the nesting place of the flamingo my hopes sank. Somewhere in the 800 square miles of the island's surface the colony was situated; but without some hint of its location I could spend a month in fruitless exploring. A few preliminary trips into the field failed to give any clue. During the first of these I became badly sunburned. Fresh from the rigors of a northern winter I had forgotten the intensity of the sun's rays and had paid the penalty for my lack of memory.

Much of the credit of finding the nestling place of the flamingos belongs to Mary Darling, which is not a name of affection but the real name of the bush woman who guided me to that portion of the great salt lake in the center of the island where the flamingos have their colony. Mary was a most remarkable person. Although she was a grandmother several times over, she was the most un-grandmotherly individual I have ever encountered. She was not old and feeble; quite the contrary. She lived alone in a little driftwood and thatch hut on the southern coast between Mathewtown and Lantern Head. Here she made her living by hunting the wild hogs which abounded in her neighborhood, and by making cleverly woven grass baskets and hats which she traded for certain necessities. Besides these activities she raised a few gigantic sweet potatoes, some weary looking corn and guinea grain and fished for conchs and other delicacies on the reef beyond her door. She habitually carried an antiquated shotgun which she loaded with iron slugs sawed from old ship fastenings, and which went off with a roar that could be heard for miles. When a wild hog crossed her path it was either blasted bodily out of existence or succumbed to heart failure. I was never certain which end of the shotgun was safest for it threatened to explode whenever the trigger was pulled. Beside the shotgun Mary carried a two-foot machete which gave her a most warlike appearance. She was a self-sufficient woman.

She had been recommended as the only person who could

solve my problem and I set out to visit her as no one seemed to know when she would take one of her very infrequent trips to the settlement. I found her near her hut trudging up a donkey trail with a fifty-pound load of palmettos on her head. With typical northern impatience I asked her to halt her task and take me to the flamingo. She puffed on her pipe for a minute, considered, and said it could not be done until next Monday.

I did not want to wait until next Monday so I offered her an extra dollar, which is as much money as she would have made in a couple of weeks' steady labor. Mary shook her head. I made it two dollars but no other day but Monday would do. I knew it would be a long time before Mary could make two dollars so quickly. But money meant little to Mary, so for nearly a week I cooled my civilized heels waiting. If I had offered her a hundred the result would have been much the same. Quite probably at the moment I approached Mary she did not need a dollar, so there was no use working for one. As I discovered later she spent the interval making a few grass baskets and catching up on her sleep!

But bright and early Monday morning she turned up with two donkeys, which she called Helen and Samson. Before I was finished I knew Helen and Samson as well as I knew my closest relatives. I slept with them and drank out of the same bucket, greatly preferring that to the alternative which was to die of thirst. Helen and Samson were almost as temperamental as Timonias had been but Mary had much better control over their peregrinations. Her running comment to these donkeys was a source of wonder; she coaxed, she wheedled, she pleaded, spoke terms of endearment, cursed and blasphemed, shrieked and howled, whispered and sang to attain her end.

"Now yo Samson, please be genleman fo de white mon. Samson, yo gives me a pain; if yo don behave I break yo dom neck—donkey yo shoulden do dat—come back heah fore I slay yo daid—"

I began to perceive that the management of donkeys was a fine art and was more than willing to turn this delicate task over to Mary's attentions.

We headed down a narrow trail directly into the interior. The usual flocks of doves began fluttering before us and wild hogs frequently blundered away. The trail began to narrow; the bushes grew closer and thicker. Spines from gaunt thorn trees caused us to edge carefully through their interstices; the ground became littered with pumpkin-shaped short round fat cacti with reddish top pieces reminding me of the fezzes of Turks—the turk's head cactus. These grew in shallow holes in the bare rock where the thorn trees thinned. The heat began to rise to amazing heights; a small pocket thermometer registered 108° in the shade. Samson and Helen were streaked with moisture and gobs of lather dripped from their tongues. The bare rock underfoot was so hot it could scarcely be touched.

By noon I had consumed nearly three quarts of water and we refilled our jugs from a hole in the rocks. Mary was a genius at finding water. From a thousand depressions she selected the right ones, and usually, when she had scraped away the accumulations of brown leaves and black soil, there was a little skim of moisture in the bottom. This water was dark brown; it crawled with insects and it stank. But it was wet and I moistened my lips and followed this stout female into the bush.

The next day we reached the last waterhole, at the base of a tamarind tree, with the vilest taste of any liquid I ever sipped. Mary calmly filled a big bucket which she had been carrying on her head and watered the donkeys—the hole was too deep for them—and then refilled it for our own use. She then broke a twig of aromatic thorn leaves and dropped it in the liquid to keep it from splashing. The bucket contained at least seven gallons and must have weighed fifty pounds but Mary heaved it to her head and then with superb posture and exquisite balance swung down the trail without spilling a drop. While engaged in this feat she picked up a dead stick in her toes, which were as dexterous as fingers, transferred it to her hand without tilting the bucket and in one stride went after Helen who had strayed off the trail. Not bad for an old girl who must have been close to half a century!

The smooth barren rock altered to a fine layer of silt and apparently at some not very distant date the great lake must have expanded miles from its present shoreline, for in places the ground was littered with the bodies of thousands of small fishes which had become stranded. These had become segregated in small ponds which had dried, leaving them in the hot sun to die. Although the temperature was well above a hundred and the sun glared directly on their corpses, the bodies of these fishes had not decayed. The soil and the silt were so impregnated with salt that they were pickled. Only the eyes and soft bellies had caved away. At certain angles the shafts of sunlight glinted brilliantly on their scales, giving the ground the appearance of being carpeted with silver coins.

Later in the day, close to sundown, we reached the edge of the lake. It lay very quiet and still, for the wind had fallen away to a calm, and it was of a pale green color, yet almost not green, of a hue that lies midway between emerald and light ultramarine. The lake gave the sensation of great expanse. It seemed to sweep away into infinite distance, silent, unmoving; the horizon was obscured by haze and the water appeared to merge with the light blue of the boundless sky. One had the feeling of being in a shallow liquid bowl without top or border.

Not far away were two diminutive islands, mere vestiges

of vegetation in a liquid world. Nestling between these was a long thin line of pink—the flamingos at last! Forgetting my weariness, I left Mary and the donkeys on the nearest island to make camp and waded into the lake before it became too dark to see. The water was quite shallow, reaching about to the knees, and the bottom was composed of loose sand and hard rock. Crawling over the lake floor were millions of Ceritheum, enough to feed a hundred thousand flamingos.

Soon the pink line became more clear. For nearly a mile it stretched out; the flock must have numbered about a thousand birds. Before long I could hear them, a queer sound like the gabbling of geese, with which were mingled the cries of a dozen other species of birds. Flocks of laughing gulls, clean in their black and white plumage, swept over my head, screeching in raucous chorus; pelicans dived headlong for fish, making tremendous splashes as they hit; graceful terns wheeled and uttered their plaintive calls; sandpipers stood in droves along the shallows and made the air musical with their twittering and whistling. Pure white egrets and the more somber bodies of herons stalked all about and dozens of ducks paddled like fleets of boats over the surface.

But it was the flamingos that held the center of the picture. Through my binoculars I could see them stalking about, dipping their queer shovel-bills in the water, scooping up the Ceritheums as they moved. Their gorgeous color made them stand out above everything else. Pure pink of the most delicate hue, the color changed with the light. While I watched, the sun faded behind a cloud and the pink suddenly altered to scarlet, to vermilion and finally to a seething line of bloody red against a background of pale blue sky and green water.

The sentinels of the flock saw me coming. The gabbling noise increased and the red line began to shift. I moved closer. Every head was in the air, watching, and nervously the flamingos began to stalk back and forth. Soon I was a hundred yards away, then fifty.

A roar of sound suddenly burst across the water and a thousand pairs of scarlet wings beat the air at once, throbbing, and the flock went screaming into the sky. It was the most breath-taking sight I have ever witnessed. The skin at the base of my scalp crept at the magnitude of it. In long skeins, a hundred crimson birds to a line, the shrieking flocks soared into the heavens. Higher and higher they mounted, wheeled, and in a colorful deluge poured over the horizon.

The spectacle was so magnificent that I stood open-mouthed for some minutes. Recovering, I moved on to the tiny islands where the flock had stood and there, only a few inches above the water, on some barren rocks, found a few nests. These consisted of mounds of mud about a foot in height. On the top of the mounds was a slight depression, and in each depression a single egg. The eggs were chalky white and about three times as large as a hen egg. One egg had been trampled by the flock and the yolk was drooling from the crushed shell. It was not yellow, but deep sickly red.

The birds were just beginning to lay. A few nests were in process of construction. I was interested to observe that they were reinforced with layers of lake weed which the birds packed into the mud while it was wet. This was a note which none of the ornithology books mentioned and may have been an Inaguan peculiarity. I examined the place for photographic possibilities and decided the only way to photograph the birds satisfactorily would be from a blind. But there was no room on the rocks for a hiding place nor materials from which to build one. The only solution was to construct some sort of boat, place a shelter on it and anchor it close to the colony.

I lied to Mary, told her the birds had not yet laid their

eggs—for I knew she would steal them for food—and returned to Mathewtown to give the flock time to get a better start, construct more nests and become thoroughly attached to their colony before disturbing them further. With some canvas and strips of plywood purchased from the Ericksons, I built a boat of sorts. It was little more than a flat-bottomed skiff, blunt at both ends, and very wobbly. By necessity it had to be light to be transported to the lake, so I had to sacrifice sturdiness for portability.

To take the boat over the trail Mary and I had so laboriously followed was out of the question, so I had it carried on a donkey cart to an arm of the lake which extended to within about eight miles of the settlement. From there it could be poled or rowed the fifteen or twenty miles to the flamingo colony. I loaded it with food and water, with a tent and a quantity of photographic equipment. By the time I had it all ready the trade wind began to increase in intensity again, daily growing more violent until on the date I scheduled for the departure it was blowing a full gale. The shore where the boat was grounded was piled waist deep in billowy foam and short but steep waves pounded against the sand.

With some difficulty I dragged the scow through the breakers and tried to climb aboard. The makeshift craft, overladen with heavy equipment, plunged heavily and began to ship water. The only way to save it was to jump out and lighten the load. There was no help for it, nor any use in waiting until the wind calmed; it might blow thus for weeks. Shedding my already sodden clothes I started out pushing the boat ahead of me to prevent the waves from slapping into my face. There was no shelter from the wind, the lake was open from one side to the other. Very distant on the horizon were some low islands, and I estimated that by steady plodding I might make them by sundown.

Hour after hour I forged ahead. It was grueling work. While the water was not particularly deep, it reached over my waist, making footing difficult. The heavy boat had to be kept continually in the wind for as soon as it went slightly broad-side it became unmanageable. To make matters worse the waves began breaking over the top and I had to bail continually, using my shirt as a sponge. The excessive salt irritated my skin and made my eyes burn; in addition the sun created a glare that very soon gave me an excruciating headache, although I am not normally susceptible to this malady.

About three in the afternoon I was nearly out of sight of land, although the island on the horizon had loomed a little higher. I felt completely out of my element and was beginning to grow very weary. The waves were running as high as ever and the bottom had dropped slightly until only my head and shoulders protruded. Progress was maddeningly slow; I could just catch enough purchase with my toes to make a little headway; at times I stepped into holes and had to swim for a few yards until I could touch bottom again or drift back to the edge where I dropped off and circle the depression. At an hour before dark I estimated I had waded eight or ten miles and I was bordering on exhaustion. The island was still a mile or two distant; as far as I could see the lake swept on and on; I was very nearly in the center of it.

When I reached land just as it was growing dark I was so tired I could scarcely stand and when I found that the borders of the island were beset with an impassable barrier of prickly pear yards deep, I sat down in the mud by the shore in disgust and despair. I could not spend the night sleeping in the slime and water so I unlimbered my machete and hacked gingerly at the soft pads. The sharp spines pierced my fingers and stuck into my legs, but eventually I cut a narrow path through the barrier and slumped on the dry sand behind. But

I did not sleep long for the hum of mosquitoes quickly brought me to life again. Trudging back to the boat I gathered the tent and its poles, a jar of water and a few tins of food. Half asleep and fighting the insects, I somehow managed to erect the tent in the dark and crawl inside. Behind the netting there was relief. I devoured a tin of fruit and then relaxed on the canvas floor where I fell into a deep slumber.

In the morning the heat of the sun aroused me. The lake was as calm as a sheet of glass. Hurriedly, to take advantage of the smooth surface, I lowered the tent and set out again. But I had hardly left the island when the wind resumed its vigor. In a half hour the waves were whipping up again, but the bottom shoaled to my knees and I made much better progress although the resistance of the water was very tiring. Around eleven o'clock I caught sight of the flamingos in the distance. The shimmer of their plumage was visible long before the birds; the horizon appeared laden with pink down. When I was still about five miles away I saw my first mirage. A group of six or eight flamingos close to a small islet far to the left of the main group gradually enlarged until they appeared about four times as great as in life, then above their heads appeared an equal number inverted. The inverted birds walked in an inverted lake and imitated the actions of their brethren below. When fully extended the heads of the upside down flamingos almost touched those beneath. The optical aberration lasted for almost half an hour when it faded slowly away. Strangely, the water in which these mirrored birds were wading looked quite calm, and when I approached I saw that it was sheltered from the wind in the lee of a dry sand bar.

I was in for a great disappointment. Late in the afternoon I reached the island where I had camped with Mary Darling and made myself comfortable for the night. As I expected to stay for several days I made the tent secure and prepared a

decent meal. As soon as the sun set I turned in to recoup some
of my dissipated energy; the miles of wading while pulling a
heavy boat had made me too tired to be interested in flamingos; for that evening, at least, I would relax. The air was
very heavy, and although I faced the tent into the wind I did
not sleep well and awakened several times. This camp was one
of the most exciting of my entire outdoor experience. The
moon was out again and between the clouds it sent long shafts
of blue light scurrying over the black waters. It had hardly
risen when a vast tumult of bird voices began to fill the air.
These started with a light peeping refrain of sandpipers and
the plaintive calls of plover and killdeer. The gallinules took
up the concert and their cackling broke in a dozen wild
choruses over the lake. One by one other birds added to the
tumult. The clatter of rails and squawk of little green herons,
accompanied by myriads of faint splashings and whistlings,
made the lake seem alive. As the minutes passed the sounds
increased until the lake was an unbelievable bedlam. This
was rather amazing for the remainder of Inagua was extraor-
dinarily quiet at night. Except for the wind, the ground clatter of the crabs and the occasional sweet melody of a mockingbird, a migrating Maryland yellow throat or other warbler
singing in its sleep, the evenings were deathly still.

The bedlam increased until the flamingos joined in. From
that moment the lake became a vast roar, a dark empty space
surging with waves of seething noise. The nearest common
approach to the sound was the tumult of a crowd at a major
football game. No football crowd, however, ever gave the
sense of majesty that came out of the lake that night. The
combination of all the sounds blended in a mournful minor key
that sent cold shivers up and down my spine. I have experienced
the same effect from certain passages of Sibelius and from
the blood-chilling cadences of *Götterdämmerung*.

Early in the morning it quieted down somewhat, and I awoke conscious that a new tone was swirling off the lake. It was the flamingos. They were no longer gabbling to themselves as though engaged in endless conversation; instead their notes were louder, more penetrating and goose-like, shortened and, it seemed, frightened. Crawling out of the tent, I walked down to the shore and listened. Beyond the flock I could hear a loud splashing as of some heavy creature. The flamingos heard it too, and their voices raised in alarm. Waves of sound broke over the flock, swept over acre after acre of birds and then died down again only to start once more. Then, all at once, there was deathly stillness, a quiet that seemed more intense after the noise that had gone before. The silence lasted for almost a minute, then with a thunderous burst there was a shriek of a thousand voices and the throb of a thousand pairs of wings. Like a great dark cloud the flamingos burst into the sky, blotting out the stars and shielding the light of the moon. The sound was such as I would imagine would fill the sky on judgment day when all the graves of the centuries would open and yield their doleful inhabitants to the heavens. A great and sorrowful wail went echoing into the spaces of the night and was lost in the emptiness.

I took the boat and went over as soon as I finished breakfast. The colony had grown since I first found it and a dozen or two new nests were plastered over the boulders. These had all had eggs in them but the panic of the night before had destroyed them. In their hurry to get away the birds had trampled on the shells and the ground was littered with broken fragments, crushed embryos and bloody yolks. Out of the entire lot only four eggs were still intact.

In the hope that the main flock would return I went back to the camp and slept most of the day where I would be out of sight. But in the evening there were still no more birds, although a few small flocks flew overhead as if reconnoitering. The next day I tried to get some pictures of the few flamingos that remained but the wind became so violent that my make-shift boat blind was shredded apart and the fluttering cover only served to alarm the birds so that they would not ap-proach. That night complete disaster overtook the struggling colony, for the waves broke over the heaped-up nests and washed the shells into the water where they drifted away.

Flamingos build their turreted nests to safeguard against this very eventuality but their breeding colonies are always subject to flood and are located in places where the change of water level may vary overnight. An extremely heavy rain may destroy a colony of a thousand nests in a few hours, or an extremely brisk wind blowing a great mass of water in one direction, as happened in this case, may cover nests that would normally would be quite safe.

A completely empty lake greeted my eyes the next day. In every direction there was nothing but green water and blue sky. There was no indication where the flock had gone; a more lifeless landscape would be difficult to imagine. The prospect of setting off once again in that waste of shoal water was not very encouraging. As I had done several times before on Inagua I asked myself what the impelling force was which led me on and on under the most uncomfortable conditions. In the incident of the exploration of the island it was pure curiosity, coupled with a sense of duty to salvage something out of the fiasco of the expedition. In the case of the flamingos it was a desire for beauty, nothing else, for I was no longer bound to duty. Beauty and discomfort do not always go hand in hand, but the flamingos of Inagua Island are one of the world's truly grand and inexpressibly lovely spectacles. If the great flock of this island were readily available to the people of the earth so that it might be reached without having to endure sun and thirst and the sting of salty water, it would be a mecca for hundreds of thousands. But that will never be, for when civilization comes the flamingos depart forever; this most marvelous of all avian sights will remain the privilege of the few, a half dozen naturalists and inquisitives who have tucked in their bodies an unquenchable thirst for the unbelievably exquisite, the ultimate of loveliness.

Flamingos are the waning remnants of a once considerable group that had their being as far north as the present polar regions. Time has eliminated all but small portions of the numerous species that once roamed the world. Farther and farther back into the lonely and desolate regions they have been crowded until at the time of this writing there are remaining only a few great colonies in this hemisphere. There is still a large colony on the island of Andros and some scattered groups along the sandy coast of Brazil; the Inagua colony is the greatest and the most magnificent of all. Here, unless fate hurries the inevitable by the medium of a great hurricane or exploitation by man, the flamingos will make their last stand before they, too, will take their final flight into the misty passages of time along with all the other wonderful creatures of the past, with the dinosaurs and pterodactyls, the saber tooths and the great sloths. The people of the earth, in spite of war and famines and pestilence, are steadily crowding out the wild things; new modes of transportation are pushing back the frontiers. Only those creatures which are exceedingly adaptable can survive man's companionship outside zoos and reservations. Flamingos are not adaptable, and unless they are accorded permanent and strict seclusion, the hour is not far distant when they will be gone. And nature as if realizing that these flamingos are probably the last of their kind has created in them the most completely gorgeous of all living birds of equal size. If they are exterminated in the next

century or two, as I believe they will be, their line will depart
in a blaze of glory.

It is not sufficient that nature has created in the flamingo
one of the most beautiful birds of the earth; she has made it
also a paradox. Where most birds feed with bills extended
forward, reaching toward their prey, the flamingo does exactly the opposite. Its bill is a remarkable adaptation for feeding on ceritheum snails and is bent backwards at an obtuse
angle. This peculiarity gives them an exaggerated aristocratic
appearance reminding one of the cartoons picturing middle-
aged Englishmen of the nobility; camels have a similar expression. The feeding is accomplished by swinging the head
in a series of arcs while walking slowly along and scooping
up the shells on the backward stroke. The edge of the bill
is equipped with a comb or screen which separates the shells
from the mud, permitting the excess water and silt to escape.
Equally odd is the fact that these ceritheum snails are exceedingly small, the palm of the hand will comfortably hold several
hundred; I have seen birds one tenth the size of flamingos devour prey many times as large; only the astronomical numbers
of ceritheum make it possible for the flamingos to exist on
such microscopic diet.

In reality flamingos are perfectly fashioned for the life they
pursue. Their long legs are ideal organs for wading endless
hours in the lakes and ponds; their equally lengthy necks are
the result of the legs; the height of one is compensated by
the lowering ability of the other. By pedal elevation and oral
depression they are able to exist dry and comfortable in a
world of splashing liquid; by any other arrangement of anatomy their niche in life would be much more difficult.

Discouraged, I climbed the only tree on my islet, a gnarled
and twisted specimen that leaned toward the west, and scanned
the horizon with the binoculars. Rotating slowly, I carefully

examined the entire 360 degrees of the lake's rim; everywhere was emptiness, miles of whitecaps and long streamers of foam. There was no sign of flamingos. Once again I circled, standing on tiptoe to gain added height, stopping now and then to recover balance, for the binoculars upset my equilibrium. I was about to give it up when far in the north I imagined I saw a faint reddish haze. Strain as I might, I could make nothing further out of it. At times it disappeared entirely and I wondered if I had actually seen it. The haze was so vague that I was tempted to disregard it, and was almost on the point of returning to the settlement when I decided it might be the flamingos after all. Truthfully, I was so discouraged and tired that I did not particularly care if it was.

Nevertheless I loaded the boat and set out into the waste of water once more. To my dismay the bottom dropped away again until I was neck deep, and worse, it became rough and jagged. The wind meanwhile was blowing at least thirty miles an hour and my head was under water as much as on top of it. Finally I could stand the buffeting no longer and I did the only possible thing. I lightened the boat of all unnecessary equipment, dumped all the food overboard, about twenty pounds of it, threw a canvas cot away, though I recovered this several days later on the far end of the lake where it drifted, and retained only my camera and films, a gallon of water and the tent which was very light. This raised the freeboard enough to accommodate my weight so I crawled in and lay panting on the bottom. The wind meanwhile swept me rapidly down the lake farther and farther from the spot where I had seen the pink mist. Unless I got busy I would lose in a short while all the miles I had gained the first day I set out. Scrambling to my knees and balancing carefully, I seized a tent pole and began battling the waves. Progress was almost nil, and I realized that unless I could stand up and push with all my strength, I would be swiftly and surely drifted to the far end of the lake.

Throwing caution to the winds and risking everything on the slim hope of maintaining balance I rose to my feet and pushed away. Several times I nearly capsized and only saved the boat by quickly jumping overboard and climbing in again. But presently I got the hang of the motion so that by flexing my knees and giving myself up to the roll of the waves I was able to keep upright very nicely.

By putting all my reserve into the task I crossed the deep section and reached a place where the water was shoal again. I had been so busy with the boat that I had not thought to look for flamingos and when I jumped overboard and glanced at the horizon I was elated at what I saw. The whole northern sector was lined with birds. Regiment after regiment trooped across the skyline. They were still far distant but I could see that this congregation surpassed anything I had yet witnessed.

The lake bottom shoaled very gradually until it indefinably merged with the dry land where the flocks were standing. This made progress much easier and the majesty of the sight revived my sagging spirits. Soon I was within a mile of their outposts. These retreated at a pace equal to my approach, sending up series after series of low notes. The main flock at first paid little attention, but as I came closer, greater and greater numbers of loosely knit companies began trooping toward the main body. A vast murmuring began to fill the air. It was mournful and wild in its tenor and once again I could feel the flesh crawl on the nape of my neck. The sun slid behind a cloud and the great scarlet army turned into a mass of seething red, an angry shade suggestive of the color of blood.

When I was about a hundred yards away all motion in the colony ceased and every bird stood quiescent, lined up in a solid front. I stopped also, overawed by the phalanx. As nearly as I could estimate there were at least three thousand flamingos. Every eye was turned in my direction; I suddenly felt self conscious and, I must admit, almost afraid. I knew, of course, that flamingos were absolutely harmless, yet the spectacle of three thousand scarlet birds lined up in an immense army as though ready to charge was a little unnerving. I know now how the men of Lexington must have felt when they saw the regiments of scarlet-clad British.

Slowly, trying not to make a splash, I crept toward the flock. A sudden hush settled over the universe. The birds remained motionless, their heads high in the air. Fifty yards. Then thirty. I unslung the camera, opened it and held it in my hand. Then the whole world burst into flame. With a resounding roar the three thousand birds catapulted into the sky at once, and the entire firmament was sheeted in crimson. Instinctively I crouched, as I would have if a blast of fire had suddenly swept out of a volcano. Even at thirty yards I could feel the rush of air created by the wings. The great multitude poured in an immense swathe over my head, and a long slow rain of pink feathers, dislodged by the sudden action, floated all around on the water. The flock swirled out into the lake and then settled like a vast pink snowstorm on the surface. When I recovered from the spell of their going, I was amazed to discover that I was trembling all over. Nothing that I have ever witnessed in all the realm of nature has ever quite come up to this incident.

To my chagrin, when it was all over, I realized that I had completely forgotten the camera. It was still clutched in my hand, untouched. Tying the boat to a boulder I walked over to the shore where the flamingos had been and saw then that I had at last found the main nesting colony. Hundreds of conical nests were arranged in low rows on ridges of rock that ran parallel to the shore and which were separated by narrow lanes of water. The nests were all new and many still showed the wet marks of feet and bills where they had been patted and moulded into shape. There were a few eggs, but not many. The colony had just been formed; I was a little too early.

Quietly, so as not to frighten the flock any further, I retreated to the boat, pushed off and went drifting down the lake on the wings of the wind. As I swept away the flock once again rose, circled, and then settled on the nests. Through my binoculars I could see individual birds at work, scraping up the mud and patting it with their feet. Those that had laid eggs settled awkwardly in place and began brooding their spawn. This was the last I was ever to see of them.

After two weeks I returned and went directly to the colony. There was not a bird in sight nor an egg—only broken shells and empty nests. In the soft mud between the nests was the evidence—the prints of bare human feet. Natives had found the colony and cleaned it out for the eggs. I spent nearly a month looking for another nesting site but found nothing but small companies of non-breeding birds.

The natural dangers of existence such as floods, wind, disease and downpouring rain are all the evils with which the flamingos can successfully cope. When the disaster of human interference during their breeding period is added, the hope that these most magnificent of birds can survive continued molestation is remote. The number of flamingos on Inagua has visibly decreased during the last eight years, and unless the Bahaman Government can educate its natives to protect these creatures, if for no other reason than the added beauty they give the island, it will be only a short time before one of the world's most sublime sights will have disappeared from the earth.

CHAPTER XIII

The Great Reef

THERE are two sights on this earth that are so unusual that they do not seem credible. One of these is the flamingos; the other the fantastic and exquisite world of the undersea barrier reef viewed from the point where the ocean bottom falls away into the great depths off the coast of Inagua. It is a strange paradox that the island of Inagua, which is so drab and forlorn in many respects, should harbor in its few square miles two of the earth's most magnificent spectacles. While I am writing these words I am trying to think of something with which to compare them—and I fail completely. The awe-inspiring display of the aurora borealis comes to mind, but this is too pastel and ghostly; and I also think of the beautiful bay of Samana in the Dominican Republic with its royal palm forests and curving bays of indigo blue water, where there is lovelier scenery per square mile than any place I have ever visited—but this, also, lacks the final touch of sheer splendor that is an integral part of the great reef.

Many hours have I spent beneath the sea, in helmets and in diving suits, in massive steel cylinders with thick glass windows, in the dark green water of the Chesapeake Bay and in the limpid waters off the coast of Florida, but I was wholly unprepared for the sublime vista which spread before my eyes when I descended from the deck of a dirty Inaguan sailboat anchored on the outer edge of the reef some miles from the settlement. From the deck there was no hint of what lay beneath, though I should have suspected something unusual for the top of the reef was magnificent in its own right. On the ocean side the water was dark blue, of the deep shade that women use for blueing and is born of great depth and darkness beneath. Down, down, the bottom dipped—two thousand fathoms the chart read—down to the blackness of everlasting night. From out of the ocean came great swelling waves propelled by the trades that swept steadily from the east. Suddenly these mounted high in the air and dissolved in thunderous fury on the jagged edge of the coral. On the inside the water was calm and green, emerald of the most intense hue, reflecting sunlight and smooth sand in liquid vividness. This blended into lighter greens and the pure white of an undisturbed tropical beach. Behind, etched in paler green against the sky stood a curving line of cocoanut palms swaying in the wind. The upper reef was a scene of pristine beauty—but it was as nothing to that which lay beneath.

The captain and owner of the sailboat, an inky black Inaguan, was considerably upset by my intentions.

"Boss mon," he pleaded with me in his funny island dialect, "boss mon, I wouldn't go down dere foh anyting—dey's shark and dey's barracuda down dere as big as dis boat."

With his hand he indicated the blue water beneath our anchorage. I grinned, looked at the length of the sailboat—it was at least twenty-five feet long—and scoffed.

"O.K., boss, it's yo hide, but I wouldn't go down dere foh a million shillins."

But I had returned to Inagua and traveled no less than 1800 miles just for the purpose of going "down dere" and I was not to be thwarted by the warnings of the sailboat captain. Together we unloaded the eighty-pound diving helmet, eased it over the gunwale, fixed it in position and connected the air line and pump. I plunged overboard and came up spouting water and shivering. After the hot tropical sunlight the water felt cold. The black captain signaled that he had the pump going so with a blowing of bubbles I ducked beneath the helmet and came up inside. I waved my hand in token that I was ready and slid gently down the life line. For a fleeting second there was a glimpse of the palms on shore, a snatch of blue sky and towering clouds, and a deep roar as a huge comber piled up in frothy whiteness on the jagged coral.

Then utter silence and quiet, a silence that seemed more intense because the only indication of life that came from the upper world was the faint pulse of the air pump that kept me alive. I looked in the direction of the comber breaking on the reef and caught my breath. It had splintered into a million, million bubbles which sprayed downwards in fountains of color—greens, reds, blues, all the hues of the spectrum, highlighted by the rays of the sun from the world above.

For a scant second the bubbles held their position and then raced toward the sky. The bigger bubbles reached the surface first and disappeared as through a molten silver wall. Then there was a period of inaction when nearly all the globules had vanished, a momentary quiet when only a few trickles of imprisoned air moved laggardly toward the surface. Suddenly without warning, the whole surface broke again, abruptly tearing apart into a chaos of color and driven froth. But the fact that was most astonishing was that there was not a sound, although I knew that only a few feet above the air was filled with a sullen roar.

Turning, I glanced away from the area of the surf. Above my head was the bottom of the boat, festooned with moss and bits of feathery seaweed. Beside it long shafts of golden sunlight pierced the water, flashed momently and disappeared. All around was a world of limpid pastel blue, the most exquisite hue I have ever seen. I felt drowned in it, as though I were floating in space with pure azure above, below and beneath. Nor was it a depressing blue, but a blue that seemed alive, a pearly sort of color that shimmered with a faint luster that was conceived of clarity and sunlight. I hung suspended, lightly grasping the life line. In the distance the sheen faded imperceptibly into a pale golden silver through which rays of misty sunlight penciled downwards in long streaks which came and went as the facets of the waves captured and directed them on their courses. I looked below me and gulped in amazement.

I was hanging on the very edge of a deep canyon, a drowned dark space that tumbled dizzily toward the center of the ocean. For seventy feet I could see clearly. Each rock and stone stood out in vivid relief, but beyond that objects became progressively dimmer, less and less visible, until in the farther reaches of out-of-focusness I could discern only the blurry outlines of phantom shapes, shadowy crags, and queer forms that flitted from place to place. Further down was empty darkness that seemed more mysterious because there was nothing tangible.

Gingerly I let myself down a few feet and became conscious that I was swaying back and forth like a pendulum. Then I noticed that everything in the canyon was swaying too. First one way and then the other. Not forcefully but very gently, back and forth over an arc of ten or twelve feet. For a second I would be poised over a mound of hard white sand, and then slowly and quite helplessly, I would sweep out over the steep walls of the canyon until I was suspended over thirty feet of nothingness. It was a most surprising sensation to be wafted thus like the lightest feather, and for nearly five minutes I hung suspended, enjoying the sensation. On a return swing I dropped the remaining distance to the mound of white sand and landed with a gentle bump on its surface. But only for a second. For a brief moment I poised erect and then was dragged from my perch by the current.

Only by quickly dropping to my knees and grasping a lavender sea fan was I able to maintain my position. I hung dizzily on the edge of the canyon until on the return swing I let go and was swept well away from the edge. Twice I repeated this process. Then I was certain that I would not roll over so I stood erect and gave myself up to the surges. Like a dancer in a slow motion picture I found myself able to give a little hop, drift airily for ten feet, land gently, poise for a second, and hop back exactly to my original position. In a little while I became accustomed to these aerial, or "waterial," excursions and had opportunity to look about.

To see the surf upside down was startling enough, but the scene that stretched before me held me speechless in wonder. Against a background of pale cerulean blue was a fantastic forest of yellow coral trees that reached leafless branches in indescribable confusion toward the surface. Row upon row extended into the intangible distance. In between the great trunks were dark caves and open blue patches with other trees beyond. This was a forest that would have done credit to the most imaginative fairy tale. I was reminded of the woods in which Snow White found herself while fleeing from the wicked Queen. And between the trunks of these nightmarish yellow trees of coral was filing a host of fishes of all the colors of the rainbow. Brilliant yellows and azures, vermilions and emerald greens, burnished silvers, purples and lavenders, iridescent pinks and mauves, all combined into a melee of unbelievable color. It was as though some artist, gone mad, had prodigally spattered a picture of some wonderful fairyland with his most intense pigments and then suddenly endowed that picture with life. Only no artist, however mad, could conceive or execute so variegated a pattern. Since this dive I have been undersea half a hundred times in the shadow of this same reef and each time my feeling is one of great awe.

Nowhere in the world of upper air is there such a conception of color or color values. Sunsets and the brilliant foliage of autumn are lovely, but in contrast they are garish and crude. There is something indescribably soft and untouchable about these coral reef hues, a shimmering pearly quality which is so evanescent and intangible that it baffles accurate description. A few feet away a school of mackerel of some unidentifiable species was pouring from between two great stone trees. When they came from the shadow they were faint lustrous pink tinged with a suggestion of silver and lavender, but when they emerged into the full rays of a stream of sunlight they suddenly but softly altered to brilliant yellow that flared and dimmed from flaming gold to reddish copper as the sun caught their scales at full right angles or obliquely.

Perhaps the most entrancing effect of the entire scene was the utter lightness of everything. Even the great stone trees, ponderous though they must have been, had an air of delicacy. Their branches extended out and out in lacy filagree becoming, queerly enough, more fragile as they went towards the direction of greatest force, the point where the surf was breaking. Land trees of equal delicacy and weight in similar position would not have lasted ten minutes. The bottom was strewn with hundreds of purple and yellow sea fans, and with the long feathery plumes of gorgonians and sea pens which gracefully swayed back and forth, not rapidly, but ever so gently in the most artistic undulations. I noticed that every sea fan was placed in precisely the same position, exactly parallel to the coast. Like the reef, like the beach and the sand dunes back of the palms on the shore they had oriented themselves at right angles to the wind and waves. Between the fans were other hundreds of purple sea-plumes which looked like feathers torn from some gigantic bird and planted helter-skelter by a childish hand. But the simile of feathers faded away when I bent close to one and saw the hundreds of tiny tentacles protruding from the shafts marking the presence of the stinging colonial animals which, bound together in feather-like association, go to make up the entirety. These sea-plumes were the most beautifully curving creations I have ever seen. Never in all their waving back and forth did they assume an ungraceful or awkward position.

The fishes, too, took on this same air of lightness. They soared without effort, flitting carelessly between the branches. Most amazing were some wrasses which were nibbling on algae on the rocks. At the beginnings of their swings they would nibble, pulling the vegetation from the boulders, and then sweep out into space, preserving the exact spacings as when they were eating, reach the perihelion of their swaying, and then return to the precise points which they had deserted when they once again resumed their interrupted feeding. Even a big jewfish, a dark brown fellow fully three feet long and weighing a hundred pounds or more, seemed to partake of this buoyancy. I first saw it far back in a deep dark hole in the farthest recesses of the coral. Only its head protruded when I discovered it but when I grasped a sea fan to anchor myself, I could see that for all its ponderousness, it too was airily swinging with the water. Without moving a muscle the fish would float motionless in its hole and then gracefully glide out head foremost to a position midway between two great coral trees and then slowly tail first back to exactly the same position. I watched the jewfish for five minutes and in all that time never saw it move so much as a fin, yet it always returned directly to its hiding place.

I tried walking down the avenues of sea fans but found it nearly impossible. From the deck of the boat the bottom had seemed quite smooth, or at most slightly rolling. Instead it proved to be a great jagged hillside, cleft with deep ravines and pitted with dark caves. Paradoxically, and unlike the hillsides on land, the tree line was on the upper slopes instead of the lower. Besides the swaying of the water which dragged me from place to place was the complication that I could not judge distance. The refraction was too great. I was surprised to find that sea fans for which I reached in order to steady myself and which appeared to be within arm's distance were really six feet or more away. To my discomfort I found myself time and again placing my foot on mounds of white brain coral which simply were not there. Although I have been undersea many times this reef was the most confusing place of my experience. Repeatedly I fell helplessly and slowly into deep holes. This was disturbing because usually as a result of some trick of the current I fell in backwards and could not see where I was tumbling. I was afraid of landing on a nest of sea urchins whose poisonous spines I could see jutting out from the crevices. Once I brushed against a smooth brownish coral which burned like nettles. I was worried about cutting my legs on the sharp stone. I knew what that would mean. Undersea in the tropics is no place in which to be bleeding, for the scent of blood drives some of the carnivores mad.

But presently I began to get the hang of the thing. I found the best way was to aim for a smooth mound of rock, gauge the distance carefully, and then leap into space allowing for the swing of the water. So near balance was I that, even though I was carrying nearly eighty pounds of lead, I could, with a light spring, float upwards and out for ten feet or more, drift gently through space and come down again like the lightest feather. Later when I became practiced at the art I found that twenty-foot leaps were quite feasible.

Once I started an underwater landslide. I had reached the edge of a deep valley, a vertical wall hung with sea fans and pink anemones, when my feet dislodged a rounded head of brain coral that had long since died and was falling to pieces. Slowly it rolled over and went bounding down the slope. I clawed at the water to keep from following it and turned in time to see it reach the bottom. It landed with an easy bump, rolled once or twice, and came to rest upside down. Then a peculiar incident occurred. Every fish within fifty feet raced to the boulder and began tearing at the upturned base. Still others darted to the trail of the avalanche made visible by a whitish cloud of silt and nibbled at the torn and crushed debris in its path. Carefully, I scrambled down to the fish and thrust my way through their milling bodies. Then I understood. About the base were the crushed bodies of dozens of sea worms whose tube-homes had been torn apart. In a split second these fishes had sensed the disaster to the worms and had come to feed. This gave me an idea. I worked my way back to the base of the reef where I had seen a number of sponges growing, looking for all the world like big black rubber balls. With a bit of a struggle I pulled one loose. Instantly a writhing six-inch green and scarlet worm shot out of the base and squirmed toward the shelter of another sponge. It did not get three feet. A brilliant red and yellow wrasse darted out of the coral and savagely attacked it. It was joined by another and by a school of small yellow fish which snatched at the crumbs. In this manner I soon became the center of attraction of a whole host of fish which followed me from sponge to sponge.

Deceit and subterfuge were farthest from my thoughts when I found a quiet spot between two mounds of brain coral. I had snuggled between them to get out of the reach of swaying current and was just making myself comfortable when to my amazement a piece of the bottom detached itself between my fingers and swam away. I felt much as you would if a portion of your dining-room floor would suddenly wake up and amble off into the kitchen. For a second I stared incredulously, and then smiled to myself. A flounder, of course. I should have known. So perfectly did the creature match the white sand that even when it settled a few feet away I had difficulty locating it. Nor could I begrudge it its little deceit, for I knew it was its sole means of securing a livelihood and protection from its enemies.

The flounder gave me a good demonstration a short time later of how it employed its camouflage. A young bluehead, a brilliant fish of yellow, blue and black, left the shelter of a cluster of coral and idly drifted over the sand in the direction of a towering finger sponge. The flounder was quite out of sight and the only indication of its presence was a slight rise in the surface of the sea floor. By looking carefully I could just discern the creature's eyes mounted on low turrets. As the bluehead approached these moved very slightly and focused on the victim. Unsuspecting, the fish floated nearer until it hovered exactly over the spot where the flounder rested on the bottom. There was a quick motion and with a swirl of white sand the flounder seized the bluehead, gave a few quick gulps, and then settled on the sand again where it wriggled slightly until the sand flowed over its fins. Briefly, after devouring the bluehead, the flounder altered color, assuming a light brown tone, but this soon faded away and it once more merged indistinctly with the piles of coral and the loose grains.

I began to look for other forms of deception and realized I had entered a whole world of it. Near my elbow, growing out of a piece of dead meandrina coral was an informal garden of maize-colored flowers whose petals unfolded in a graceful spiral. These petals were long and delicate and were faintly barred with alternate rows of black which gave the blossoms a most artistic and unusual pattern. I reached out to touch one but before my fingers contacted it, their shadow fell across the petals. The blossom was jerked back into the stone so rapidly I could barely see the movement. I reached for another, and it, too, was pulled out of sight. Where the blossoms had been were only a number of slight round holes. I knew then that the blossoms were not flowers at all but sea worms, long wriggly creations of peculiar form that spend their entire lives hidden in the interstices of the rock. The sensation that this sight afforded is the same as one would have in a garden should one try to pick a daisy or a nasturtium and have it suddenly yanked into the ground. My arm, casting a moving shadow, was all that was necessary to send dozens of these creatures hurtling into their burrows. Imagine walking through a hothouse and having the flowers fold up as you progressed. Yet more strangely, when the sun went behind a cloud, and cast a shadow identical to that produced by my arm these worms moved not at all but merely swayed and curled with the flow of the currents.

The flower-like petals are really the means by which the worms seize the microscopic prey on which they feed and carry it to their mouths. Life for them is principally a question of waiting patiently with tentacles expanded for the currents to bring them food. The usual connotation of the word "worm" conveys something mean and low, or a slimy creature that frequents the damp and dark. The worms of this Inaguan coral reef are almost all lovely. Why they should be so exquisite is hard to answer unless it is because everything else on the reef is so gorgeous that to be ugly would seem out of place.

The worms were not the only flower-like animals that practiced deceit. Brilliant sponges of red, emerald green, maroon and lavender pretended to be mosses and plastered the rock wherever there was space. Bryozoans played at being lichens, and their lacy filagree covered eroded spots on the coral and bare spots on the stems of sea fans. Only, unlike the lichens, these bryozoans contained no commensal algae and had no green coloring. A crab topped the list when it made a show of being an entire garden! I discovered it when a complete set of vegetable-like animals and mosses got up and walked between two lavender gorgonians and then sank down again a foot or so away. If it had not moved I would never have suspected it. Planted on the creature's shell were several small anemones, a dainty finger sponge, and a cluster of yellow seaweed.

Struggling up the slope again I made my way back to the nook between the brain corals. I had hardly seated myself when I noticed a wave of excitement pass over all the parrot-fish. There were quite a number of these, in assorted groups of red and blue. Up to this time they had been contentedly feeding, munching the algae off the rocks, like so many azure and scarlet cows. The simile of cows is not altogether inappropriate for parrotfish spend their hours grazing on the algae which they scrape off the rocks with their great white protruding teeth. These teeth give them a rather "horsey" appearance and they wear a stupid bovine expression in keeping with their habits. As one fish they streaked for narrow holes in the coral. I looked to see the cause of the disturbance. Off in the obscure distance was a great gray shape that swam just beyond the point of clear vision. In a moment it had melted into the haze and was gone. A big shark possibly, I do not know, for it did not reappear immediately and before long the parrotfish were back at their interminable munching. In some way they sensed that all was not well and that an enemy was near. Strangely, none of the other fish showed any indication of alarm.

The behavior of the parrotfish, however, gave the clue to life on the reef. Everywhere there lurked some sort of danger. Everything fed upon something else, something smaller or more helpless than itself. The sand-colored flounder on the sea floor, the vegetable-like anemones and worms, the garden-simulating crab were all examples of deception for a purpose, to hide from enemies or to catch prey more easily. Even the unmoving coral trees passed their existence in a similar manner, for the millions of tiny polyps that covered the yellow branches in a living skin harbored stinging tentacles that instantly killed the small prey that came within reach.

In time I began to notice that there was a definite order to everything about the reef. Life was divided into rigid groups or castes. The fishes that had their being near the sea floor were not the same as those that flitted among the upper branches of the coral trees. The sea floor group might be portioned into three main classes—the munchers, like the parrotfish and the triggerfish which made their living by feeding quietly on the filmy vegetation that covered the rocks; the probers, such as the goatfish, which seemed to spend their time incessantly roaming over the sand and rocks, tapping the bottom with their barbels until they located some microscopic tidbit in the soil when they quickly burrowed and snatched it up; and the lurkers, typified by the flounders, which hid in the sand; and finally by the jewfish and groupers, which concealed themselves in deep holes waiting for some luckless muncher or prober to pass.

The jewfish and groupers probably had the best system of all. They are tremendously fat fishes with gaping cavernous mouths. I discovered their strategy quite by accident when I was watching the progress of a pair of golden angelfish. The angels swam slowly by a jewfish's den. Suddenly, and quite unaccountably, one of the angelfish simply disappeared. Into

thin air—or water—as it were. I blinked and looked at the
jewfish. It had not moved a muscle and yet I could have sworn
that I saw the angelfish vanish into its mouth. I waited patiently for another victim. Soon a demoiselle with a brilliant
yellow tail came near. It passed within three feet, stopped to
feed at a sea fan, and then turned back again. This was its undoing, for it came close to the cavernous mouth. Abruptly and
without warning, it was sucked into the swaying jaws. Then I
knew what had happened. The jewfish was operating an underwater vacuum cleaner! I saw it clearly. The fish merely
opened wide its tremendous gill flaps, creating a suction into
the yawning mouth. The jaws snapped shut and the demoiselle was no more.

Quite in contrast to the bottom fishes were those that hung
in mid-water well up into the interstices of the coral. There
were numerous sergeant-majors, little fellows striped vividly
in jet black and yellow like off-colored barber poles. These
filtered in and out among the branches along with a few score
silver moonfish, a host of bright blue tang and some azure
Beau-gregorys. These Beau-gregorys were the bravest fishes
on the reef. Certain little portions of the coral they claimed as
their very own, and these they guarded as territory inviolate.
One of the tang, which resembled nothing so much as flat
blue dinner plates which had fantastically become equipped
with fins and taken to an underwater existence, ventured too
near a branch of coral which a Beau-gregory had appropriated. With fins bristling with rage the midget dashed out and
attacked the tang. The larger fish, much to my surprise, turned
tail and fled.

A few minutes later I saw this same Beau-gregory coura-
geously assail a Spanish mackerel which was fully twenty times
its size and which was armed with a long row of sharp teeth.
The mackerel almost seemed to have a look of hurt surprise,

and, like the tang, fled ignominiously. But the mackerel amazed me still further by gliding to the surface and there snapping up a glistening silverside which was peacefully idling just below the surface film minding its own business. This lesson "in what might have happened" had no visible effect on the Beau-gregory, for shortly after it was busily engaged in driving another intruder from its domain.

Still another category of life about the reef had its existence in the few feet just beneath the surface. Here a considerable galaxy of organisms hung forever suspended between the wrinkled mirror of the top of the sea and the regions lower down. These were even graded according to their distance from the waves. Farthest up were the houndfish, which were long streamlined creatures equipped with double rows of murderous-looking teeth. They are savage carnivores belonging to the genus *Strongylura* and although the whole of their activity took place within a narrow zone they were so swift and well equipped that they garnered a good living by preying on the hundreds of silversides, bumpers and flyingfish, which also were restricted to this area. The energy of these houndfish, once they got into motion, was amazing. They appeared as living arrows, as indeed they were. At such great speed do they move that they have been known to injure fishermen severely into whose boats they have blundered during some of their spectacular spear-like leaps after flyingfish. Their prey was usually caught crosswise in their bills, crushed and shaken until dead and then momentarily released to be turned head foremost for easy swallowing.

The roof of this liquid world was a network of living creatures. There was an endless procession of small fishes continually passing to and fro at all conceivable angles. Some of these passed hurriedly, rushing by as though the very devil were after them, as indeed they may have imagined. Others drifted slowly, pausing frequently, spiraling or sidling off on all sorts of side excursions. Suspended between these moving forms was an innumerable assemblage of baby fish of a hundred varieties. Every inch of this upper strata contained at least one transparent fishlet or equally glass-like crustacean visible to the naked eye, not to include the literal billions of microorganisms on which these small fry feed. The water was a living soup; and the diatom feeders, those peculiar fishes that are equipped with natural sieves and scoop nets within their gaping mouths, were busily crisscrossing, gathering the manna which, instead of falling from heaven, strangely floated as though the laws of gravitation had been inexplicably and suddenly repealed.

A most magnificent cavalcade crossed this area when a school of six large tarpon, gleaming burnished silver on their large scales, went by without stopping. The tarpon were followed by a tremendous school of mackerel, which as nearly as I could determine by the appearance of their well-separated dorsal fins and small curved tails belong to the genus *Auxis*, or frigate mackerels. Each was about a foot in length and was streaked with a line of intense yellow which flamed in iridescent glow just above their lateral lines. The school was so huge that its passage temporarily darkened the water, and the excitement occasioned by its passage caused a veritable deluge of small fishes seeking to escape this finny hurricane. Long after they had gone the more sedentary surface fishes went periodically into small local flurries; their frenzied activity sent myriads of darting forms whirling about in a contagion of fear which spread in widening circles.

But the main impression of the reef was one of peace. Except for the occasional forays of the houndfish and the amusing angers of the incautious Beau-gregorys there was no sense of strife or danger. Rather, the reef was a cosmos reigned over by color and beauty. Everything appeared relaxed, at ease, swaying back and forth with the water.

I worked my way into the coral down an avenue of limpid blue. On the way I was surrounded by a large school of flashy blue and golden snappers. They darted fearlessly between my legs and under my arms. I amused myself by carving up anemones with my knife and feeding them the pieces. They greedily snatched the fragments from my fingers and crowded closer.

Then, when I leaned over to dig at another I suddenly suspected that something was wrong; an instinctive sixth sense caused me to look up. The snappers, like the parrotfish some minutes before, had all deserted me and were swimming off in between close-set barriers of the coral. I peered about for the cause of their fright but saw nothing. But presently, far off in the hazy distance, I recognized the same dim gray shape that had alarmed the parrots. With my mouth I squirted a quantity of salt water on the glass of the helmet to secure better vision, as it had become slightly clouded from my warm breath. The shape was still indistinct but it was surely moving closer and closer. Slowly and leisurely it emerged from the blue depths and flowed up a narrow misty valley. I glanced at the bottom of the boat suspended from the rolling silvery ceiling. The air line and rope curled down into the water beside it, but it was too far away to attempt to reach it. Whatever the *thing* was, it could get there quicker than I.

I sat tight, one hand clutching a sea fan and the other on the life line ready to go. The gray form came closer, swept up the valley and then turned toward the reef. Then, although the object was still blurred from the distance, I could see what it was. It was a tremendous shark, species unknown.

I remembered the warning words of the sailboat captain, and grinned a sickly grin into the emptiness of the helmet.

At the same time there flashed into memory the recollection of the body of a ten-foot shark which I had once found on a Florida beach with its stomach neatly bitten out in one piece by some monstrous creature. I crouched close to the ground and the beast curved up the last rise of the valley and swept on parallel to the ridge. I was quite helpless, for before I could use a knife the animal could have made mincemeat of my unprotected body should it choose to attack. But the creature glided on, paying me not the slightest attention. As it passed within twenty feet I could see the whites of its eyes rolling as it peered about. Once it swerved slightly in my direction while I stared breathlessly. But it swerved back again and I limply watched it pass. From its size and the deep pit at the base of its tail I guessed it to be one of the *Galeocerdo* or tiger sharks.

The Inaguan had not lied, the creature was at least fifteen feet long. Above it was softly mottled, beneath pearly white with a suggestion of delicate pink. There was not a blemish on it. Through the sleek back I could see the great muscles rippling as they twisted the long caudal fin. Strangely, with the exception of the snappers and the parrotfish, and a few other forms of equal size, none of the other reef fish seemed to be alarmed at its presence. They went on feeding as usual and a pair of silly-looking trunk fish even swam under its belly as it passed. Perhaps these last felt secure in their triangular bodices of bony armor. The shark soon disappeared in the distance. Later, from a number of dives in this same spot, I discovered that this individual spent much of its time patroling back and forth along this section of reef. From the surface through a water glass I saw it no less than a dozen times. I waited cautiously, thinking it might reappear, saw the parrotfish and the tang resume their feeding, and then climbed hand over hand up the line.

The Inaguan beamed in triumph. "Yoh wouldn' listen to me," he caroled. "I tol yo."

On deck my courage revived and I reminded him that, after all, the shark behaved like a gentleman. There are, undoubtedly, a number of well-substantiated cases of shark attack, but from my several experiences, the first at Sheep Cay and later on the barrier reef near Mathewtown, and from the discussions I have had with other divers, the possibilities of sharks attacking a normally behaving man clad in a helmet or full suit are somewhat remote. Most of the smaller sharks are afraid of the strange figure of a diver and give him a wide berth.

After resting a while I went below again. This time I landed on the edge of the canyon, teetered drunkenly, and then swung out over the depths. Instead of swaying back to the wall I decided to drop to the ocean floor and explore the shadowy crags below. The valley turned out to be deeper than I supposed and when I landed with a slight bump the pressure was very perceptible. The surging flow of the current, however, was largely stilled; apparently the influence of the inrolling combers did not extend beyond thirty feet. It was a great relief to be able to stand without danger of being carried away, and although the pressure was uncomfortable and the water much colder, I began to look about with interest.

The valley might well have belonged on Mars, or on the rim of one of the craters of the moon. It was shrouded in gloomy azure, purple shadows merged with the deep blacks of underwater caverns in producing an other-world aspect. I would have liked to have entered some of these caverns, but try as I might I could not gather quite enough courage. Several times I approached the mouth of one, tried to peer inside and then edged back. The fact that there was nothing tangible on which to gaze rendered the undertaking more frightening. Man is always more afraid of the invisible than the real. So I excused myself on the grounds that I had no flashlight, and besides I had no desire to provoke an unwarranted combat with an angry moray or some other large carnivore that might be lurking in the dark. The appearance of the valley itself was sufficient to melt my already partially dissipated bravery. There is no place in all the world so efficacious as the depths of tropical undersea for deflating the human ego. One feels so helpless and out of element.

The valley was interesting in that it marked the boundary line of the distribution of a great many creatures. The closer one approached the surface the more abundant and varied was the life. Down below variety was compensated by size. It seemed that the older fishes preferred a more quiet and subdued life away from the flash and turmoil of the resplendent reef. The upper edge of the ravine also marked the fringe of the true vegetation. The last carpet of moss and algae terminated at the brim. These plants required light for their wellbeing; and although the valley was lighted, this illumination was much too wan and weak. This was the farthest down of vegetable life; everything beyond was animal. From the valley floor one left behind all vestige of the world of the upper air.

I had never realized before how very important light was nor how dispiriting the color blue could be. On the reef itself the blue was alive, for it was fused with a shining abundance of sunlight; down there it was heavy and depressing. I am confident that a person kept continually in deep blue light would shortly go mad with melancholia; to have the blues is a literal description.

The very center of the valley was occupied by a towering crag that was topped with a small coral tree. It reminded me of the absurd stone castles that people place in goldfish bowls, and like those ornaments, it was pierced with carved grottoes at the base. One of the grottoes held a solid culture of the most immense tang I have ever seen. All the ichthyological textbooks place the size limit on tang at about twelve inches; none of those in the grotto were less than sixteen inches and some were closer to eighteen, with all due allowance for the refraction of the water. The tang were packed like the proverbial sardines and were all aligned in the same position, facing the entrance. This gave them the most ridiculous appearance. Tang are very round and flat but are highly compressed in a vertical direction, and when they are examined head on they seem to be only thin vertical lines. When I first saw them all I could discern was a large number of dark blue streaks out of which peered twice the number of golden brown eyes and an equal number of pale whitish lips. The tang were slowly opening and closing these lips as though eternally, and soundlessly, mouthing the word "oh" over and over again. I tried to make them desert their shelter but they would not be moved. Even when I thrust my leg squarely into their packed bodies, they only glided slightly to one side and then closed ranks again. These were evidently resting, for there seemed to be no other reason to congregate in this sheltered nook, though there may have been. We know so little about the habits and behavior of undersea creatures.

My life line began jerking and I was nearly dragged from my feet. Turning to gaze back I saw that I had reached the end of my tether, the entire coil of the air hose had been used up. Following its twisting course I crept back toward the reef. It seemed very far away, a glimmering line of fantastic tan trees poised on the very edge of the drowned cliff. Even as I looked a great school of yellow snappers rushed out from between the massive trunks, rank after rank, file after file of them, and poured like a flood into the depths. At the very moment they reached the edge of the cliff a ray of sunlight caught their scales and transformed them into an array of gleaming motes. It was as though an army emblazoned in gold were marching into the sea. For a brief second I saw them; and then a cloud passed over the sun, drowning my world in even more melancholy blue.

CHAPTER XIV

In Defense of Octopuses

I FEEL about octopuses—as Mark Twain did about the devil—that someone should undertake their rehabilitation. All writers about the sea, from Victor Hugo down to the present, have published volumes against them; they have been the unknowing and unwitting victims of a large and very unfair amount of propaganda, and have long suffered under the stigma of being considered horrible and exceedingly repulsive. No one has ever told the octopuses' side of the story; nor has anyone ever defended them against the mass of calumnies which have been heaped on their peculiar and marvelously shaped heads. We have convicted them without benefit of a hearing, which is a most partial and unjust proceeding. I propose that octopuses, and their near relatives the squids, are among the most wonderful of all earth's creatures, and as such are deserving of our respect, if not our admiration.

My personal interest in octopi dates back to the moment when I turned to climb out of the drowned ravine at the base of the Inaguan barrier reef. I had reached the lower portion of the final slope and was about to seize on a piece of yellow rock to steady myself when I noticed that from the top of the boulder was peering a cold dark eye that neither blinked nor stirred. In vain I looked for eyelids; the orb apparently belonged to the rock itself.

Then suddenly, I felt a chill wave creep up my spine. Before my gaze the rock started to melt, began to ooze at the sides like a candle that had become too hot. There is no other way to describe the action. I was so startled at the phenomenon that it was a full second or two before I was conscious of what I was watching.

It was my first acquaintance with a live, full grown octopus. The beast flowed down the remainder of the boulder, so closely did its flesh adhere to the stone, and then slowly, with tentacles spread slightly apart, slithered into a crevasse nearby. The head of the octopus was about as big as a football, but as it reached the fissure, which was not more than four inches in width, it flattened out and wedged itself into the opening. It seemed somewhat irritated at my disturbing it, for it rapidly flushed from pebbled yellow to mottled brown and then back to a livid white. It remained white for about twenty seconds and then altered slowly to a dark gray edged with maroon. I stood stock-still but it made no overt motions and I slowly edged away. Quite possibly it might have been a nasty customer, for the tentacles were about five feet from tip to tip.

This last statement may seem a contradiction to my opening paragraph; and, I must admit, that is the way I felt about the octopus at the time. However, since that hour I have collected and observed a number of these creatures, including the squids. I have found them animals of unusual attainments and they should be ranked among the most remarkable denizens of the sea. They are endowed with considerable intelligence and they have reached a system of living all their own which they have maintained for approximately 500,000,000 years. As far back as the Ordovician period of geology we find their ancestors, and there is good evidence that at one time the forefathers of the present octopi very nearly ruled the world. Had they been able to pass the barrier of the edge of the ocean as the early fish-derived amphibians did there might have been no limit to the amazing forms which would have peopled the earth.

Within the bounds of pure speculation, however, the fact remains that the cephalopods, as the entire octopi-like group of animals is termed, have missed the status of brainy intelligence, of which man is the highest criterion, only by a very narrow margin. There is reason to believe that they are the most keen-witted creatures in the ocean and had they developed an opposable thumb and fingers instead of suckers with which to manipulate various objects the entire course of the earth's existence might have been altered.

There are some very curious similarities between the development of intelligence in man and in the modern cephalopode. Both acquired brains after their individual fashions because the course of organic evolution left them without adequate physical protection against the vicissitudes of nature. Man, the weak and the puny, without claws and rending fangs to battle the beasts and without long legs with which to flee, had to acquire cunning or perish. That marvelous addition, the opposable thumb, made possible holding and using tools and gave a stimulus to cunning that nothing else in the mechanics of evolution could have provided. The thumb is by far the most remarkable portion of man's anatomy. Literature, music, art, philosophy, religion, civilization itself are directly the result of man's possession of this digit.

Like man, the modern cephalopods have been thrown upon the world naked and without the armor protection of their ancestors. For cephalopods are shellfish, blood brothers to the oyster, the clam and the conch; they are mollusks which have been deprived of their shells. The only present day cephalopods which still retain their shells are the Nautiloids which are direct descendents of the ancient types whose fossils are found in the tightly compressed rocks of the Upper Cambrian. Over three thousand fossil nautiloids have been named, an imposing group ranging in size from a tiny seven millimeter creature called *Cyrtoceras* to the immense 14 foot cone of *Endoceras!* Only four closely related species of this mighty shelled host remain, all occurring in the South Pacific.

To compensate for the loss of their shells, which were their bulwarks against fate, these unclothed cephalopods have developed, like man, cunning and intelligence. Alone among the molluscs they have acquired by concentration of their chief nerve ganglia what may be truly considered a brain. With the casting aside of the shell they have also gained their freedom, speed and mobility.

Safety often goes hand in hand with degeneration. It is a curious circumstance that those creatures which live completely guarded lives also have a very dull existence. What, for example, could be safer and more stupid and sedentary than an oyster, clad in its house of lime? The loss of a shell not only rescued the cephalopods from dullness but it probably also saved them from extinction. The most highly ornate shelled cephalopods of all time, the gracefully coiled Ammonoids, which are so named because of their resemblance to the ram-like horns of the deity Jupiter Ammon, and which developed during the Upper Silurian and lasted until the close of the Age of Reptiles, went out of existence because the extent of their external sculpture and complexity of septation rendered them so specialized that they failed to respond to change. Some of these fantastic Ammonoids, of which six thousand species are known, possessed coiled shells more than six feet in diameter!

"Cephalopods," the scientific name of the octopi and squids, immediately characterizes them as something unusual, for it signifies that they walk on their heads. This is precisely what they do, for their tentacles or "feet" are located between their eyes and mouths. No other animals on earth utilize this position or method of progression.

However, it is in their mode of swimming that the motion of these weird beings is most amazing. They are beautifully streamlined when in action, and can dart about at remarkable speed. I recall once being out to sea in a fishing trawler off the Virginia Capes. I was sitting in the dark on deck watching the stars and swaying to the slight roll of the boat when suddenly I heard a rapidly reiterated splashing in the sea. The sound was slightly reminiscent of the pattering noise of flying fish. I knew that I was too far north for any quantity of these volant creatures. I went below and returned on deck with a flashlight. Its beam pierced the dark and glowed on the wave tops. The ship was passing through a school of small surface fish. They were being prayed upon by hundreds of *Loligo* squid. The squid were shuttling back and forth through the water at incredible speed. Most wonderful was the organization with which they seemed to operate. Entire masses of these cephalopods, all swimming in the same direction, would dart at the mass fish, quickly seize and bite at them, then abruptly wheel as a unit and sweep through the panic-stricken victims which scurried everywhere. Some of these squid were traveling so rapidly that when they approached the top of the water they burst through and went skimming through the air for several yards, falling back with light splashes. In the morning I found several on the deck of the trawler where they had jumped, a vertical distance of at least six feet! There is another record made near the coast of Brazil of a swarm of squids flying out of the water on the deck of a ship which was twelve feet above the surface and which was further protected by a high bulwark, making a minimum jump of fifteen feet! Several score were shoveled off the ship when daylight came.

The cephalopods and particularly the squids might be compared to living fountain pens or animated syringes, for they accomplish their flight-like swimming by pulling liquid into their body cavities and squirting it out again. Their likeness to a living fountain pen is even further heightened when one considers that some of the cephalopods contain ink and a quill.

Nor is this all, for nature, not content to offer all these wonders in one creature, has ordained that they may swim, not only forward like all other creatures of the sea, but backward! They can swim forward and sideways, too, but the normal mode is stern foremost.

The quill of these mobile fountain pens is the remnant of the shells of their prehistoric ancestors, and it persists, like our vermiform appendix, as a useless but telltale evidence of former usage. The quill, reduced in the octopi to two chitinous rods, and in the squid to a long narrow fluted pen, remarkably resembling an old fashioned quill, is buried deep within the tissue. In a sense, the octopi and squids are shellfish which have surrounded their shells.

It is in the ink of these cephalopods that we are confronted with a true paradox. This ink, basis of the familiar India ink, is utilized for two diametrically opposite purposes. It is intended to provide concealment and, diversely, to enable the animal to keep in touch with its fellows. When there is fear of an attack by enemies, the ink is expelled into the water to form a "smoke screen" behind which the cephalopod flees to shelter. Thus the modern military technique of employing the smoke screen to conceal retreating movements was conceived by the cephalopods as early as the Jurassic, as is proved by a beautifully preserved fossil of that period which shows the ink bag prominently limned in the highly compressed tissue impression of a squid. However, when night closes down on the water shrouding the blue vastness of the deeps in impenetrable gloom it is by means of this same ink that the members of a school of squids are able to keep in contact with one another. It is believed that the ink is extruded in very small quantities and is picked up by unusually sensitive olfactory organs. The more solitary octopi use it in much the same manner to locate their mates.

I had no idea of the efficiency of this inky fluid until my

third or fourth meeting with the octopus of the valley. I had been going down for a half hour or so each day near the same spot in the reef and almost always finished the day's dive with a final excursion to the limit of the hose on the base of the ravine. In these trips I saw a number of octopuses, mostly much smaller than the first. These seemed to live in the crevasses near the base of the reef, and often all that I saw of them was a tentacle or two twitching or writhing languidly from a fissure. Some I discovered by the neat piles of mussel shells and other mollusks near the entrances to their hiding places. Some of these shells were, surprisingly, unopened and, it can be assumed, were being stored against an hour of larger appetite. Also, most interesting, the only localities on Inagua where the mussels were to be found in any abundance was in the area of the surf, a living habit that might be attributed to the ceaseless raids of octopods on colonies in more peaceful localities. The mussels, in self defense as it were, had established themselves in the only place where they might live undisturbed, which was, in contradiction, the most violent area of all the world of underwater. They were, so to speak, between the devil and the deep blue sea, or to be more exact, between the devil and the hot dry air.

Most of these octopods were exceedingly shy, fleeing into their shelters at my approach, and drawing far back out of reach, a reaction quite at variance with the accepted theories of ferocity and malignancy. I tried to capture some of the smaller ones, but they were too fast for me. The big fellow on the slope of the ravine, however, while it did not seem quite so timid always gave me a wide berth and invariably, the few times I encountered it, withdrew to its fissure where it was never quite hidden, but was revealed by a portion of the body and the restless arms. At first I left it strictly alone, but curiosity about its peculiar color changes, prompted me to come closer.

It always seemed irritated at my presence. Its nervousness may have been caused by fear, for it certainly made no pretense of belligerency, and it constantly underwent a series of pigment alterations that were little short of marvelous. Blushing was its specialty. No schoolgirl with her first love was ever subjected to a more rapid or recurring course of excited flushes than this particular octopus. The most common colors were creamy white, mottled Van Dyke brown, maroon, bluish gray, and finally light ultramarine nearly the color of the water. When most agitated it turned livid white, which is I believe the reaction of fear. During some of the changes it became streaked, at times in wide bands of maroon and cream, and once or twice in wavy lines of lavender and deep rose. Even red spots and irregular purplish polka dots were included in its repertoire, though these gaudy variations seldom lasted for long.

I had heard that a light touch on the skin would leave a vivid impression of color and I was anxious to see if this were the case. From the boatman I borrowed a long stick and dropped down to the sea floor again. The octopus was still in place and I walked over to it with the pole in my hand. At first I was hesitant about the experiment. The creature had behaved so nicely that I almost decided to give it up. But the old curiosity prevailed and with my pole I slowly reached out and stroked it along the side of its body.

Then things began to happen. The stick was snatched from my fingers and went floating to the surface. The octopus flashed out of the fissure and ejected an immense cloud of purplish ink. For a brief moment I saw it swimming away, long and sleek in shape, and then I was surrounded by the haze. The fog was not opaque but imparted much the same quality of non-vision as thick smoke in dry air, except that I did not notice much in the way of wreaths. In fact, I was so confused and startled, that my only thought was to get away. From underneath the helmet there arose a faint odor quite unlike anything else. Fishy musk is the nearest description I can think of. The color was most interesting, as I had always been under the impression that cephalopod ink was black. Rather, it appeared dark purple which later faded to a somber shade of azure. I can also remember, when it thinned considerably, seeing vague shafts of reddish when the rays of sunlight far above caught the substance at oblique angles. The ink spread out in a cloud extending over several yards; and, in the still depths of the ravine took quite a time to dissipate. Actually it floated away as a hazy smudge before it evaporated.

I was not able to continue my observations on color changes until several days later when I netted a baby octopus from some turtle-weed growing a few yards from shore near the place where the reef reached its final termination in a mass of sandy shoals. I transferred the mite, a youngster of seven or eight inches spread, to the tidepool near my old house where I kept it for several days. It took to its new surroundings very gracefully and made no attempt to escape but made life miserable for the numerous small crabs and fishes that shared the pond. The crabs were its principal prey which it captured by stealth and by lying patiently in wait. Patience was its most evident virtue, and much to my disgust it would sit for hours in one spot without moving, staring endlessly at the moving forms in the water. It used a great deal of intelligence in securing the crabs and selected a spot to lurk where it had ready command of an entire corner of the pool.

The rocks of its dwelling were creamy brown, and this was the exact hue it assumed while waiting to make a capture. It had perfect control of its pigmentation. In comparison the renowned chameleons are but rank amateurs. The mechanics of this alteration of hue are very complex but are controlled by the expansion and contraction of a group of cells attached to pigmented sacks, known as chromatophores, residing in the outer layers of skin over the entire surface of the body. In addition there is scattered over the body another great series of cells capable of reflecting light. These are yellow and impart a strange iridescent shimmer, slightly suggestive of the glow of pearls. The chromatophores, which are of a variety of colors, are opened and shut at will producing any or all colors of the rainbow.

These color cells are manipulated by highly sensitive nerves communicating with the brain and with the eye. The eye principally dictates the choice of color although emotion also seems to have a definite influence. When frightened the octopi usually blanch to a whitish or light tone; irritation will cause them to break out in dark pigments. No other creatures in the world can alter their color as quickly and completely. Emotion will cause a human being to flush with anger or become pale with pain or anxiety; but no one can hold his hand and will it to be green with yellow stripes, or even yellow or plain brown, let alone lavender or ultramarine. An artist may paint a picture; only an octopus can color its skin with the portrait of its emotions, or duplicate exactly the pattern of the soil on which it rests. Only a very highly organized creature, one with a brain and an unusually well co-ordinated nervous system could accomplish the mechanical marvel of operating several thousands of cells at once, rapidly opening and closing them in proper order.

The cephalopods are not limited to color change but are also credited with being able to produce the most brilliant light known in the realm of animals. While this luminescence is limited to a very few deep sea species of decapods, which are the ten-armed squids, their light is so vivid that they outshine the fireflies. These lights organs may be found on any portion of the body, including the eyeball itself, and oddly enough, even in the interior of the animal! In these last forms the body tissues are quite transparent, so the light is not necessarily concealed. These light organs are quite varied, some being but mounds of glowing fluid, others complex and carefully constructed lenses with mirrors of reflecting tissue. As yet very little is known of these abyssal octopi and squid, though a few captured specimens have been observed burning with a strong light for several hours. Some day when the means of exploring the vast deeps of the ocean comfortably and safely has been devised we will learn more of these unbelievable cephalopods.

Quite unseen, my octopus would wait until a crab ventured near. Then it would either swoop quickly over the victim smothering it in its diminutive tentacles or suddenly dart out an arm and seize its meal before it had time to flee. It seldom missed but when it did it usually retrieved its dinner by a quick pursuit before it had gone far. Before twenty-four hours were up the entire bottom of the pool was littered with the hollow carapaces of crabs. Peculiarly, the animal almost always devoured its victim bottom side up, biting through the softer lower shell with its small parrot-like beak and rasping out the contents with its filed tongue before casting the empty shell away. The legs and feet were seldom eaten and were usually torn off and discarded. Little of this feeding was done during the day. At high noon I even saw a crab crawl over the relaxed tentacles without being molested or becoming aware of the danger it was courting. In the evening, however, particularly just before sunset the octopus seized everything within reach.

The capture of fish was not nearly so easy, and although I saw it make a number of attempts its only successful capture was a small goby that very injudiciously decided to rest a few inches below the octopus' chosen corner. As in the case of several of the crabs it was blanketed by a mass of writhing tentacles. Once the fish was grasped by the vacuum cups of these tentacles it was finished, for in their method of attacking, the octopi utilize one of the most efficient systems devised, a principle more certain than curving claws or the sharpness of teeth. Only the hand of man with its opposable thumb is superior.

The feel of these vacuum cups on the bare flesh is most unusual. It is not unpleasant, and in a small specimen, gives the sensation of hundreds of tiny wet clammy hands pulling at the skin. The strength of the suckers is amazing. When I tried to lift the youngster off my wrist it clung tenaciously and even when I had dislodged all the tentacles except one I still had to give a strong pull in proportion to its size to release the suckers. There have been cases in which the tentacles have been torn apart before the suckers released their grip. These suckers, which operate on much the same principle as the little rubber cups with which we attach objects to automobile windshields, are actuated by a muscular piston. The rim of the cup is fastened to an object, then the floor of the center is raised and retracted to form a vacuum. The cups, I found, would slip easily from side to side but when pulled directly exercised considerable power. In the octopods the suckers are sessile, or are mounted on low mounds; the squids carry the mechanism a bit further and produce them on stalks. In the giant squid the rim of the suckers are even equipped with fine teeth to render them more efficient. Whalers have recorded capturing whales with dozens of circular scars on their heads, inflicted in gargantuan battles with these monsters of the open ocean. Some of these scars have measured over two inches in diameter so that the creatures that possessed them must have been huge.

How large do the squid and octopi grow? There is an authentic record of a North Atlantic squid which measured fifty-two feet over all! Its tentacles had an abnormal reach of thirty-five feet and the remaining seventeen feet was taken up by the cylindrical body which had a circumference of twelve feet. The eye of this fabulous animal was seven by nine inches, the largest visual organ in the world. The suckers had a diameter of two and a quarter inches, and as some of the scars on captured whales have exceeded this measurement it is not unreasonable to assume that there may exist somewhere in the abyssal depths of the North Atlantic still larger squid of perhaps sixty or seventy feet. Even these amazing squid, however, are preyed upon by the great sperm whales which tear them apart with their long shearing teeth. In that old classic and favorite "The Cruise of the Cachalot," the author, Mr. Frank Bullen, gives a vivid description of a battle between a large sperm whale and one of these squid.

"At about eleven A. M.," he writes, "I was leaning over the rail, gazing steadily at the bright surface of the sea, when there was a violent commotion in the sea right where the moon's rays were concentrated, so great that, remembering our position, I was at first inclined to alarm all hands, for I had often heard of volcanic islands suddenly lifting their heads from the depths below, or disappearing in a moment, and . . . I felt doubtful indeed of what was now happening. Getting the night glasses out of the cabin scuttle where they were always hung in readiness, I focused them on the troubled spot, perfectly satisfied by a short examination that neither volcano nor earthquake had anything to do with what was going on; yet so vast were the forces engaged that I might well have been excused for my first supposition. A very large whale was locked in deadly conflict with a cuttlefish or squid almost as large as himself, whose interminable tentacles seemed to enclose the whole of his great body. The head of the whale especially seemed a perfect network of writhing arms, naturally, I suppose, for it appeared as if the whale had the tail part of the mollusk in his jaws, and, in a business-like methodical way was

sawing through it. By the side of the black columnar head of
the whale appeared the head of a great squid, as awful an object as one could well imagine, even in a fevered dream. Judg-
ing as carefully as possible, I estimated it to be at least as large
as one of our pipes, which contained three hundred and fifty
gallons; but it may have been, and probably was, a good deal
larger. The eyes were very remarkable for their size and blackness, which, contrasted with the livid whiteness of the head,
made their appearance all the more striking. They were at
least a foot in diameter, and seen under such conditions looked
decidedly eerie and hobgoblin-like. All around the combatants
were numerous sharks, like jackals around a lion, ready to share
the feast, and apparently assisting in the destruction of the
large Cephalopod."

Unfortunately Bullen does not tell the result of the combat
but one might assume that the whale was the victor, for the
food of sperm whales consists almost exclusively of squid.

If the squid and octopi are accused of being fearsome and
savage, it might be argued that they live in an underwater
world in which savagery and primitive instincts are the most
common passions, and the only way to exist is to conform to
the mode. There is no doubt that an enraged large cephalopod
could be a formidable antagonist. The authentic instances of
octopi or squid attacking human beings or divers, however,
are so rare as to be considered non-existent in spite of a large
literature to the contrary. Most of their savagery is confined
to securing their food, which is a normal and reasonable function.

The tentacles serve still another and more wonderful purpose, for it is by means of their arms that these unorthodox
creatures are able to perpetuate their race. The arms that serve
in this function are known as hectocotylized arms and this
name was derived from an honest and understandable mistake

by Cuvier. The name also signifies the arm of a hundred cells, and the mistake was made when the detached portion of one of these many-celled arms was found clinging in the mantle cavity of a female paper nautilus where it was erroneously thought to be some new sort of parasitic worm. The strange worm was named a hectocotylus and the error was not discovered until further researches had been undertaken in regard to the animal's breeding habits. It appears that the arm of the male paper nautilus is extended during breeding time until it looks like a long worm-like lash. This lash is charged with the fertilizing spermatophores. When the male and female meet they intertwine their tentacles in a medusa-like embrace, and when they disengage from their fantastic lovemaking, the end of the lash is deposited under the mantle of the female, where it is held for a time, for the female is not yet ready to spawn. When her eggs are eventually extruded, they are fertilized by the waiting sperm. The broken arm is not completely lost, for the male can grow another and still another.

The cephalopods are so delightfully versatile that they have still other systems of reproducing. In some forms the hectocotylized arm is not detached but is specially modified so that it can develop and transfer spermatophores to the females' mantle cavity near the oviduct. The spermatophore is itself the most remarkable creation of all this complex mating. It is a long tubular structure loaded with sperm, an apparatus for extruding it, and most wonderful a cement gland for attaching it to the female. It can be utilized at will; a thoughtful provision considering that the female may then take her good time in depositing her eggs under favorable circumstances. In other species the spermatophore is grasped by the male as it passes from his mantle and is placed in her mantle cavity or to the membrane around her mouth where the eggs are sometimes fertilized.

Some of the cephalopods show an amazing amount of mother-love and parental care. The common octopus *vulgaris* has been observed in aquaria guarding its eggs which were attached to the stone walls. It fiercely resented any interference and kept a constant circulation of water flowing, over them to insure that no parasites would take hold and that proper oxygenation would occur. The eggs were not even left long enough for the mother to secure food even though the period of incubation lasted for a considerable time. So intense was this guardianship that another octopus in the same tank which ventured close too frequently was set upon and slain. Mother-love in an octopus seems a strange and outlandish emotion, but no doubt it is actuated by the same flame that causes human parents to sacrifice their pleasures and desires that Junior, or his sister, for example, might go to college.

Cephalopodian care of the egg is responsible for another of the truly paradoxical things about these creatures. In the genus *Argonauta* the female carries about with her a beautifully coiled and graceful shell. This seems a contradiction to an earlier statement that the modern cephalopods are creatures which have cast aside their shells. Actually the shell of the Argonauts is not a true shell but is an egg case formed on the spiral shell pattern, which is mechanically a very strong and structurally efficient shape. The Argonaut is not bound to the shell in any way, for it may leave it whenever it desires, which it has been reported to do under certain conditions. No other mollusk is so equipped. Imagine an oyster, for example, opening its valves and stepping out for an airing! The shell is held in position by two arms which are specially formed for the purpose. Only the female possesses this protection, and she forms the shell, not with the mantle as do all other mollusks, but with her two modified arms with their expanded membranous disks. When the Argonauts are first born they have no shells and they do not begin its construction until they are a week or two old. Unfortunately for the natural history of Aristotle, they do not sail over the surface of the sea like miniature ships with the arms held as sails as that ancient and inquiring naturalist so quaintly believed, but creep and crawl along the bottom or swim by means of their siphons like any other cephalopod. While the eggs of the Argonauts are well protected and carefully mothered the adult has paid a reverse penalty for its acquisition of a shell, even though that shell is not a true one. The Argonauts have lost some of the intelligence and freedom of other octopods, for they appear to be the most sluggish and stupid of their class.

Inagua from above the sea gives no hint of the host of octopods that must harbor in its reefs, or of the tiny frond-colored squids that shelter in the growths of sargassum weed that float ceaselessly by on the currents, or of the larger and more appalling-looking decapods that move about in small groups in the open water. Nor is there much indication even to the diver of their presence. Unlike the reef fishes they are mostly nocturnal. During the bright hours they lie quiescent, curled up in the crevasses of their coral homes or float suspended and still, in the magic manner of underwater between top and bottom, waiting patiently with staring round eyes for the sun to drop and extend vague shadows over the blue depths. Then they creep from their dens and go slithering over the coral boulders or swim like living arrows through the green waters, pouncing on their prey and doing whatever amazing things fall to the lot of cephalopods.

Whenever I think of the great barrier reef of Inagua I think always of two things; first, of the fairyland of the coral itself and the pastel colors, and second, of the octopus of the drowned ravine with its weird eye and rubbery body. More than any other creature, the octopus is the spirit of the reef; unreal themselves, completely fantastic, unbelievable, weird, they are fitting residents of a world in which all the accepted routines are nullified, in which animals play at being vegetables, where worms are beautiful, where the trees are made of brittle stone, where crabs pretend to be things they are not, where flowers devour fishes, where fishes imitate sand and rocks and where danger lurks in innocent color or harmless shape. That they should, also, be inhabitants of the shadowy night places is the final touch on their characters. The octopi fill a niche of creation claimed by no others and a niche which they occupy to perfection.

- -

CHAPTER XV

The Marvel of a Tide

ALL living, when looked upon in a large sense, is a tide. Ebb and flow is one of the inevitable characteristics of existence. The growths of nations and their declines, the boiling sweep of conquests and their recessions, the rise and fall of cultures are manifestations of the turn of tides in the affairs of men. The Dark Ages and the Renaissance that followed were opposite halves of a single flow of energy just as the devastation of the hordes commanded by Chepe Noyon had its counterpart in the brilliance of the court of Kublai Khan. Only time pours ceaselessly in one direction; but even the march of the hours leaves behind a trail of risings and fallings, of comings and goings. The geologic eras bear bountiful evidence of the fluctuations of existence. Great waves of life washed up on the shores of eternity and fell back again; the extinct dinosaurs and amphibians, the fossils of armored fish and the billions of long buried trilobites are proof of this. Even individual lives are only tides in miniature; birth, growth and swelling maturity, decline and dissolution are separate phases in this phenomenon.

I have often wondered if the ancient and very primitive religions which recognized the existence of Selene, the goddess of the moon, did not have as their origin an instinctive recognition of the immense power of that satellite over the ceaseless pulsing of the tide-controlled sea. The phases of the moon and the correlation of the creeping of the waters into bays and lagoons could hardly have escaped the attention of early man, who was highly conscious of natural phenomena and who was just becoming aware of a sense of power and articulation. The moon worships date far into the recesses of unrecorded history. Many of the primitive peoples of today to whom the printed page is an inexplicable mystery have a keen appreciation of the relationship of the tide to that orb and regulate their activities accordingly.

The flowing of a tide to anyone familiar with the sea, and with the least grain of perception, is an impelling and inspiring event. The tides of time are discernible only from a distance, but the surging and falling of a sea tide is a potent and tangible happening. Perhaps the inexorable character of a tide is its impressive quality, but I think the emotional response to the occurrence goes deeper than that. The newly formed embryo of a human being bearing its telltale marks of ancient gill clefts harks back to the time when our ancestors, no matter how far removed, strove and battled fin and tail with the tide. If you have never leaned over a ship's rail and watched the soft swirl and eddy of the tide-urged water flowing past a rudder you cannot fully appreciate what I mean. If you have, and were at all aware, you will know that the sight of a moving tide is a stimulating experience.

Here at my typewriter, far from the flow of moving water, the feel of a tide is a difficult emotion to catch and imprison on a sheet of paper. If a tide boomed and crashed like the surf it would not be so hard. But a tide is *silent;* it cannot be heard except faintly when interrupted by a rudder or a ship's bow; it cannot be smelled nor touched. A tide is best seen though it is more readily *sensed* than visualized. Its very vastness makes it difficult to grasp. In my mind's eye I see barren sand bars lying idle in the sun with fiddler crabs moving about, or boats lying on their bellies in the sand; I picture seaweeds trailing toward the mouth of a river or whirlpools eddying about a buoy and I say "this is a tide." But it is not. These are only small manifestations of a tide. A complete tide is a stupendous awakening, a gargantuan breathing of the whole ocean, or a monstrous wave running the circuit of the earth extending from pole to pole. It is a swelling giant that sends millions of creeping fingers into the hollows of the land, bringing life to those hollows and as regularly withdrawing it again. A tide is the pulsing bosom of our planet. The Norsemen grasped the idea better than we when they believed it to be the breathing of the earth-serpent, Iörmungander, a monster so enormous that it encircled the globe and held its tail in its mouth to make room for that appendage.

> "Beneath the lashings of his tail
> Seas, mountain high, swelled on the land."

It was a tide that wrecked me on Inagua when I thought all danger from the ocean was past, and it was to the tide that I turned for one of the most entertaining days I spent on that island. Near Mathewtown, toward the south and in the direction of the opening of the Windward Passage, the coast of Inagua makes a last turn before sweeping away in a long spit toward the desolate frozen sand dunes of the weather side of the island. At the last point of the turn the rock cliffs by the settlement crumble away, and a little beyond, the interminable arcs of the barrier reef take up their existence and fling away toward the infinite horizon. Here the full force of the tide, sweeping in twice a day from the wastes of the Atlantic Ocean and from the turbulent deeps of the blue Caribbean, meets in a boiling mass of currents and counter-currents. When all the remainder of the coast was calm and smooth this point was flecked with foam and with the peculiar lapping waves of tide-rips. This was the final meeting place of east and west where the debris and flotsam of two oceans mingled before being swept into the blue depths or piled on the high white beach which was already littered with the fragments of a hundred thousand sea tragedies.

The diving at this rendezvous of the seas promised to be good, so I lugged the heavy helmet with its hose and line down to a little shelf on the very edge of the breakers. Instead of diving from a boat I decided to crawl from dry land to the depths on foot, so that I might experience the full sensation of the transition from dry to wet and examine the structure of the cliff wall and its life on the way. A small oblique opening in the sloping rock made an easy entering wedge without making it necessary to battle the full force of the surf. In addition, the opening was well padded with algae on its upper slopes and was reasonably free of the ubiquitous spiny sea urchins.

With a tremendous heave I hoisted the eighty-pound helmet on my head and settled it on my shoulders. It was so top-heavy that I staggered and nearly fell. The native boy that I hired for the task, started the pump, and, like a drunken man, I felt my way across the padded algae and stepped into the first gradient of the slope. The foam whirled slightly about my knees and then about my hips. In a second I had advanced to my shoulders and the intolerable weight was suddenly lifted. Once more I assumed control of my feet. I paused a moment at eye height gazing at the strange sight of a world divided in half and enjoying the unusual perspective of being exactly at the level of the water. Most impressive was the definiteness of the division; above was dry air and sunshine, all the familiar sights, flowers and white clouds; below was a strange blue cosmos of tumbled rocks, vague shadows and dancing bubbles. The surface was as rigid a barrier for most life as if it had been made of hard metal instead of the light-transmitting, yet opaque, film that it appeared from beneath.

The amount of life that clung to the film itself was surprising. On the upper side it was dusted with yellow grains of pollen drifted from the bushes on shore, and with down and winged seeds that had floated too far on the trades. There were also a few dead bugs, the frayed and broken wings of a butterfly, and some beetle elytra, little else. For the land creatures the top of the sea was death and failure. But a mere fraction of an inch beneath, the reverse was true; the under film was a marine maternity ward. For clinging to the burnished ceiling was a host of just-created things: baby fishes scarcely a quarter of an inch in length, transparent as glass and as helpless as the current-swirled plankton; microscopic lacy crustaceans aglow with jets of iridescent color; round globular pelagic eggs with long filaments and dark specks of nuclei; small blobs of pulsating jellies just released from their rock-dwelling, hydroidlike, animal-flower parents; and other myriads too small to be identifiable to the naked eye but made apparent by the rays of sunlight they caught and refracted. This final yard of open sea before the beginning of dry land was a veritable hatchery of sea-life.

Swiftly I dropped into the wedge and entered the frothing line of bubbles. These hurled about in all directions and I had to seize a rock to keep from being smashed against the sheer wall. The waves retreated and came plunging in again forcing me to cling tightly, digging in toes and fingers like one of the Grapsus crabs against the swirling retreat. Six times I crouched against the onslaughts before there came a lull and I was able to step lightly into space and float downwards to a ledge eight or nine feet below. I had hardly landed when the seventh wave came in and I had to fall on my knees to keep a firm hold. Once more there came a period of quiet and again I jumped, pausing momentarily on a round mound of meandrina before I gave a final seven-league step and landed thirty feet below the surface on the level white sand at the base of the cliff that was the foundation of Inagua.

Catching my balance and my breath I looked about. Sea-

ward a smooth plain of dazzling white sand leveled off into a
blue immensity, dipping slightly at the point where it went
out of vision. To the right the southwesternmost crags of the
island lay piled in gigantic fashion, torn loose in great blocks
by some heavy force. On the left a similar but smaller bluff
jutted out into the azure world. Like the first it was scarred
and pitted, festooned with a tremendous mass of living objects.
Long fronds of exceedingly lacy algae alternately drooped listlessly, then flung skyward as the advancing pulse of a wave
hit and rushed upward, deflected by the stone. Looking at
the combers from below I was interested to observe that it
was the wave form that moved, not the water itself; the great
bulk of blue liquid seemed to throb forward slightly but always
came back to its original station. I ascertained this by watching
some floating bumpers that hung close to the watery ceiling.
Only in the last few yards did the inverted wave-mounds fling
themselves in their entirety at the cliff. In the open the wave
shapes advanced ceaselessly; their power seemed to be transmitted from particle to particle, but the particles remained in
their relative positions. Were this not so the destruction that
would be wreaked on the land would be so tremendous that
the islands and the continents would be quickly eaten away.

In order to take in the entire vista of the base of an island
resting on its bed of sand I moved forward towards the open
plain and stepped from the shelter of the twin bluffs. Instantly,
and unexpectedly, I was met by a blast of water that threw
me off my feet, rolling and twisting on my side over the smooth
sand bottom. My helmet filled with bitter salt water. I gasped
for breath and fought to stand erect. With a jerk I came to the
end of the light rope that I was trailing between my fingers,
then was startled to find myself yanked off my feet, and
streamed out on the end of the line like a rag in the breeze.
Fortunately my flight into open water brought me erect again

and with a final splash the liquid subsided in the helmet so that I was able to catch my breath once more. The savage current caught my lightly balanced body, swooped it in a great arc nearly to the surface, swirled me towards the shore where it slackened and let me drop again on the sand.

Then I became aware that beyond the shelter of the crags a great assortment of objects was floating by at a dizzy rate. I had noticed them before but they had made no impression. Between the cliffs the current was barely perceptible except as a cool back eddy from the main stream. Once more I tried to breast the flow but was thrust back as if by a heavy hand. There was a solidity to the pressure that was unequaled by any other flow of energy with which I have had experience. Wind in a violent storm pushes and buffets one about, but water moving at one-twentieth the speed of a gale of wind would level everything in its path and tear up the ground besides.

The sand out in the swath of the tide was moving too. Close to the bottom the grains were rolling and bumping, creating small dust storms—a strange phenomenon under water—and long curving ridges and valleys a foot or more in depth which formed in endless parallel arcs at right angles to the course of the water. On a larger scale they were precisely like the smaller ripples seen on the mud bars when the tide is out. The whole ocean bottom seemed on the move, as though it were alive and were creeping towards an unknown destination.

Crouching in the shelter of the outermost boulder, I made myself comfortable and sat down to contemplate this stupendous event. For it was exactly that. All along the hundreds of miles of coast all over the world this same action was taking place. Great rivers of liquid were surging past thousands of headlands into bays, creeks, rivers, and lagoons, over shallow bars and in the hollows of deep channels, rolling countless sand grains and bringing oxygen, food, life and death to millions of swarming creatures. I remembered another tide I had watched in the murky green waters of the Chesapeake Bay in Maryland. In comparison to this Inaguan tide, it was a dull slow affair, but before I was through witnessing it from the windows of a steel cylinder hung from a barge anchored in the mouth of the Patuxent River near Solomons Island, I was completely overwhelmed at the mass of life it had brought past my small sphere of vision. The Chesapeake at that time was full of ctenophores, wraith-like comb-jellies belonging to the genus *Mnemiopsis*. The range of vision from the window of the cylinder was limited because of the haze to about six square feet. With a companion I began counting these organisms as they swirled helplessly by on the rising current. For six long hours we tabulated ctenophores and found that an average of 48 went by every minute or over 23,000 for the entire period. Then by computing the width of the river and the square surface of the tidal flow in a line across the river at its narrowest point, we reached the almost astronomical figure of 1,218,816,000 ctenophores! This did not consider any of the other forms of life which abounded in the water. This was only one small river, so unimportant that it does not even appear on a map of the Eastern United States. When we realize that every inch of this tide-impelled water all over the oceans from the poles to the equator is swarming with similar billions of living things we can only be silent with awe.

The Chesapeake tide, however, had none of the gigantic sweep and force of this Inaguan occurrence. It was a small scale flow, performed in a landlocked bay. This, of Inagua, was a full-fledged deep sea current with the pressure of two immense oceans forcing it on. While I watched, it increased in intensity until even the backwaters of my quiet eddy began to circle and tug at my bare flesh. The algae on the outer rocks were all streamed in one direction, straining at their fastenings as though they would momentarily tear loose. There was none of the gentle swaying and graceful undulations of the sea fans that I had seen on the reef. The actions of the marine plants and organisms gave the impression that a vast underwater hurricane was brewing and that they would all be shorn away into the blue abyss beyond. Some had been pulled from their anchorages, for large heads of orange-colored algae went swirling past and were lost in the haze. Clinging to one of them was the curved, ringed torso of a spotted seahorse and the saffron colored carapace of a small crab. They were battling bravely to maintain their positions on the rotating fronds, but they were probably going to a certain death. Sooner or later the buoyant tissues would lose their freshness, become limp and watersoaked, the particles of enclosed gas would escape and the seahorse and crab would coast with the plant to the deep sea bottom far off shore away from their accustomed habitat. Somewhere down in the blackness they would be snatched up by a hungry deep sea creature or would slowly deliquesce amid the abyssal ooze and slime.

While the tide was disaster for the tiny cosmos of the orange algae-head, it was the high road for the larger more vigorous fishes which took full advantage of the current to carry them on errands best known to themselves. A few fish attempted to breast the tide but large numbers permitted themselves to be carried on its strenuous course. How like people they were, taking the path of least resistance, going full speed towards an intangible goal, to be returned again when the tide changed. In just this way human action follows the main stream of thought, climbing on the fashionable bandwagons of a particular movement. Large numbers of big hogfish, gaudy fellows splattered with reds and deep oranges went by in a steady stream. Several times vast schools of blue-striped grunts, gleaming with brilliant iridescence, obscured the sand, so closely

packed and so numerous were they. These were followed by a
scattering of immense amberjacks which may have accounted
for the excessive hurry the grunts were in. Some very stout-
hearted fishes were breasting the current, but they were not
making a very good job of it. Most numerous of this rugged
group were the common and vividly colored spot snappers.
They moved along in a narrow file, or in congregations of
thirty or forty, close to the bottom, taking advantage of every
depression or place where the rush of water was moderated
even slightly. Their fins vibrated at high speed as they crept
along, gaining a few feet, holding their own for a space, then
inching forward again. What could have been so important to
cause all this expenditure of energy I could not guess, though
I rather suspect that the fishes themselves did not know. In
many respects they are like sheep and blindly follow the leader.
It is even questionable if the leader is fully conscious of its
activities, for if by some alarm or other interruption the direction of a schooling mass is changed, the leader relinquishes its
place and becomes the led, imitating the motions of the nearest
member of the school. There is much that is not understood
about the phenomenon of schooling in fish; it has been suggested that the occurrence is a form of natural communism
organized by a scheming nature as a means of protection. It is
a simple task for a marauder to follow and seize a lone individual, but much more difficult to grasp that same individual when
it is one of a great mass of darting, scurrying forms. Numbers
mean confusion to the enemy, a sort of primitive and defensive
"united we stand, divided we fall." It is a curious fact, however, that very few of the big carnivores resort to gregarious
living; the greater number of fishes of this type are the preyed
upon. However, like all communisms, the individual is sacri-
ficed for the purposes of the mob, and we have the spectacle
of spot-snappers following their leader in a useless and energy-

spending task.

Not all of the upstream creatures, however, were as foolish as the snappers. Some of these wiser ones were exceedingly cunning in their method of attaining their end. These were mostly small fishes, like the red, dark-eyed squirrel fish, and the silvery burnished moonfish and lookdowns. They went well out of their paths to avoid the current, circling in the lee of rocks, catching the back eddies, pushing through narrow holes and crevices, pausing frequently to catch their breaths, as it were. Of all these the lookdowns were the most amazing. They were characterized by the constancy of their numbers. Whereas the other fishes came singly, in vast schools or in isolated groups of six or seven, the lookdowns always appeared in twos. There is magic in numbers. Seven is a favorite numeral in certain folklore, thirteen forebodes evil, and all good things are supposed to come in threes. The number two will always bring to mind the silvery bodies of these fish. When I first saw these peculiar creatures during some diving in Florida, they were swimming in pairs and I have seldom observed them otherwise. Always two by two, side by side, moving as one individual, they are an underwater Damon and Pythias. Their duality is complete. If one dipped downwards, its companion did likewise; when they turned they turned together; moving or quiescent, what one did so did the other. I can think of no logical explanation for this piscine twinning, for these fishes are not known to pair off and build nests in the manner of some fish.

Even in appearance the pairs were identical. They seemed to have a sad expression, and their name was in keeping with their faces. The forehead sloped steeply downwards and they looked as though they were continually searching for some treasure lost on the bottom. From the tips of their backs long lacy filaments went trailing off in graceful arcs. Not the least remarkable characteristic of these fishes was their thinness. When swimming directly toward or away from one, all that was visible was a narrow line extending in a vertical direction. It was fascinating to watch the thin line suddenly form into a broad oval and then as quickly fade as the fishes wheeled and turned. A sort of now-you-see-me and now-you-don't.

Although the tide was whirling a vast horde of larvae fish and transparent spawn towards the outer wastes of the open ocean, it was also bringing a bounty to the many fishermen crouched on the rocks. Not human fishermen these, but an array of fantastic creatures of considerable variety. They were armed with an astonishing assortment of hooks, entangling snares, poisoned arrows and cleverly designed nets. Among the netmen were those most enchanting, highly successful and amazing creatures, the barnacles. Superficially, nothing is more stupid than a barnacle. Yet these doughty animals are clever enough to maintain themselves all over the world, from the frigid Arctic to the equally frozen Antarctic. There is almost no place in the sea where one cannot expect to find them at their interminable net casting. They think nothing of taking a world voyage on the bottom of some dirty tramp, or to go frolicking off on the hide of a whale. Certain species of whale barnacles are so fastidious that they will most often reside on the whale's lips and the front edge of its flippers, while others are said to prefer the throat and belly to the exclusion of the rest of the animal. Still other species are known to take to the air on the persons of flyingfish, and not the least unusual are certain forms that attach themselves to the umbrellas of large dead jellyfish.

As seen from underwater barnacles are creations of considerable beauty, not from their color, for they are always drab, but from the exceedingly graceful and lacy form of their fish-nets. These nets, which are really legs which have been transformed by the mechanics of need into living seines, must be seen to be appreciated. A barnacle's legs—even though these appendages resemble feathers more than they do legs—are as important to a barnacle as hands to a person, fins to a fish, or wings to a bird. Although walking is unthought of, their entire existence is dependent on their limbs; their breathing is possible because these organs circulate the water necessary for the separation of oxygen; and the status of the barnacle's stomach is directly in ratio to the functioning of the legs. A barnacle lives because it kicks.

Contrary to popular belief, a barnacle is not a shell fish, although it spends almost its entire life period tightly encased in a shell. Instead it owes allegiance to the great Class *Crustacea*, and in its family tree are the lobsters, the shrimps, and our other friend of the epicures, the edible crab. The name of its sub-class is the Cirripedia, which means, literally, the "feathery-footed."

Biologists, not being above error, for a long time considered the barnacles as aberrant relatives of the mollusks, and it was not until some thoughtful soul undertook to study the early stages of this creature that the truth became apparent. It was discovered that, after hatching, the young barnacle was so unlike the adult that it seemed impossible that the two could be parent and progeny. The infant had no shell at all; it swam and it looked like nothing on earth quite so much as an outlandish mosquito. It was studded with hairs and bristles, with spikes and long trailing appendages. But it obviously was a crustacean, for it was segmented and resembled the young of certain other crustaceans. In time the microscopic monstrosity molted, then again and again, altering its shape until oddly enough it grew a small shell on each side of its changed anatomy. At this period of its development it wandered about seeking a place to settle down to begin housekeeping as a full-fledged, calcium-enclosed barnacle. When, by instinct or simple chance, it discovered a proper locality it turned on its back, firmly cemented itself in place, surrounded itself with a house and began kicking—an activity that it continued to the final chapter. And its legs—which in any other crustacean would have become claws, paddles for swimming, or hooks for grasping—spread out, fringe apart and wound up looking like so many feathers.

I worked my way out to the boulder where there was a considerable colony of barnacles and watched them snaring the manna brought on the tide. They looked like so many active volcanoes, with puffs of light brown smoke beginning to issue from the tips of the cones only to be suddenly snatched in again, as though the eruption had gone inexplicably in reverse. Peering closer I could see that the momentary puffs of smoke were really the interlacings of the feet which were extruded and then quickly withdrawn fully expanded and curved inward to prevent the escape of any life that they had snared. The excess water escaped between the interstices of the fibers.

With my fingers I touched one of the delicate cirri, as the feathers are properly termed. With a snap it was retracted and the entrance barred with two plates of solid ivory. These plates fit so closely that they are airtight and watertight, sealing the barnacle in its shell until it once again desires to open. Thus barnacles can survive low tides when they are helplessly removed from their native element. Crashing surf, preying enemies are all the same to the barnacle. I have often thought that barnacles have their advantages. How nice it would be if we could escape undesirable situations, tax collectors and such, by merely closing our doors and going to sleep!

By this time the chill of moving water began to penetrate every fiber of my being. Some of the current seemed to be welling up from the depths for it carried bands of warm and cold. As the tide increased the cold became more pronounced until I was shivering. So I called a recess for a half hour.

When I again dropped below a great change had taken place. The current had become so violent that I had difficulty in keeping my position, even in the shelter of the boulders. Practically all the fish had disappeared. Those that were still about were swimming close to the rocks or were snuggled down in depressions where they were slowly undulating their tails. Great numbers had retreated into crevices and fissures in the cliff where they hung motionless. No big fish were in sight, except a half dozen large blue parrotfish that were bunched together in the shadow of a crag. The water had become a veritable avalanche and its speed was so great that even the fish did not consider it prudent to fight against it but took refuge in a philosophical retreat.

I did not descend again until just a few minutes before the tide began to change. The water which had flowed so swiftly before was barely moving. It was nearing the full flood. The aqueous dust storms had all subsided and the limit of visibility had extended thirty feet or more. Only the long curving rows of sand ripples remained to remind one of the deluge. I could stand without danger of being swept away.

In ten minutes all motion ceased and a perfect calm settled over everything, except at the surface where the waves still rolled over the rocks. The greatest change, however, was in the fishes. They no longer hung hidden in deep holes or lay quiescent in hollows on the bottom. The grunts were back again from their indefinite errands, though the amber-jacks that pursued them did not return. Most of the fish were busily feeding. A number of brilliant triggerfish had mysteriously appeared from nowhere and were gliding from place to place munching on small tidbits which they scraped from the algae-

adorned rocks. Their strange dorsal spines, I noted, were
folded well out of the way, and were raised only occasionally.
These spines, which comprise the first dorsal fin, are constructed in a most ingenious manner. At their bases is a complicated locking device, so cleverly arranged that when the
first spine is erected it cannot be lowered from without until
the third is depressed. When this is done the entire fin automatically folds down with it. I watched them carefully for
a long time hoping to catch some hint of the reason for this
strange contrivance. It is considered as a protection against
enemies, though this theory does not account for the unlock-
ing action of the third spine. Unless this is first lowered, however, when pressure is applied the other spines will usually
break before they give.

Between the triggerfish were swarming large numbers of
porkfish, handsome striped creatures, gleaming with iridescent
color. Like the triggers they were feeding off the algae, but
their method and food was quite different. The triggerfish
were scraping low lying mosses; the porkfish confined their
activities to the larger, more rounded heads of vegetation
where they seemed to search carefully, probing between the
fronds, snatching up the small crustaceans, worms and other
invertebrates that made the algae their homes.

With a five-pointed spear that I took down with me I tried
to add one of these porkfish to my collection. I missed it completely but on a second try snared one through the top of the
back. Before I could grasp it to place it in the mesh bag I carried tucked in my belt for the purpose it had twisted loose,
and squirming in pain it floated lopsidedly past the cliff wall.
Before it had drifted very far there was a rush of fins and it
was seized by a rock hind, a large mottled fish covered with
reddish spots which, unnoticed by me, had been lurking in a
wide crevice. The hind returned to its shelter carrying its vic-

tim with it and I went to try for another porkfish. To my surprise they would not permit me to approach. Previously they had swum freely about my legs, but now they kept their distance. Before I had been considered some strange new kind of fish; I was now regarded as a potential enemy. I have observed similar behavior among the snappers.

Most fish, however, are quite unconcerned about the death of their neighbors. Tragedy may strike within a few inches and they will continue feeding or idling or whatever their activity might be, as though nothing had happened. The next fish that I tried to spear exhibited a most surprising reaction. The barbed point scraped along its side, removed several scales and retained a small speck of flesh on the point. The victim, which was a yellow grunt with a flaming scarlet mouth, darted away, then turned, snatched up the floating scales and bit at the flesh on the point of the spear. Even when I jabbed at it again it did not flee but glided to one side and nosed the blades which had become buried in the sand! I marveled at the contrast between the two species; one perfectly sure of itself and the other timid and untrusting once danger had been proved.

Spearing fish is not as easy as it might seem. Although most fishes appear utterly relaxed, they are ever on the alert for anything that moves with directness. I have jabbed a spear into a school of fish, so densely packed that to miss seemed impossible, only to find that my barbs did not touch a scale. Yet the school, itself, moved scarcely at all. Usually there is a localized flurry which lasts for a brief moment and subsides.

After my failure at snaring the grunt my attention was attracted to a pair of small dull-colored fish which were cavorting between two sponge covered masses of dead coral. They were blennies of the same type that I had found at Lantern Head. They were the most unfish-like creatures I have ever seen. They skittered about the rocks assuming the most unusual attitudes. Heads up, then down, vertically or horizontally, they slithered in and out between the algae like restless insects. In a moment they gave a most remarkable performance. They had climbed down—they seemed to walk rather than swim, so closely did they stick to the moss—to the sand at the base of a boulder. Here they faced each other with only an inch or two of space between. For a second they remained motionless, then began a strange little hopping dance, using their pectorals as stilts. Round and round they went in a circle with their mouths as the axis. Occasionally they halted as though attempting to stare each other down.

Their mouths, which up to this point had been tightly closed began chattering as if in conversation. Once again the hopping and skipping began and continued for some time. When they again stopped, instead of chattering, they protruded their mouths until they touched. It was a perfect kiss! No such amatory caress was intended, however, for, shortly after, the blennies touched lips once more, established a firm contact and began shoving. The kiss was really a trial of strength, and apparently was their method of establishing ownership over a certain territory, for after quite a bit of pushing one of the blennies suddenly turned and fled, leaving the victor triumphantly poised over its tiny kingdom of a square yard of sand and an equal amount of coral encrusted rock. This seemed a very safe and sane way of settling the question of ownership without resort to bloodshed.

The instinct of curiosity, I am certain, is very highly developed in certain fishes. Sharks possess it in a great degree and so do the gurnards and sea-robins. This victorious blennie was the most inquisitive fish I have ever encountered. When I sat down in the sand close to its domain it come over and very carefully inspected each of my fingers outspread in the loose soil, tiptoeing delicately from one finger nail to the other. It nudged each very gently and then proceeded to crawl over my foot where it examined minutely an old scar inflicted by the sharp edge of an oyster shell years before.

Life in this tide-swept land clung almost exclusively to the rocks. The outer sand with its curving ridges was too completely unstable to house any permanent organisms. It was a watery no-man's land, a barren sheet of white against a background of blue. However, in the temporary quiet of the full flood, a number of fishes were deserting the rocks and making short excursions into the open. With the exception of the larger and more able types, few strayed any great distance. The sergeant-majors, blueheads, and the demoiselles were restricted to within eight or ten feet. Within this range they seemed very confident, frequently passing within easy reach of much larger forms. They knew that with a twist of a fin they could dart into the safety of a crevice. The only small forms that strayed with impunity into the open sand were the trunkfish, which no doubt felt secure behind their solid casings of jointed armor, and the porcupine fish, which are the nearest things to a living pincushion except the sedentary sea urchins. These were utterly without fear, and little wonder, for even to touch one would be to invite a painful puncture.

The open water was also inhabited by a small group of swellfishes, drab prickly fellows with gullets capable of tremendous extension when they are alarmed. These fish are supposed to be very stupid, yet in the Chesapeake Bay I have observed close relatives of the West Indian forms attacking large blue crabs in mass and biting with their sharp teeth through the crabs' hard shells, a task that would be exceedingly dangerous if attempted singly. No creature that is capable of such organized action can be considered stupid.

Most of the fish that patrolled the outer waters were large carnivores that swept ceaselessly back and forth waiting for

some rock-dweller to venture too far. They were not very
numerous, but most were capable of great speed. Among this
group were a cornet-fish about three feet long, not including
the long filament attached to the end of its tail, an equally
long trumpet fish which chased a tiny butterfly fish into the
shelter of a crag, and the long slim torso of a barracuda.

For a half hour the water at the base of the submarine cliff
remained quiet and motionless. The fishes glided about, moving and turning in an easy effortless way. Then faintly, imperceptibly, the tide began to swing. At first I did not notice it, so
gently did it start. But soon I became aware that the algae no
longer drooped listlessly. They began to point their delicate
fronds in the direction of the distant and invisible island of
Mariguana. I noticed that the sea fans on the rocks were bending too, and that, unlike the sea fans on the great reef, they
were all aligned at right angles to the shore instead of parallel
to it. Here the tide, not the surf, was the dominating force.
Out on the sand the long ripples began to reform, reversing
the position of their slopes, gradual on the upstream side, steep
on the lee. The parrots, demoiselles, and other rock feeding
species began to drift over to the sheltered side of the boulders
where they temporarily resumed their interrupted feeding.
The easy relaxation of the past half hour began to disappear.
The underwater gale was approaching, and in preparation the
fishes and even some of the invertebrates, including a half
dozen wandering hermit crabs, began to vanish into little holes
or fissures where they drifted into that wide-awake yet apparently restful sleep of the creatures without eyelids. The trunkfish and swellfish came out of the sand to settle down on a
smooth spot where the swellfish buried themselves until little
more than their eyes were showing. I could not help but wonder what sort of perilous life the creatures of this outermost
point must lead, forever hedged in by marauding, patrolling

enemies, limited above by the boiling surf, and twice daily forced to battle, or sustain, an almost irresistible deluge of flooding water. I was reminded of the people of Flanders, or of Alsace, who are periodically overwhelmed by floods of conquest or counter conquest, who bravely or hopefully continue living there, building new homes to replace those destroyed by shells or gutted by flames, and who after a time see them destroyed once more and are faced with the necessity of doing it all over again. Yet the comparison is not a completely true one, for a sea-tide is a river of life, not of death, a manifestation of nature which is a normal state of affairs for millions of creatures all over the world.

It was fitting that, as I returned to the dry earth again to avoid the rush of water rapidly welling to its climax, the last creatures I saw before my helmet broke the surface were the *Aurelias*, the moon-jellies. They were the first and only moon-jellies that I saw near Inagua. Their appearance at this opportune moment was significant. More than any other living creatures could have done, they expressed in their filmy iridescent tissues the symbolism of a flowing tide. There were six of them slowly drifting with slight pulsations of their hemispherical umbrellas on the bosom of the current towards the open sea. Pale and glowing they resembled the moon after which they are named; in a translucent shining galaxy they floated aimlessly off into watery space. Like the currents of the ocean they were giving themselves completely and passively to the pull of the invisible moon; the responsive tide was their life, their complete world and their means of conveyance.

CHAPTER XVI

The Incredible Sharks

SHARKS are beautiful in much the same sense that tigers or dive bombers are beautiful. They may be savage, cruel, blood-thirsty and sadistic beasts, or like the bombers, precise engines of destruction, but the fact remains that a free, ocean-living shark is perfection of line, the ultimate of grace. Streamlining is not new; it is only a modern application of an art developed by the sharks long ages before man was ever dreamed of, let alone created. There are, of course, a few sharks that have strayed from the elegant symmetry of their race. The hammer-heads and the bonnet-sharks are among these variants, but, by and large, the family of sharks has upheld the first rule of its form—harmonious proportion.

A shark strung up on a fishing line or lying dead on the deck of a ship is not lovely. Like any other dead thing it is so much twisted flesh and crumpled tissue. Only life endows them with their most conspicuous characteristic. I have questioned numerous individuals about sharks, fishermen and naturalists, and find that very few seem to recognize the fact of their grace. Perhaps this is because only a mere handful of people have seen sharks in their natural environment, and on the same foot-ing. With even these, some of them, the legendary fear, the accumulated distrust augmented by a large literature of shark stories has made it difficult to recognize beauty. Similarly, only one person in ten thousand can see beauty in a serpent although it unquestionably exists. Also the man who is about to have explosives dropped on his head by a Stuka is hardly in a position or mood to think of the airplane's design. Only when fear and distrust are divorced from the mind is it possible to think of sharks or of serpents or Stukas objectively. I reiterate; sharks from the viewpoint of architecture are among the earth's most carefully designed animals.

I do not propose to enter the interminable discussion as to whether sharks do or do not attack human beings. There seems to be good evidence for both arguments. There are a few authentic cases of attack; many hundreds of records which are neither authentic nor accurate and a large number that are definite fictions. Many of the instances of attack credited to sharks are really to be attributed to barracuda, about which there is no question of their ferocity and savagery. Most sharks are entirely harmless, including several of the largest species. True man-eaters are rare.

I once held to the common thesis that all sharks are to be avoided and are objects of repugnance. My metamorphosis into an Elasmobranchophile began at Sheep Cay where, because of my ignorance, I was thrown into such a panic, and blossomed into genuine interest with the adventure of the tiger shark at the barrier reef. Do not misunderstand me; I am not of that strange genus of humans who has any desire to hobnob with sharks nor tackle them with a knife, as did one individual for the sake of making a motion picture; nor do I tempt fate by hitting them on their tender snouts to shoo them away as another writer claims to have done. Rather, I have a deep respect for all sharks. I prefer in my underwater excursions to efface myself as much as it is possible in a metal helmet gurgling with a stream of bubbles, and to sit quietly back in the interstices of some well-protected coral where undisturbed and more or less unseen, I can watch the activity about me.

Sharks about Inagua do not swarm so I cannot truthfully tell any tale of being surrounded and hemmed in by schools of these animals. On the contrary most sharks are distinctly solitary, although some types do move in large groups. It was seldom that I saw more than two individuals at a time, though once I saw five moving leisurely along the face of the reef. When I think of the Inaguan sharks I think of most of them as associated with some definite place. The tiger shark patrolled the reef face where I first went down; week after week it could be found in that neighborhood. The sandy area just beyond the surf north of Mathewtown was the feeding ground of a pair of nurse sharks. An isolated patch of brain coral that grew all by itself midway between the shore and the place, a quarter mile out, where the bottom dropped away to the great depths, not far from the location of my old house, was the hub of existence for a six-foot ground shark which seemed to go on numerous trips but which always returned to its coral castle to rest or to swim idly about, weaving its tail in graceful, slow undulations. There were also a few species that were impermanent, true drifters and wanderers. These made their appearance and immediately disappeared or hovered around for a day or two at most before taking off into the misty distances.

Chief among these wanderers was a large blue shark, and it was this particular individual that first brought to my attention the fact that sharks are undeniably beautiful. It appeared on a day when an unaccountable shift of the current brought large masses of sargassum weed drifting in from the direction of Cuba just below the horizon. On this particular day I did not have sharks on my mind at all but went diving for the sole purpose of examining some of the floating gulf-weed from underneath, hoping to see some of the famed sargassum animals clinging to the bright yellow fronds. I was hanging lightly suspended from my life line just a foot or so beneath the surface watching the drifting masses go by. An unusually large clump came within reach and I wedged it between the keel of my boat and the line hoping thus to keep it there while I examined it frond by frond. Like so many sargassum patches, this clump contained none of the fantastic sea horses or yellow crabs which frequently make it their home. Disappointed, I released it and turned to wait for the next mass.

As I turned I saw floating about twenty feet away the sleek torso of a blue shark. It was approximately eight or nine feet long, fully adult, and it was watching me, not moving a muscle. My first reaction was the usual one; I was a little startled. But this was followed by a second and opposite sensation. This shark was the most exquisite and rhythmically formed animal of its size I had ever seen. It was a symphony in blue. From the tip of its smoothly rounded dorsal fin to the curve of its pure white belly it was deep radiant blue, an indefinable shade that was neither azure nor indigo; Gulf Stream blue is the closest comparison of which I can think. The rays of the sun breaking through the top of the water caused the rounded skin to glow with an unearthly light, a phenomenon seen only underwater. The belly also carried a delicate sheen, at times pale yellow, at others pink and even light mauve, which ran in evanescent waves over the tissue, glowing and fading, sweeping in soft bands across the white. This creature blended perfectly with the sphere in which it lived; it was a blue shadow in a blue world.

Its color was only one feature of its beauty; grace was its crowning accomplishment. The fish hung motionless for perhaps sixty seconds and then flowed into action. There is no other way of describing it. It did not merely move; it flowed from its pointed nose to the tip of its attenuated tail. Progression was effected by an inexpressible curvature of the caudal portion of the body, a long arc that swept to a perihelion, paused for an infinitesimal fraction of a second and then elegantly curved in the opposite direction. The motion was very gentle and the shark pulsed ahead until it was almost out of sight, banked in a long sweeping loop, twisting its whole body as it did so, and then passed in front of me within fifteen feet. As it went by I could see that the pulsing of its muscles, easily visible, kept perfect time with the action of the fins. It was delicately balanced. Once when it decided to veer slightly to the left it merely altered the position of its long pectorals a bare inch or two, bent the tail a little further and with hardly an effort went sliding off in that direction.

Once again it swam nearly out of vision, turned and was swimming back when something alarmed it. I am not certain what, perhaps a noise in the boat above, something it sensed, or possibly it simply got an idea in its head. Unexpectedly it put all its energy into motion and with tail lashing out with tremendous power it shot by at incredible speed and hurtled into obscurity. From a series of lazily curling arcs it became in an instant an engine designed for speed, in a medium where speed is acquired only by excellence of form and by perfect co-ordination of nerve and muscle.

It is little wonder that the sharks have succeeded in attaining underwater perfection, for they have had longer to do it than any other fishes. Sharks go back to the very beginning of things. The fossils of their ancestors may be found among the rocks of the Paleozoic. It seems a far cry from a flyingfish with its long multi-rayed pectorals or a scarlet parrotfish munching on reef vegetation to a carnivorous shark, yet there is evidence that all our modern fishes are derived from a shark-like ancestor.

Sharks, more than any other fish in the sea, fill me with a sense of awe. When one considers that they have maintained themselves, almost unchanged, down through the misty flights of the ages, undiminished and as vigorous as ever, one must give them respect, if only grudgingly. Four hundred million years is no mean record for any group of creatures. When one contemplates the fact that they were pursuing their prey and engaging in the activities of their kind when the solid earth was nothing but an empty space of slimy mud or dusty desert, where nothing moved or stirred and where no voice broke the stillness, that respect must be tinged with wonder.

Eventually, when the land did become carpeted with vegetation, when the amphibians had their grotesque hour and then disappeared, to be followed by the still more weird reptiles—by the gigantic dinosaurs, the ichthyosaurs and the pterodactyls—when the ocean was the abiding place of the ferocious mosasaurs, which descended from the land into the sea, the sharks maintained themselves as they had from time immemorial. When the reptiles were gone in their turn, and when the dawn of the age of mammals broke upon the face of the earth just as it is now in our time rapidly coming to a swift and unfortunate close these persistent sharks blossomed into a numerical abundance which must have been amazing, if we could only have been there to witness it.

My earliest memories of fossil hunts bring recollections of finding myriads of shark teeth. At the base of the famous blue cliffs of the Miocene in Maryland along the shore of the Chesapeake Bay I have in a single day picked out of the sand and clay a thousand shark teeth from a strip of cliff and beach several hundred yards long! Sharks must have swarmed in legions to have left so many teeth in one spot. These ranged in size from tiny points a quarter inch in length to large triangles five inches from apex to root. It has been estimated that these latter teeth must have been borne by animals ranging from a hundred to a hundred and twenty feet long, the largest living organisms of all time? A man could have easily sat in the open mouth of one of these monsters. They apparently persisted into comparatively recent times for hundreds of similar teeth have been dredged from the ocean bottom. We have no indication of what force, or series of circumstances, drove these greatest of all beings from the face of the earth. Perhaps by their very ferocity they may have devoured everything within their geographical range and then eliminated themselves by cannibalism. Perhaps some unknown elasmobranchian disease may have vanquished them. Some smaller and equally hungry creature may have destroyed their young or they may have become too specialized in some manner to breed with facility. We do not know.

Perhaps one of the reasons the sharks have persisted so long is because of their simplicity. Some of the most efficient machines are the least complex. The sharks in their truly incredible style have managed to remain quite primitive, yet remarkably facile. Many of the animals with which they started their history became exceedingly intricate, exceedingly specialized—and also exceedingly extinct. The early sharks, which were the starting point for a very diverse group of fishes, including practically all modern forms, provided the basic architecture on which these later creatures were patterned. The sharks, too, have evolved but they have been very conservative about it. One is reminded of the architecture of the Greeks. It has been the inspiration of much that has followed, yet few modern structures are as exquisite as the Parthenon with its essential simplicity. This is why the sharks are still found wherever there is sufficient sea water to hold them. From the sunlit surface to the blue-blackness of a thousand fathoms and from the berg encrusted arctic to the tropics, sharks thrive and thrive efficiently.

Sharks to land dwellers seem rather nebulous, yet not an hour's travel from the Atlantic Coast in the vicinity of New York and Philadelphia, there are legions of them. Once, in the winter, I spent a week on a trawler operating out of Norfolk, Virginia. The trawler was out after porgies and similar food ishes for New York consumption. The trawl nets were dragged for a full week over a stretch of several hundred miles. Every half hour the drag was lifted and emptied of its contents. It took seven days to secure enough edible fish for a skimpy boat-load to port. Nearly every time the trawl was lifted, it was bulging with sharks, hundreds to the haul. We waded in shark bodies up to our knees. The fishermen beat them, clubbed them, slit them with razors until the decks ran with blood, trying to destroy them and cursing them, for each haul meant lost money. It was a futile proceeding, for the next net, like the first and the next and next was packed with sharks. For seven days we skipped over the ocean hoping to outrun them, nor did they begin to thin out until we reached the vicinity of Cape Hatteras far to the south. The ocean floor must have been literally carpeted with their undulating bodies.

Most animals eat to live. Sharks live to eat. It is their constant insatiable hunger that has brought them so unfavorably to attention. I frequently watched the nurse sharks on their sand bar. From the shore they appeared to spend their time merely gliding about, restlessly pacing back and forth between the beach and the depths. Hour after hour they continued their peregrinations, dark shadows against the gleaming bottom. They even came in to the last few yards of surf in search of carrion and crustaceans. Here their fins and broad lobed tails could frequently be seen cutting the surface. But they never hurried, except when I occasionally frightened them by throwing conchs at their bodies when they came too close to shore. Then they exerted themselves to the utmost to be away and splashed out of the shallows with lightning speed. Usually their progress was a series of interminable weavings from side to side, economy of energy their characteristic.

From the helmet they were beautiful to watch. They prowled close to the bottom skimming just above the sand. Their coloration was rather light so that against the sand bottom they were very inconspicuous. At times their shadows were more visible than the owners. Most interesting was their ability to stop instantly in their flight. I never quite discovered how it was managed. Their pectorals were spread apart as checks or brakes but not to the extent it seemed necessary to halt a hundred pounds of gliding fish. They could also make a complete reversal within their own length, though I only saw this done once. Usually they banked steeply, rolling slightly to one side and then came about in a long graceful sweep.

By way of entertainment I gathered a group of prickly sea urchins from some rocks near shore and carried them under me along with a five-pronged spear. With this instrument I crushed several and rolled them along the bottom. Then I retired twenty or thirty feet away. For a long time I waited. Nothing happened except that in the meantime a group of small fish began tearing at the broken urchins and soon had them all eaten up. I gathered some more which I beat into an oozy pulp with a rock. This time I had better luck although hardly ten seconds had elapsed before the bait was surrounded by a dense cloud of fish. There was no shooing them away so I withdrew, hoping against hope that my bait would last until the nurses got the scent. They did. A few seconds later I saw their shapes devolving out of the blue sunlit haze. They were no longer moving leisurely but were sweeping along at considerable speed although they did not give the impression of being in a rush. One approached directly head on and I was interested to observe that it did not move in a straight line but was weaving from side to side. Apparently its sense of direction was dictated by the use of alternate nostrils. When it received the strongest stimulation on one side it swung in an arc until the other was affected. As soon as it saw the bait the weaving ceased. With a rush it swept up with its companion, glided over the urchins, cattering the snapping fishlets which fled a short distance and hovered, hoping to catch some of the crumbs.

Both sharks carried remoras, which is a contradiction to the belief that these peculiar parasites are not to be found when two or more sharks swim together. These dropped off before their hosts had time to turn and busily dug their noses into the urchins. They had only a brief second, however, before the nurses were back. The sharks immediately snatched up the bait, giving it several hard shakes before gulping it down. The spines of the urchins did not seem to bother them for they devoured the pieces, spines and all.

The remoras glided busily about in front of the nurses' mouths, snatching at small fragments that they dropped, but keeping alertly just out of reach. When the bait was all gone except for a few crumbs, the nurses appeared tremendously excited, twisting and weaving about the place where the bait had been. Not finding any more they began circling and then approached me, possibly attracted by the urchin scent on my hands. They made me feel somewhat uncomfortable, but fortified by the knowledge that they were harmless. I stood my ground. The shadow of the boat seemed to cause them some disquiet for they avoided it scrupulously. Twice they went around, whirling in opposite directions, ogling me with their tiny eyes but not venturing closer than about twelve feet. I remained perfectly motionless, fascinated by their grace. Their appearance was only marred by their barbels, a peculiarity of the nurse sharks, one on each side of the mouth, which gave them a slightly sneering and disdainful expression. At the beginning of the third turn around I decided I had had enough of their attentions and suddenly raised my arm, hoping they wouldn't get an idea to eat it. With two mighty surges they turned in their tracks and went bursting away into the haze. As they went I could feel the rush of water from their caudal fins and its force was sufficient to stir up the sand at my feet in little clouds of silt.

Quite unexpectedly, the remoras, which were still restlessly searching among the urchin crumbs, did not follow but persisted in their quest. They remained around for perhaps five minutes longer and then, one after the other, melted into the azure distance. They neither followed the paths of the nurses nor seemed to be aware of what direction they had gone.

At first examination there is not much relation between beefsteak and sharks. Yet I am certain that but for sharks our interest in beefsteak would be very casual. For as far as we know sharks invented teeth, and without teeth our beefsteak potentialities would be limited to gulping and hasty swallowing, assuming that we would even be eating this delicacy. In fact, a shark may be truthfully and literally described as being an animal which is covered from one end to the other with teeth; skin teeth to be exact, or as they are more properly termed "dermal denticles."

The hide of a shark, which appears so smooth and velvety, is not soft at all but tough and rasping with a touch like a file. I know one old-fashioned cabinetmaker who so preferred his well-worn piece of shark-skin for certain finishes that he would use it in preference to sandpaper. Shark-skin was a common polishing agent long before sandpaper was conceived. This roughness is caused by the presence of hundreds of thousands of miniature "teeth" which protrude through the skin. These teeth, which en masse are known as shagreen, are true teeth in that their structure exactly resembles that of the dentition of all animals above the grade of the sharks. Like true teeth these skin teeth contain a "pulp" with blood vessels, nerves and connective tissue, dentine which is that ivory-like substance characteristic of all teeth, and finally on the outside a layer of hard enamel. Happily, sharks are not subject to toothache.

It is these skin denticles which give us the clue as to the method by which chewing, grinding and cutting teeth were evolved. The gradual transition from skin denticles to actual teeth is readily observed in the embryos of certain sharks, where, if one follows with a glass the curve of the mouth from exterior to interior, the denticles become more and more altered, larger, and finally perfect and functional teeth. The peculiar teeth on the swords of sawfish, which are close relatives of the sharks, are derived similarly from the skin. These teeth are greatly enlarged skin denticles which have grown in alternate positions on the blade of the sword. The teeth in the mouth of a shark are frequently laid in series, row after row, sometimes to the amount of four hundred. These advance continually, replacing those worn out or lost. Only the outer series are used.

Depending on their usage, the teeth of shark and their relatives show a great variety of form. Some of these are little more than tiny pointed needles, others have become blunt, or even hexagonal while some are triangular with razor-sharp saw edges that cut like a knife. A bite from one of the latter would shear flesh into ribbons. Strangely, one of our very largest sharks, the whale sharks, which reach a length of forty feet and a recorded weight of 26,500 pounds, have teeth which are on the average less than a quarter of an inch long. These fish are quite without means of protection and certainly, in spite of their huge bulk, are among the most inoffensive of creatures. I once saw one of these huge fellows basking in the sunlight on top of the ocean about half way between Inagua and Haiti. It was beautifully checkered with a series of light polka dots and rectangular cross lines. The ship missed it by inches. A moment later the monster sounded and went hurtling into the depths. Little is known of this species and it has been seen only a few times. Its food is believed to consist of small plankton, organisms that float freely with the waves and current. This accounts for the minute dentition, for plankton feeders have little or no use for teeth.

Fins in most fish serve as rudders, balancers, brakes, or ailerons. It remained for the sharks to put them to a more remarkable and important purpose. The ventral fins of male sharks are produced into a long rod-like process which possess a hollow groove. The function of these modified fins, or claspers, as they are commonly termed, is to carry the life-creating sperm to the body of the female where the eggs are fertilized. Consider what an intelligent provision this is. It is not only a means of insuring proper fertilization of the waiting ova, but is a distinct economy. There is none of the terrific waste common to so much marine life, none of the lost millions of sperm cells cast loose to drift away on the tide, their destiny unfulfilled. Nor is there the corresponding loss of eggs because of lack of union with the fertilizing element. This is another reason why sharks thrive undiminished while other fishes have their seasons of scarcity and why they have continued where more complex types have gone out of existence.

Life and arithmetic are associated in exact proportions. The number of young that the shark produces, just as in other fishes, is in precise ratio to their chances of survival. In this respect the sharks maintain an almost human ratio. Some of the viviparous species are known to produce only two or three young; a dozen is usually considered a maximum family. Contrast these figures with those of a cod which must extrude up to 9,000,000 eggs to keep its race alive. While the fertilization of shark ova is accomplished in most of the species in much the manner described, they are still somewhat versatile in their methods of reproduction. A great many forms bring forth their young alive—a surprising action in such a primitive animal— and an equal number lay eggs. Here again we see the laws of mathematics applied, for the egg laying forms, being subject to greater loss, must and do produce a larger number of spawn to maintain themselves.

The eggs of sharks, and the affiliated skates and rays, are encased in tough leathery covers, usually rectangular in shape with long fibrous tendrils which are caught about marine vegetation or solid objects to prevent them from being drifted away. Others, however, are formed in a peculiar ridged spiral resembling somewhat the curled forms of certain sea shells. Every Atlantic beach at certain seasons of the year is strewn with the black remnants of these cases.

Not the least curious of all fin developments is that belonging to those most original of all hoboes, the remoras, itinerant and unwanted companions of the sharks. They attach themselves to their elasmobranchian freight trains with an oval disk located on the flattened upper surfaces of their heads. These disks are made up of a series of fleshy partitions which by muscular retraction create a semi-vacuum. The disk is simply a dorsal fin which by an amazing transformation has become modified into a sucker.

The thresher sharks, however, have the most unusual fin development of all. The upper lobe of their caudal fin is equal to the length of the remainder of the animal. Its purpose has not yet been discovered, although it is believed by some to be utilized as a flail to herd the small schooling fishes on which it feeds into a compact mass where they can be attacked with ease. The common stories that the blade-like tail is used to beat porpoises to death is utterly without foundation. There is also the possibility that it is one of those freaks of animate existence which has no sensible purpose but which was caused by an outlandish mutation, a going astray of the genes and chromosomes of a distant ancestor. We will not know much of these creatures of the sea until some way is devised of observing them in their own element. The ocean will remain to the very last the farthest boundary.

The subject of shark fins is by no means exhausted with mention of the threshers. For there remain the rays and skates, including the giant devil fish, which are little more than sharks which have become modified for a bottom existence. A ray or skate is, in a sense, a set of shark pectorals equipped with an almost indistinguishable body; they are all fin. The transition from shark to skate is proved by the existence of the angel sharks which are neither true sharks nor yet quite progressed to the point of being full-fledged rays. There were large numbers of these skates and rays all about Inagua, and at the settlement they frequently came to within a few yards of shore to feed on the entrails and other refuse which the local fishermen cast into the water while cleaning their catch.

One of these rays gave me quite a fright. I was walking in the shallow lagoon behind the barrier reef looking for shells. Suddenly I felt something rubbery beneath my foot. Startled I jumped high in the air and came down just in time to miss the lashing tail of a large stingaree. The fish went dashing off into deeper water, swimming rapidly with graceful undulations of its broad wings. I was very happy not to have stepped in the way of the tail for it was equipped with a dangerous, saw-edged spine which can inflict a nasty and very painful wound. These wounds often take months to heal because the spine is frequently coated with a layer of germ-ridden mucus that starts a festering infection. This spine is simply one of the skin teeth of their shark relatives which has become enlarged as a weapon of defense.

If I were to make a catalogue of strange and wonderful animals, I would place the hammerhead shark that I saw late one afternoon at the top of the list. I had been diving for about an hour in a spot midway between the patrolling grounds of the nurse sharks and the coral castle of the ground shark and was interesting myself in some huge razor shells that jutted out of the sand. I was down quite a depth, nearly forty feet. These shells were larger than any I had seen washed up on the beach. Although they were imbedded in soft sand they were fastened firmly by the strands of their byssus and I had quite a time prying them loose. My bare hands, softened by the water, were not equal to the task so I returned to the dory and secured a hook of iron. After warming myself in the sun for a while I dropped down again with the instrument and made my way over to the spot where several huge shells were clustered together. Carefully, so as not to injure the delicate shell I inserted the curved iron bar in the sand until it engaged the tangled byssus threads, and then pulled. To my disgust the shell crumbled to pieces and the hook emerged with the flesh of the mollusk adhering to its point. I tried another, being exceedingly careful, but the result was the same. Another fared likewise as did a fourth before I began casting around for another method. It then occurred to me that the most satisfactory attack would be to excavate the creatures complete. With the iron I began scraping at the bottom and was soon surrounded by so dense a cloud of silt that I could not see. Nevertheless I continued. On my hands and knees I dug at the chalky close packed soil until, with a slight heave, the shell came loose and I rose holding it in my hand and tried to peer through the murk. There was very little current at this spot and the cloud hung around like a pall.

I was about to turn and climb up the life-line when I discovered that I had dropped it during my digging and it had drifted out of sight. This did not particularly disturb me, for I knew that if necessary I could climb the hose curling up from under my shoulder. Preferring to locate it, however, I groped around in circles waving my outstretched arm back and forth.

After a few seconds I found it again and tucking the shell in my belt started to go up the line. I had scarcely ascended ten feet when I saw an indistinct gray shadow surging through the water. Not knowing what it was I felt that prudence was the sensible course and went rapidly up to the surface. Under the keel of the boat I hung long enough to dispose of my shell and then dropped down again about six feet to be clear of the bubbles breaking against the bow.

I looked down. The bottom seemed a long distance away, an illusion created by the refraction of the water. In the very center of the limits of vision was the cloud of silt I had stirred up. It was slowly clearing and about its periphery was a cloud of fish. They were obviously excited about something and, as I watched, others arrived out of the blue and joined the milling circle. This in itself was extremely interesting because when I first went down there was hardly a fish in sight; the ocean bottom seemed peopled with only the half buried razor shells and a few isolated conch.

Suddenly one entire sector of the circle burst asunder and out of the silt emerged the form of a small hammerhead shark. The smaller fishes dashed in all directions, waited until the hammerhead was several yards away and then reformed ranks. But they were not to have much peace for the shark suddenly doubled on its tracks and with mighty thrusts of its tail went into the haze again. Then it dawned on me what it was after. Like the other fish it had smelled the juices of the mollusks, and attracted by the promise of an easy meal had come on the scene. That it had arrived first testified to the keenness of its senses. Before I stirred up the bottom the water had been so clear that I could see a hundred feet in either direction. The shark had scented the mollusks and reached the place of their demise in less than four minutes. This seemed incredible for the current was flowing slowly. Even presuming that the shark was just beyond the range of vision it must have come at terrific speed. Perhaps it was just as well that I was surrounded by haze when it approached for to have looked up suddenly and seen a hammerhead rushing on me like a bolt out of the blue would have been too much.

In a few seconds the silt began to settle and I could see the creature swooping just above the sand, nosing the spot where the shells had been. Its energy was astonishing, not for a second was it still. Taking a deep breath and crossing my fingers for luck, I slid in a long drop down the life line and checked myself just above the bottom, blowing hard through my nostrils to relieve the pressure that had suddenly built up in my ears. It corrected itself with an audible squeak and I dropped the remaining six feet to the sand. Trying to feel just a little brave, I turned and consciously composed myself. Inasmuch as the hammerhead was less than six feet long I felt reasonably safe, though if the shark had been much larger I think I would have cast bravery to the winds and scrambled hurriedly into the boat. But this was the only live hammerhead I had seen on Inagua, or anywhere else for that matter, and I did not want to forego the opportunity of making its acquaintance.

It was the most grotesque animal I have ever seen. From its gill clefts backwards it was a normal shark, graceful and sleek. From this point forwards it was all out of reason—a travesty of a fish. Its eyes were set on the distal extremities of its outlandish head, and its nostrils, unlike those of all other sharks, were visible as long narrow slits along the entire front edge of the hammer. With such elongated sensory organs it was little wonder that it had smelled the mollusks as quickly as it did. When it rolled over I could see that the mouth was situated well back of the head projections. Underneath it was yellowish white, above dark brown with the slightest suggestion of mottling. I was inordinately interested in the use of the amazing head anatomy but saw nothing that even suggested its purpose.

Whatever its function, the creature's bow was certainly no hindrance, for it was one of the most active sharks I have ever seen. The nurse sharks are the Southerners of their family; nothing except fright ever makes them move beyond a certain leisurely pace. The hammerheads, by comparison, are metropolitan New Yorkers; they are bursting with impatient energy, restlessly scurrying here and there, working like the very devil to make a living, rushing through life as though their very existence depended on speed. Already excited by its easy meal of mollusks, the hammerhead was circling and swooping at a dizzy rate. Its appetite must have been whetted, for it began pursuing several small wrasse which, attracted by the scent of the mollusks, had injudiciously left their clump of isolated coral faintly visible in the distance to seek food. One of the wrasse escaped by diving headlong into a hole in the bottom which had been constructed by some sort of animal, for there was a considerable circle of piled up silt around the entrance. The other was not so fortunate. It made the mistake of dashing in a straight line for its coral home. The shark then gave one of the most masterly exhibitions of water acrobatics I have ever seen in all my hours of diving. It lunged after the wrasse which was vibrating its tail so rapidly that it could scarcely be seen. The midget was putting its last ounce of energy in its dash for life. But it was no equal for the hammerhead. The big fish swooped over its tiny prey, hovered for a split second and then dived. The wrasse, sensing the tragedy over its head, suddenly halted and with a violent twist of its body reversed its direction. But too late. The hammerhead did a magnificent Immelmann turn, curving backward in its own length, and then coming down again in a rushing dive gave a half turn, opened its mouth and snapped it shut on the wrasse. Without a stop the shark did another twist before it hit the bottom, missing it by inches and causing a temporary flurry of loose sand before it flung into a wide arc which, with diminishing speed, carried it to a point midway between the surface and the ocean floor where it hung motionless for at least sixty seconds. I saw it gulp once or twice and watched a silver scale trickle from its jaws. The scale went slowly drifting down through the azure water catching momentary flashes of sunlight as it rocked back and forth before it finally settled on the floor of the ocean.

The effect of this tiny mote and its slow descent after the rush of action that preceded it was startling. The nearest common happening to which I can link it is the silvery tinkle of tiny fragments of glass falling to the ground after the rending, sickening crash of a bad automobile accident. I vividly remember the same sensation when a car in which I was riding, and which was driven off the road by a reckless driver in another machine, collided with a telephone pole and snapped it off at its base. Fortunately no one was hurt but the most realistic recollection of the whole affair was not the thunderous boom of the actual contact but the delicate trickling of minute pieces of the windshield and headlights as they slid across the crumpled metal in the comparative quiet that followed. Whenever I hear the tinkle of fine glass I automatically wince. Similarly whenever I think of hammerheads there immediately flashes to mind the silvery scale slowly dropping through the azure water.

The shark poised in midwater for perhaps five minutes and then with a mighty surge of its torso pulsed off into the unknown. The last I saw of its retreating body was a three quarter view when it swerved to inspect something beyond my ken. I felt as though I were looking at a creature which did not belong to my world; it seemed a shape that was properly snatched out of the recesses of the past to spend a brief hour in the present. Yet I know that it is not improbable that the sharks, living as they do in the depths of the unchanging ocean will be swarming the waters of the world when our man-made cities are crumbling mounds of earth and that they will be feeding, as they do now and have been doing for breathless ages on the crustaceans and the fishes, in a time when man will be a forgotten, precocious creature who, for a brief space of time, nearly upset the balance of nature.

CHAPTER XVII

Night Beneath the Sea

At half past nine on the evening of May 14th I was, I must admit, just a little uneasy. A peculiar crawling sensation in the pit of my stomach, somewhat like the emptiness of extreme hunger caused me to feel ill at ease. I have long ago passed the period in life when I am disturbed at natural phenomena. Storms still fill me with awe; I respect them and avoid them whenever possible, but I am not afraid of them. Spiders and snakes cause me not the slightest quiver. I have studied them long enough to know that they are—most of them—perfectly harmless; I regard them with interest and with an eye to beauty. Likewise with most other natural creations; I have already written my reactions to sharks and octopi.

Before the darkness had come I had rowed out beyond the breakers near the settlement and watched the sun plunge beneath the horizon in great sheets of gold and vermilion. While it was sinking, casting purple shadows over the dark line of the shore and temporarily painting the usually white beach with crimson, the trade wind had slackened and the white caps which all day had been marching toward the west ceased their movement. The waves became rolling, and as darkness came rushing blanketwise out of the east the waters grew still, then slick with only a slight heave to suggest the turmoil of the day. In the brief space between half-light and dark, while the stars appeared one by one, I had unloaded my diving equipment, placed the helmet in position over the gunwale, connected the air hose and pump, adjusted the life line, and then sat down to wait for the coming of full night.

The water turned from light blue to blue gray, gray, then dark and finally somber opaque ebony. The shore which, up to this time had been plainly visible, became a black line suggested more than revealed by the loom of the stars. There was no moon. That satellite would not appear for another week; it was hidden on the other side of the earth. I turned and contemplated the surface of the ocean. Its blackness was complete. Once more the crawling at the pit of my stomach began. I had come out beyond the breakers with the avowed intention of diving beneath the surface to see what was going on in the ocean during the dark. Now that the accomplishment was only waiting for my action, I hesitated. Even in full daylight the undersea is a world in which man definitely does not belong. Then, when visibility is at its utmost, one is frequently beset with a feeling of helplessness. How much more so at night when one's eyes are completely useless, and when clear vision is further complicated by the limited perception directly in front of the helmet.

In a last minute check-up, and to gain time to revive my waning courage, I tested the fastenings of my underwater flashlight. This was an ordinary searchlight encased in sheet rubber with a lens cemented over the bulb, so arranged that by feeling through the rubber I could turn it on and off. Satisfied that it was in proper working order, and finding no further excuses for delay, I issued some last minute instructions to my black helper, and told him that regardless of what happened he was to keep pumping steadily. Turning away, I poised on the gunwale, stood still long enough to hear a rooster on shore crow halfheartedly as though it knew it was hours too early, felt a wave of perfume redolent of jasmine and lavender come swirling off the beach in a breath of warm air, and then stepped over the side into the depths.

The cold water plunging over my head shocked me into

activity, and with a spurt of energy I stroked my way to the surface where I located the boat and swam over to the gunwale. Now that I had actually made the first step the feeling of fear left me somewhat though I still felt keenly aware of being out of element. I groped along the side for the life line, curled it about my hand, once again patted my belt where the flashlight was hung to make sure it was there, acknowledged my readiness in a low voice and permitted myself to be helmed. The sibilant rush of pulsing air assured me that the pump was functioning properly, and with a last minute roar of breaking bubbles in my ears, I let go and was plummeted into the spaces of watery night.

In a long sweep I allowed myself to drift downward for about twenty feet. Then with ten feet of inky water still between me and the bottom I halted my descent with a slight pressure of my fingers and hung motionless. For a few seconds I swayed back and forth, twirling slightly, and came to complete rest.

I peered out of the glass. Try as I might I could discern nothing. I was poised in the center of empty space. There was neither light nor movement, only a still solid blackness. Thus might the world have been on the first day of creation. The feeling of terror surged through my senses again. The skin at the back of my legs quivered as though some sixth sense warned that something was rushing silently at me out of the night. I twisted around and saw nothing except the same utter void; my nerves were playing me tricks. Revolving to my original position I saw a very wonderful event. Out of the darkness that covered the deep there suddenly blossomed into being a tiny pinpoint of light. It flared for perhaps a sixteenth of a second, reached a brilliance made all the more vivid by the dark all around and was extinguished. Here in a few seconds was re-enacted the first portion of the drama of genesis; the prelude to all that followed.

Then, as my eyes adjusted themselves to the dark, I began to see other flashes, minute explosions that burst suddenly into being and then passed forever out of sight. Reaching for the searchlight I extracted it from its carrying hook, raised it at arm's length and pressed the button. Instantly a long beam of strong white light pierced the gloom and went penciling off into the distance. I looked in vain for the makers of the tiny flashing lights but they were nowhere to be seen. A few drifting motes, slightly resembling sunbeams, floated through the ocean, watery counterparts of the dust that drifts in the air over the land. Turning the beam off, I waited until my pupils had once more expanded to their fullest capacity. Sure enough the lights became visible once again, only this time I saw many more, until on my straining retinas the world registered as a galaxy of little star-points, a cosmos of pale Fourth of July sparklers without the glowing stems. The lights were the energy-burstings of hundreds of microscopic animalcules, whose bodies too small to be visible under natural illumination were betrayed by the energy they expended.

Turning on the flash again I swept it in a wide arc. The lovely evanescent blue of daytime was gone; in its place was a long beam of yellow surrounded on each side by purplish gloom. The water, however, was crystal clear and the rays brilliantly brought into vision any objects within their reach. Arching my back so I could see above me I pointed the light toward the surface. It was as molten and as impenetrable as ever. Casting the light in another direction I focused it in mid-water, started to sweep it in an arc down to the bottom—then held it rigid.

A brilliant flash, many times brighter than the rays of the electric bulb suddenly burst back at me. It lasted for only a second and then vanished. Its source was far away but in the space of an eyewink it was followed by another and another until the water was blazing with them. The owners of the flashes, still unseen, moved as though animated by invisible heliostats. These were no microscopic explosions but large blazes of colored fire.

The flashes came closer, shooting across the beam with lightning rapidity, flaring and disappearing, approaching ever nearer. Finally one stopped only a few inches away. It was glowing from one end to the other with unearthly light, the most brilliant undiluted lavender I have ever seen. I recognized this lovely creature as an anchovy, a fish about three or four inches in length. It did not seem possible that this glowing animal could be the source of the dismal mess known as anchovy paste. Yet a quick glance at the creature's long undershot jaw identified it beyond all question. No opal ever gleamed with more intense fire; even as the anchovy moved the lavender was replaced with a shimmering pink and finally with a bright silver as it sped away.

The coming of the anchovies is an event that I shall long remember. There must have been some magnetic quality about my searchlight that they could not resist. The silversides, long minnows with broad bands of burnished silver running down their sides, were affected similarly. In less time than it takes to write this sentence, I was surrounded by a deluge of silver-lavender forms that milled about the lens in a whirling cloud, rushing headlong at the glass, bumping it and turning in sudden fright to dash away, only to be magnetized once more. The accumulated reflection of their shining bodies lit up the darkness for several yards around; ripples of rose-colored light flickered through the murk.

Within five minutes there must have been several hundred of them, but these were completely eclipsed when from the surface of the ocean there rained down a large school which must have numbered several thousand. These came so quickly, so compactly, and flared into brilliance so suddenly that I instinctively ducked when they hit the aura of the light. For yards around the sea was packed with their close-set bodies. Most beautifully, they were swimming as one fish, veering and turning together, a great pink and lavender wheel that circled round and round.

Unfortunately their circling did not last for long, for like javelins out of the night a group of small houndfish burst through the school, snapping and gulping their prey as fast as they could swallow. The anchovies scattered in all directions and for several minutes the water was streaked with lines of flashing color which marked the trail of the fleeing fishes. While the houndfish worked their carnage, they were followed by a half dozen flying-fish which surprisingly appeared out of nowhere and then, realizing their mistake, suddenly turned and shot like arrows toward the surface. As strong an attraction as the light was, it was not enough to keep them in place; their fear of the houndfish was something to behold. They were crazed with terror, and in a vibrating, scintillating blur they passed out of my sphere.

The pure ferocity of the houndfish exceeded any similar savagery I have ever seen. Their appetites were insatiable. Back and forth they lunged, striking, slaying, maiming, sometimes not pausing to swallow their prey before dashing on to another. They gorged themselves until their gullets were distended, then continued to kill and injure. More than any other sight, this massacre of the anchovies brought home the cruelty, the age old barbarity of the ocean.

Presently, back in the dim haze beyond the flashlight, I began to be conscious of moving forms, some which reflected the light and others which appeared as dark, heavy shadows. These flitted from place to place, appearing and disappearing, as though attracted by the activity around the light but not daring to approach. Their very vagueness caused the queer feeling in the pit of my stomach to arise once more, and rather than tempt any larger animal to join the activity of the lunging houndfish, I felt with my fingers for the flash button and switched off the current.

The blackness that followed was more intense than any that had gone before. Hordes of scurrying silversides and anchovies, frantic with panic, brushed against my arms and against my exposed legs, sending tiny cool currents across my flesh. For several seconds I could feel their bodies, and then the tickling of their fins ceased and I hung once more in lifeless space. Slackening the grip of my fingers, I allowed the strands of the rope to slide slowly past. Down, down, until with a slight bump I felt the pressure of sand beneath my feet. Here I let go, and leaning slightly against the tide walked several feet.

Once more I turned on the light. Its beam glared across the bottom casting long shadows, throwing the tide ridges into high relief and bringing into prominence objects that I had never seen before, though I had dived at this place a dozen times. Deep craters, which in the light of day would not have been conspicuous, pitted the bottom everywhere. Holes in the sand were visible as round black patches and from some of these little currents, laden with specks of silt and tiny plankton, could be seen pulsing in and out. Their molluscan or crustacean owners, whichever they were, were busy at work sucking in and expelling the water by which they derived their oxygen and food.

In order to get a better look at one of these underwater ventilating systems I slid to my knees and then lay on my stomach, arching my back so the water would not enter the helmet. I had hardly settled myself when there suddenly appeared a strange apparition. Its head was clad in plates of mail and these were chased and engraved in the most unusual patterns, reminding one of the etchings of snowflakes, or of some of the mineral crystals which have a radiating design, or better yet, of a cartoonist's idea of an exploding bomb, dozens of lines issuing forth from a common center. These plates were further studded with grotesque short spines which gave the face a lean angular appearance. But most peculiar this medieval armored physiognomy, which was coming head on, appeared to have no body and was walking on a series of six spidery legs. The legs appeared jointless and flexible and were being advanced one after the other in the most dainty yet consecutive precision. The rays of the lamp cast further incongruous shadows over the creature, gnome, troll or whatever it was, and accentuated the already weird features. It was not until it had advanced to my finger tips and turned partly around that I recognized its true character—a sea robin belonging to the genus *Prionotus*.

Walking fish are always of sufficient rarity to be interesting. This one had mastered the art to a fine degree. It made no attempt to swim and held its broad, spotted wing-like pectoral fins stiffly out at right angles to its body. These were of large size and seemed all out of proportion to the owner. The creature's curiosity was overpowering. It tiptoed up to the lens of the light and stood staring at the illumination. Unlike the anchovies nearer the surface, however, the light did not seem to excite it in the slightest degree. When it finished its examination it backed away, reminding me of a ballet dancer, and then came over to the rope which was curled like a long serpent in the sand. It walked back and forth over this and then stepped over to my hand which was partly buried in the sand. When it had walked completely around the periphery it topped its performance by stepping across my bare flesh. The pectoral rays tickled as they went across and the ends felt sharp. When it reached the other side I made a sudden grab for its body. I was too slow, however, for it quickly folded up its walking rays and put the fins to their normal use—swimming. Settling again just beyond reach, it dropped airily to the sand and stood there eyeing me.

Rising to my feet again I plodded over to the great shadowy mounds of boulders that marked the lower ramparts of the island. The moss covered crags towered high into the air—water rather—and the algaes and sea fans were dipping and swaying just as they had done in the daytime. But it was not the same world. There was a noticeable difference. At first I credited it to the darkness and the long shadows cast by the flash. These, of course, changed its appearance considerably, altering an already strange landscape into another of still more weird proportions. The crags which during the day might well have fitted into a valley on Mars, at night were almost lunar in their aspect. Everything was delineated in sharp, vividly contrasted outlines. Brilliantly scarlet gorgonians, that normally melted inconspicuously into the general melee of color, merging with yellows, blues and greens, now stood out in all their crimson glory against a background of jet black. There is no richer combination in the world than scarlet and black. The old Chinese craftsmen long ago realized this and have made ample use of it in their incomparable lacquers. The lacy fronds of the algaes' tendrils looked even more fragile now that they were silhouetted alone; they appeared to be doing some sort of filmy dance, forever flinging their graceful arms upward in supplication and bowing them to earth again. The dark entrances to a hundred underwater caverns gaped open-mouthed between long curving ovals of brilliant yellow. Stony rainbows fringed with the pale white stems of hydroids and encrusted with purple and lavender finger sponges arched away into the somber distance. Long rows of yellow sea fans running along the crest of the rock ridges flexed and bowed with the pulse of the waves; their glow reflecting against the molten surface above sent soft bands of voiced light running across the sand at the foot of the rocks where it was focused and shot down by the facets of the waves.

Everything was either colorfully lighted or shrouded in gloom. There were no half tones to break the contrast. The distance between high visibility and complete dark was less than a half inch; only the reflection from the surface softened the shadows, and this accentuated rather than relieved the obscurity. The factor, however, that imparted a sense of difference to the locality was not the alteration of the main color scheme, as striking as this was, but the change in the residents. Practically none of the daytime fishes were about. In vain I turned the searchlight over the rocks looking for them. They were nowhere to be found. In their places were other forms which heretofore had been seen only as lurkers in shadowy holes and deep fissures. Chief among these were the squirrel fish, brilliant red, with wide open dark eyes which gave them an over-cosmeticized appearance. These were actively filtering in and out among the rocks and were accompanied with another scarlet species, a round-bodied fish, with eyes so big and soulful that it gave the impression that it was about to burst into tears at any moment. The fish's common name, the Deep Big Eye, describes it exactly. I was rather surprised at seeing these, for I had always understood them to be deep water fishes. Yet here they were only a few yards from the surf. It was odd, too, that they should be associated with the squirrel fish, and even more peculiar that the two forms, both apparently nocturnal, should be colored red. I remembered that some of the deep sea fishes and crustaceans which live in regions where night is eternal are also colored in this hue.

The blue tang were still about but these were not very active. There were several masses clustered together in the midst of a large crevasse where they hung in midwater like a living ball. The ball floated lazily up and down with the action of the surf but the individuals held their exact positions to the fraction of an inch. Each fish was facing in the same direction, and while I watched, the entire group slowly revolved as though on a pivot.

I let my light play over their motionless forms and then switched it to the crevassed floor and back along its slope to the mouth of a narrow festooned cave. Here I was startled to see a row of seven pairs of gleaming teeth floating in mid-air with no evidence of bodies. Two pairs were bright bluish green, four were whitish and one had a very perceptible rosy hue. They suggested nothing quite so much as the nightmare of an inebriated dentist on the verge of delirium tremens. The teeth backed into the cave until they were nearly out of sight; and following, I climbed over an immense sponge and pointed the light directly into their shelter. The seven pair of teeth then resolved into the bodies of seven pairs of assorted large parrot-fish, four olive green fellows at least two feet in length, two red ones with prominently marked scales and one of variegated hue.

Backing out again I examined other holes and fissures. Nearly everyone was filled with fish, some of these were floating quite motionless except for slight wavings of their pectoral fins. Others, including the sergeant-majors, readily identifiable by their vivid yellow stripes, were restlessly pacing back and forth, but remaining well within the limits of their abodes. A cluster of eleven butterfly-fish had the most unusual sleeping arrangement of all. They did not elect to dispose of themselves in the dark of the cave but had taken up their positions under a stone arch, shaped somewhat like the famous Natural Bridge of Virginia. Here they had arranged themselves in a vertical column poised midway between the bottom and the top. If the position of the lowermost fish was north, the one above was north by east, the next northeast, and so on around the compass in an ascending scale. The result was an exceedingly graceful spiral. The spiral, keeping time with the great ball of living tang, rocked slightly with the current but maintained its relative position. What the reason was for this formation I could not guess unless it was so arranged as a protection in order that there would be a butterfly-fish facing in every direction to give warning of the approach of an enemy. But if this were so, why then did the tang ignore the rule and all face the same way?

While I was watching the butterfly-fish I suddenly sensed a great swirling movement behind me. Frightened, I whirled around expecting to see the large form of a barracuda or other predator. Instead, I was relieved to see that it was only a tremendous migration of schoolmasters, which were fishes about a foot in length marked with a brilliant blue streak placed just below their eyes from their lips to the edge of their opercles. Their eyes gleamed like jewels and as the school twisted and wound its way into the dark, the mass effect was of a thousand glowing coals gliding into the depths. The school was proceeding very leisurely and sliding along close to the bottom like a great long rope. The fishes were packed so close together it seemed they had scarcely room to waggle their tails. Apparently they mistrusted the light for they made a long circle around the spot where its beam was focused on the ocean floor.

The reaction of various marine organisms to artificial light is an absorbing study. Anchovies, silversides, menhaden, free-swimming worms and certain crustaceans seem to find it irresistible, some of these, like the worms, are driven mad by it. Other forms shun light like the plague, or at most, hover uncertainly about its further edges. Strangely, weak light attracts more life than excessive brilliance. It cost me about forty dollars to find this out. During my experiments in the Chesapeake Bay I conceived the idea that a five thousand watt light assembly would bring a vast assortment of marine life to my observation post. Accordingly I purchased a number of expensive electric bulbs, special waterproof wire to carry the current, and suitable fuses and switches. When the apparatus was lowered in the water and turned on, it produced a tremendous glare, lighting the water for yards around. It improved visibility tremendously but little came to its beam. In disgust, I gave it up and returned to the old method of using flashlights, which was much more satisfactory.

After the schoolmasters were gone I was deluged for about ten minutes with a crowd of half-beaks. These came from near the surface and were one of the types that found the light an irresistible attraction. They must have been traveling in a loose-knit school for they arrived within a few seconds of each other, dropping in out of the darkness above like silver and green comets. Their greenness was most unusual. It shimmered over their scales with a delicate glaucous iridescence, and the border of each scale was outlined in vivid emerald. These same fish when taken out of their element are plain silver but few fishes appear underwater as they do in the open air. Some day I would like to prepare a color chart for the quick recognition of tropical fishes in their natural element. It is most confusing to read in the identification keys that mullet, for example, are silver with faint gray stripings only to find when viewed on their own level and in their own element that they are not silver at all but gorgeous flaming lavender; or that Spanish mackerel are not olive platinum but are adorned with body-length streaks of fiery yellow which disappear when they are taken out of water, leaving no hint of its existence.

The glaucous tone of the half-beaks was not nearly as unusual as the appearance of their heads. Their lower jaws were extended all out of proportion to the upper, being equally as long as the remainder of their heads. This gave them an odd, though not ungraceful, shape. They were long and streamlined, reminding one of miniature swordfishes. Unlike swordfishes, however, their attenuated bills were not sharp and hard at the ends but were finished off with a scarlet tip which was soft and fleshy. The purpose of the tip is obscure; it may be used for a sensory organ or as a probe. The food of half-beaks seems to be principally vegetable matter mixed with a few small crustaceans. How they manage to feed with their long bills thrust in front of them is something of a mystery.

Dropping to my knees I crawled along the lowest border of rocks to see what the invertebrates were doing. They were almost all awake and active. The barnacles were still casting their nets, extruding and withdrawing their feathery feet. Light and dark meant nothing to them encased in their thick shells of carbonate of lime. Food and oxygen were their concern; sleep would wait for a full belly. At any hour of the day or night the barnacles can be found busily at work. Likewise the anemones. These were all out in full blossom, slowly waving and pulsing; their poisonous tentacles loaded with fiery darts were patiently waiting for some incautious crustacean or swimming worm. The flower-pretending worms, too, were all awake with cirri expanded for whatever fate and the currents would bring them.

Not all the worms were bound to the rocks, for my light was rapidly becoming surrounded by a maze of their undulating forms. Swimming sea worms are among the most unappealing of all earth's creatures. My fingers, long used to grasping all manner of insects, spiders and reptiles, instinctively recoil at the vibrating bodies of swimming worms. Some of them sting when touched, others bite with long sharp extrusible jaws, and all of them send shivers through my flesh on contact. They are covered with such a maze of bristles, antennae, legs, odd fibers and cirri, all vibrating at high speed, that they possess something of the appearance that I imagine a bolt of electricity would have if suddenly and unexplainably endowed with life and tissues. The comparison of sea worms to electric arcs is not as farfetched as it might seem, for their activity is stupendous. Whatever their imaginary amperage may be, their visible voltage is high. The worms which were darting about my light were becoming frantic in their excitement. Looping, undulating, vibrating, shaking and shivering, they whirled about the lens in a vermiform frenzy. My nerves, already slightly on edge, revolted when a long body slithered along the curve of my forearm and burst into the light leaving my flesh tingling from the contact. It was a brilliant worm of light scarlet fronted with a yellowish head, and it was being rowed along with several scores of triangular green oars composed of fibrous bristles. From its fantastic head covered with whisker-like blue cirri to its pointed, feathery tail it was about seven inches long. In the rays of the flash it shimmered and scintillated with iridescent light.

I had barely recovered from the shock of its bristly touch when it was joined by two others which dashed over to the first and began looping over and over its body. Round and round they went in a blur of activity. They were joined by others until the beam of the lamp was filled with a swirling mixture of revolving bodies. In between the larger worms fifteen or twenty smaller individuals of several species darted back and forth on straight paths. These gave the moving design an additional pattern of horizontal streaks, flashing lines of green and pink. Hastily I tried to remember their characteristics in the hope that I might identify them later, but gave it up as impossible. The larger worms I am confident were some type of *Neirids*, but the indentification of sea worms is at best an uncongenial task. I can patiently count the scales of a fish, or enumerate the location and position of its spines and rays; but the characters which determine the nomenclature of sea worms are so technical and vague as to cause me invariably to throw up my untaxonomic hands in despair.

Events undersea, like certain forms of trouble, generally occur in bunches. The galaxy of worms which had collected in front of my light were the forerunners of a considerable mass. Possibly the continued burning of the light attracted them, possibly the behavior of the worms already there, but whatever it was they came swarming from all sides. They were followed quickly by the scarlet bodies of the squirrel-fish and the big-eyes which made the most of the unexpected provender. The worms did not flee but seemed intent on nothing but their interminable whirling about each other's bodies. I am convinced that they were in the throes of their reproductive cycle, for I noted that certain individuals were giving off exceedingly faint emanations, somewhat like smoke, which must have been either unfertilized ova or male sperm. When a newly advanced worm hit these miniature clouds it went into a blind frenzy which made its previous activity seem mild.

Minute after minute the horde of gyrating worms increased in number. Unable to stand the sensation of their squirming against my bare flesh and alarmed at the activity of fishes that I had stirred up, for the squirrel-fish were followed by larger and more active forms, including the huge bulk of a beautifully barred Nassau grouper, I turned off the light and climbed hurriedly up the line. I quickly ducked out of the helmet and flopped over the railing into the bottom of the boat.

When I checked my watch I found that I had been under for sixty-seven minutes. The wind had picked up again and the boat was pitching and plunging at its anchor. I realized that I was tired and satiated with the black depths of the ocean.

ooking again at the ebony surface, I shuddered slightly at
he memory of the feel of the swarming worms, and decided I
ad enough for one night. I would have given much for the
trong curved sides of my steel cylinder with its big plate glass
vindow. With its aid I could have watched the drama of the
vorms to its conclusion. But it was a thousand and a half miles
way, drawn up high and dry on a Chesapeake Beach. So with
he aid of my pump operator, I gathered in the anchor and
owed to shore where I dropped into bed and fell into a deep
lumber. Here I lay without moving until the rays of sunlight
tealing through the open window announced the coming of
ull daylight.

I did not go diving at night again until almost three weeks
iter. The moon, at first wan and thin, had nightly climbed into
he sky, expanding steadily, until it was round and gleaming.
ts rays lighted the dry salinas and turned the sloping shell-
tudded beaches into pale white ribbons that stretched away
nto the indefinite darkness. The surface of the reef, moaning
vith the might of the curling breakers, was plainly visible and
ven the shallow waters of the lagoons were sufficiently il-
uminated to show the differences between the depths and the
hallows and the locations where the patches of green turtle
rass grew. Only the ocean beyond the reef was completely
lack; down in the great depths the sand and rocks were too
ar away to reflect the moonlight. But even its somberness was
elieved by the sparkle of moonbeams on the wave facets and
y the momentary whiteness of hurtling whitecaps.

We anchored a few yards from the face of the reef, and
itching and tossing waited until the slack of the anchor rope
vas taken up by the drift. A flying-fish, disturbed in its surface
loating, or perhaps alarmed by the cable, suddenly whizzed
ut of the night, skimmed across the hollow of a wave valley,
vas silhouetted against the sphere of the moon, and with an

audible plop fell in the water several yards away. It was followed by several more and all around we could hear their pat-
terings as they rose, flew, and returned to their proper element.
Further away a heavier and more sullen splash marked the
place where some larger creature, perhaps pursuing the flying-
fish, had lunged through the surface and fallen back again.

The ocean seemed alive. Gleams of silver flared briefly up
from the depths, thrown back by the bright scales of schooling
fishes. Close by the hull a twice repeated swish of rippling
water gave evidence of the presence of some large moving
organism whose fins had broken the surface. Shadows even
blacker than the general tone of the water glided under the
hull and merged with the liquid emptiness beyond. High above,
between the stars and the reef, the faint call of migrating sandpipers came filtering down through space and once, in the direction of the breakers, a tarpon leaped high in the air, shook
itself, and landed on the water with a loud crash.

The same feeling of uneasiness that had come upon me in
my first night dive swept over me again. But the thought of
seeing the great reef in the moonlight was so tempting that I
pushed the crawling fear into the background of my consciousness. This time I was descending fully clothed and with
a strong pair of shoes to ward off the spines of sea urchins that
I might not see in the dark. Also, I decided to carry a short
spear to prevent the unwelcome attentions of any large fishes
which might become too curious.

I delayed my dive into the water long enough to allow an
acre-wide swarm of thimble-jellies to float slowly by. They
were packed so closely together that their sides touched, and
in the fifteen minutes that elapsed before they passed under the
keel their denseness never diminished. Each square foot contained several hundred; the swarm must have contained well
over a million. When they were safely by I vaulted over the

il and donned the helmet, hoping they would not be fol-
owed by another school, for to be engulfed in several hun-
red thousand jellies at night seemed too strange an experience
o be contemplated with the equanimity which a similar event
ould occasion in the full light of day. Besides, although the
ings of thimble-jellies are reported to be very mild to the
uman skin, I did not feel like experimenting with them in the
ark.

A coral reef during the day is unbelievable. At night and
ghted by a tropical moon it is so utterly fantastic that there
re no superlatives in the English language nor similes with
hich to make an apt comparison. Imagine a world in which
ll color is gone, where shadows assume the shapes of twisted
iants, where nothing is still for a moment, where the sky is
olid burnished platinum, where phantom figures, clad in pale
omber gray, hover restlessly in mid-air in the shelter of nar-
ow caves dripping with stalactites, which do not hang mo-
ionless but sway eerily to and fro. Imagine the atmosphere
lled with a pale soft glow, an unearthly sheen that has no
isible substance but which increases and dims as shafts of
earl gray light run like ghosts from surface to bottom, creat-
ng halos of visibility as they reach the sandy soil.

This was the scene that met my eyes when I slid slowly
lown the rope and came to rest over my usual drowned valley.
Catching a loop in the line and placing the arch of my foot in
t, I relaxed and permitted myself to be swayed slowly back
nd forth. The beautiful blues, reds, lavenders and golds were
anished as utterly as if they had never existed. The rays of
he moon filtering down through the clear water cast long
wavering shadows into the ravine which seemed more gloomy
nd mysterious than ever. The great stone trees stood like a
ow of silvery ghosts. Their jagged fingers, each outlined with
 white line of glowing light, reached pleading hands up to the

ceiling where the surf was breaking. There the water was being churned into livid mercury. Great windrows of melted
platinum and frosty aluminum swirled into one another, mark
ing the positions of large bubbles or fine atomized froth. It was
a scene in monotone. Silvers, grays and liquid blacks were the
pigments. Lustrous near the surface, they became more and
more vague and indeterminate as they faded toward the depth
until at forty feet there was nothing tangible, nor even sug
gested.

The coral forest with its upper branches wreathed in ani
mated silver held the center of attraction. During the day the
glory of upside down surf, brilliant as it was with all the hue
of the spectrum, was dulled and overwhelmed by the color of
the reef beneath. In the moonlight the reverse was true. Then
all the fury, the power and the turmoil of breaking water were
expressed in one medium—cold icy light. Boiling, surging
frothing and tearing into a thousand fragments the breaker
spread out as a great gleaming line reaching across the zenith
But again, as in the daytime, the silence was overwhelming
More than the sight of rushing, glowing bubbles this created
sense of awe. It seemed impossible that there should be so much
violence and no sound. But then, when I looked downwards
away from the turmoil and the froth, down toward the un
fathomable depths, I knew this was as it should be. Foreve
drowned, forever separated from the upper air, this world had
no place for sound. No place for sound and only a little for
light. A few yards away, a few feet down the slope both light
and sound were vanquished; down below was only still empty
darkness. A chill sensation crept over my flesh. Shuddering
little, I tore my eyes from the depths and concentrated on the
coral.

As in the daytime, and unlike my first nocturnal dive, hun
dreds of fish were moving about the branches. But they were

ot the fish I was familiar with. These were merely shapes and hadows, moving wraiths in monotone, or at best momentary leams of silver or soft pearl gray. All the identifying colors vere gone. Blue and red parrotfish, gold and orange snappers nd grunts, were toned exactly alike. Only the pale and apropriately named moon-fish were instantly recognizable. Vhile I looked one rose from a deep hole, arched slowly hrough space, reached the summit of its course, and slowly, ke its heavenly counterpart, set over a rim of earth. To make he imitation more complete it rotated as it went across the vatery sky. At first it appeared new and thin. As its revolving ontinued it became more and more round, reached the full nd finally disappeared as a narrow crescent line.

Only shape and method of movement were the clues to pecies and genera. In some cases I had to rely on swimming lone. In the half-light the bodies of the sergeant-majors and he butterfly-fish looked exactly alike; they were instantly eparated by their manner. The sergeant-majors had an internittent bouncing flight with numerous stops and starts; they vaved their fins leisurely except when startled. The butterlies were erratic and vibrated all over when they moved. Angelfish soared, as angels should; the similarly shaped, roundodied tang floated and drifted. Other types like the needleish could best be described as darting arrows; the flying-fish nd trumpet-fish also belonged in this category. The snappers, grunts and porgies trailed close to the bottom in a slow undulating style, sinuosity their characteristic; still others forged teadily on their paths without hint of slackening pace. Among hese last was the large body of a tarpon, possibly the same that eaped in the air when we first anchored. With a little study I pelieve most fishes, like birds, could be instantly distinguished by their swimming.

Several times, however, I was badly fooled, as when the

arrow-like form of a fish came darting by and I automatically assigned it to the houndfish group, I was startled to discover when it turned and came in full view that it was a barracuda instead. In the dark it looked grimmer than ever and I was much relieved when it kept going and disappeared. The barracuda, however, did not give me nearly as much of a scare as the big jewfish which I had observed previously during the day swinging airily in its den.

Tiring of my pendulum-like position on the life line I withdrew my foot and slipped down to the bottom. Here, carefully retaining my grip on the rope to prevent a mishap in the current, I hopped and skipped over to my favorite sea fan where I sat down, clutching it between my legs. From this position I could see the creature's hiding place, but the gloom inside was too great to make out any details. Knowing that it was nocturnal I wondered where the jewfish was and started revolving around the fan to see if I could find it. It suddenly loomed up a few inches from the helmet. I let out a yell which, if emitted on the surface, would have been heard a couple miles away, and gave a great jump that carried me nearly to the surface. The leap shot me out over the ravine and as I floated down I came to an abrupt, though easy, halt when I reached the end of my tether. I then swung in towards the perpendicular and towards the jewfish which was still waiting near the brink. By this time, however, I had recovered my mental equilibrium and came to a gentle rest on the rock bottom a few feet from its body. It backed away a short distance and then hovered again.

I felt a little chagrined for reacting the way I did but the sight of that monstrous black body so close to mine, even though I was looking for it, was more of a shock than my nerves could stand.

The jewfish regarded me for a minute or two and then

lowly moved its great hulk back into the shadows. When it was
one, I made my way over to a large mound of brain coral
where I had frequently sat during the day and wedged myself
gainst its roundness. Here at least nothing could approach
me from the rear. Feeling a little safer, though with nerves still
n edge, I settled down to watch.

It was fitting and wholly like the happenings in this dark
world of underwater that the next event should be one of
delicate splendor. In fact it was so in contrast to the ugliness
nd fright of the jewfish adventure, that I caught my breath
nd held it in wonder. While I was sitting trying to distinguish
he characteristics of the shadowy forms darting over the bot-
om, the light suddenly faded away. Thinking a cloud had
passed over the moon, I arched my back and glanced up. Then
saw that the surface was obscured by a vast school of fish.
They were moving parallel to the reef. The school must have
numbered several hundred thousand individuals for I could not
ee its outer edges. The lines of alternate black and silver that
hey formed as they swam past row on row, produced a glow-
ng tapestry effect, a skein of living motes. The school slowly
plit, riven by a great band of burnished light, turned and
eversed its direction. As it wheeled each of the thousands of
bodies caught the rays of the moon and focused them downwards in a broad sheet of glowing light. This briefly lit the
bottom and then died as rapidly as it was formed.

There was a second flare as the school, alarmed by something in the far distance, wheeled again and went into a brief
frenzy of fright. After it had dashed about fifteen or twenty
feet it slowed up and once more resumed its flowing march up
the coral wall. Down on the sand the record of its passing was
exhibited as a host of reflections glided over the ocean floor
like miniature ghosts. These danced and swirled as the waves
above changed the focus; the entire undersea appeared splat-

tered with fragments of light and shadow.

I looked up again. The whole school had altered its course. This time instead of following the heaving sky, it was pouring into the depths. The effect was that of a living cascade. Long threads of burnished metal and spangles of quivering silver glittered in a liquid torrent. For fully two minutes it lasted, and then, with a final spluttering of light, the fishes faded away and vanished forever.

The calm that followed the deluge of fishes was so intense that some seconds passed before I became aware of any movement. Then in the direction of the coral trees at the base of the trunks, I saw what appeared to be a long winding serpent. It was defiling from a shadowy avenue of twisted trunks and was slithering close to the bottom where it followed the contour of the rocks and crags. Neither end was visible as it squirmed and swayed into obscurity. My curiosity was aroused and although I felt safer in my corner I got up and walked slowly over. When I came close I saw it was one of the interminable schools of snappers. They did not seem to mind my presence, though I must have been a strange sight to them with a geyser of moonlit bubbles mounting from my head. I strode through the snappers but they merely separated long enough to allow passage and closed ranks again.

Where they were going in the night and for what purpose I could not guess. They seemed to be in no hurry but they were off on some errand which, no doubt, was important to them. For a few seconds I had an irresistible urge to follow but knowing that I was limited to the length of my hose, even imagining that they would permit my trailing them, I desisted and watched them vanish like the surface fishes into the abyss.

The two schools taking their separate paths to obscurity gave a hint of the tremendous activity that was occurring along the borders of the sea. In my imagination I could visualize similar schools that must be winding in the moonlight and in the shadows along the slopes of the oceans all over the world. Off Inagua alone the pulsing masses of life creeping in and out of the coral forests must be stupendous. Whenever I stand on the seashore at night I will think, not of the waves lapping at my feet, but of the winding serpents of individual fishes crawling in and out of the sea, all unseen, unnoticed and unknown. When I think again of these millions of lives going on millions of errands, with millions of hopes and millions of failures, with millions of problems, millions of ways of solving them, pursuing millions of meals, escaping millions of enemies, giving life to millions of spawn and dying millions of deaths, I can only be silent with awe.

Then, when the snappers were gone, I turned away and crept down into the valley as it had become my custom to do at the end of each trip. At the bottom I stood motionless while all around phantom shapes resolved and dissolved with the shadows. For a long time I paused. Then, when a group of large fishes went hurrying by, and I recognized them by their forms and by their gleaming horselike teeth as parrotfish, and saw that they were scurrying frantically for the upper corals, I knew that this was not my world and that I had stayed long enough.

CHAPTER XVIII

The Edge of the Edge of the World

HELMETED and visored like some knight of old, I stood motionless at the bottom of the sea on the next but last day I was to spend on Inagua and contemplated the great mound of yellow rock where I was poised forty feet beneath the surface. Slowly I crouched, stooped to nearly a sitting position, and then sprang into space. Up I soared, five feet, ten, fifteen, on up to twenty, slowly drifted to a stop and then coasted down again. I landed on a smooth stretch of sand, bounced a tiny bit and, like an actor in a slow motion picture, came to rest. Breathing a sigh of relief I turned and looked at the jagged rocks I had just cleared with my amazing leap.

I was glad I had not misjudged the distance, as an error would have resulted in badly scarred limbs. Strange, I thought to myself, the chances a man will take for the sake of curiosity. There was no other excuse I could think of for this last-minute escapade. I thought I had had enough of diving but one thing remained. For weeks I had stood on shore and looked at the place beyond the settlement where the color of the ocean changed abruptly from light green to dark blue, marking a sheer drop of 1200 fathoms, a terrifying plunge to the uttermost depths. Finally I could resist the temptation no longer; I had to see what the edge of that submarine cliff was like.

With the aid of a native boatman I loaded my diving helmet into the boat and anchored just a few feet on the land side of the brink. I was perhaps a quarter of a mile out from shore. The bottom looked a long distance away, and it was with a

THE EDGE OF THE EDGE 375

feeling of doubt that I donned the helmet and went sliding into the blue. I landed a few seconds later, deeply conscious of the pressure, and turned and looked about. A heavy weight seemed to be pressing on my abdomen and chest. The surface was a long, long distance away; my hose curled up behind me in a wide arc, a snaky black line that became increasingly indistinct until at its further end it blurred away. Even the boat was obscure and somewhat nebulous.

I peered about, trying to get some hint of direction. Above and to all sides existed nothing but blue water, a filmy evanescent blue that baffled description, unrelieved by any solid objects. Leaning far backwards, I looked towards the surface. Still nothing but liquid blue, perhaps a trace lighter than the color to each side. There was no such thing as direction. North, east, south and west were all the same. Blue water everywhere; one was drowned in it, lost in azure.

Only the sand at my feet, heaped in little piles between the rocks, helped to stabilize, to give a hint where I might find the edge of the cliff. I sensed that it was close because my naked flesh could detect a faint cold current coming up from the depths. Hesitating, I turned my body this way and that, trying to catch the direction of the current. But it was too slight, too vague to help. Then my feet gave me the clue. The bottom was uneven, very regularly uneven. I looked at the piles of sand. They were heaped in hundreds of little mounds, long waving lines that faded into the blue immensity. They were similar to the lines I had seen when I watched the tide flowing by Inagua's westernmost point. I guessed that, like those others, they would run at right angles to the shore opposite the direction of the current. My course was parallel with them.

On I pressed, leaning hard against the water. Presently the cold became more pronounced, a gentle sort of chill that merely gave a hint of what lay before, like the faint coolness that sometimes comes on dry land in September before the leaves are gone.

A feeling of loneliness swept briefly over me. I felt as though I were the only person in the world, as indeed I was, for although I knew that only seventy feet away the boatman was steadily stroking the pump that kept me alive, he might well have been on Mars, so separated were we by the thin film of the top of the ocean. And I knew that I was treading a spot where no man had ever trod before, that my eyes would be the first to see this abyssal underwater cliff that dropped away for nearly 7000 feet before it reached the floor of the ocean. Perhaps it was the deathly stillness that gave the feeling, for no sound came to my ears but the faint hiss of the air that came down the hose.

· Nervously I tightened my grip on the life line and pulled on it to make certain that it was securely fastened. It was. I could feel the surge of the boat as it bobbed up and down on the waves. Turning on my course I looked again for the boat. It was quite out of sight. Completing my rotation I searched carefully in all directions. The boatman had warned that the cliff edge was the rendezvous of huge sharks and barracuda and that I should be cautious. As I had done on the reef, I scoffed at him; though after my experience there, and now that I was by myself and lost in an azure immensity, I was not so sure.

The edge came sooner than I expected. Suddenly I was peering down into a great blue void. The soil had disappeared at my feet and the bottom had become soft and yielding. For an awful second I could see the sand drifting, sliding downwards, and frantically I seized the life line and held it tight. I knew well enough that I would not drift ten feet before I would be checked by both hose and line, but the space below looked so utterly vacant that I could not help reacting as I did.

Trembling slightly, I sat down on the soft bank and peered

downwards. It was an overwhelmingly empty space. Down, down into the terrifying blur of out-of-focusness the sand sloped away. There was nothing down there but deepness, empty dark and cold.

Like an invisible wall a chill feeling hung on the edge of the cliff. I stirred one of my feet. A little pile of sand drifted loose, gathered volume and in a creeping slithering landslide, oozed its way down the slope. A faint cloud of powdery silt arose, gently spread apart and slowly disappeared. There was something so serpentine, so creeping about that landslide. None of the rush and tumble of a slide on land—only a slow gentle falling into the depths. I imagined how horrible it must be to slide helplessly to death, should one be unable to free the helmet weights and lose the stabilizing hose and line, to drift oozily down, inch by inch, foot by foot, with the pressure increasing in a crushing horrible grip. And I could imagine the increasing darkness that would come before unconsciousness would make it complete, a gradual deepening of color, ultramarine, azure, deep azure, blue-black—and then utter darkness.

Clickety-click, clickety-click—the faint sound of the air pump brought me back to reality. I reasoned that I was perfectly safe, and curiosity began to replace the sensations of panic. I wondered what lay below and what held the soft edge so evenly in place. I looked back. In a long even plain, seamed with fissures and crevasses, the sand and rocks sloped gently towards the surface, a rise that was so gradual as to be almost imperceptible.

I reached down and picked up some of the sand, tightly clenching it in my palm to keep it from oozing from between my fingers. Holding it close to the helmet I examined it carefully. It was foraminiferous sand, not the hard quartz sand of American beaches, but sand formed from the dead and decayed shells of numberless sea creatures. In incredible billions these animals had died, dropping their calcified remains in a slow organic rain to the sea floor. The cliff was a vast funeral pile of a million, million lives. The ocean currents welling up from the depths had gathered it all there in one spot to make the edge of a world.

A shadow passed across the helmet. The shadow of the boat I thought, and let the sand run between my fingers. The boat was fully seventy feet away from the edge. It could cast no shadow!

I saw a darkened patch move slowly over the sand, slide over the rounded edge and become nothingness with the gloom beyond. I looked up and nearly yelled into the recesses of the helmet. There, not fifteen feet above my head, was a great manta, the most gigantic of all the devilfish. It was flying— there is no other word for it—flying along in mid-water like some great bat or monstrous pterodactyl, looking like a vision out of the forgotten past. Flapping its great expanded wings, it seemed to be soaring rather than swimming through the water.

I froze to the sand. The monster turned slightly, coming dangerously close to the air line, swooped gracefully over the edge, and faded into the depths. It must have measured fifteen feet from wing tip to wing tip.

I turned to grasp the life line to go to the surface and then froze again. The fish was returning. To the right I saw its huge bulk heading up out of the shadows. Up to the very brink it came, curled one great fin high, and in a sweeping curve turned up the edge of the bank. It headed straight for me, and I could see its drooping cephalic fins, looking like great horns, held straight downwards. Apparently they were being used for rudders, but the thought flashed into my mind that they were also used for sweeping prey into the mouth with its crushing rows of cobblestone teeth.

On it came straight for the helmet. There was nothing I could do. I was helpless, was not even carrying a sheath knife. In a moment it was but fifteen feet away, then ten, and then, just as I was prepared to be crushed under its great spreading black and white wings, it banked sharply, swung eerily over my head, narrowly missing the air hose again, and disappeared to the left. As it banked I could see its little pig-like eyes glinting at me, jet black pupils set in a white iris.

I rolled over and caught a glimpse of the creature flying slowly towards the place where the boat was anchored. Behind it for three feet trailed a slim, rigid, black tail held stiffly like a rod. On its body were two remora, larger than the ones I had seen on the nurse sharks. They slithered all over the creature's belly as though restlessly waiting the manta's dinnertime when they would glean their meals of crumbs from the monster's feasting.

The devilfish swung again and then came back but not so close this time. It passed within fifteen feet, steered wide of the air line, much to my relief, and turned down the edge of the bank. Rapidly it faded into the haze, became more and more faint, and finally disappeared altogether. I waited to make certain that it was gone and then went hand over hand up the life line as hard as I could go. In a moment I was safe and sound, panting in the sunshine on the deck of the sailboat.

For the second time my boatman beamed with triumph.

"Some day yo get yosef in trubble—dem tings aint nothin to mess wif," he warned.

For once, I was inclined to agree. If the manta had sheared off my air hose or had become entangled in the life line its visit might have been extremely awkward, if not tragic.

Half an hour later, after catching my breath and reviving my courage, I went down again. I found the edge rather easily this time, but in a different spot. Here a patch of sea grass extended out to the very brim, and the sand was more firm. I made myself as comfortable as possible and sat patiently, squirting little jets of water on the glass to clear the mist that was forming from my breath. At first I saw nothing but presently made a discovery.

The edge was the highroad for hundreds of fishes passing up and down the bank. The first that I saw were a large school of mackerel of a species that I could not determine. They were all about eighteen inches in length and were traveling about ten feet above my head. The glow of the sunshine filtering down through the blue caught their silvery bodies and highlighted each one with a line of gleaming yellow. I have never seen anything on dry land as brilliant except possibly the wings of certain butterflies. When I first glimpsed them they were swimming leisurely; but suddenly, as one fish, they all broke into action. In a great yellow streaking line they darted towards the surface where some slim smaller fish were idling.

The smaller fish saw them coming, and like living arrows they, too, streaked surfacewards. Looking up I could faintly make out the opaque surface film and, as I watched, the smaller fish burst through and disappeared. Then I knew them for flying-fish. Disappointed, the mackerel turned aside and resumed their march up the bank edge. I did not see the flying-fish drop in again, as the haze and the distance obscured them from view.

Suddenly my arm began burning as though on fire. Frightened, I whipped around, sending a white cloud tumbling over the earth brim. Trailing over my arm were two or three strands of gelatinous tentacles from a Portuguese man-of-war, a blue and lavender jellyfish that was drifting over my head. Frantically I ducked the remaining tentacles and managed to elude them by throwing myself on the sand. The swirl of my action wisted the soft-bodied animal around, throwing the trailing fingers out of their graceful arrangement. I gasped, rubbed my arm and was interested to observe that the man-of-war instantly retracted its tentacles, drawing them well up under its partially deflated float. The expanded tentacles were fully ten or twelve feet long and, had I received the full benefit of their discharge I would have had an exceedingly nasty arm. As it was, my arm burned and smarted for nearly two hours.

Portuguese men-of-war are as peculiar as they are malignant. They are cousins to the hydroids and the jellyfish but have the distinction of being almost the only communists to live in a completely beneficial yet unquarrelsome group. For men-of-war, as single as they may seem, are really made up of several separate individuals, all performing different functions but operating as a unit. Superficially they appear as one animal but if the colony is examined carefully it will be seen to be composed of polyps having varied shapes and purposes. One type, a tube-like structure of delicate blue, does the feeding and digesting for the entire group; another, a finger-shaped jelly, is highly sensory and functions as a tactile organ; still others serve as reproductive cells, while a fourth kind have been metamorphosed into long tentacles and streamers loaded with poisonous stings. These capture the prey and act as defensive armament. They also serve the further purpose of balancing rudders. Needless to say, the Portuguese men-of-war are let strictly alone.

But the most interesting sight, after I recovered my equilibrium, was the host of tiny fish that centered about the jelly. I identified them as the butterfish, *Peprilis*, the young of the same creatures that grace our tables. They have become associated with the Portuguese man-of-war and with other jellyfish, to which they look for protection. When menaced by larger and

hungrier fish, these butterfish slip quickly beneath the poisonous tentacles and take up a position safe from harm. Once in
a great while in the excitement of fleeing from an enemy, a
butterfish blunders into a tentacle and is immediately paralyzed.
Then the jellyfish has its innings and slowly, inexorably the
tentacles contract and pass the helpless fish to the mouth to be
devoured.

Except for accidents of this type, however, the jellies do not
seem to be aware of the protection they are affording their
slim associates. This is not true of the butterfish, for they are
acutely conscious of the stinging character of the tentacles and
exercise great care in slipping in and out. Theirs must be a precarious lot, comparable to living in a place hung with dozens
of high voltage electric wires.

This association of the men-of-war and the butterfish, as
one sided as it is, is a wonderful thing. How did such a companionship begin? What intrepid butterfish first ventured into
these portieres of paralyzing death and learned their value as
protectors? Was it a super-butterfish that first did this thing,
and then, in some unexplainable manner, transmitted the new-
found knowledge to its successors? Or did all the butterfish
come to know this all at once by some strange instinct? These
questions are almost without answer.

I was glad when the man-of-war was gone, for while they
are very lovely in their delicate lavender colors there is something very sinister about them, and they sting frightfully. There
is no group of creatures that so entirely fits into this strange
world of underwater. Filmy, delicate, fantastic in shape and
form, nearly 98% water themselves, extremely fragile, they
melt perfectly into the underwater landscape.

Relieved, I sat down and watched some margate fish come
filing out of the haze. Unlike the mackerel they traveled in
twos and threes. They seemed to find little tid-bits in the sand

elow the rim and their progress was rather leisurely, inter-
upted by all sorts of side excursions.

Once I saw a barracuda. Long and slim and graceful, it
merged from the filmy distance and came to a stop a few feet
way. Across its gill flap was a deep line which gave it a hard,
rim appearance. It eyed me coldly, hung motionless in the
vater for about three minutes, and then without visible effort
lid away into the blue. I was not as nervous over the barracuda
s I had been over the devilfish, though I might have been, for
he barracuda are the reputed tigers of the sea.

The greatest thrill came when a great green turtle, weigh-
ng a hundred pounds or more, swept by. It arrived from be-
iind me somewhere, sliding just above the sand, reaching out
vith graceful motions of its flippers. It paid me not the slight-
st attention and went by within ten feet. Great masses of
vhitish barnacles covered its shell, and it was adorned with a
ilmy carpet of greenish moss. Like the manta it was carrying
parasite, a remora attached to the underside of its shell. Hang-
ng close to the bottom, it slid over the edge and vanished in
he gloom. I could not help wondering where it was going,
)ecause I knew there was a limit to the time it could stay below.
Turtles breathe atmospheric air and must come to the surface
it regular intervals. But down it went, down into the hazy
listance and the dark.

The turtle gave a clue to another type of migration on the
:liff edge, a migration that was not as important as the long
;hore migration. Fish were gliding back and forth from the
lepths and the shallows of the bank. The most abundant of
:hese were the squirrel-fish, which I had not seen in any large
1umbers before except at night. A steady stream of them fil-
:ered out of the depths. They seemed to know where they were
going and headed straight for the rocks on shore. Others were
returning, coming to the edge and slipping over and down.

They were accompanied by red and blue parrotfish whose errands in the depths were something of a mystery, for the limit of the vegetation on which they fed was near the cliff edge. Yet there were great numbers and presumably they divided their time between the rocks on shore and some shadowy crags far below.

My last view of this edge of a world was one of the most awe-inspiring sights I have ever seen. I determined to go down as far as I dared and the pressure would permit. After a short rest I crept out to the very edge of the brim and, grasping the life line, let myself over. The sand started sliding beneath my feet, but I held fast and crept downwards. The slope was quite steep, but with the steadying line I managed to keep upright. Down I went, slowly, blowing hard through my nose to relieve the pressure on my eardrums. Down ten feet, fifteen, twenty.

I looked up. There was no hint of the surface. I was down 55 feet. Not much as modern diving goes, but a lot for the light equipment I was using. I knew that I should go no further. But something drew me down. Curiosity again, that indefinable urge to see what is around the corner, to go a few feet more and a few more. I was beginning to feel the pressure. A heavy weight seemed to be pressing against my stomach and chest, and I was breathing heavily. Sixty feet. My head began to swim. Sixty-five.

I hurriedly looked about. Down as far as I could see there was nothing but sand sloping away into infinity, sand and utter darkness, the most mysterious quiet darkness I have ever beheld. There was something terrifying about it—it was so vague, so intangible. I turned back and struggled up the slope. High above, over the rim poured a halo of golden light. My head was reeling from the unaccustomed pressure. Hand over

and I pulled myself up the line. Even as I reached the rim a
shining horde of golden motes poured over the edge. It was
a great school of fishes going to the depths. We passed midway,
for them the darkness and the cool—for me the glorious, dry,
air-breathing world of the sun.